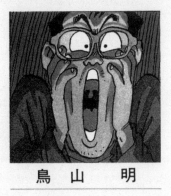

鳥　山　明

I really hate mice. I'm totally okay with snakes and spiders, but I can't handle mice. And so, our house has suddenly become a mansion for mice. Around 40 mice have been caught in glue traps, and there are still more. I'm so terrified that I can hardly work. The slightest clunk or scratching noise and I can't be in my office. So lately, my submissions have been on the late side…

—*Akira Toriyama, 1991*

Widely known all over the world for his playful, innovative storytelling and humorous, distinctive art style, **Dragon Ball** creator Akira Toriyama is also known in his native Japan for the wildly popular **Dr. Slump**, his previous manga series about the adventures of a mad scientist and his android "daughter." His hit series **Dragon Ball** ran from 1984 to 1995 in Shueisha's **Weekly Shonen Jump** magazine. He is also known for his design work on video games such as **Dragon Warrior**, **Chrono Trigger** and **Tobal No. 1**. His recent manga works include **Cowa!**, **Kajika**, **Sand Land**, **Neko Majin**, and a children's book, **Toccio the Angel**. He lives with his family in Japan.

**DRAGON BALL Z VOL. 13**
**SHONEN JUMP Manga Edition**

STORY AND ART BY
AKIRA TORIYAMA

English Adaptation/Gerard Jones
Translation/Lillian Olsen
Touch-Up Art & Lettering/Wayne Truman
Cover Design/Sean Lee
Graphics & Design/Sean Lee
Senior Editor/Jason Thompson

In the original Japanese edition, DRAGON BALL and DRAGON BALL Z
are known collectively as the 42-volume series DRAGON BALL. The
English DRAGON BALL Z was originally volumes 17–42 of the Japanese
DRAGON BALL.

Printed in the U.S.A.

Published by VIZ Media, LLC
P.O. Box 77010
San Francisco, CA 94107

10 9 8
First printing, July 2003
Eighth printing, November 2014

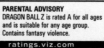

SHONEN JUMP MANGA

# DRAGON BALL Z

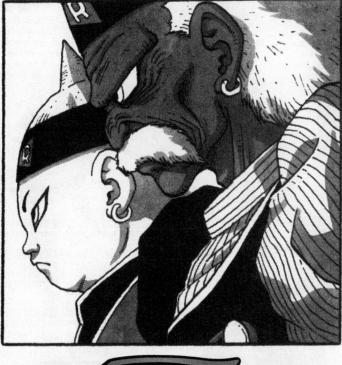

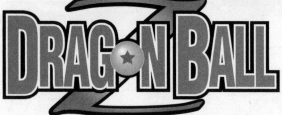

Vol. 13

DB: 29 of 42

STORY AND ART BY
AKIRA TORIYAMA

# THE MAIN CHARACTERS

**Bulma**

ku's oldest friend, Bulma a scientific genius. She t Goku while on a quest for the seven magical agon Balls which, when gathered together, can grant any wish.

**Son Goku**

The greatest martial artist on Earth, he owes his strength to the training of Kame-Sen'nin and Kaiô-sama, and the fact that he's an alien Saiyan. He was the first person to become "Super Saiyan."

**Kaiô-sama**

The "Lord of Worlds," he is Kami-sama's superior in the heavenly bureaucracy. He taught Goku the *kaiô-ken* and other amazing martial arts techniques.

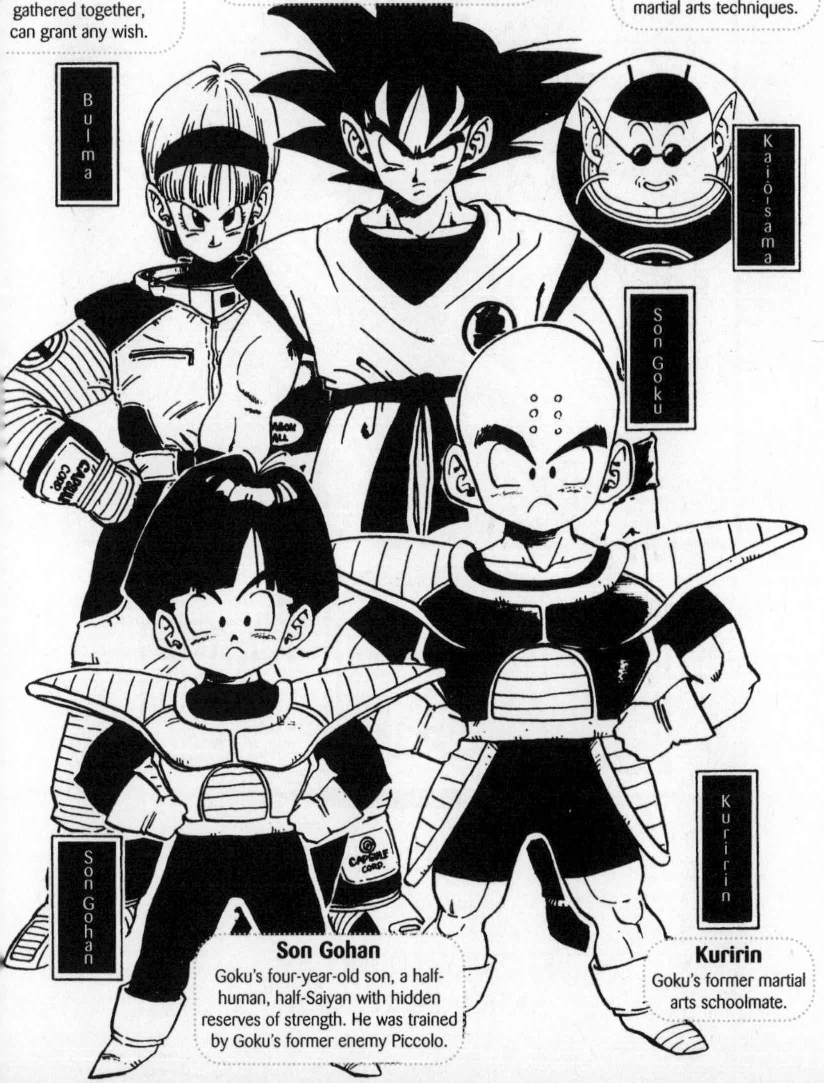
Bulma
Kaiôsama
Son Goku
Kuririn
Son Gohan

**Son Gohan**

Goku's four-year-old son, a half-human, half-Saiyan with hidden reserves of strength. He was trained by Goku's former enemy Piccolo.

**Kuririn**

Goku's former martial arts schoolmate.

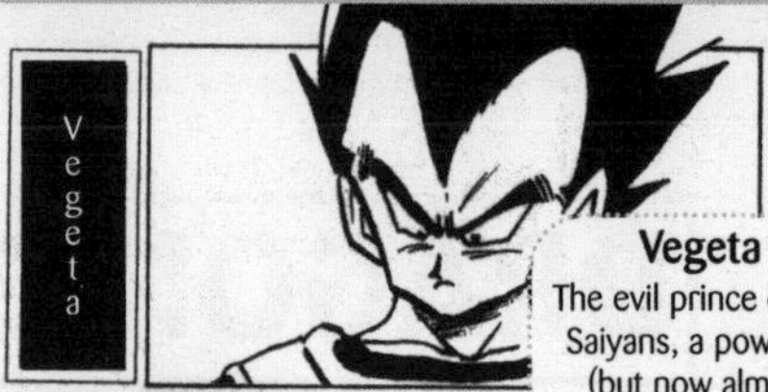
Vegeta

## Vegeta

The evil prince of t
Saiyans, a powerf
(but now almost
extinct) alien race.
yearns to defeat Gc
with his own hand

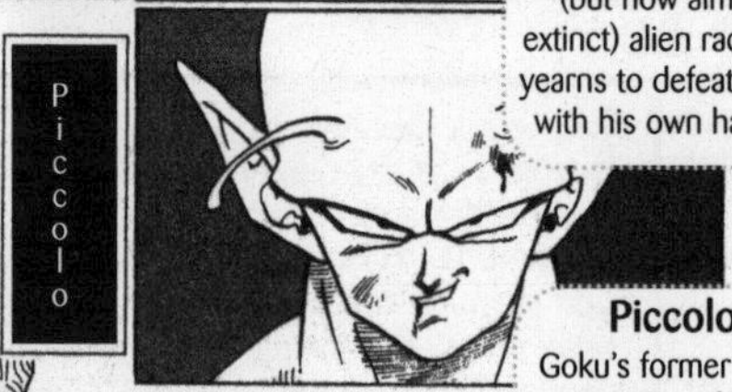
Piccolo

## Piccolo

Goku's former arc
enemy, Piccolo is
alien from plane
Namek—and the d
half of Kami-sam
the deity who crea
the Dragon Balls

## Trunks

The future son of Vegeta and Bulma, he is a half-human, half-Saiyan—and the second person, after Goku, able to become an all-powerful "Super Saiyan." In our heroes' current timeline, he's just a little baby.

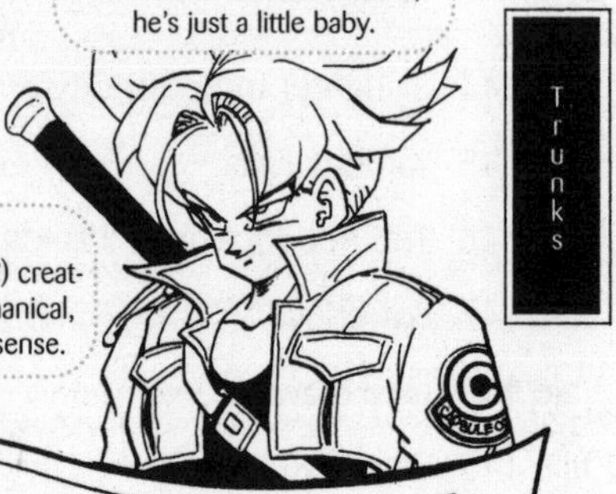
Trunks

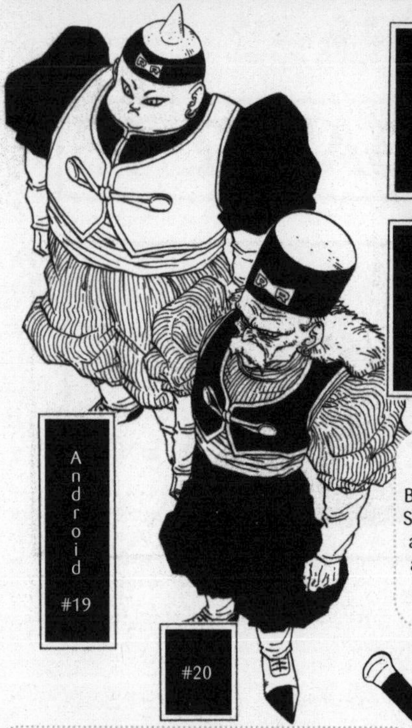
Android #19
#20

## Androids #19 and #20

Incredibly strong androids (or are they cyborgs?) created by the evil Dr. Gero. Because they are mechanical, they have no *chi* (life force) for our heroes to sense.

Son Goku was Earth's greatest hero, and the Dragon Balls—which can grant any wish—were Earth's greatest treasure. Three years ago, a mysterious young man appeared on Earth: Trunks, a time traveler from the future. Trunks warned Earth's martial artists that the world would soon be attacked by terrifying androids built by the evil Dr. Gero—and worse still, Goku would develop a deadly virus! Trunks gave Goku a futuristic medicine for his virus, but instead of stopping Dr. Gero before he could build the androids, the heroes decided to spend the three years training to see if they would be tough enough to beat them. And now, the day of reckoning has come…

# DRAGON BALL Z 13

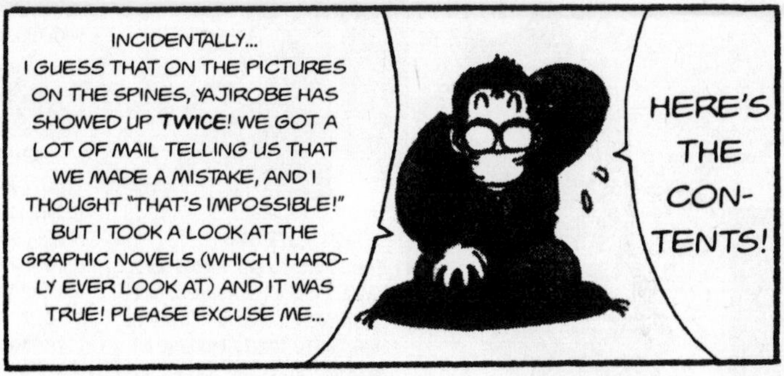
INCIDENTALLY... I GUESS THAT ON THE PICTURES ON THE SPINES, YAJIROBE HAS SHOWED UP **TWICE**! WE GOT A LOT OF MAIL TELLING US THAT WE MADE A MISTAKE, AND I THOUGHT "THAT'S IMPOSSIBLE!" BUT I TOOK A LOOK AT THE GRAPHIC NOVELS (WHICH I HARDLY EVER LOOK AT) AND IT WAS TRUE! PLEASE EXCUSE ME...
HERE'S THE CONTENTS!

# DRAGON BALL
## DBZ:144 • Slaughter in South City

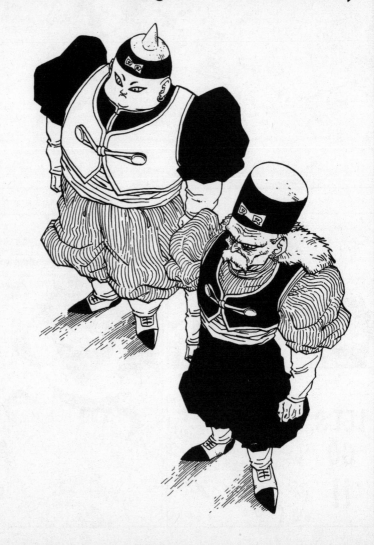

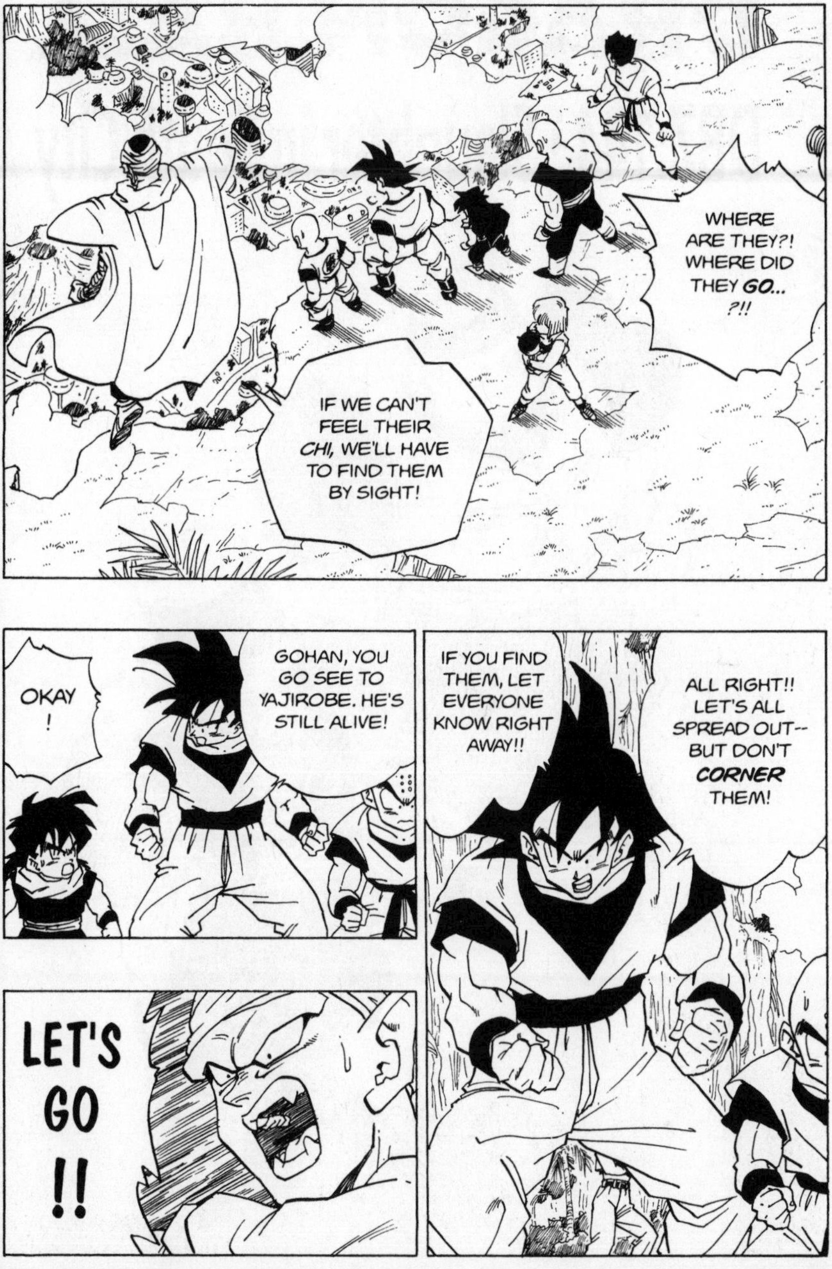
WHERE ARE THEY?! WHERE DID THEY *GO...* ?!!
IF WE CAN'T FEEL THEIR *CHI,* WE'LL HAVE TO FIND THEM BY SIGHT!
ALL RIGHT!! LET'S ALL SPREAD OUT-- BUT DON'T ***CORNER*** THEM!
IF YOU FIND THEM, LET EVERYONE KNOW RIGHT AWAY!!
GOHAN, YOU GO SEE TO YAJIROBE. HE'S STILL ALIVE!
OKAY !
LET'S GO !!

READ THIS WAY

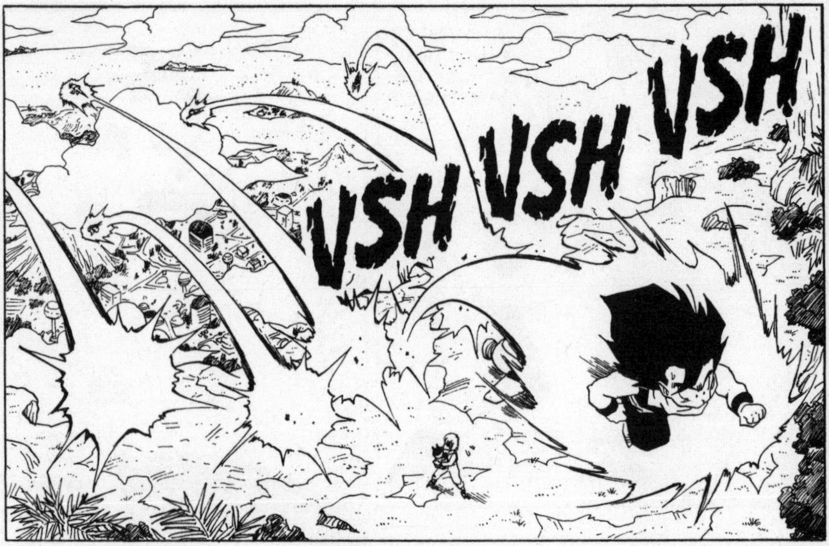
VSH VSH VSH

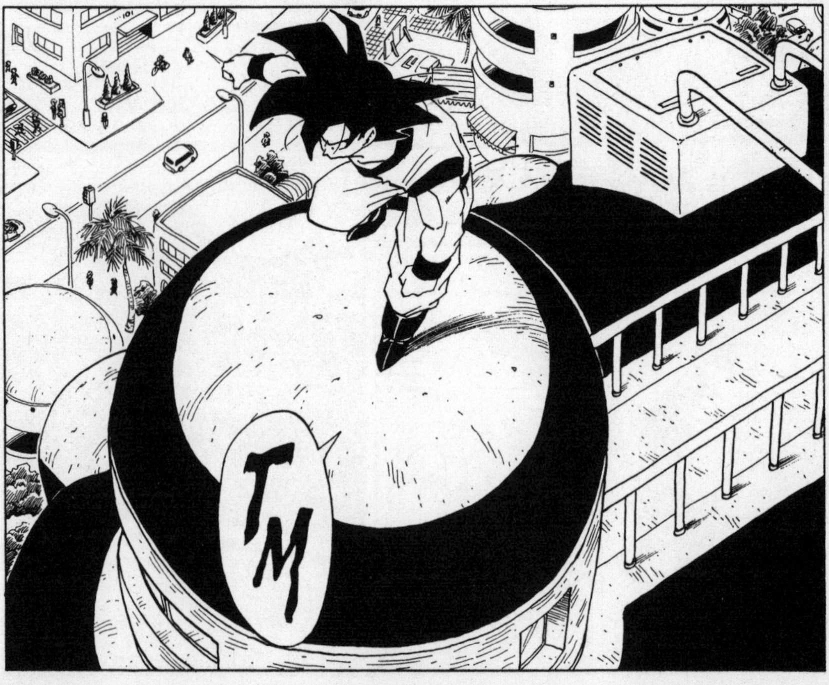
TM

READ THIS WAY

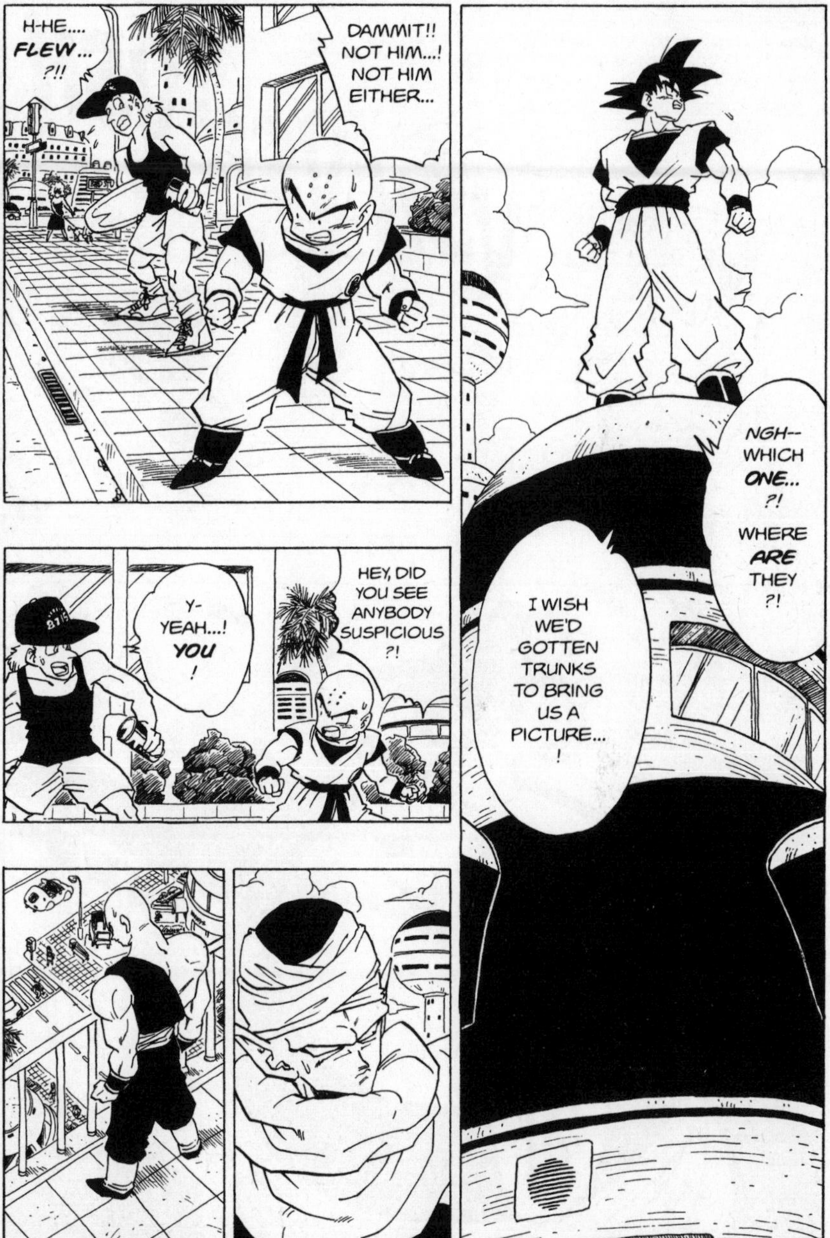
NGH-- WHICH ONE... ?! WHERE ARE THEY ?!
I WISH WE'D GOTTEN TRUNKS TO BRING US A PICTURE... !
DAMMIT!! NOT HIM...! NOT HIM EITHER...
H-HE.... FLEW... ?!!
HEY, DID YOU SEE ANYBODY SUSPICIOUS ?!
Y-YEAH...! YOU !

READ THIS WAY

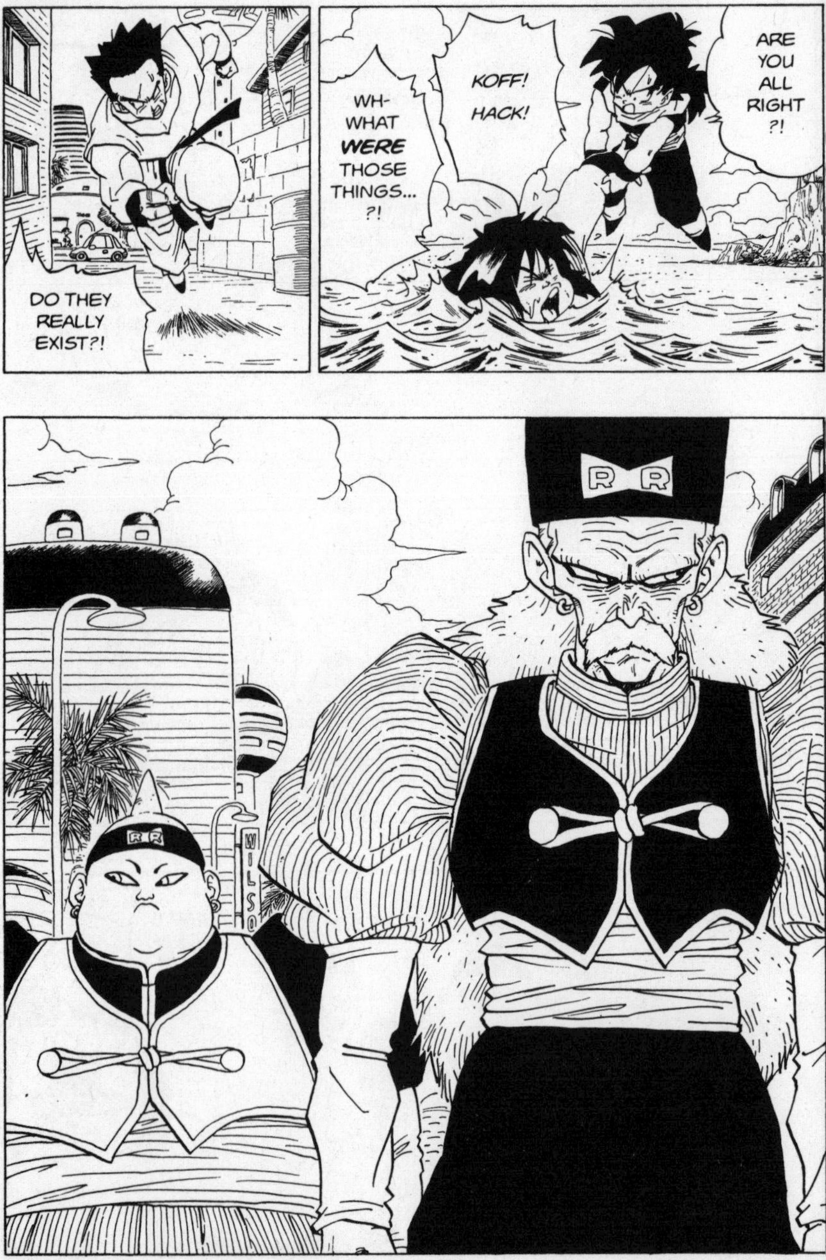

ARE YOU ALL RIGHT ?!
KOFF! HACK!
WH- WHAT **WERE** THOSE THINGS... ?!
DO THEY REALLY EXIST?!
WILSO

READ THIS WAY

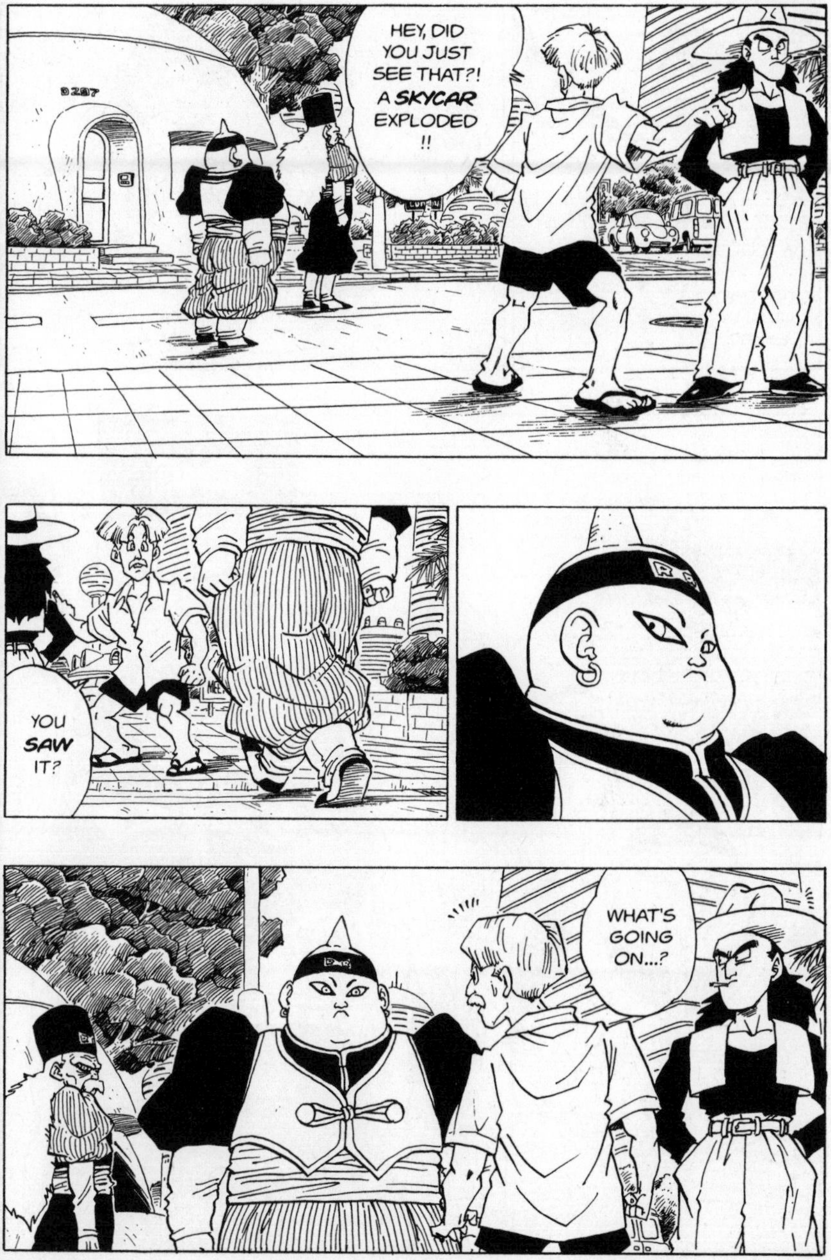

HEY, DID YOU JUST SEE THAT?! A SKYCAR EXPLODED !!
YOU SAW IT?
WHAT'S GOING ON...?

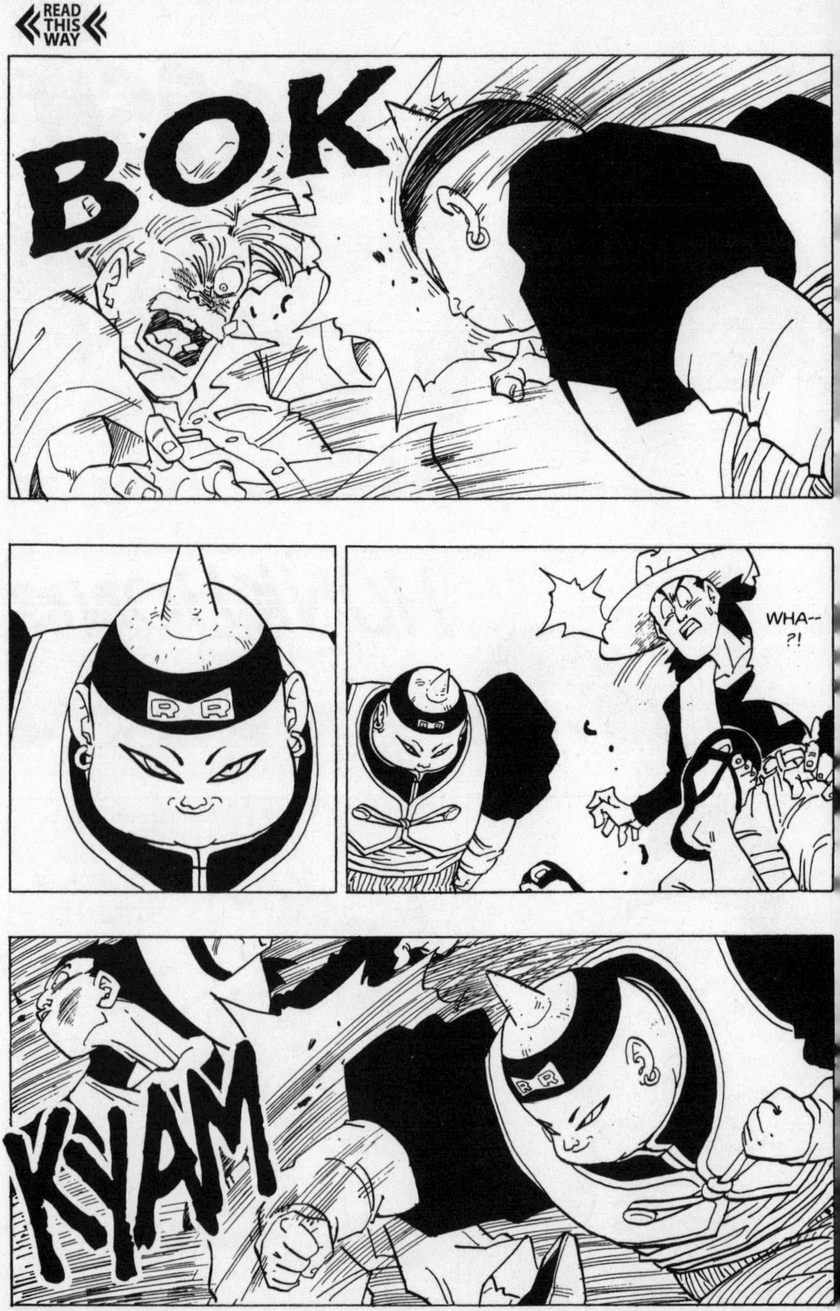
READ THIS WAY
BOK
WHA-- ?!
KYAM

READ THIS WAY

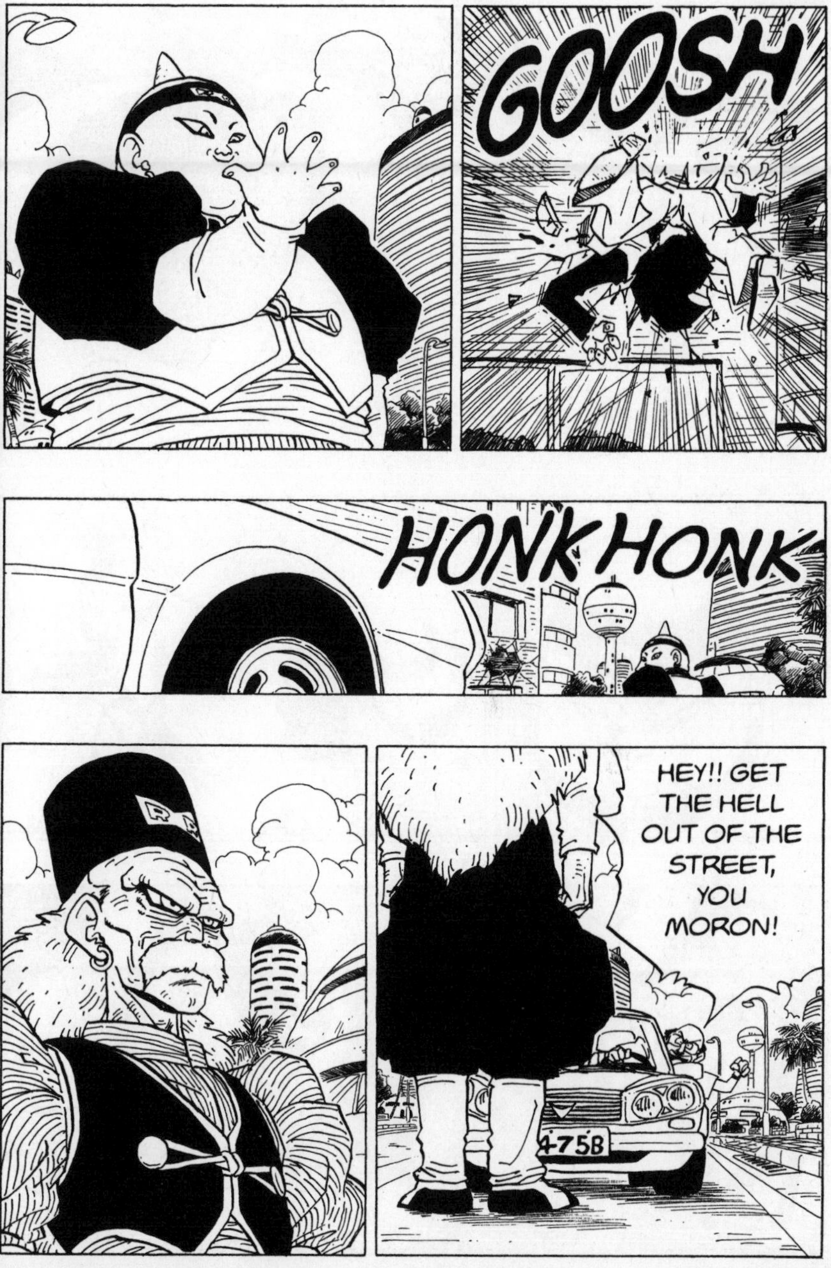
GOOSH
HONK HONK
HEY!! GET THE HELL OUT OF THE STREET, YOU MORON!

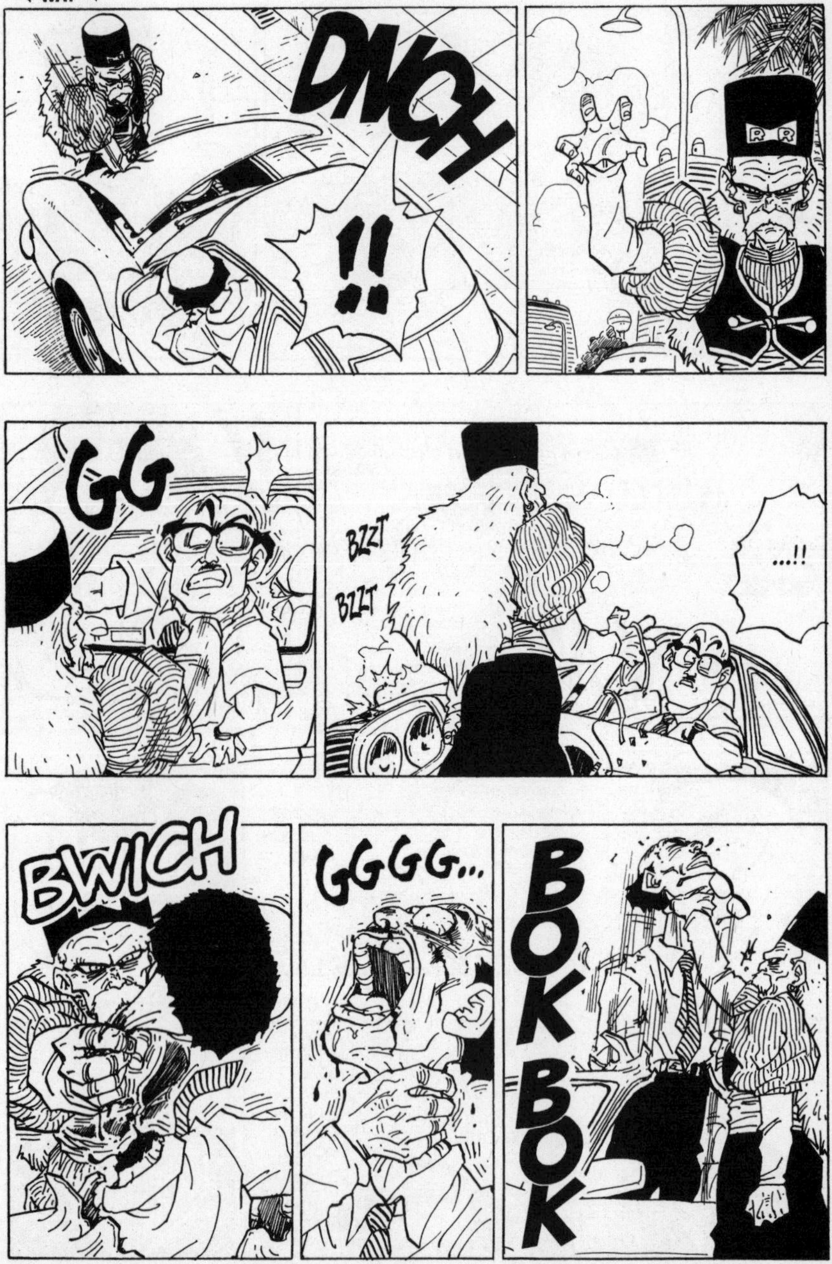
DNCH
!!
BZZT
BZZT
...!!
GG
BOK BOK
GGGG...
BWICH

READ THIS WAY

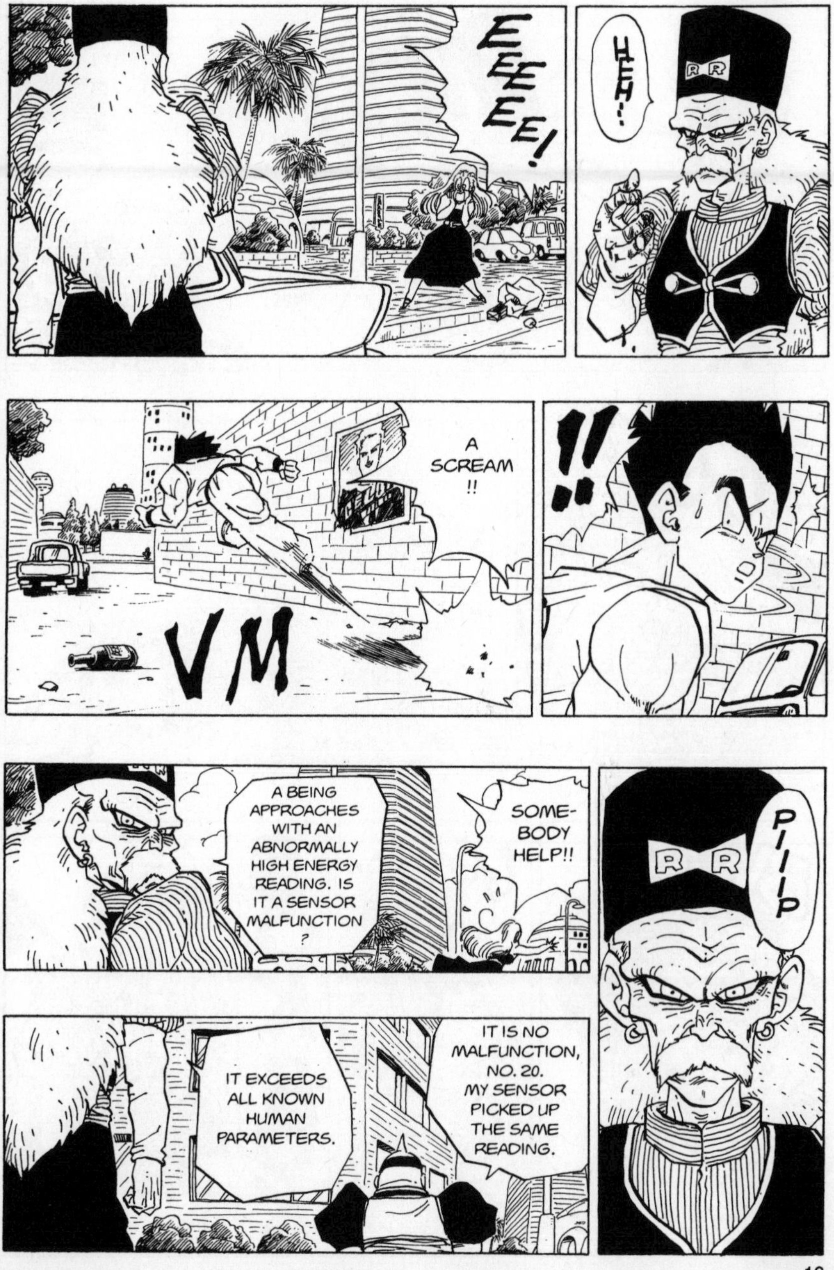

HEH!..
EEEEEE!
!!
A SCREAM !!
VM
PIIIP
SOME-BODY HELP!!
A BEING APPROACHES WITH AN ABNORMALLY HIGH ENERGY READING. IS IT A SENSOR MALFUNCTION ?
IT IS NO MALFUNCTION, NO. 20. MY SENSOR PICKED UP THE SAME READING.
IT EXCEEDS ALL KNOWN HUMAN PARAMETERS.

READ THIS WAY

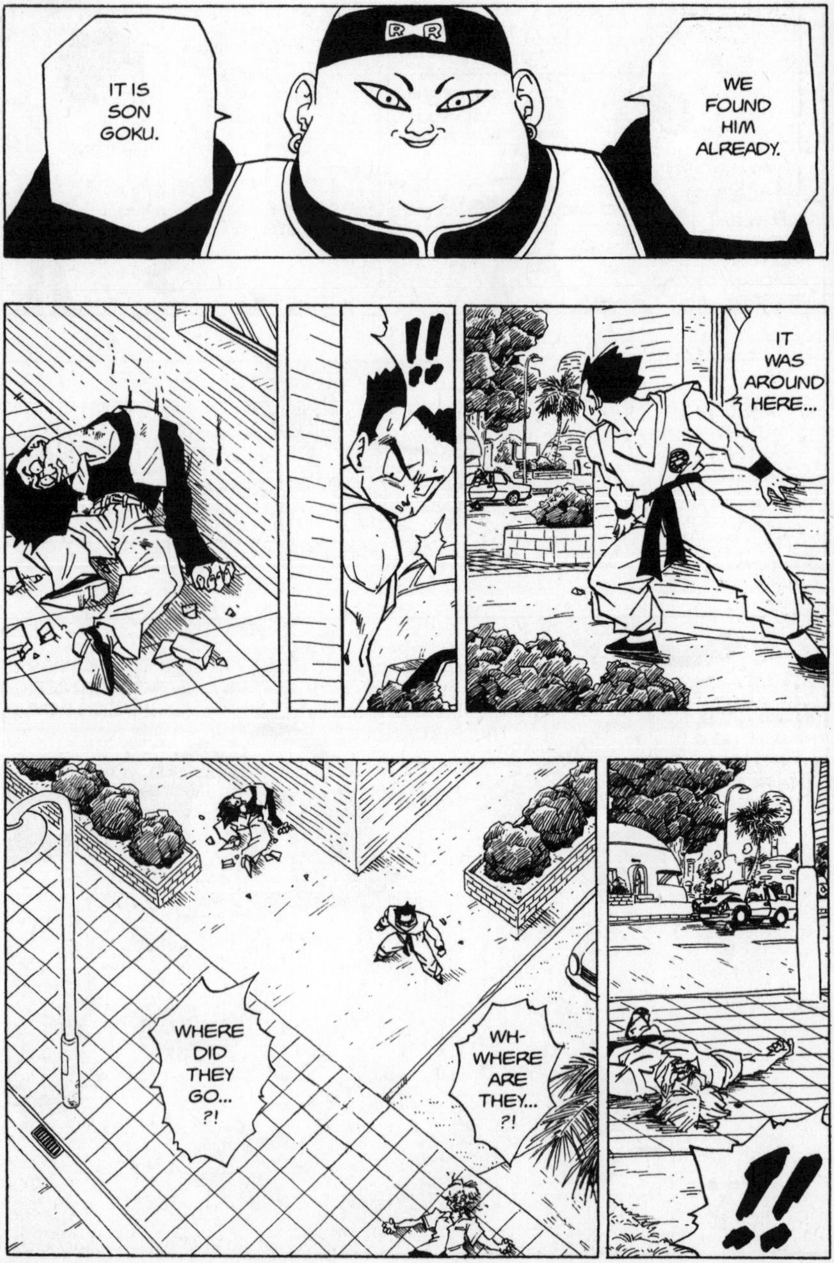

WE FOUND HIM ALREADY.
IT IS SON GOKU.
IT WAS AROUND HERE...
!!
!!
WH- WHERE ARE THEY... ?!
WHERE DID THEY GO... ?!

READ THIS WAY

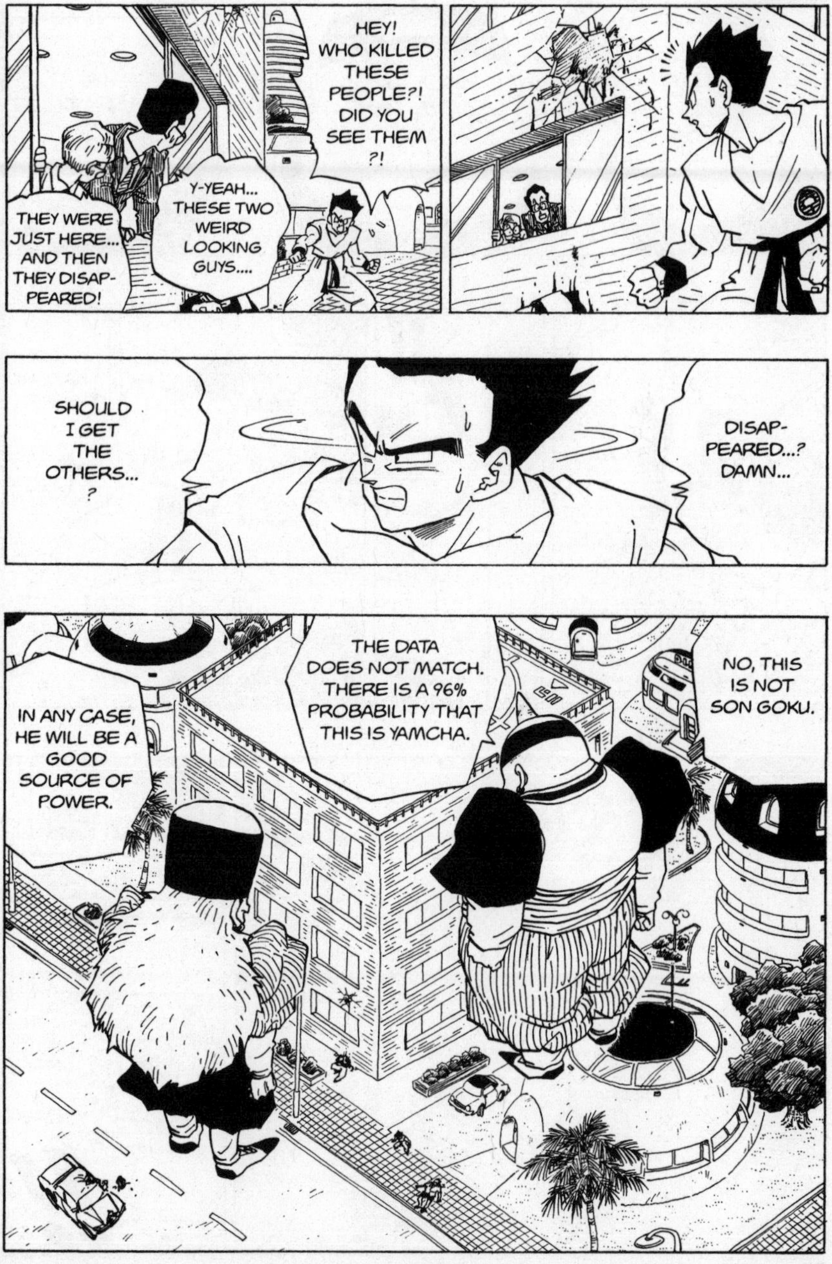
HEY! WHO KILLED THESE PEOPLE?! DID YOU SEE THEM ?!
Y-YEAH... THESE TWO WEIRD LOOKING GUYS....
THEY WERE JUST HERE... AND THEN THEY DISAP-PEARED!
DISAP-PEARED...? DAMN...
SHOULD I GET THE OTHERS... ?
NO, THIS IS NOT SON GOKU.
THE DATA DOES NOT MATCH. THERE IS A 96% PROBABILITY THAT THIS IS YAMCHA.
IN ANY CASE, HE WILL BE A GOOD SOURCE OF POWER.

READ THIS WAY

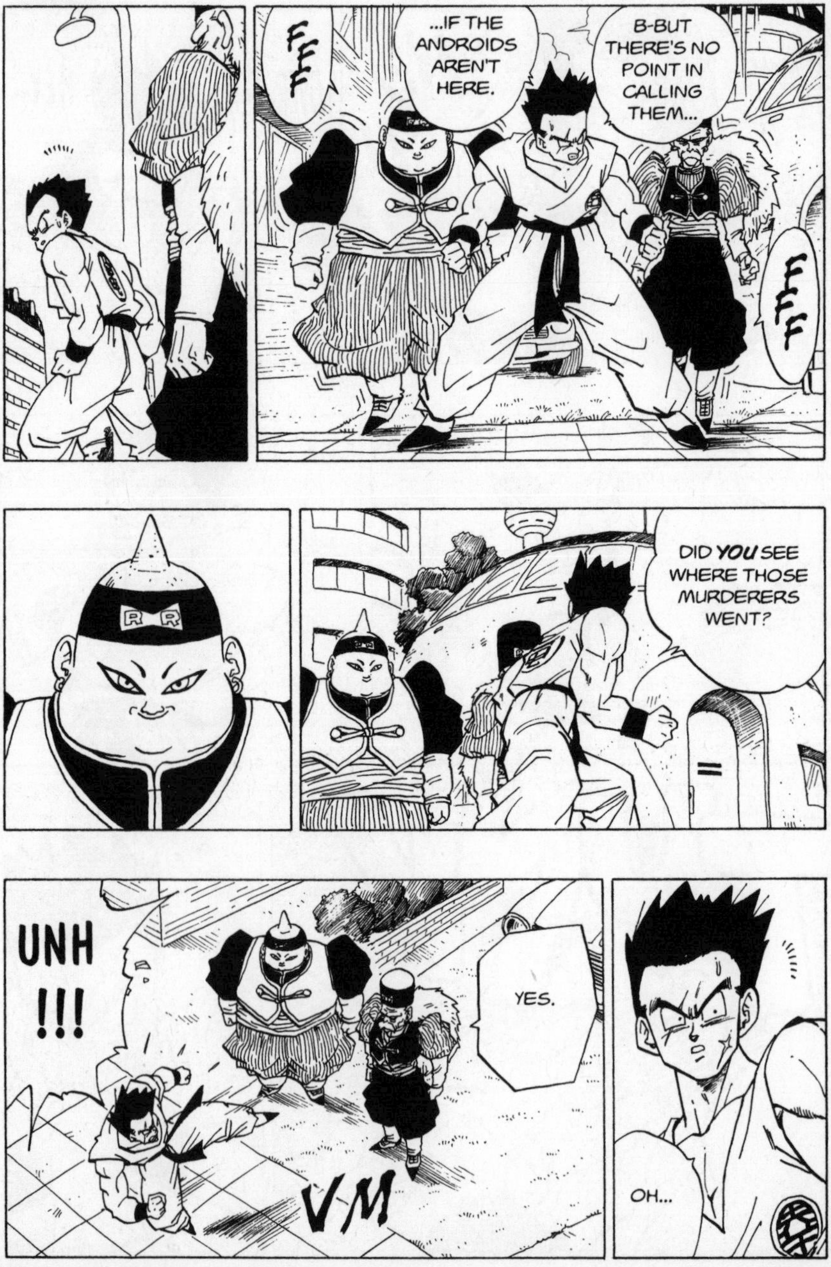

B-BUT THERE'S NO POINT IN CALLING THEM...
...IF THE ANDROIDS AREN'T HERE.
FFF
FFF
DID YOU SEE WHERE THOSE MURDERERS WENT?
OH...
YES.
VM
UNH !!!

READ THIS WAY

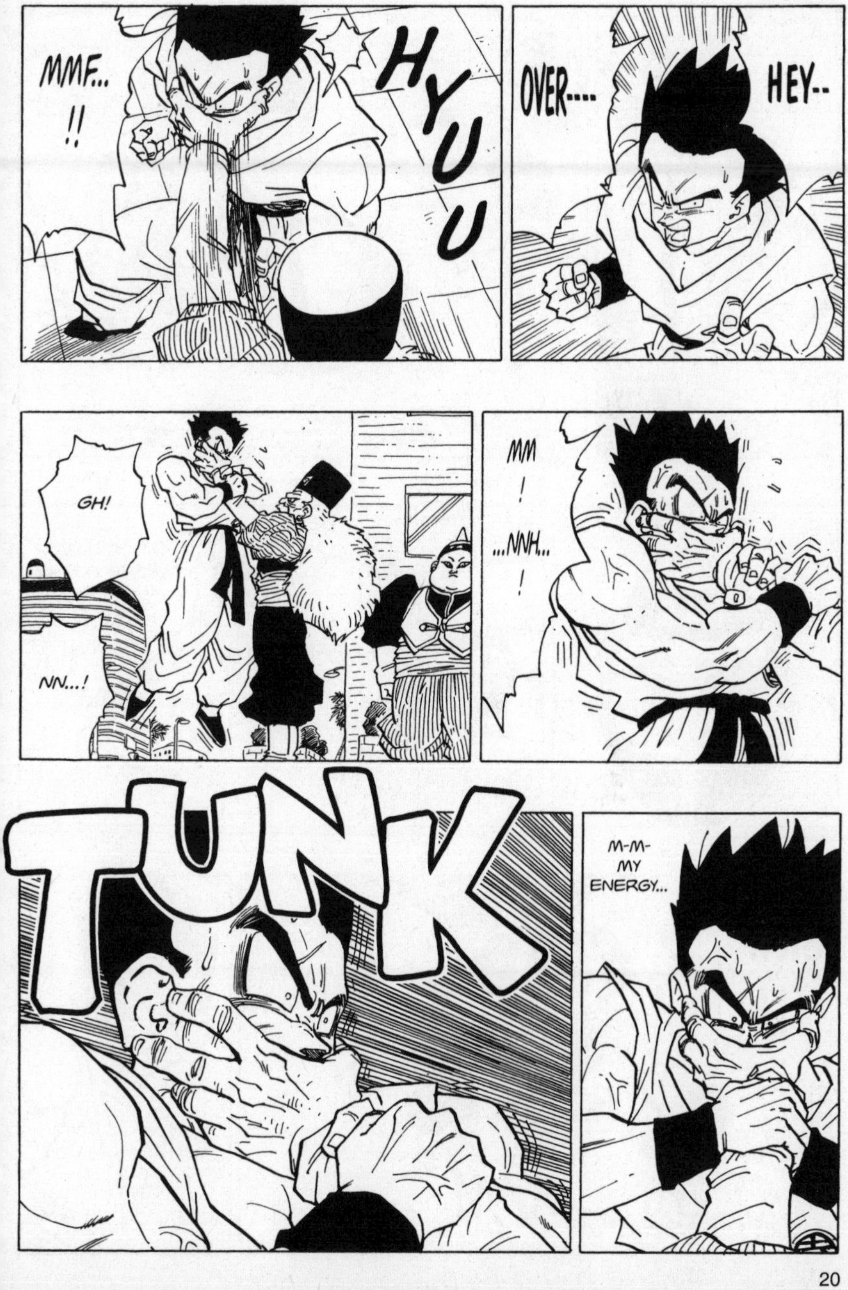
HEY--
OVER....
HYUU
MMF... !!
MM ! ...NNH... !
GH!
NN...!
M-M-MY ENERGY...
TUNK

READ THIS WAY

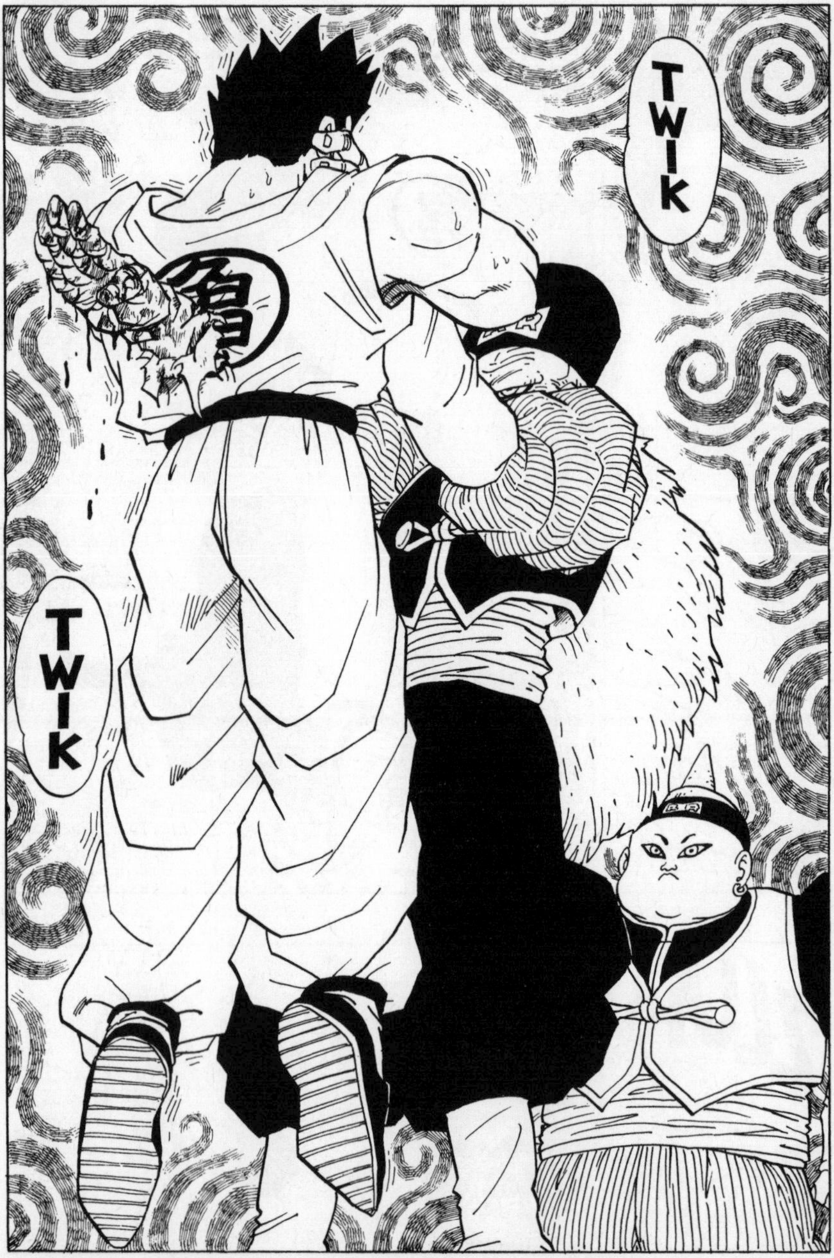
TWIK
TWIK

NEXT: The Second Death of Yamcha?

# DBZ:145 • Yamcha Falls

READ THIS WAY

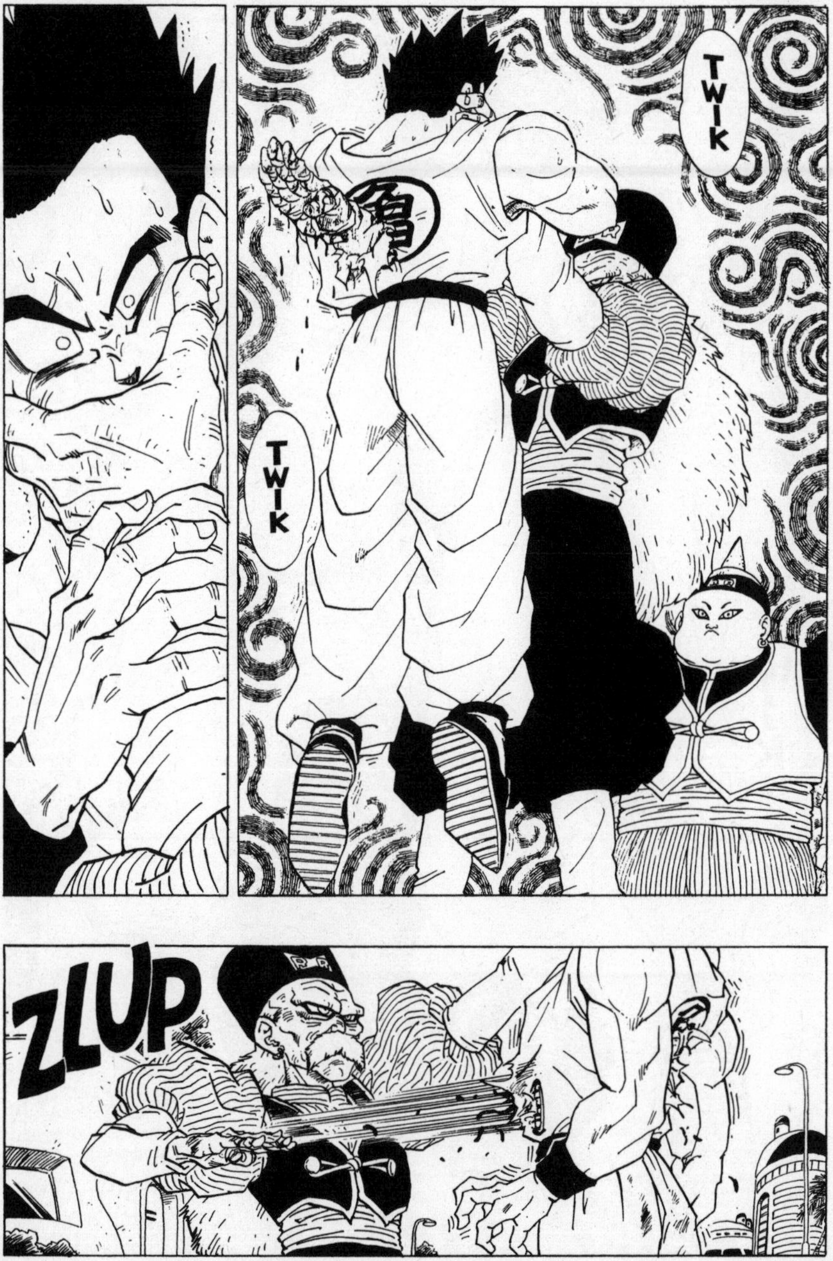
TWIK
TWIK
ZLUP

READ THIS WAY

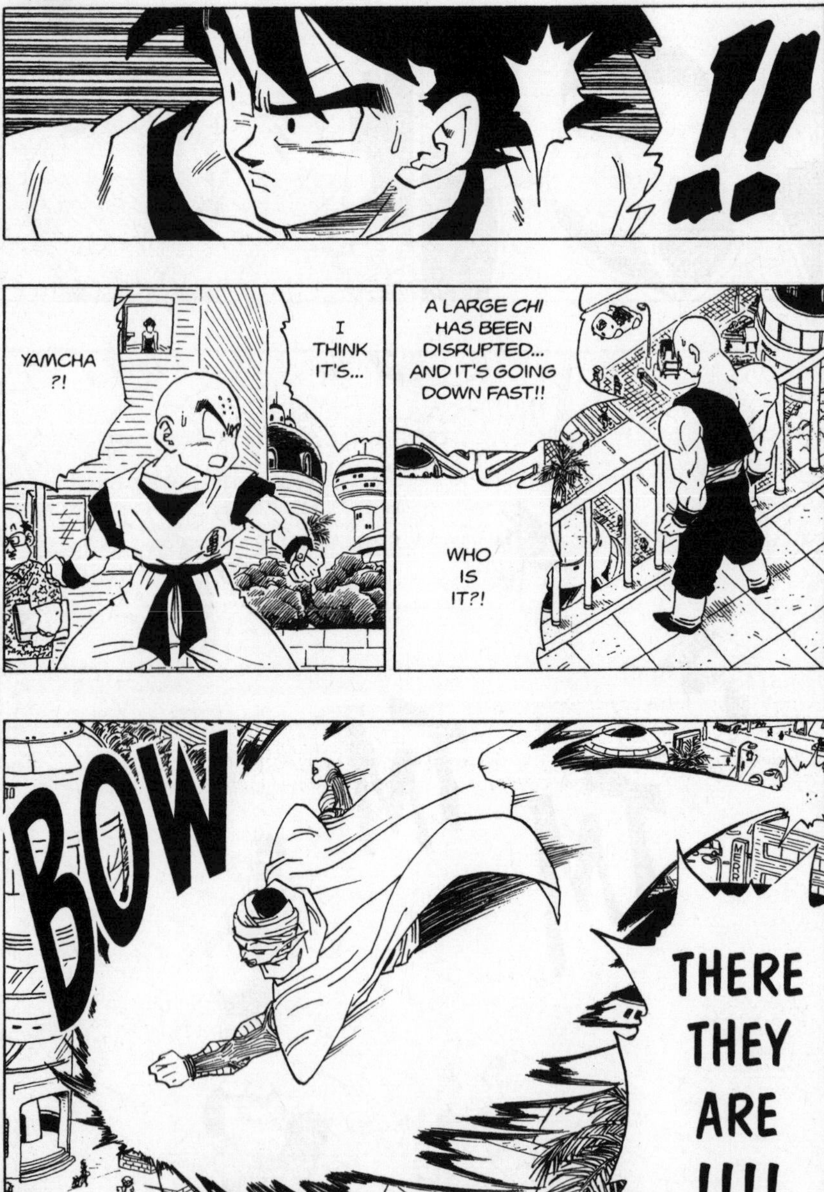
!!
A LARGE *CHI* HAS BEEN DISRUPTED... AND IT'S GOING DOWN FAST!!
WHO IS IT?!
I THINK IT'S...
YAMCHA ?!
BOW
THERE THEY ARE !!!!

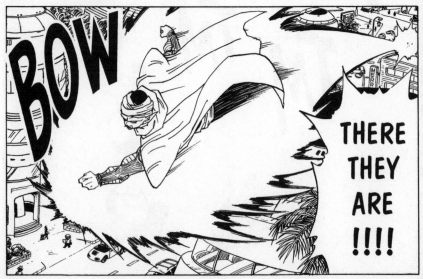

READ THIS WAY

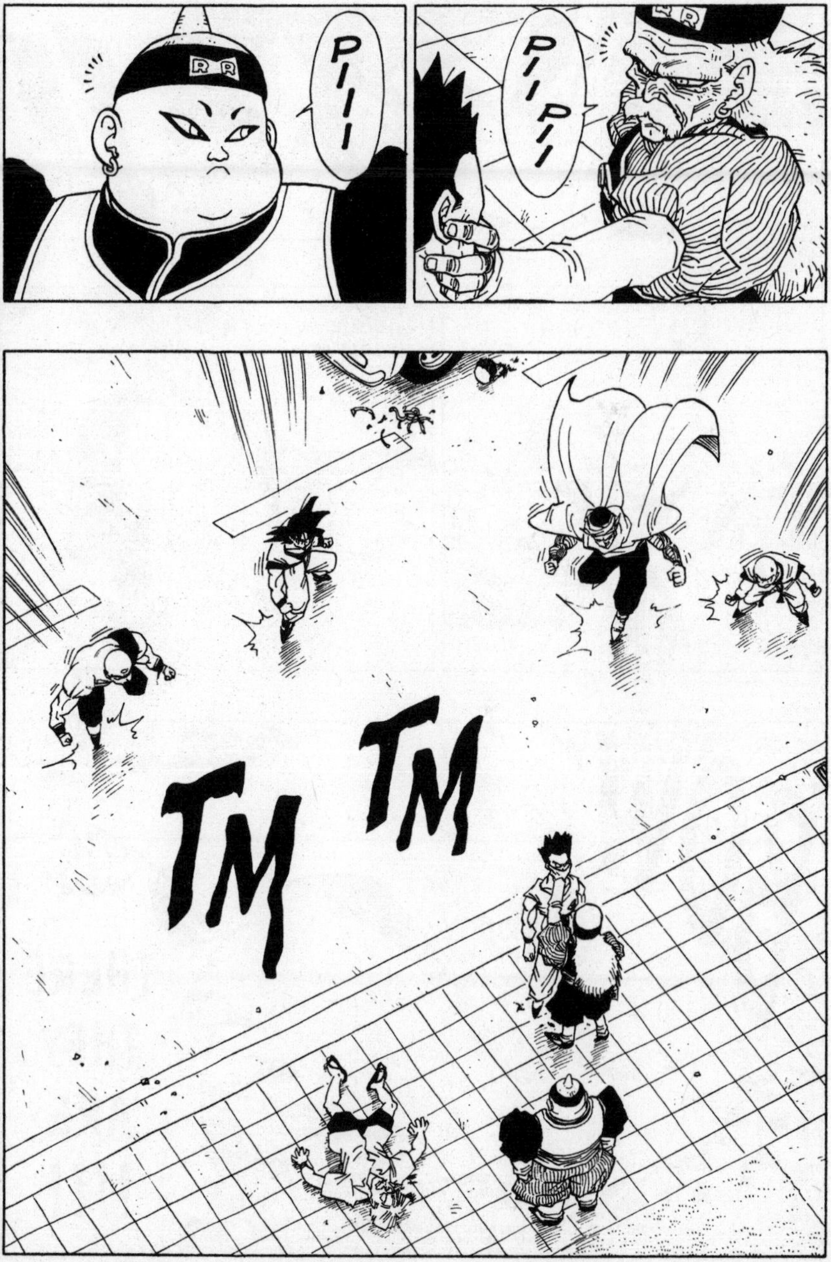
PIIPII
PIII
TM
TM

READ THIS WAY

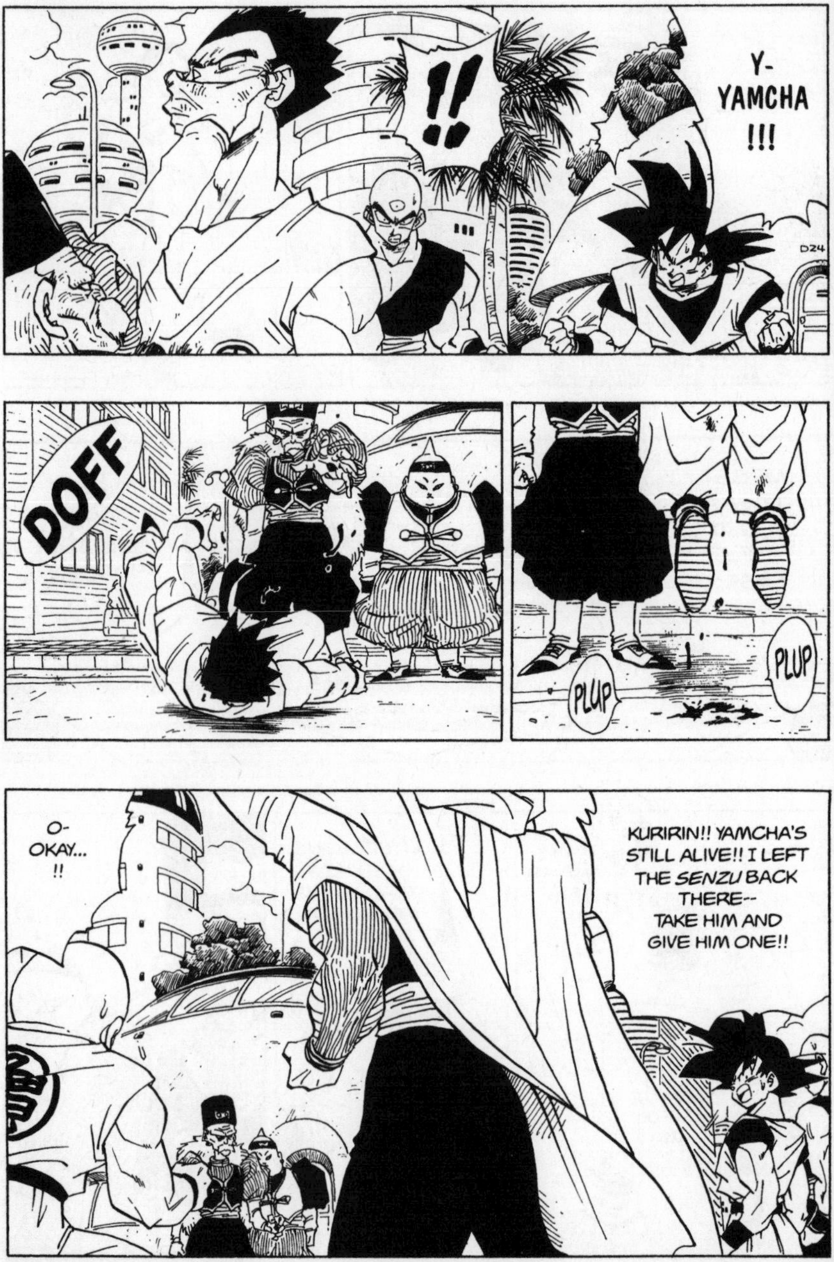

Y- YAMCHA !!!
!!
PLUP
PLUP
DOFF
KURIRIN!! YAMCHA'S STILL ALIVE!! I LEFT THE *SENZU* BACK THERE-- TAKE HIM AND GIVE HIM ONE!!
O- OKAY... !!

READ THIS WAY

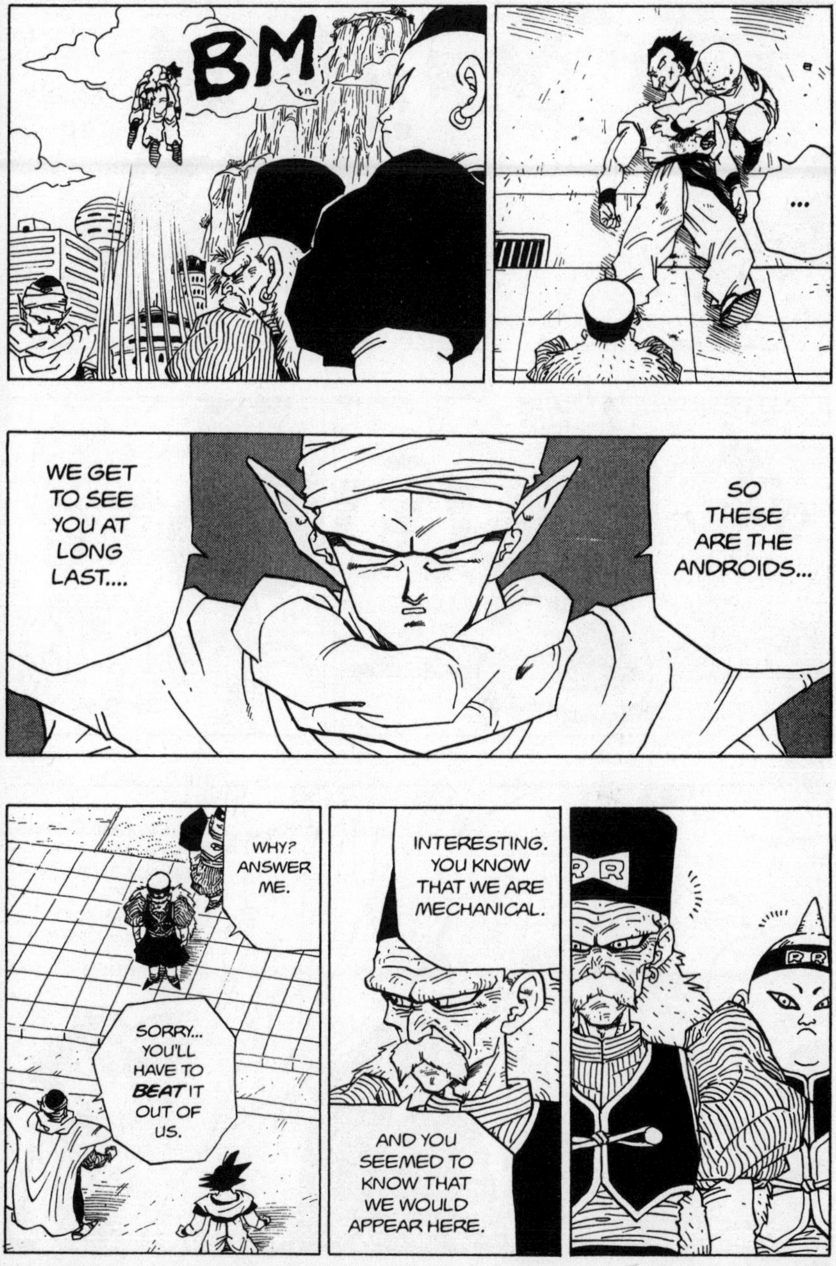

...
BM
SO THESE ARE THE ANDROIDS...
WE GET TO SEE YOU AT LONG LAST....
INTERESTING. YOU KNOW THAT WE ARE MECHANICAL.
AND YOU SEEMED TO KNOW THAT WE WOULD APPEAR HERE.
WHY? ANSWER ME.
SORRY... YOU'LL HAVE TO *BEAT* IT OUT OF US.

READ THIS WAY

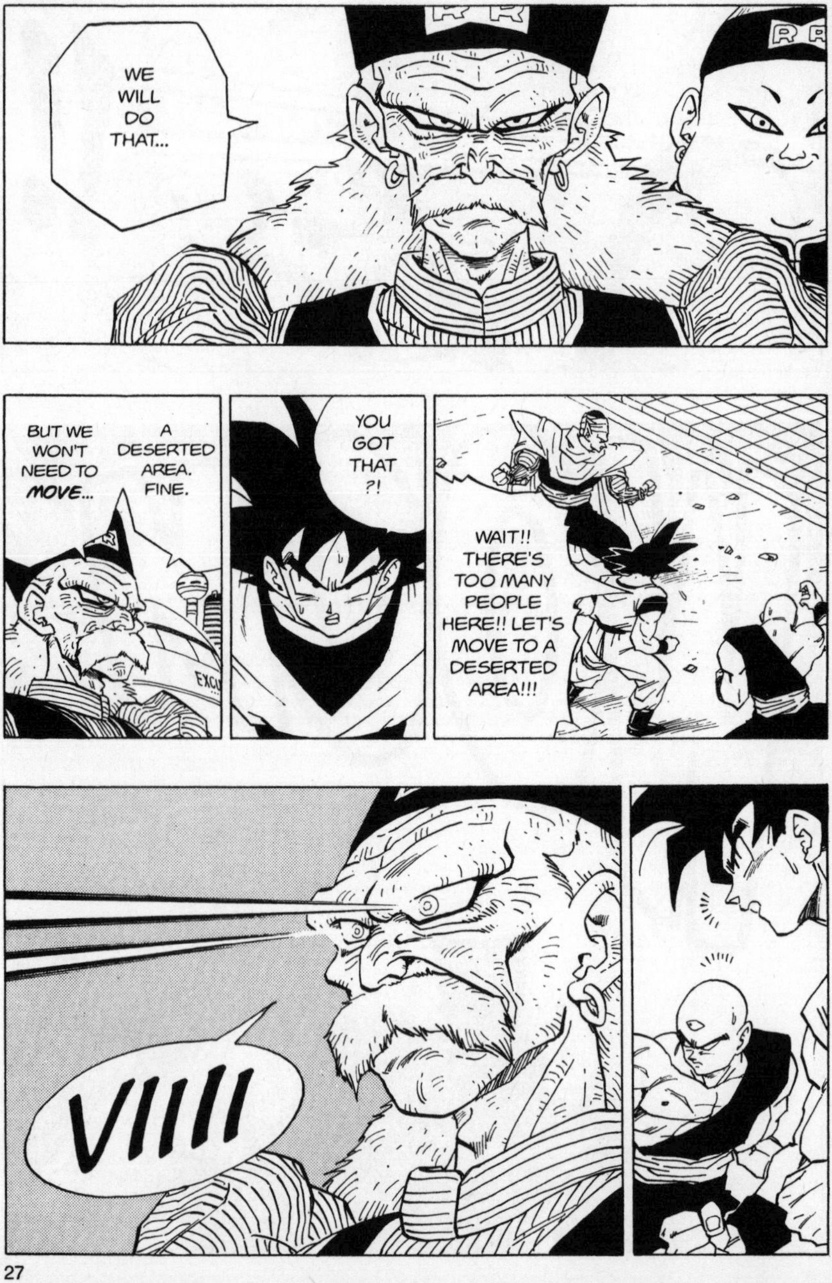

WE WILL DO THAT...
WAIT!! THERE'S TOO MANY PEOPLE HERE!! LET'S MOVE TO A DESERTED AREA!!!
YOU GOT THAT ?!
A DESERTED AREA. FINE.
BUT WE WON'T NEED TO *MOVE*...
VIIII

READ THIS WAY

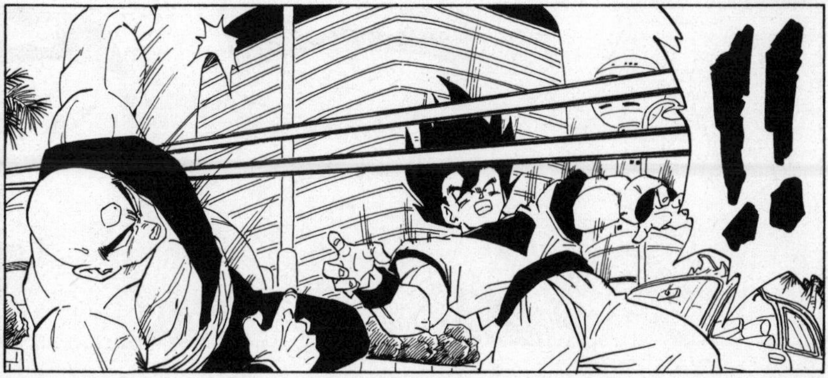
!!

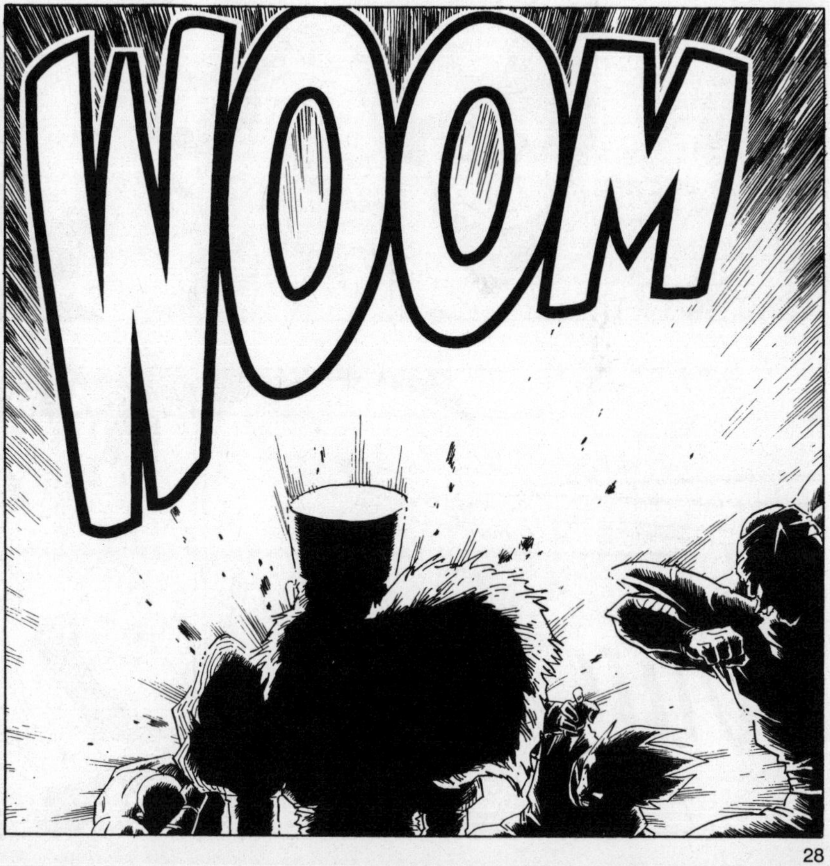
WOOM

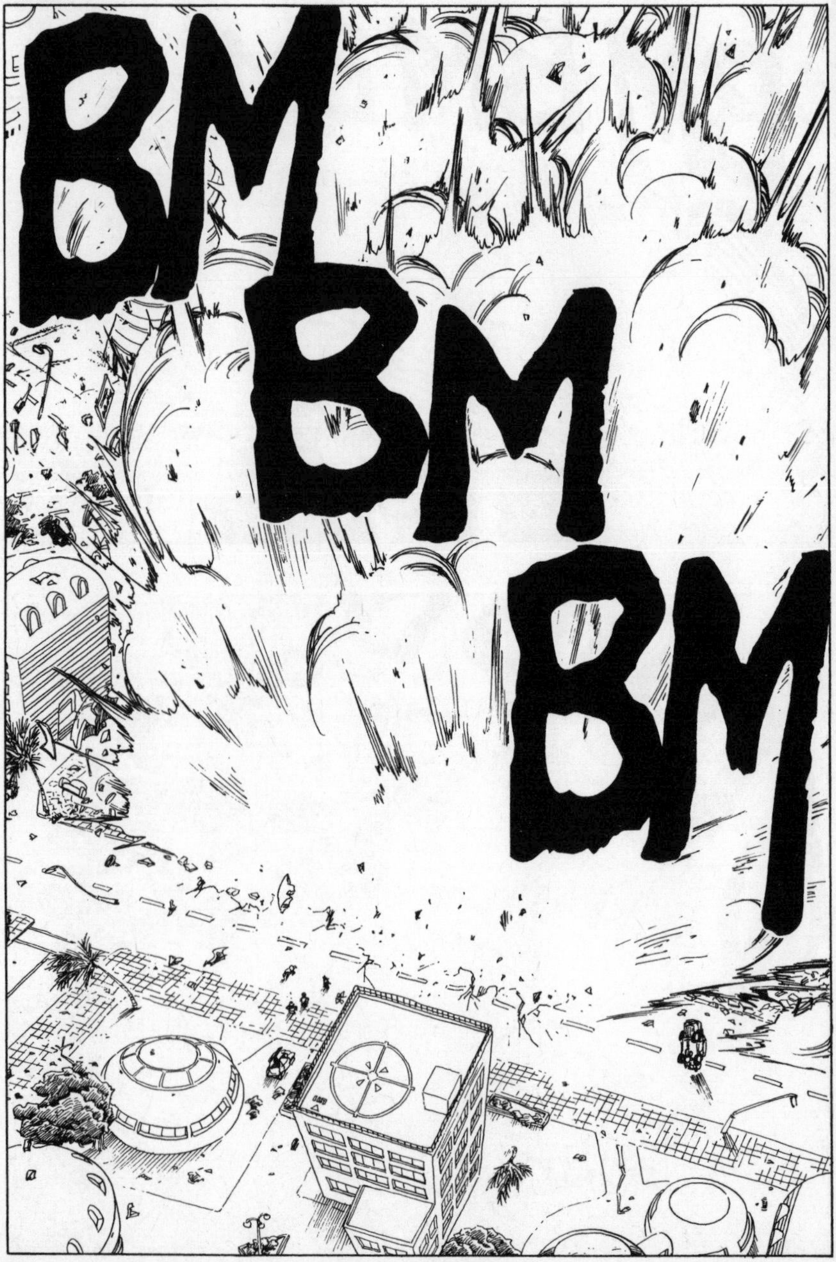
BM
BM
BM

READ THIS WAY

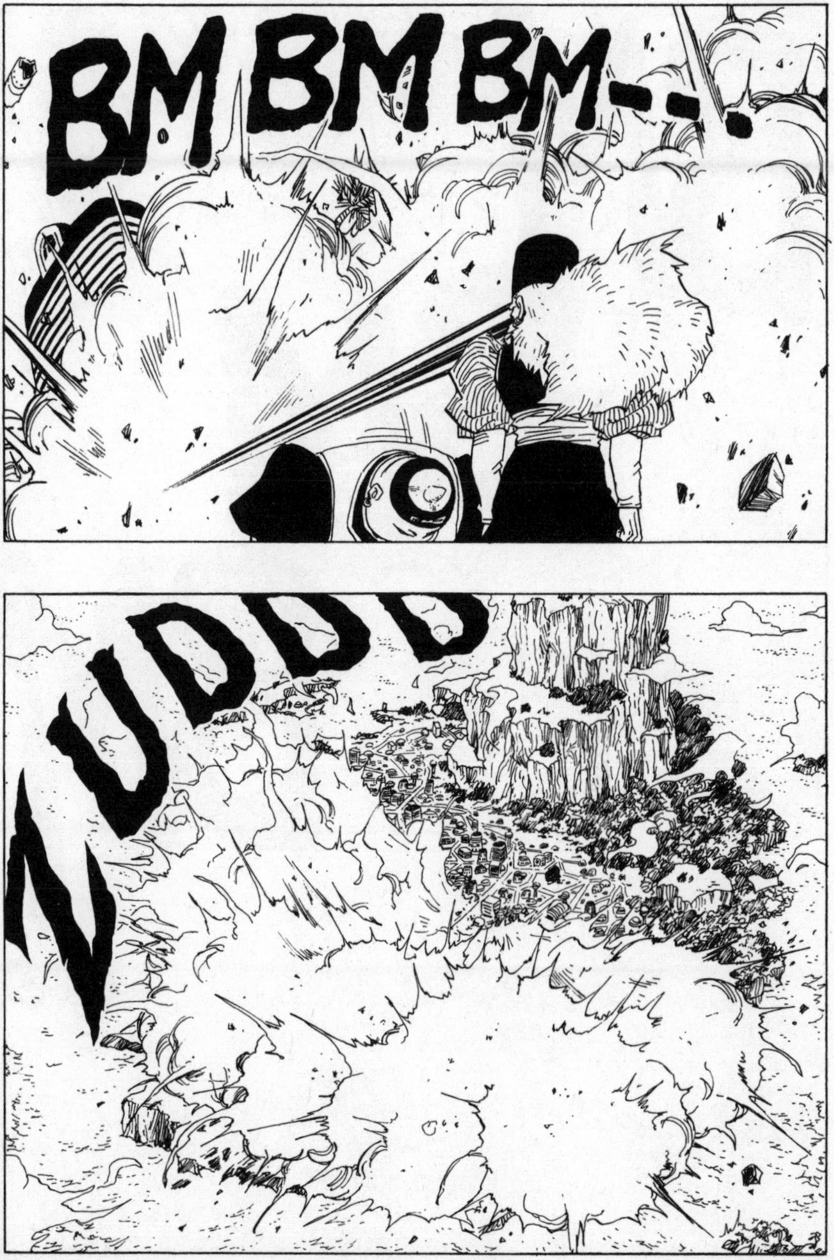
BM BM BM--!
ZUDDD

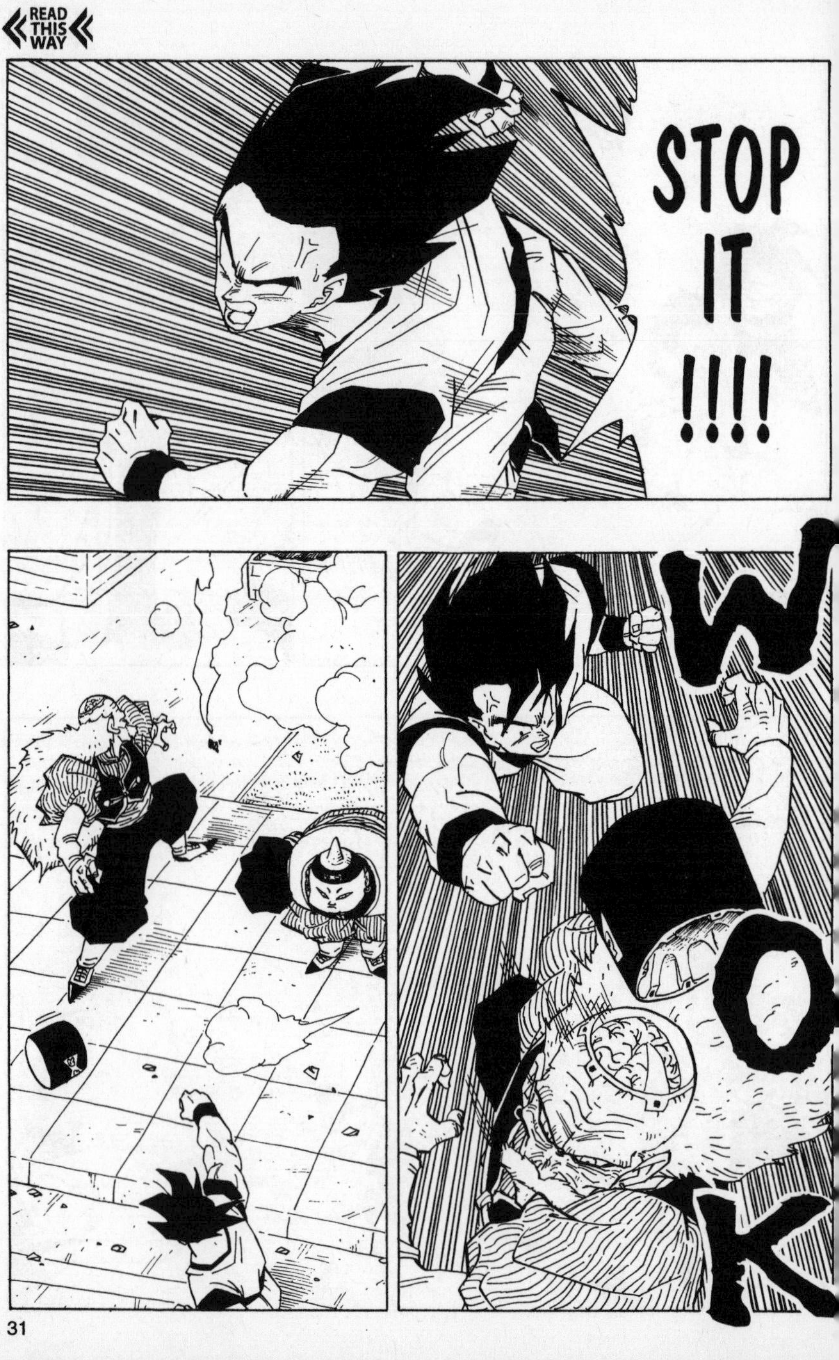
READ THIS WAY
STOP IT !!!!
WOK

READ THIS WAY

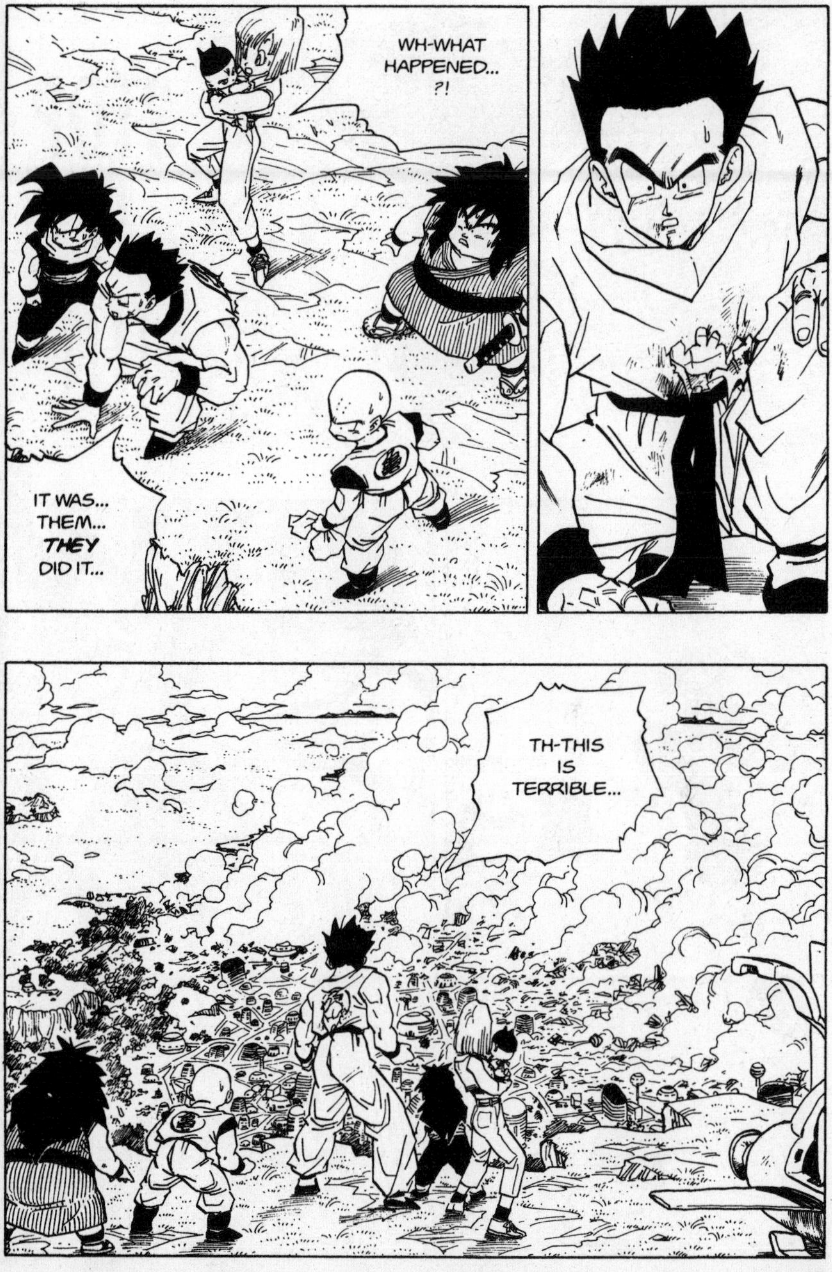
WH-WHAT HAPPENED... ?!
IT WAS... THEM... *THEY* DID IT...
TH-THIS IS TERRIBLE...

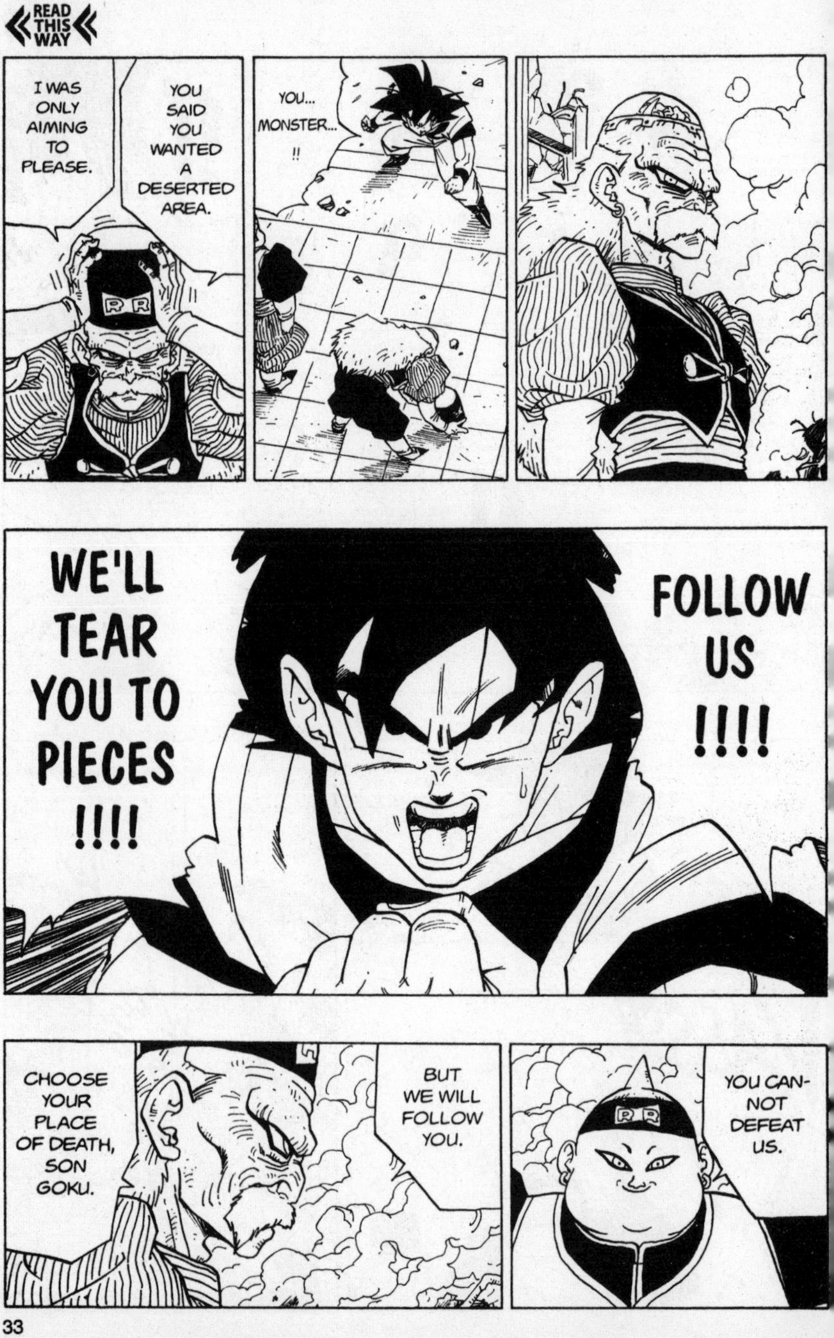
READ THIS WAY
YOU... MONSTER... !!
YOU SAID YOU WANTED A DESERTED AREA.
I WAS ONLY AIMING TO PLEASE.
FOLLOW US !!!!
WE'LL TEAR YOU TO PIECES !!!!
YOU CAN-NOT DEFEAT US.
BUT WE WILL FOLLOW YOU.
CHOOSE YOUR PLACE OF DEATH, SON GOKU.

READ THIS WAY

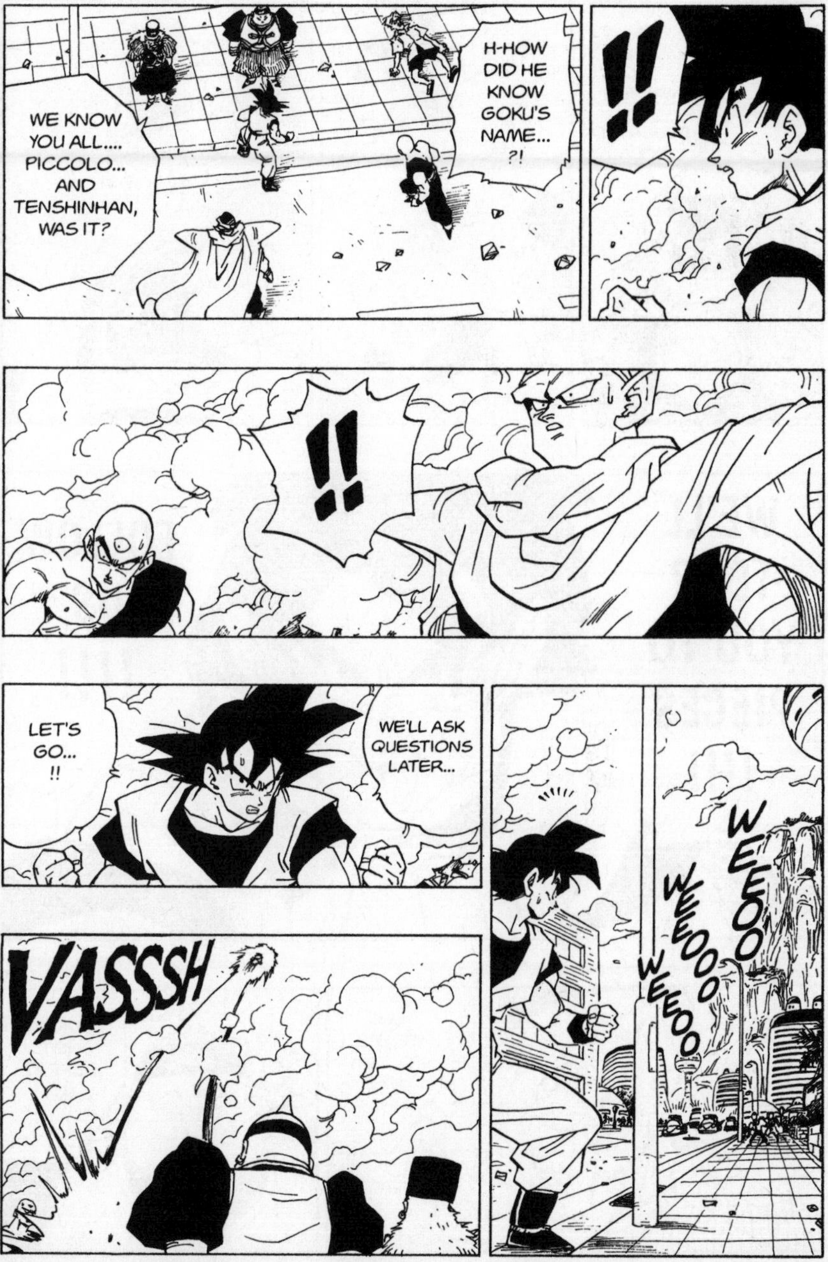

!!
H-HOW DID HE KNOW GOKU'S NAME...?!
WE KNOW YOU ALL.... PICCOLO... AND TENSHINHAN, WAS IT?
!!
WEEOO WEEOO WEEOO
WE'LL ASK QUESTIONS LATER...
LET'S GO... !!
VASSSH

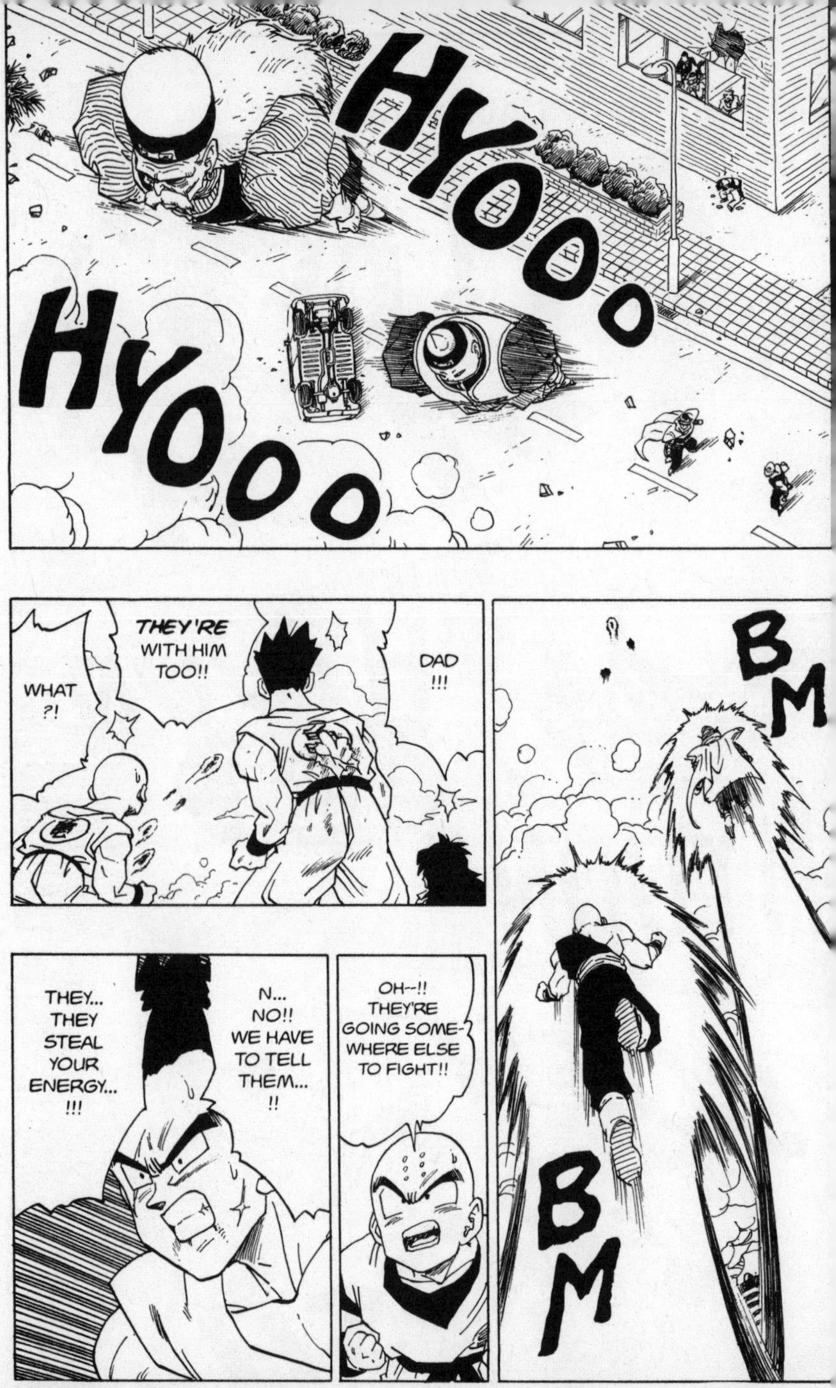
HYOOOO
HYOOOO
BM
BM
DAD!!!
THEY'RE WITH HIM TOO!!
WHAT?!
OH--!! THEY'RE GOING SOME-WHERE ELSE TO FIGHT!!
N... NO!! WE HAVE TO TELL THEM... !!
THEY... THEY STEAL YOUR ENERGY... !!!

**NEXT: Son Goku vs. The Red Ribbon Avengers**

# DBZ:146 • The Red Ribbon Androids

READ THIS WAY

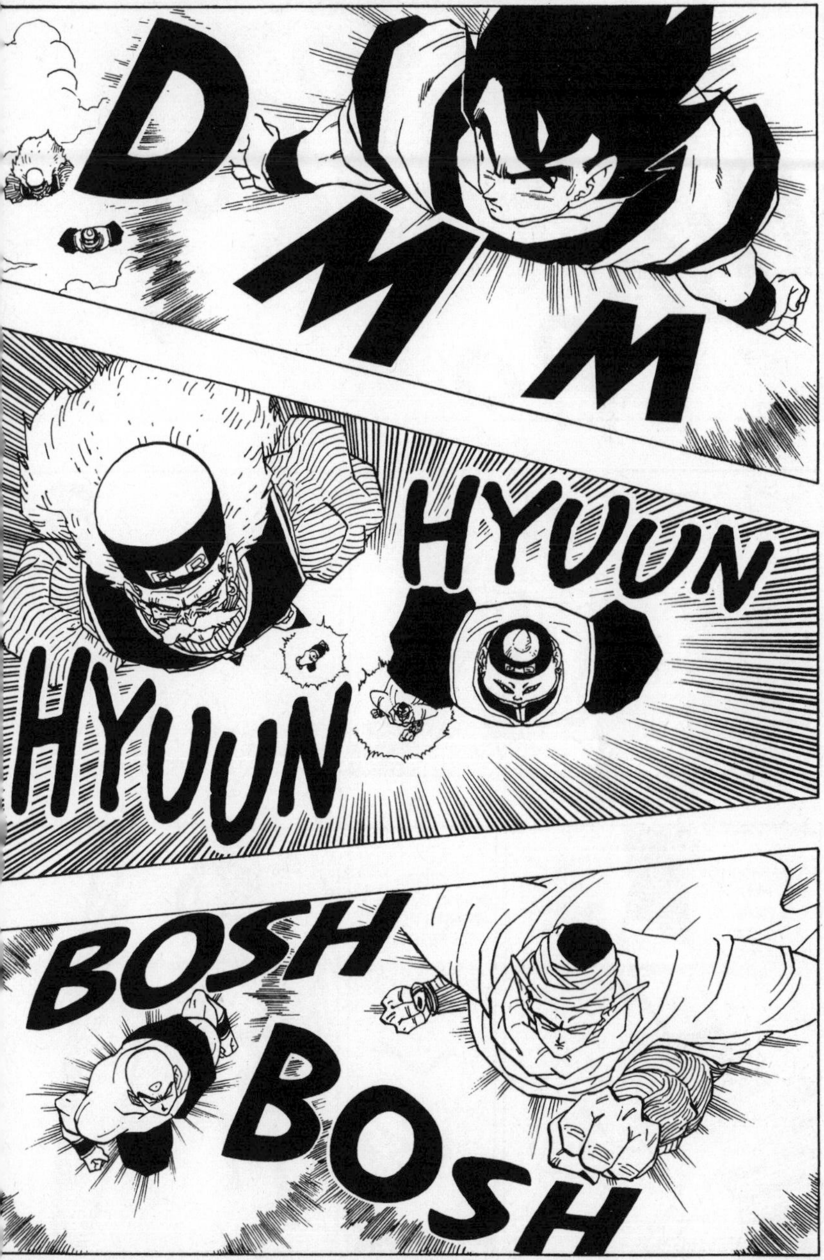
DMM
HYUUN
HYUUN
BOSH
BOSH

READ THIS WAY

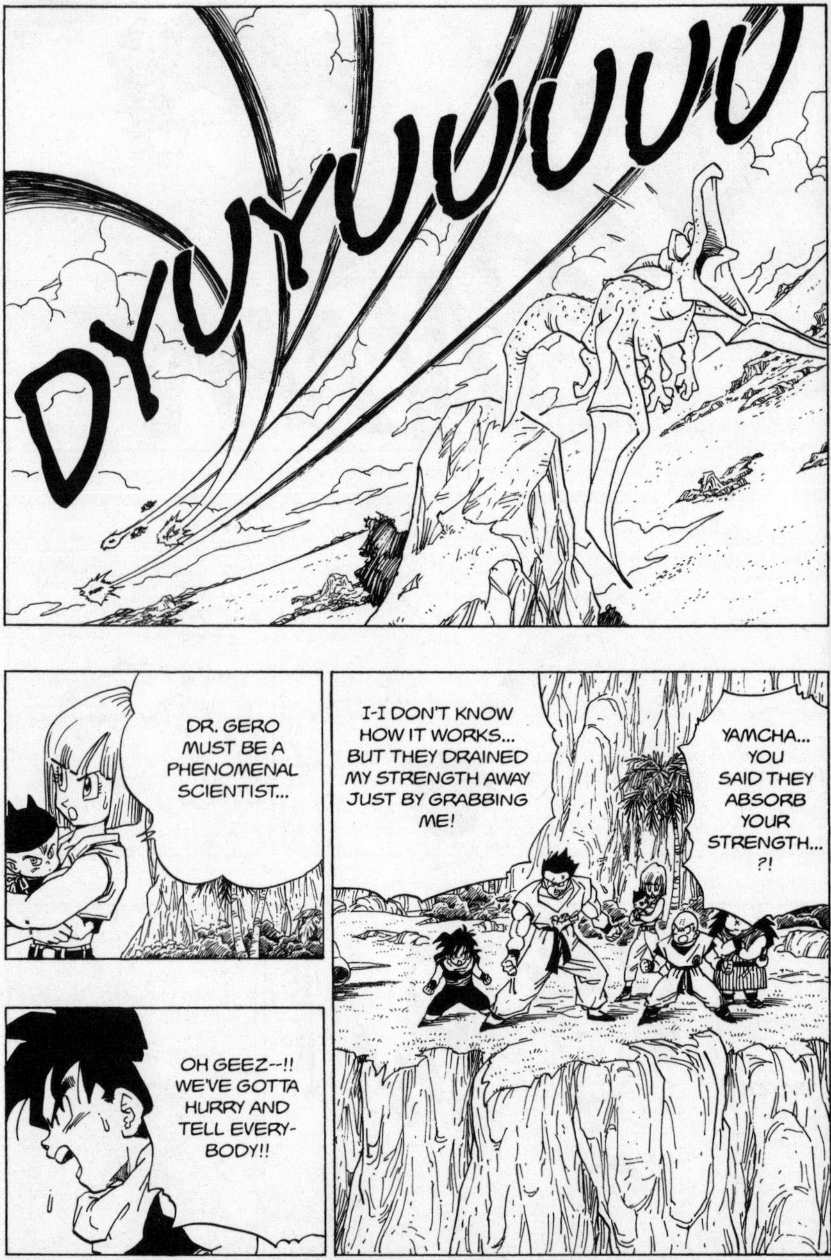
DYUYUUUUO
YAMCHA... YOU SAID THEY ABSORB YOUR STRENGTH... ?!
I-I DON'T KNOW HOW IT WORKS... BUT THEY DRAINED MY STRENGTH AWAY JUST BY GRABBING ME!
DR. GERO MUST BE A PHENOMENAL SCIENTIST...
OH GEEZ--!! WE'VE GOTTA HURRY AND TELL EVERY-BODY!!

READ THIS WAY

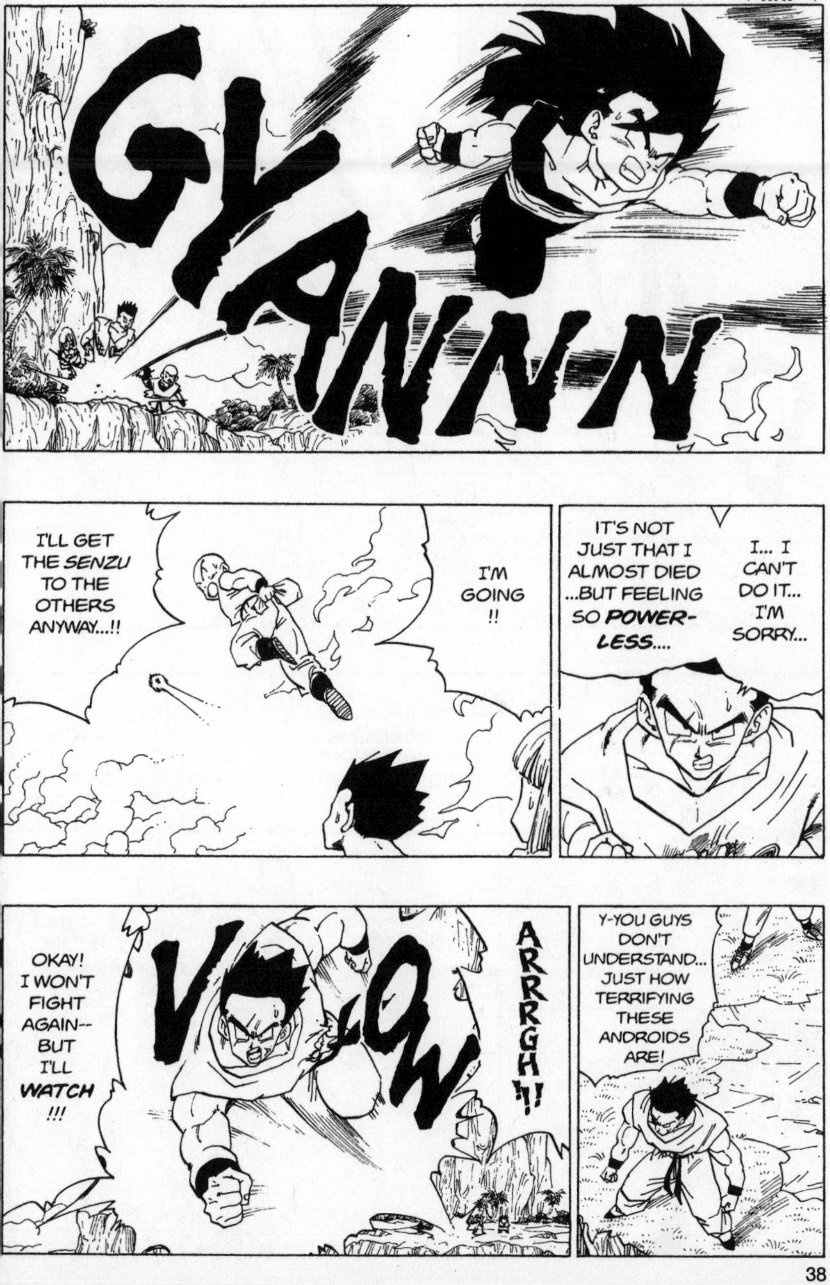
GYANNN
I... I CAN'T DO IT... I'M SORRY...
IT'S NOT JUST THAT I ALMOST DIED ...BUT FEELING SO **POWER-LESS**....
I'M GOING !!
I'LL GET THE *SENZU* TO THE OTHERS ANYWAY...!!
Y-YOU GUYS DON'T UNDERSTAND... JUST HOW TERRIFYING THESE ANDROIDS ARE!
ARRRGH!!
OKAY! I WON'T FIGHT AGAIN-- BUT I'LL ***WATCH*** !!!

READ THIS WAY

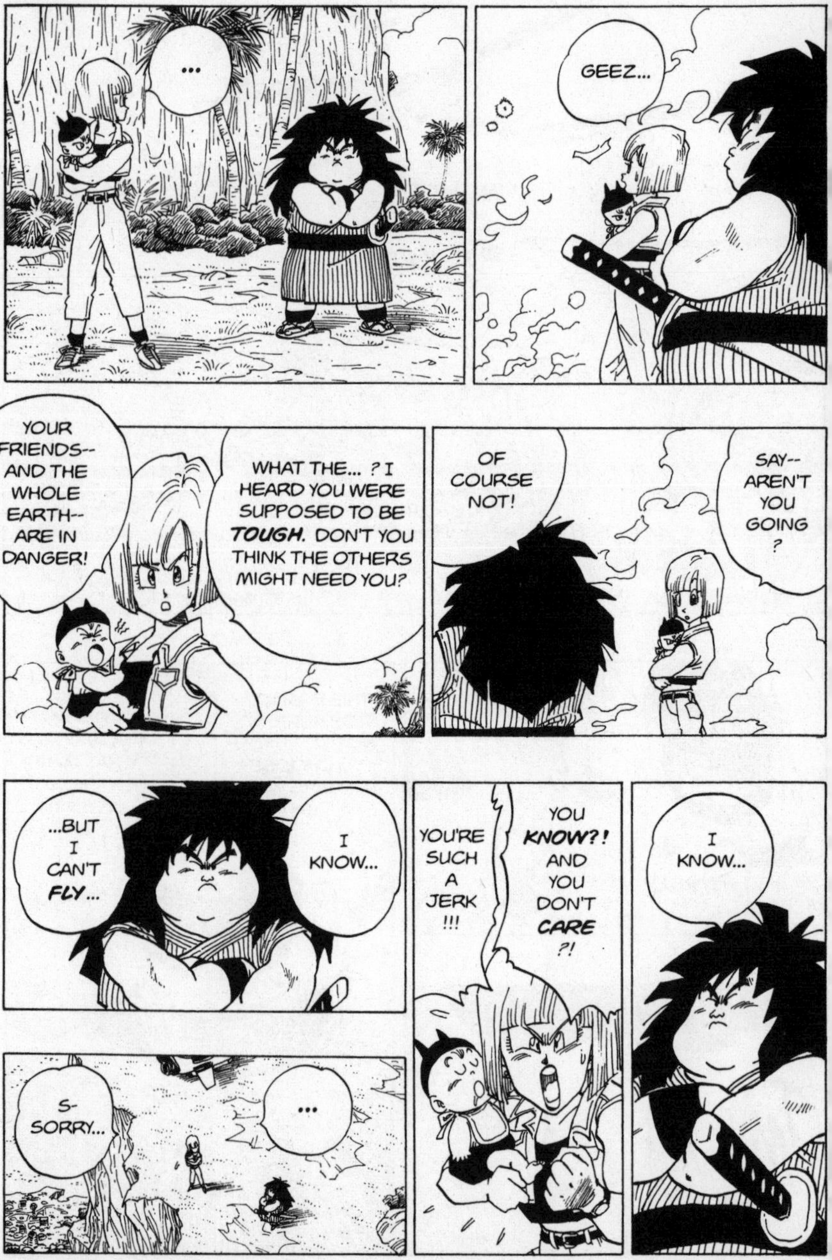
GEEZ...
...
SAY-- AREN'T YOU GOING ?
OF COURSE NOT!
WHAT THE... ? I HEARD YOU WERE SUPPOSED TO BE **TOUGH.** DON'T YOU THINK THE OTHERS MIGHT NEED YOU?
YOUR FRIENDS-- AND THE WHOLE EARTH-- ARE IN DANGER!
I KNOW...
YOU **KNOW?!** AND YOU DON'T **CARE** ?!
YOU'RE SUCH A JERK !!!
I KNOW...
...BUT I CAN'T **FLY...**
...
S-SORRY...

READ THIS WAY

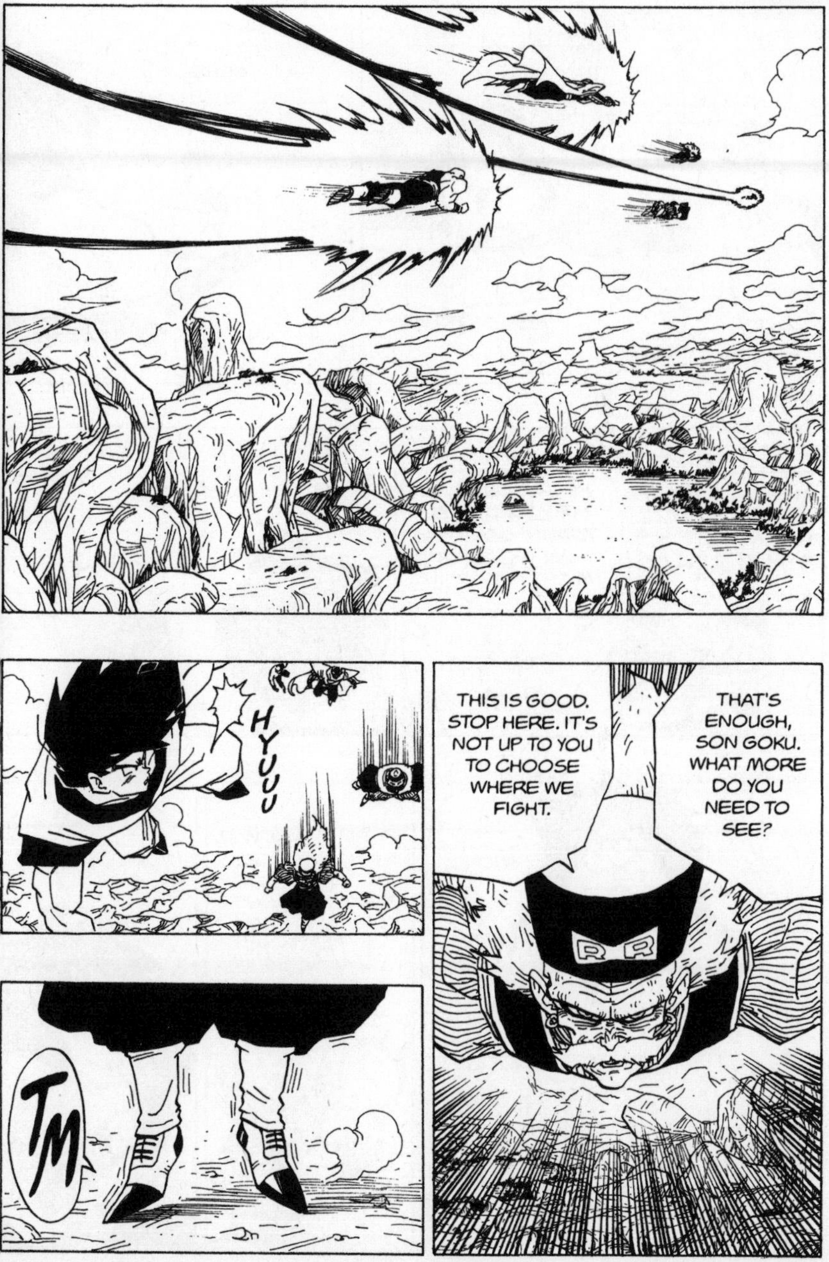

THAT'S ENOUGH, SON GOKU. WHAT MORE DO YOU NEED TO SEE?
THIS IS GOOD. STOP HERE. IT'S NOT UP TO YOU TO CHOOSE WHERE WE FIGHT.
HYUUU
TM

READ THIS WAY

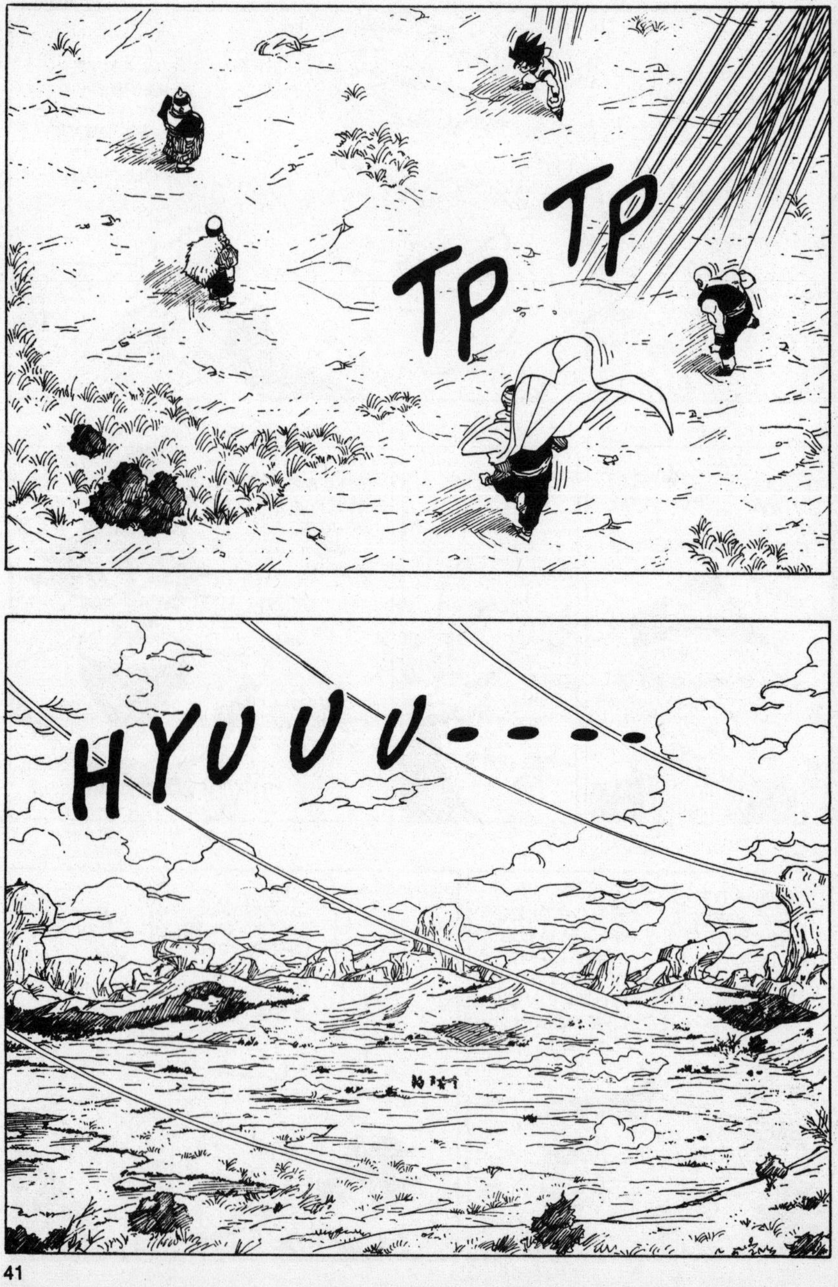
TP TP
HYUUU...

READ THIS WAY

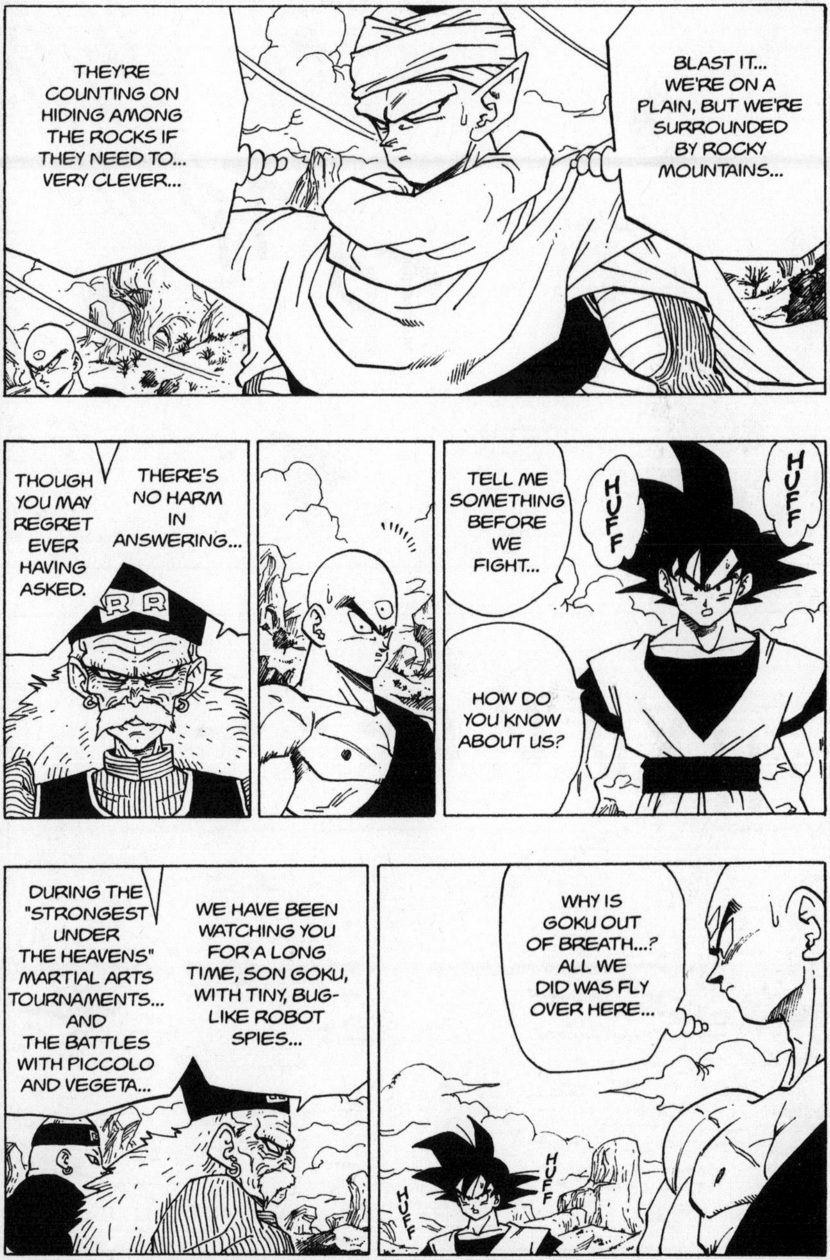

BLAST IT... WE'RE ON A PLAIN, BUT WE'RE SURROUNDED BY ROCKY MOUNTAINS...
THEY'RE COUNTING ON HIDING AMONG THE ROCKS IF THEY NEED TO... VERY CLEVER...
HUFF
HUFF
TELL ME SOMETHING BEFORE WE FIGHT...
HOW DO YOU KNOW ABOUT US?
THERE'S NO HARM IN ANSWERING...
THOUGH YOU MAY REGRET EVER HAVING ASKED.
WHY IS GOKU OUT OF BREATH...? ALL WE DID WAS FLY OVER HERE...
HUFF
HUFF
WE HAVE BEEN WATCHING YOU FOR A LONG TIME, SON GOKU, WITH TINY, BUG-LIKE ROBOT SPIES...
DURING THE "STRONGEST UNDER THE HEAVENS" MARTIAL ARTS TOURNAMENTS... AND THE BATTLES WITH PICCOLO AND VEGETA...

READ THIS WAY

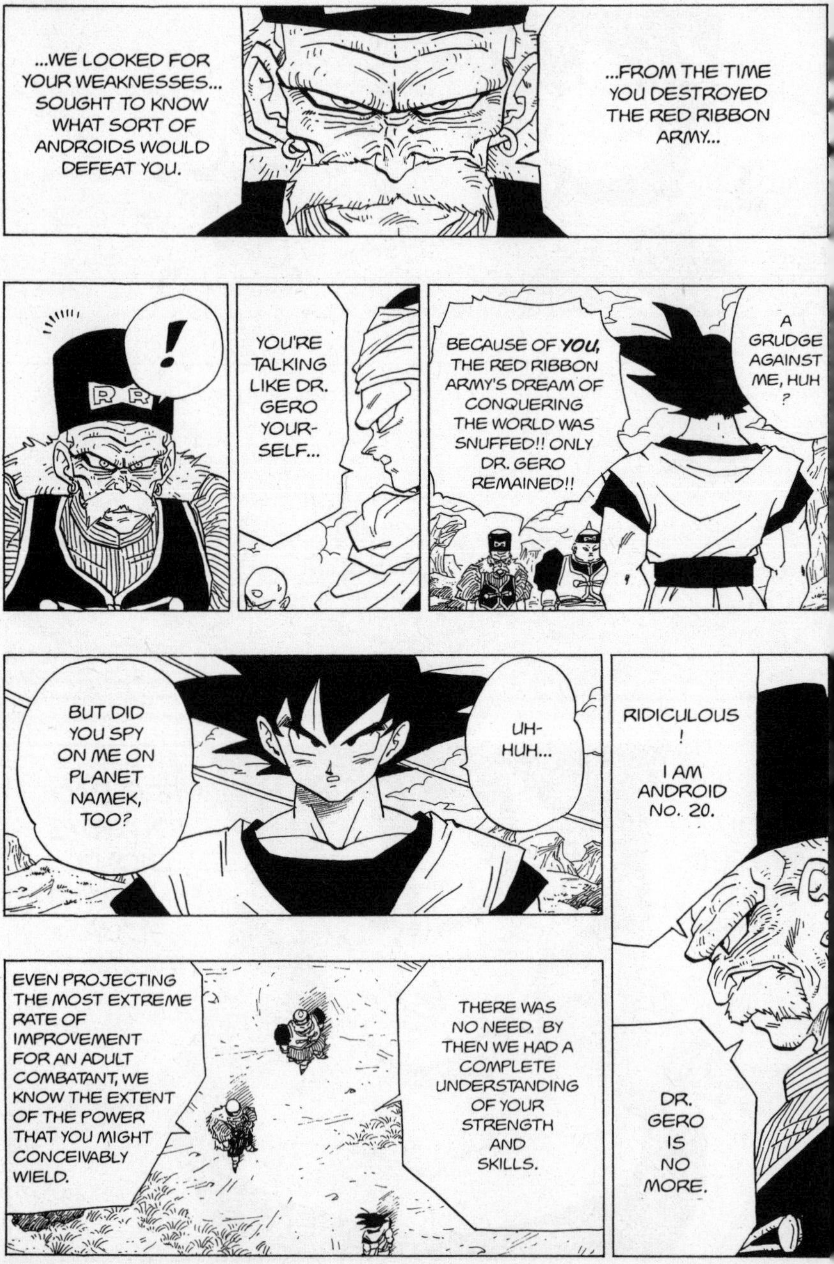
...FROM THE TIME YOU DESTROYED THE RED RIBBON ARMY...
...WE LOOKED FOR YOUR WEAKNESSES... SOUGHT TO KNOW WHAT SORT OF ANDROIDS WOULD DEFEAT YOU.
A GRUDGE AGAINST ME, HUH?
BECAUSE OF ***YOU,*** THE RED RIBBON ARMY'S DREAM OF CONQUERING THE WORLD WAS SNUFFED!! ONLY DR. GERO REMAINED!!
YOU'RE TALKING LIKE DR. GERO YOURSELF...
!
RIDICULOUS! I AM ANDROID NO. 20.
DR. GERO IS NO MORE.
UH-HUH...
BUT DID YOU SPY ON ME ON PLANET NAMEK, TOO?
THERE WAS NO NEED. BY THEN WE HAD A COMPLETE UNDERSTANDING OF YOUR STRENGTH AND SKILLS.
EVEN PROJECTING THE MOST EXTREME RATE OF IMPROVEMENT FOR AN ADULT COMBATANT, WE KNOW THE EXTENT OF THE POWER THAT YOU MIGHT CONCEIVABLY WIELD.

READ THIS WAY

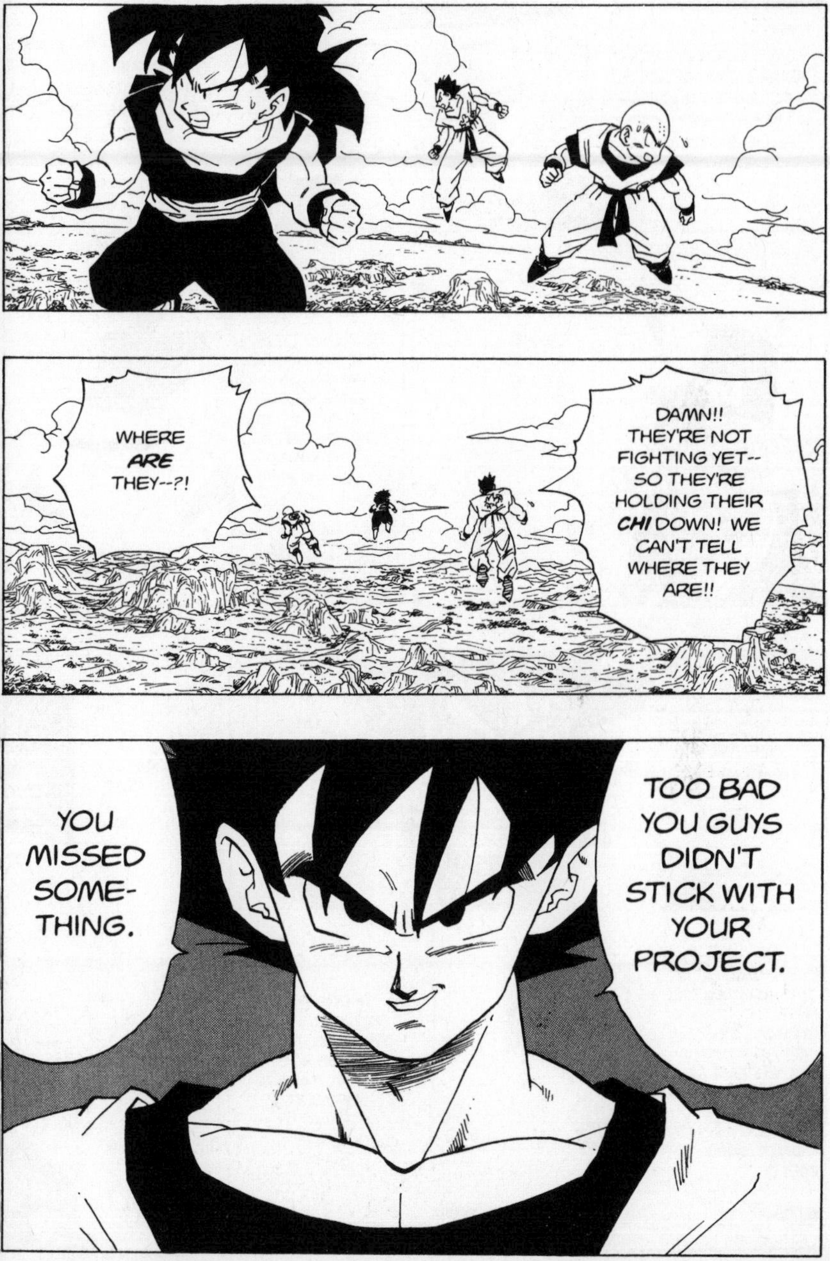
DAMN!! THEY'RE NOT FIGHTING YET-- SO THEY'RE HOLDING THEIR *CHI* DOWN! WE CAN'T TELL WHERE THEY ARE!!
WHERE *ARE* THEY--?!
TOO BAD YOU GUYS DIDN'T STICK WITH YOUR PROJECT.
YOU MISSED SOME-THING.

READ THIS WAY

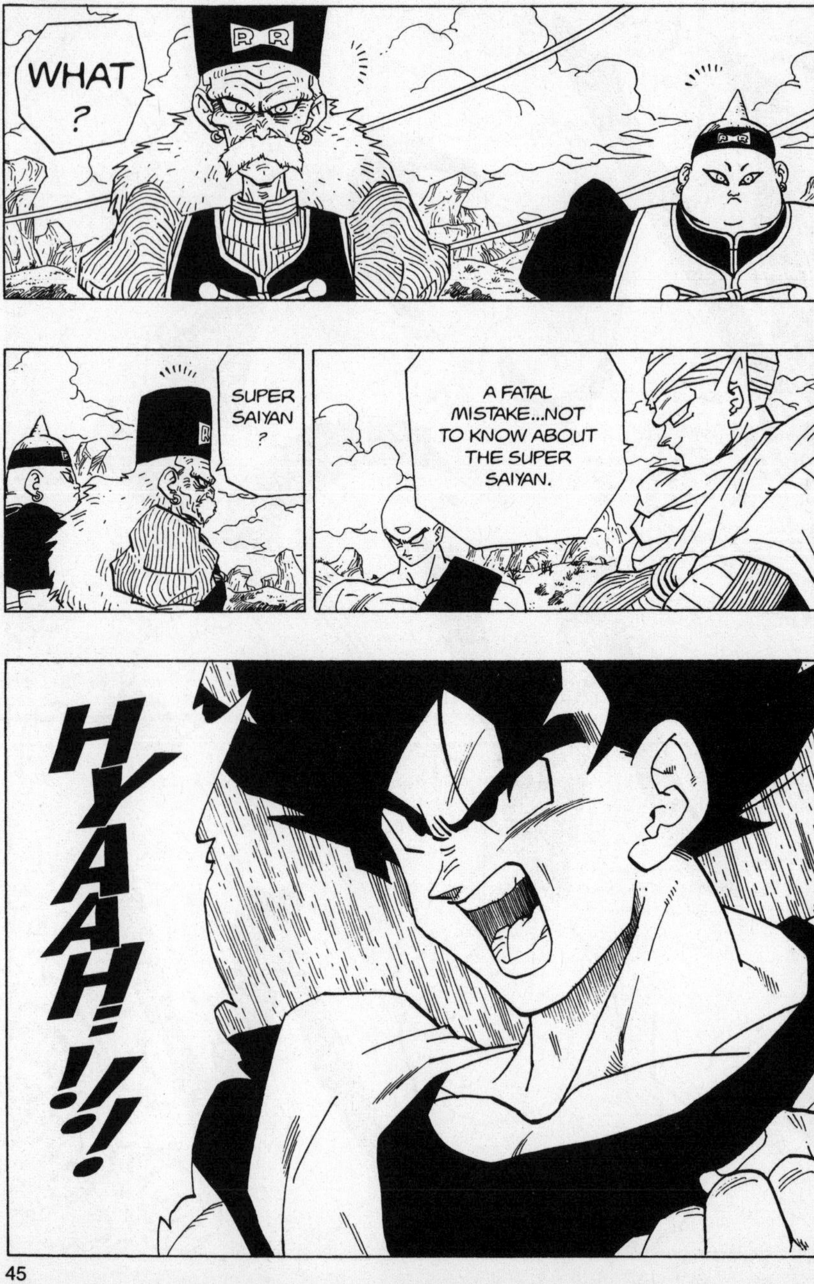

WHAT ?
A FATAL MISTAKE...NOT TO KNOW ABOUT THE SUPER SAIYAN.
SUPER SAIYAN ?
HYAAH!!!

READ THIS WAY

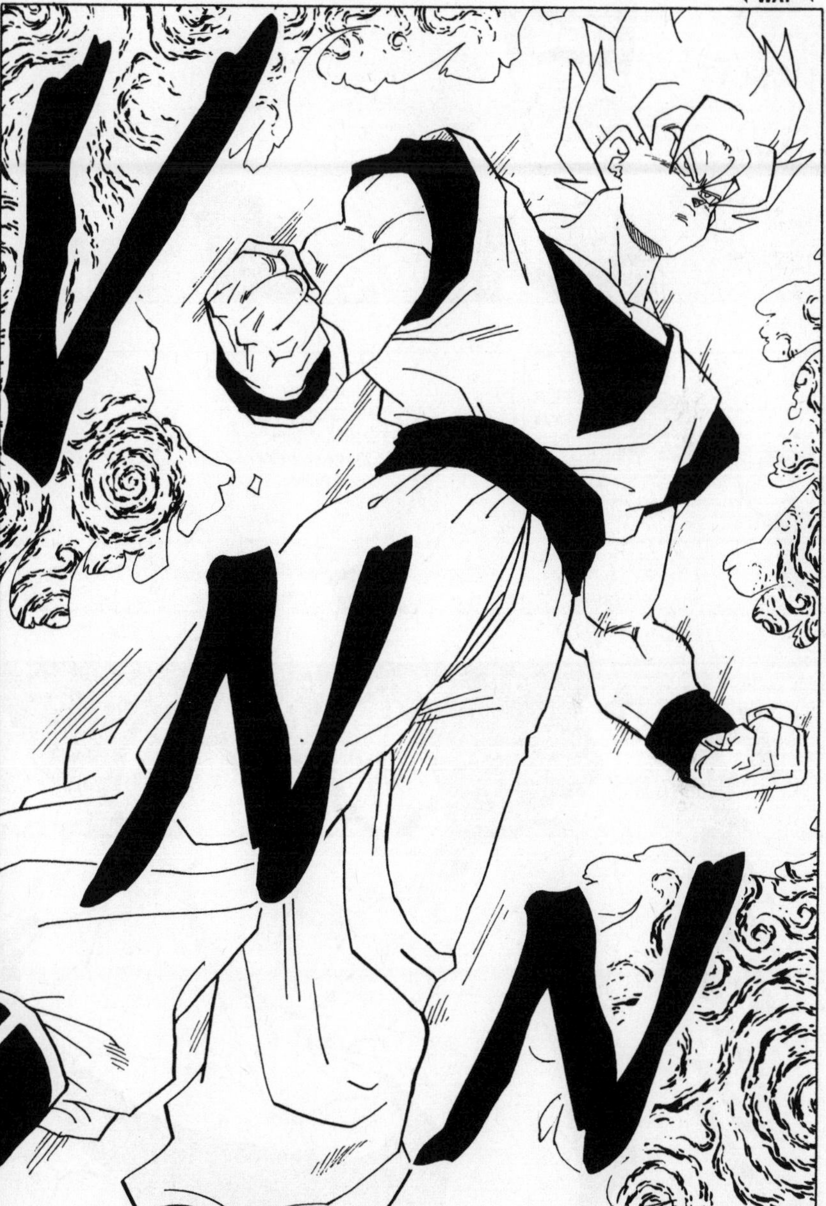
VNN

READ THIS WAY

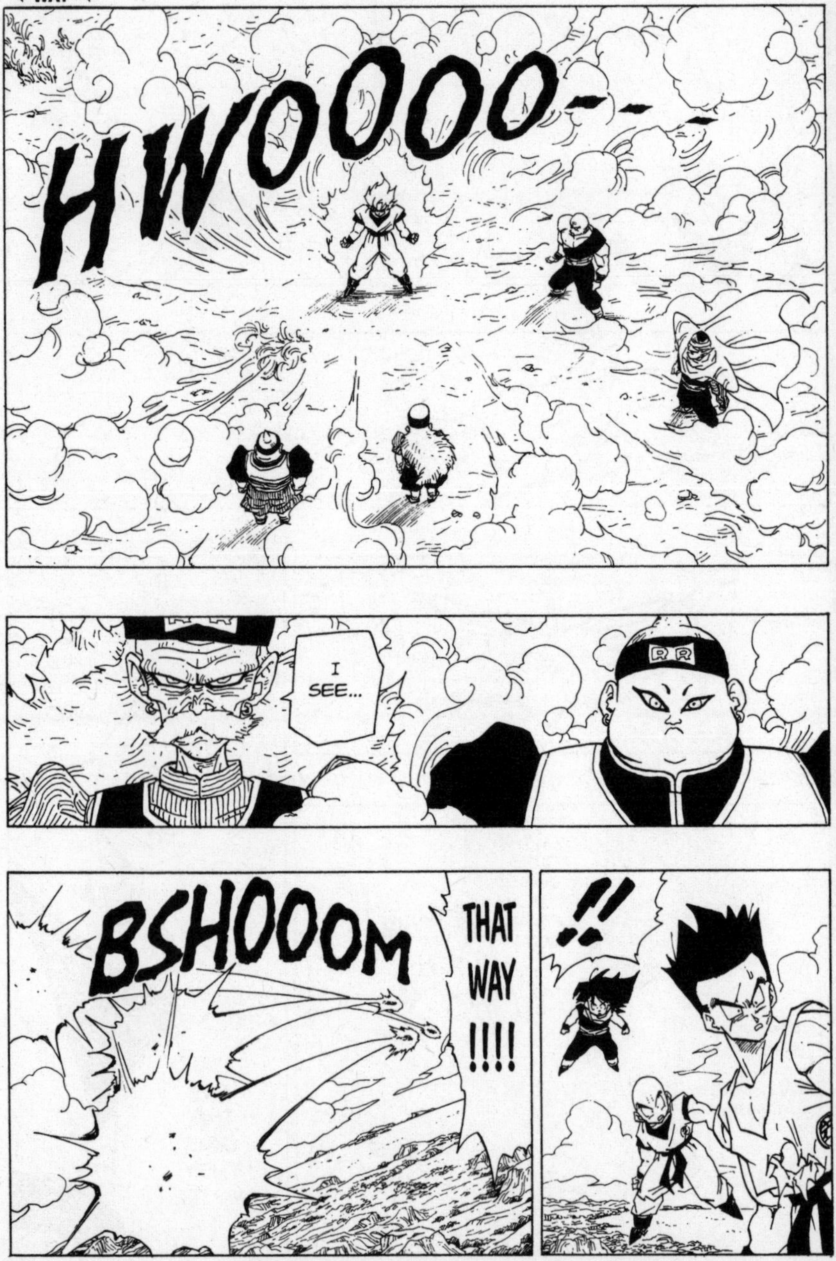
HWOOOO--
I SEE...
!!
THAT WAY!!!!
BSHOOOM

READ THIS WAY

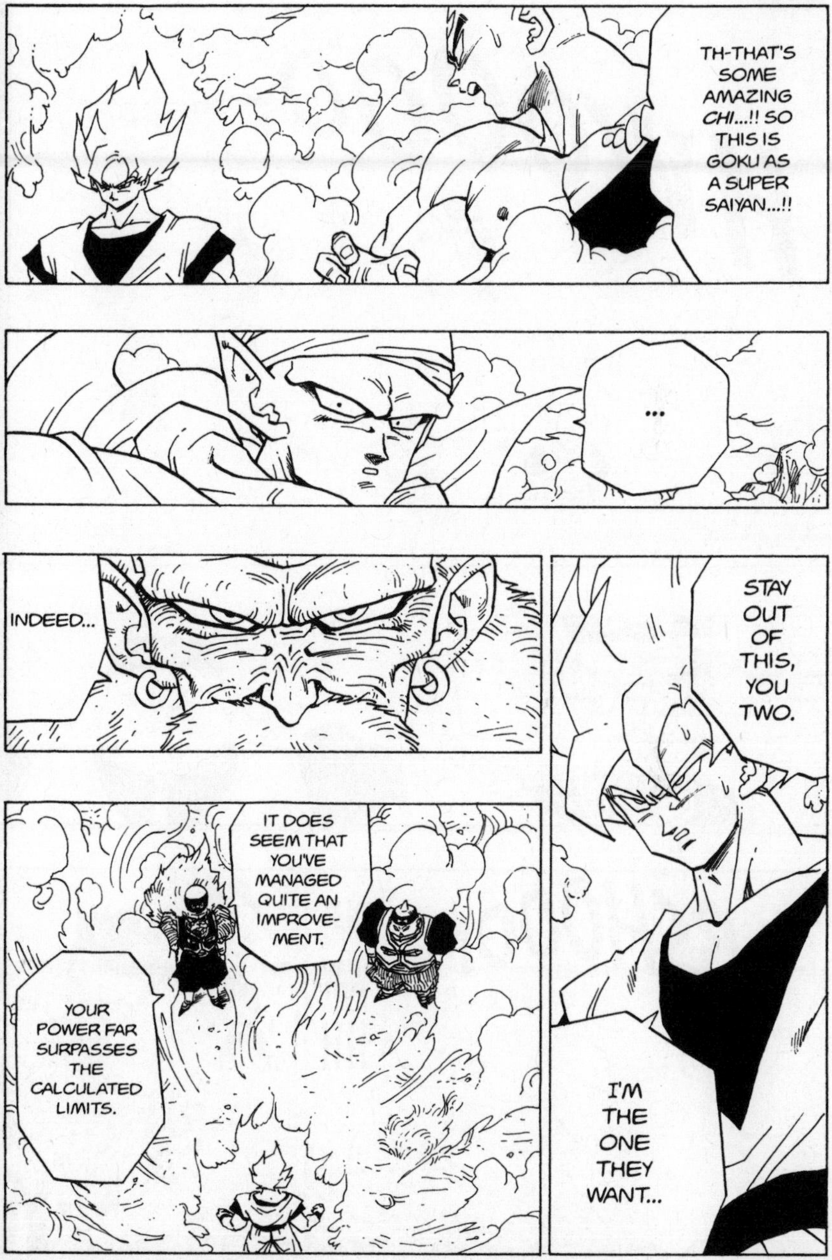
TH-THAT'S SOME AMAZING CHI...!! SO THIS IS GOKU AS A SUPER SAIYAN...!!
...
STAY OUT OF THIS, YOU TWO.
I'M THE ONE THEY WANT...
INDEED...
IT DOES SEEM THAT YOU'VE MANAGED QUITE AN IMPROVE-MENT.
YOUR POWER FAR SURPASSES THE CALCULATED LIMITS.

READ THIS WAY

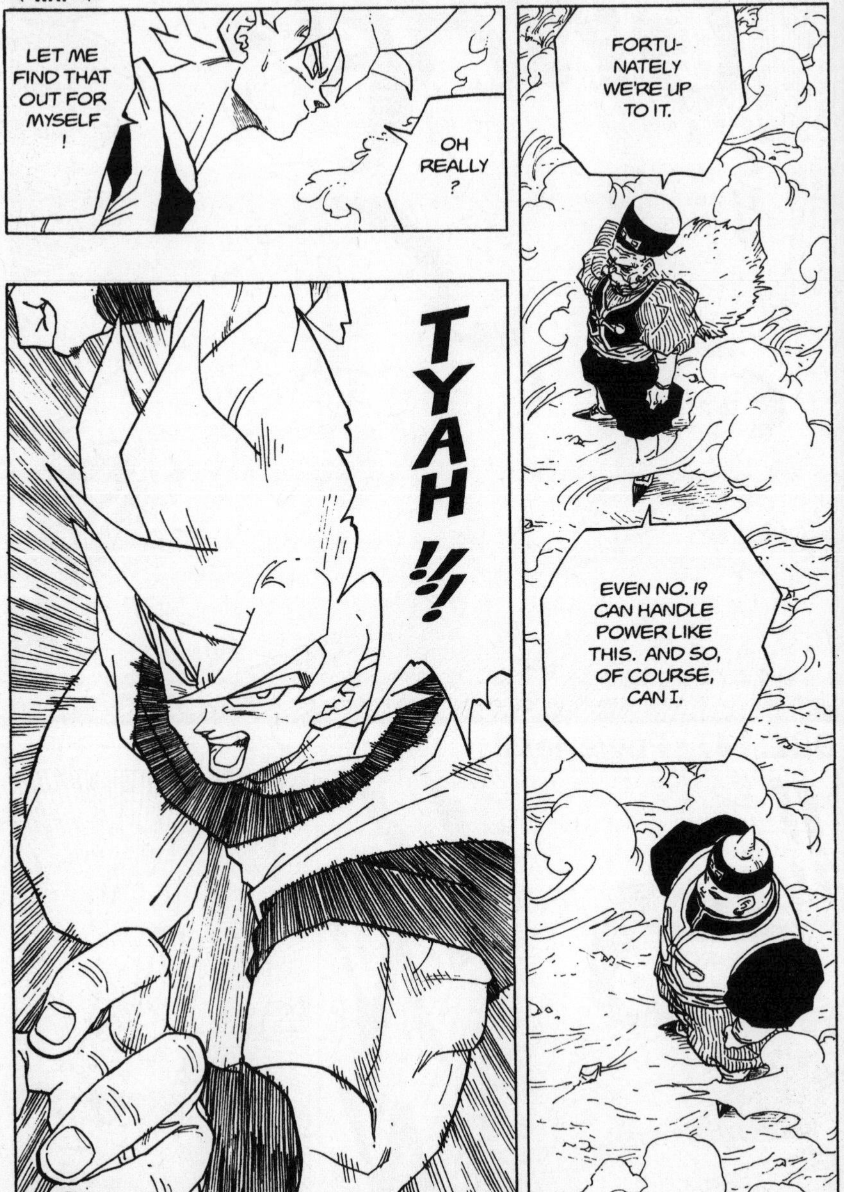
FORTUNATELY WE'RE UP TO IT.
EVEN NO. 19 CAN HANDLE POWER LIKE THIS. AND SO, OF COURSE, CAN I.
OH REALLY ?
LET ME FIND THAT OUT FOR MYSELF !
TYAH !!!

**NEXT: What's Wrong with Goku?**

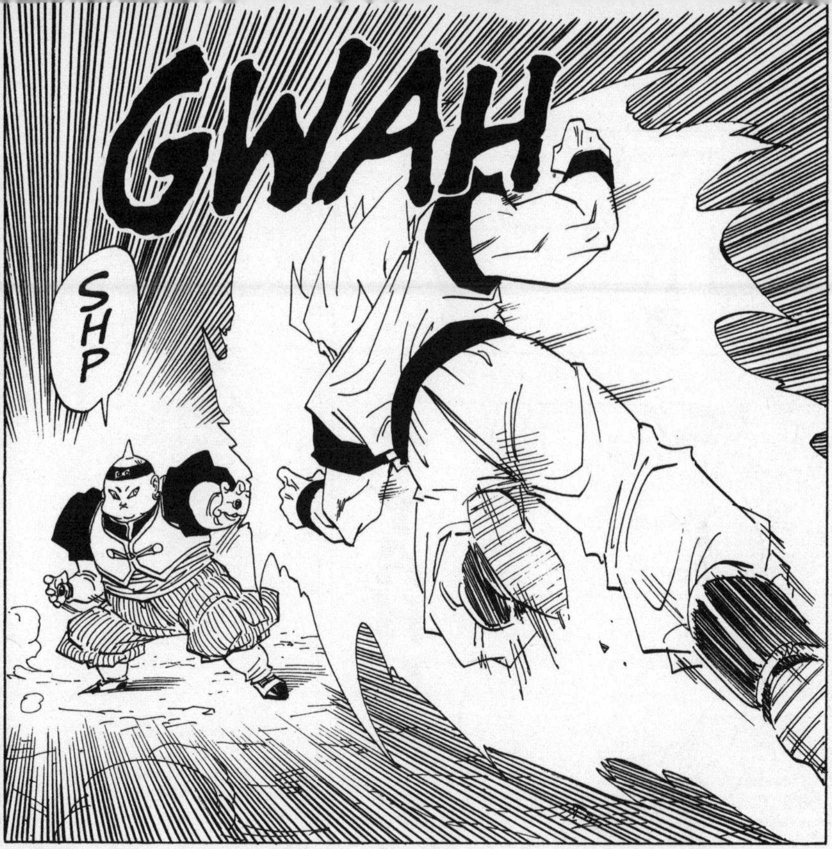
GWAH
SHP

## DBZ: 147 • Powerless!

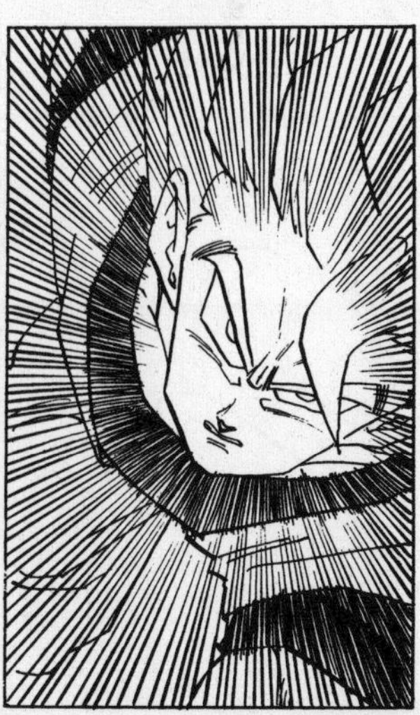

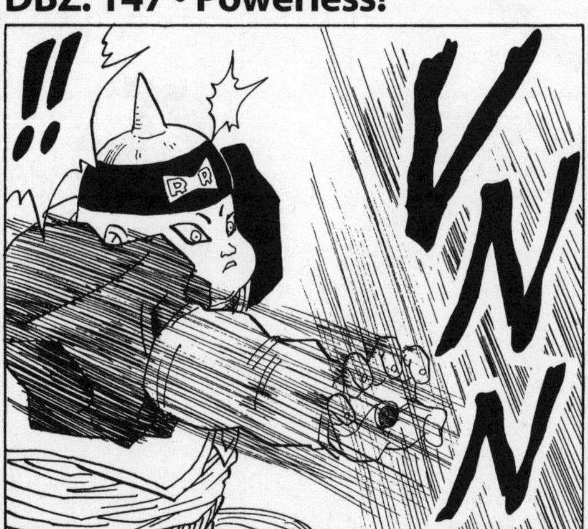
!!
VNN

READ THIS WAY

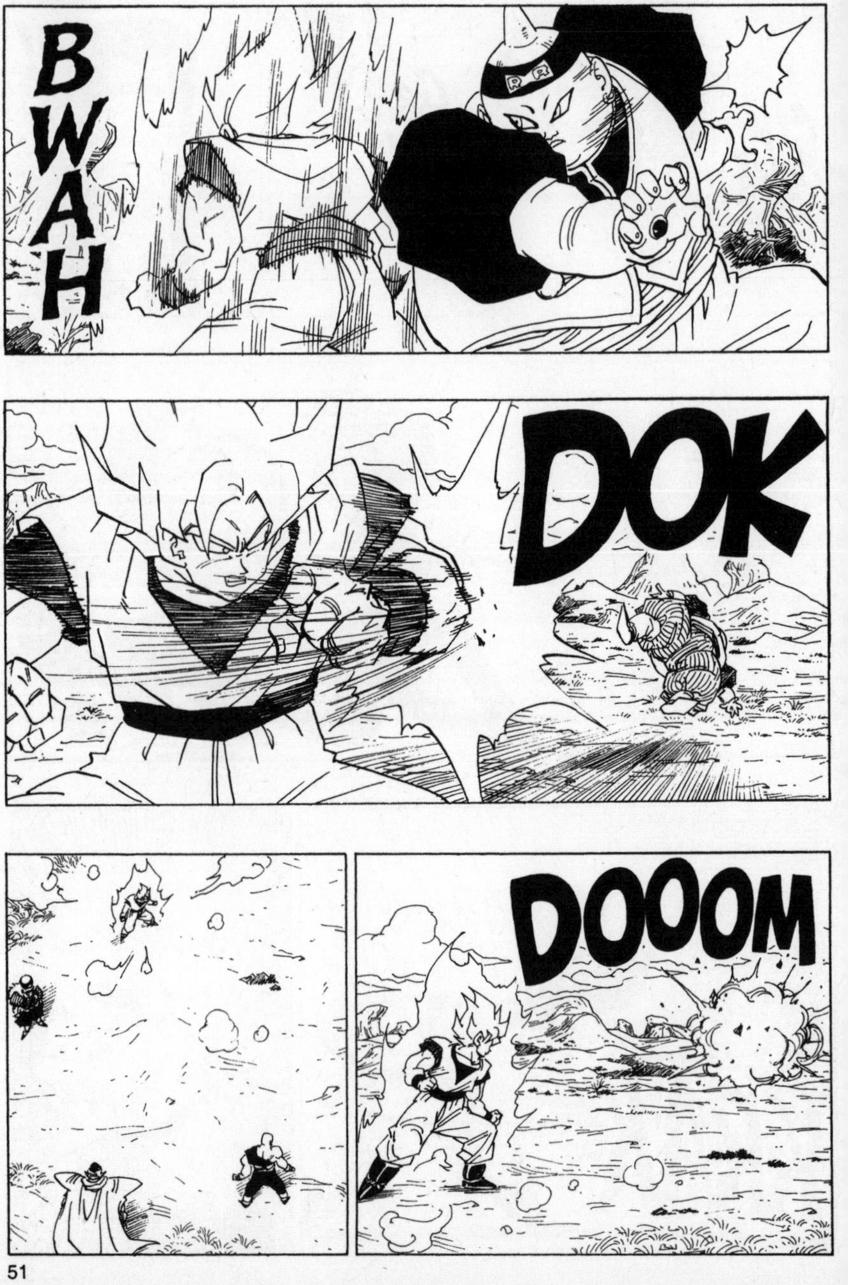
BWAH
DOK
DOOOM

READ THIS WAY

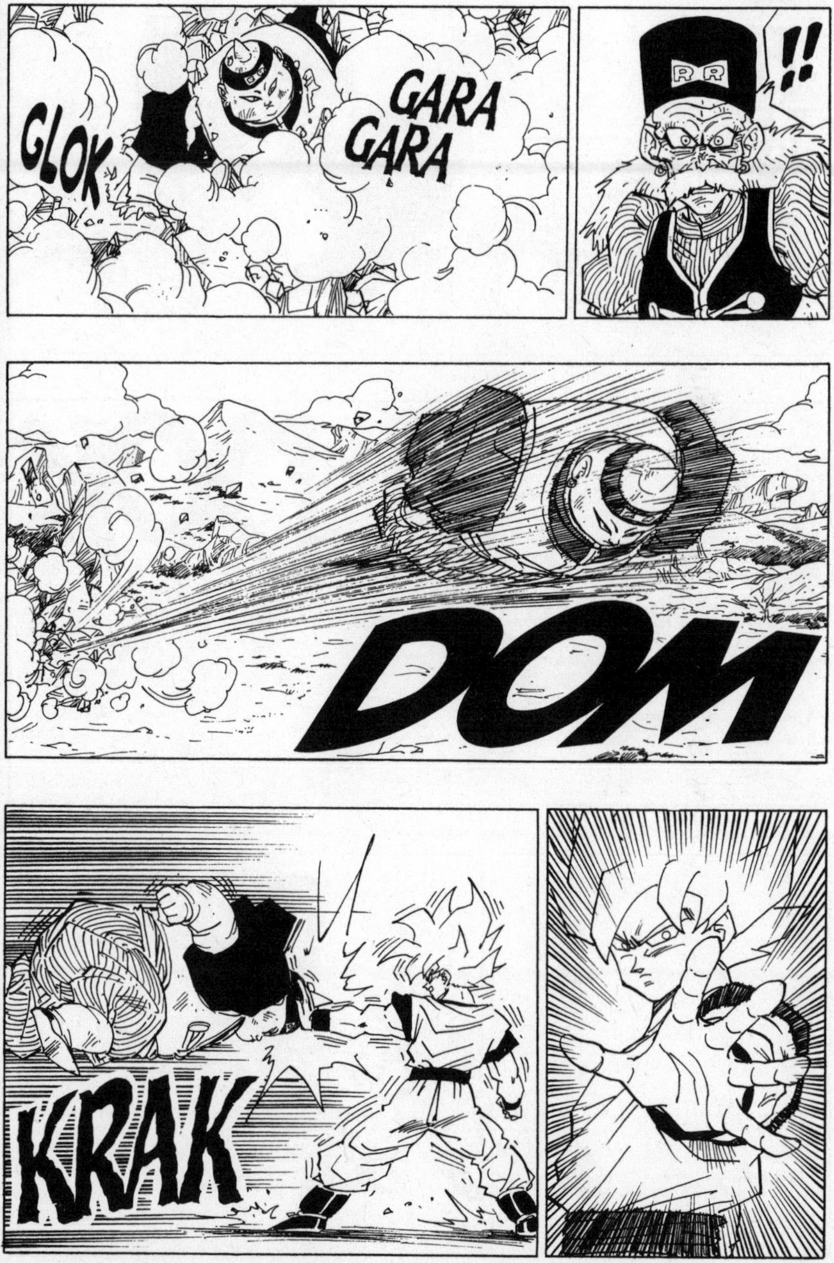
!!
GARA GARA
GLOK
DOM
KRAK

READ THIS WAY

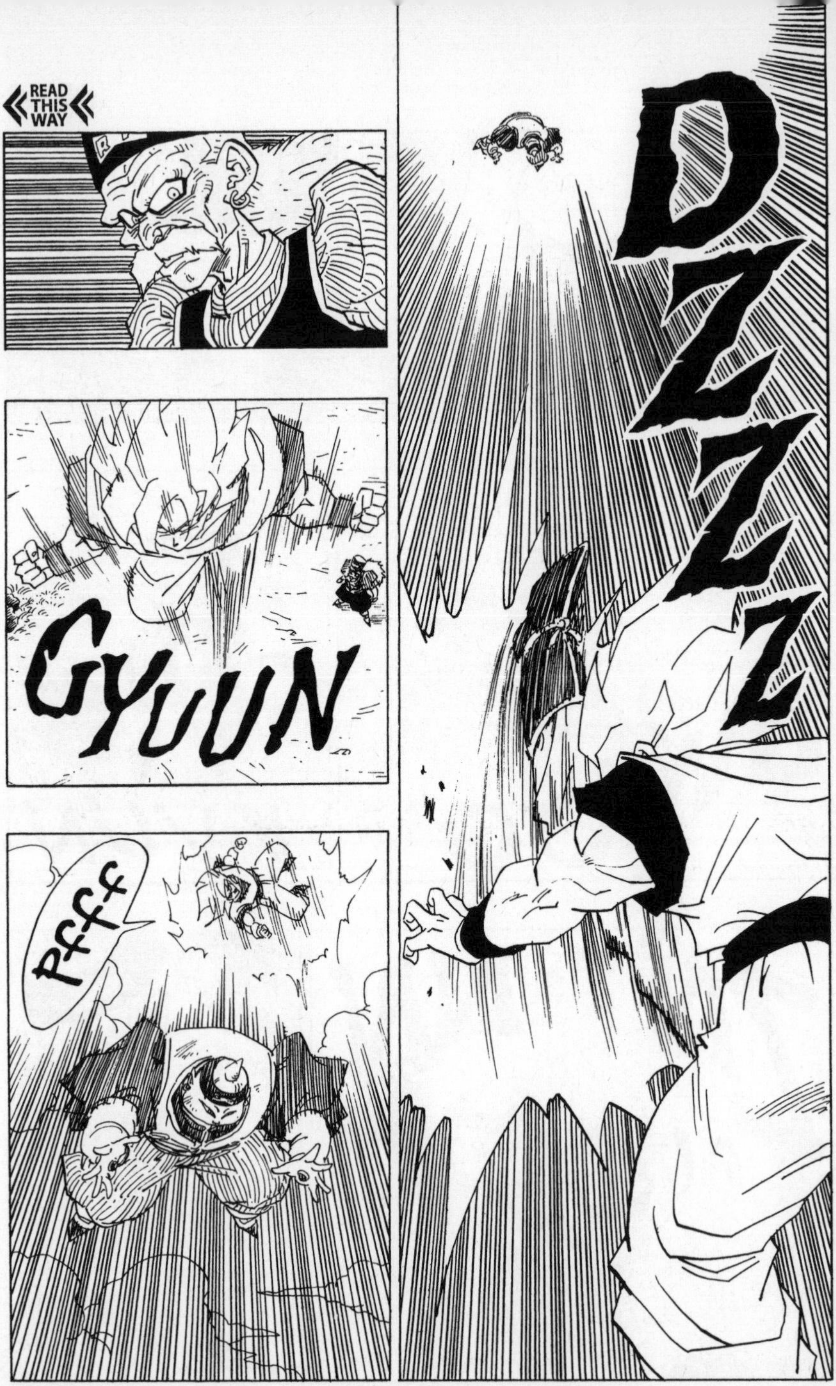
DZZZZ
GYUUN
Pfff

READ THIS WAY

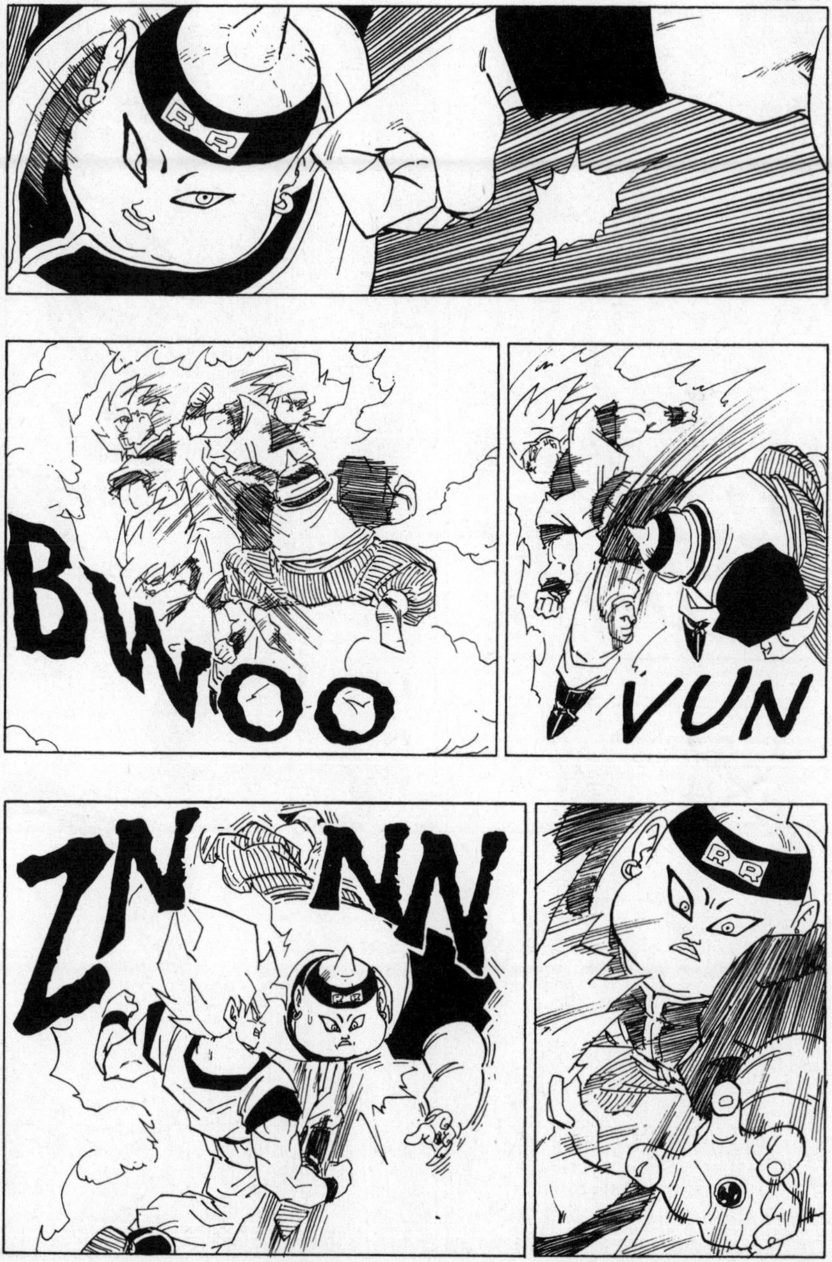
VUN
BWOOO
ZNNN

READ THIS WAY

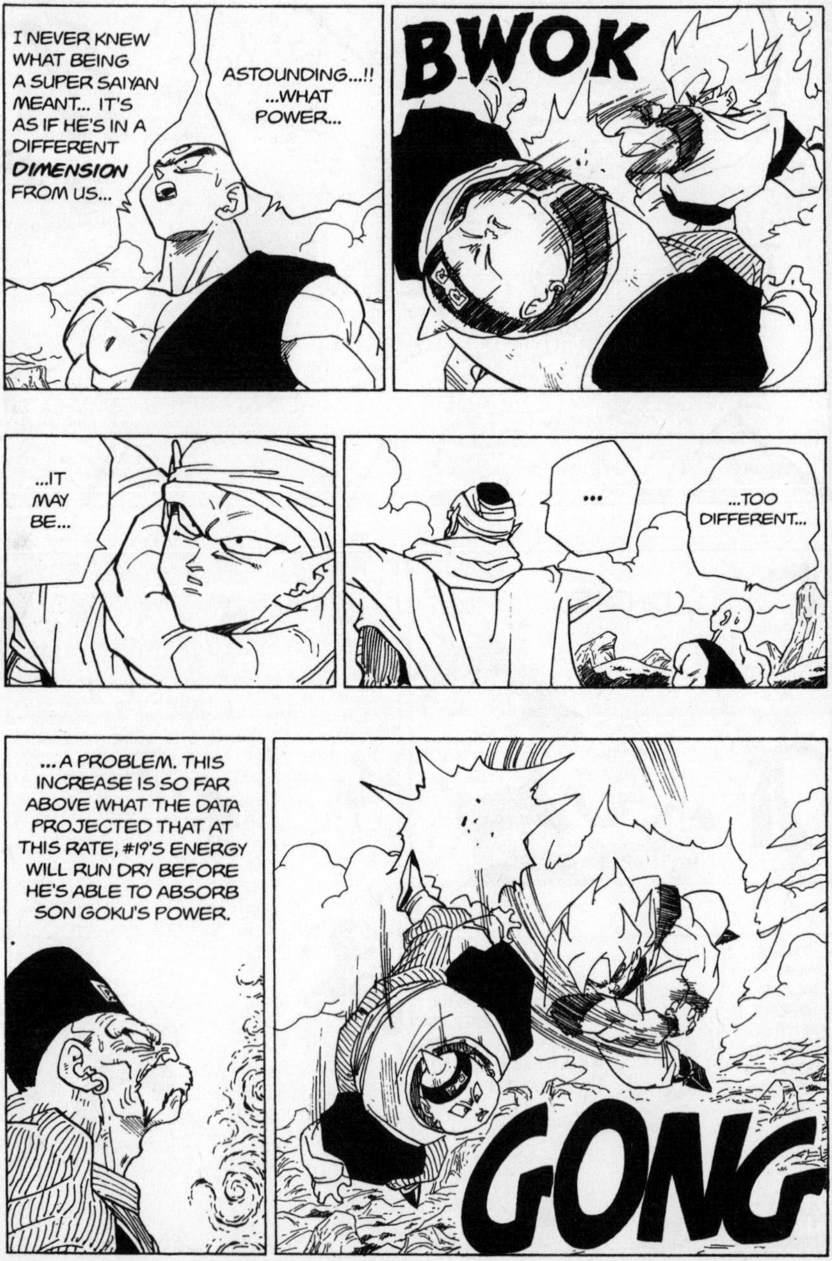
BWOK
ASTOUNDING...!! ...WHAT POWER...
I NEVER KNEW WHAT BEING A SUPER SAIYAN MEANT... IT'S AS IF HE'S IN A DIFFERENT DIMENSION FROM US...
...TOO DIFFERENT...
...
...IT MAY BE...
GONG
...A PROBLEM. THIS INCREASE IS SO FAR ABOVE WHAT THE DATA PROJECTED THAT AT THIS RATE, #19'S ENERGY WILL RUN DRY BEFORE HE'S ABLE TO ABSORB SON GOKU'S POWER.

READ THIS WAY

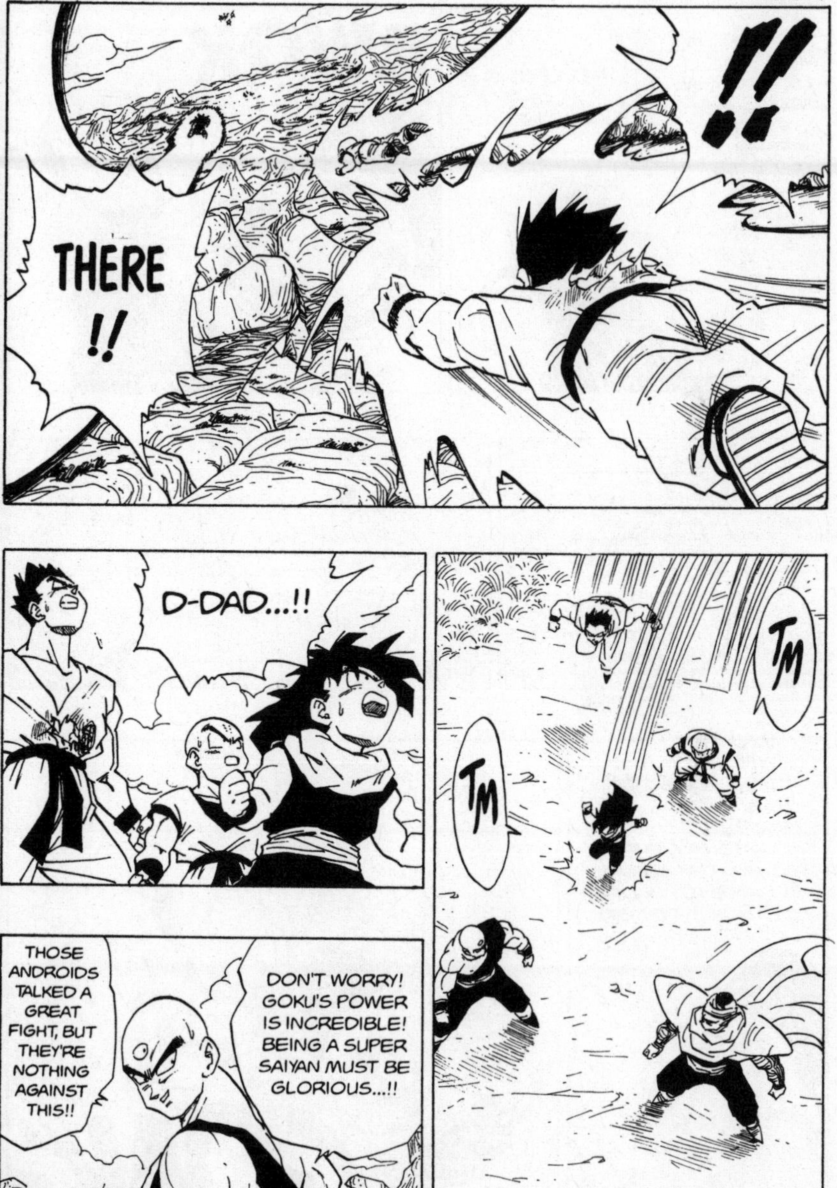
!!
THERE !!
TM
TM
D-DAD...!!
DON'T WORRY! GOKU'S POWER IS INCREDIBLE! BEING A SUPER SAIYAN MUST BE GLORIOUS...!!
THOSE ANDROIDS TALKED A GREAT FIGHT, BUT THEY'RE NOTHING AGAINST THIS!!

READ THIS WAY

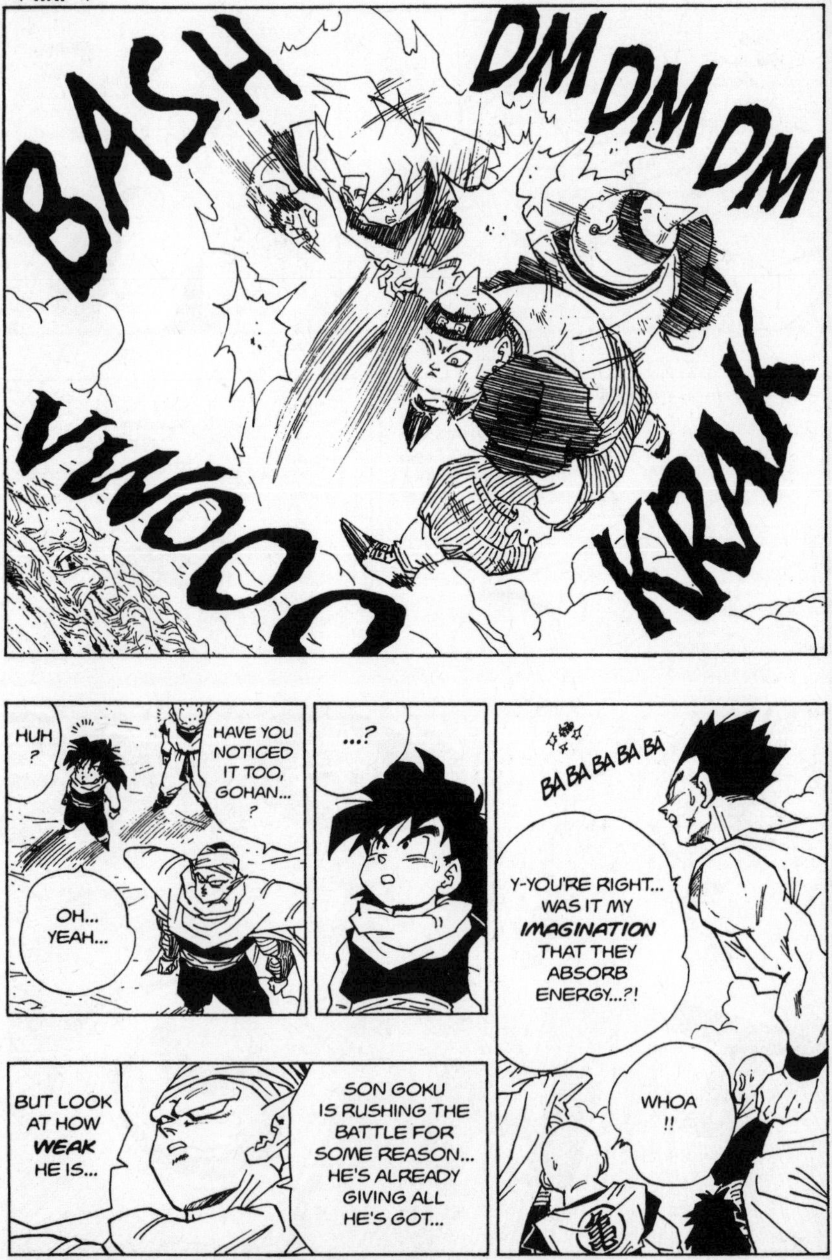

DM DM DM DM
BASH
KRAK
VWOOO
BA BA BA BA BA BA
Y-YOU'RE RIGHT... WAS IT MY **IMAGINATION** THAT THEY ABSORB ENERGY...?!
WHOA !!
...?
HAVE YOU NOTICED IT TOO, GOHAN...?
HUH ?
OH... YEAH...
SON GOKU IS RUSHING THE BATTLE FOR SOME REASON... HE'S ALREADY GIVING ALL HE'S GOT...
BUT LOOK AT HOW **WEAK** HE IS...

READ THIS WAY

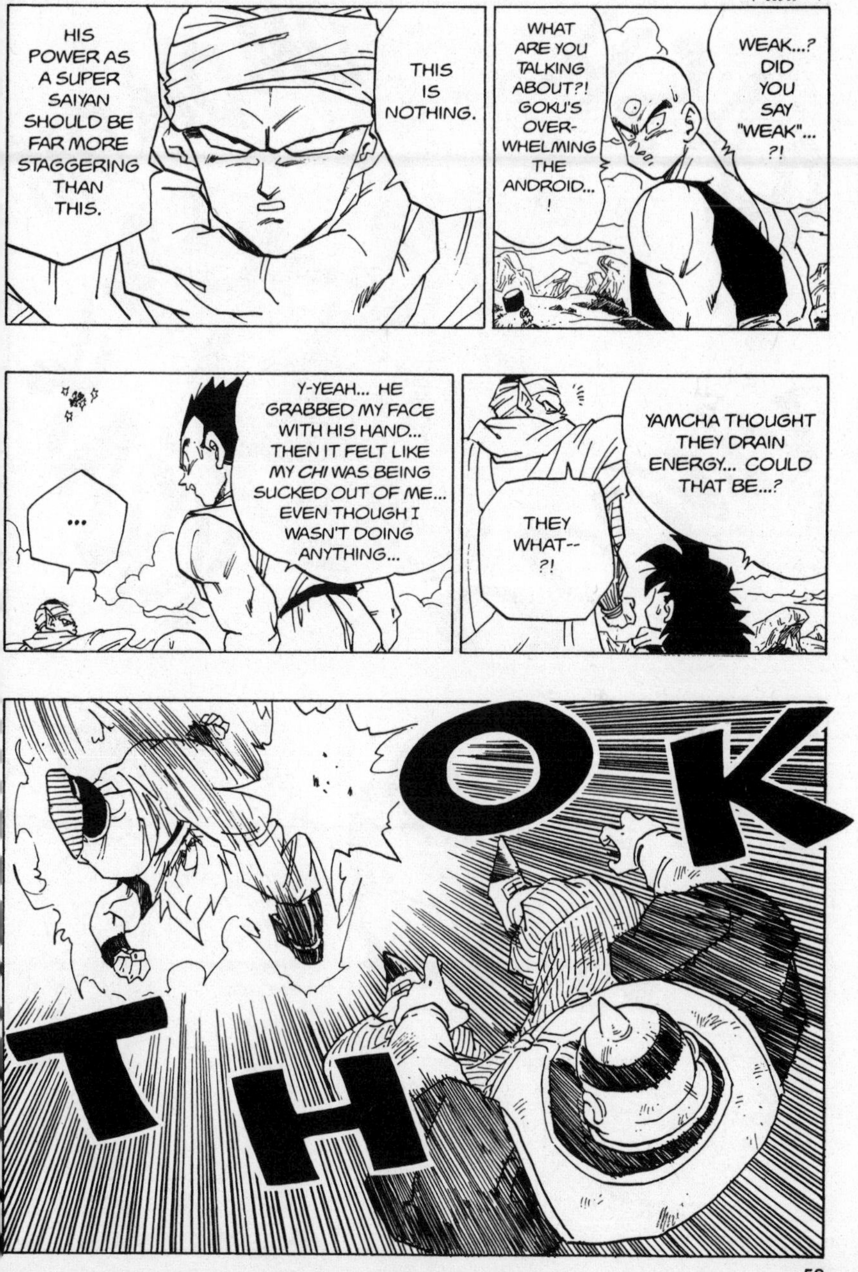

WEAK...? DID YOU SAY "WEAK"... ?!
WHAT ARE YOU TALKING ABOUT?! GOKU'S OVER-WHELMING THE ANDROID... !
THIS IS NOTHING.
HIS POWER AS A SUPER SAIYAN SHOULD BE FAR MORE STAGGERING THAN THIS.
YAMCHA THOUGHT THEY DRAIN ENERGY... COULD THAT BE...?
THEY WHAT-- ?!
Y-YEAH... HE GRABBED MY FACE WITH HIS HAND... THEN IT FELT LIKE MY *CHI* WAS BEING SUCKED OUT OF ME... EVEN THOUGH I WASN'T DOING ANYTHING...
...
THOK

READ THIS WAY

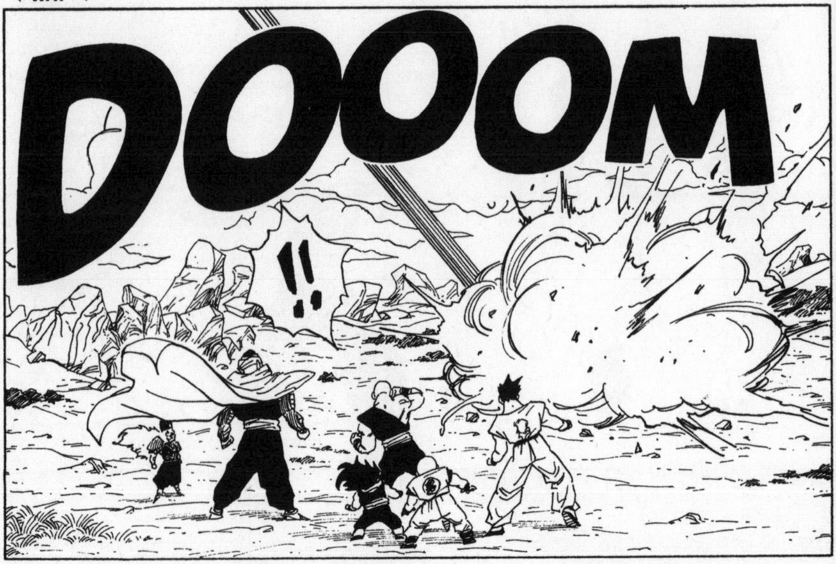
DOOOM
!!

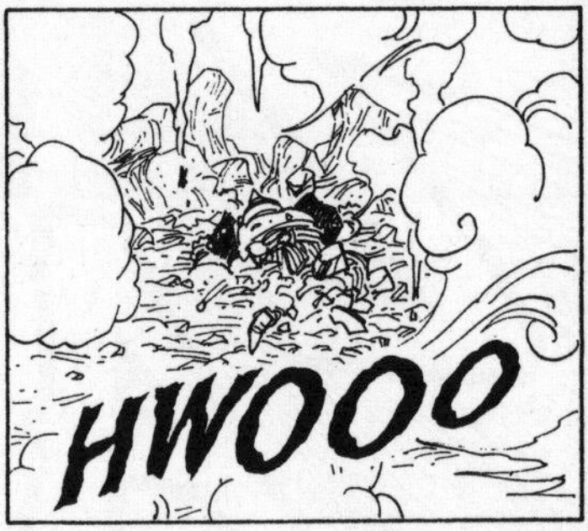
HWOOO

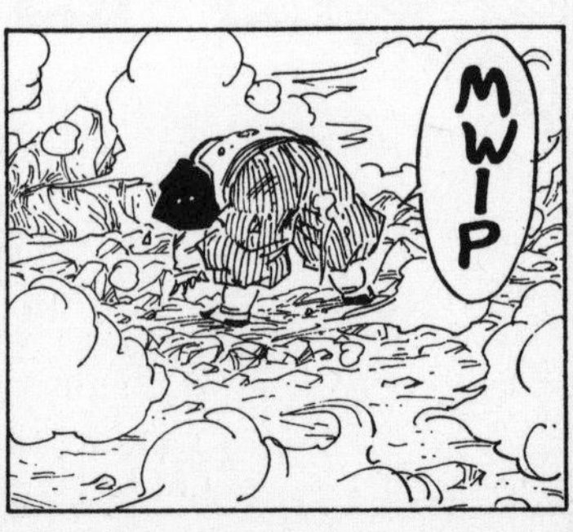
MWIP

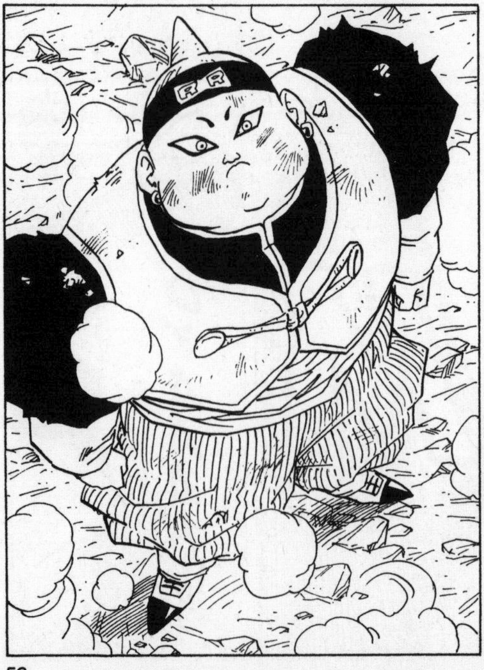

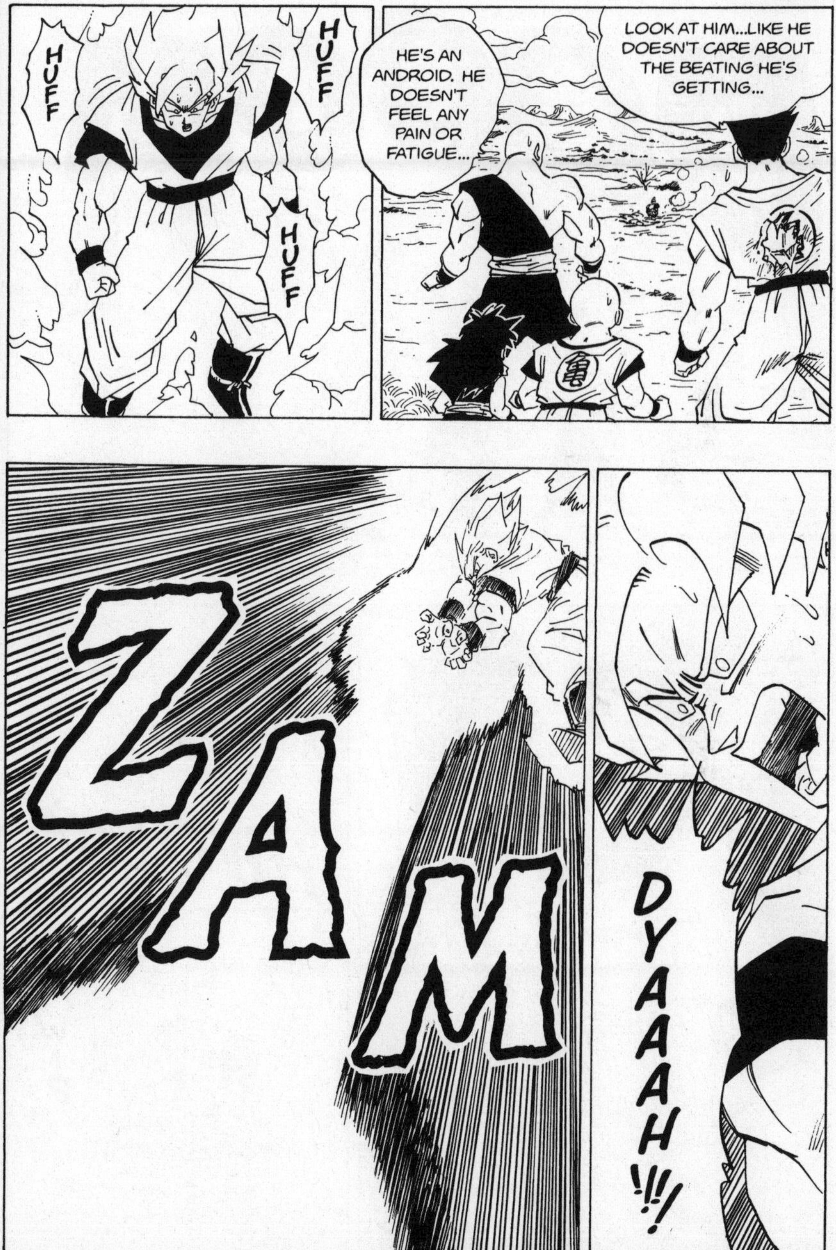
LOOK AT HIM...LIKE HE DOESN'T CARE ABOUT THE BEATING HE'S GETTING...
HE'S AN ANDROID. HE DOESN'T FEEL ANY PAIN OR FATIGUE...
HUFF
HUFF
HUFF
DYAAAAH!!!!
ZAM

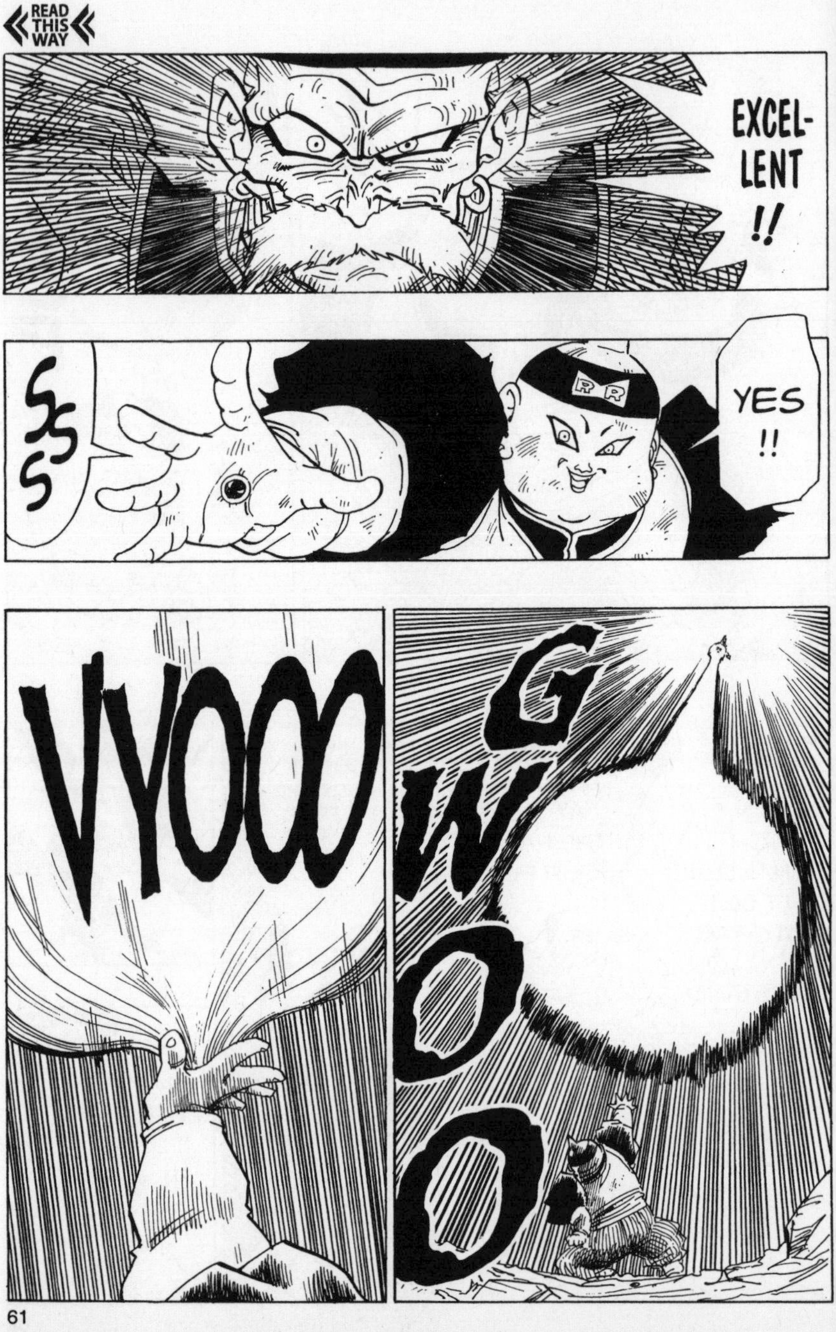
READ THIS WAY
EXCEL-LENT !!
YES !!
SSS
GWOOO
VYOOO

READ THIS WAY

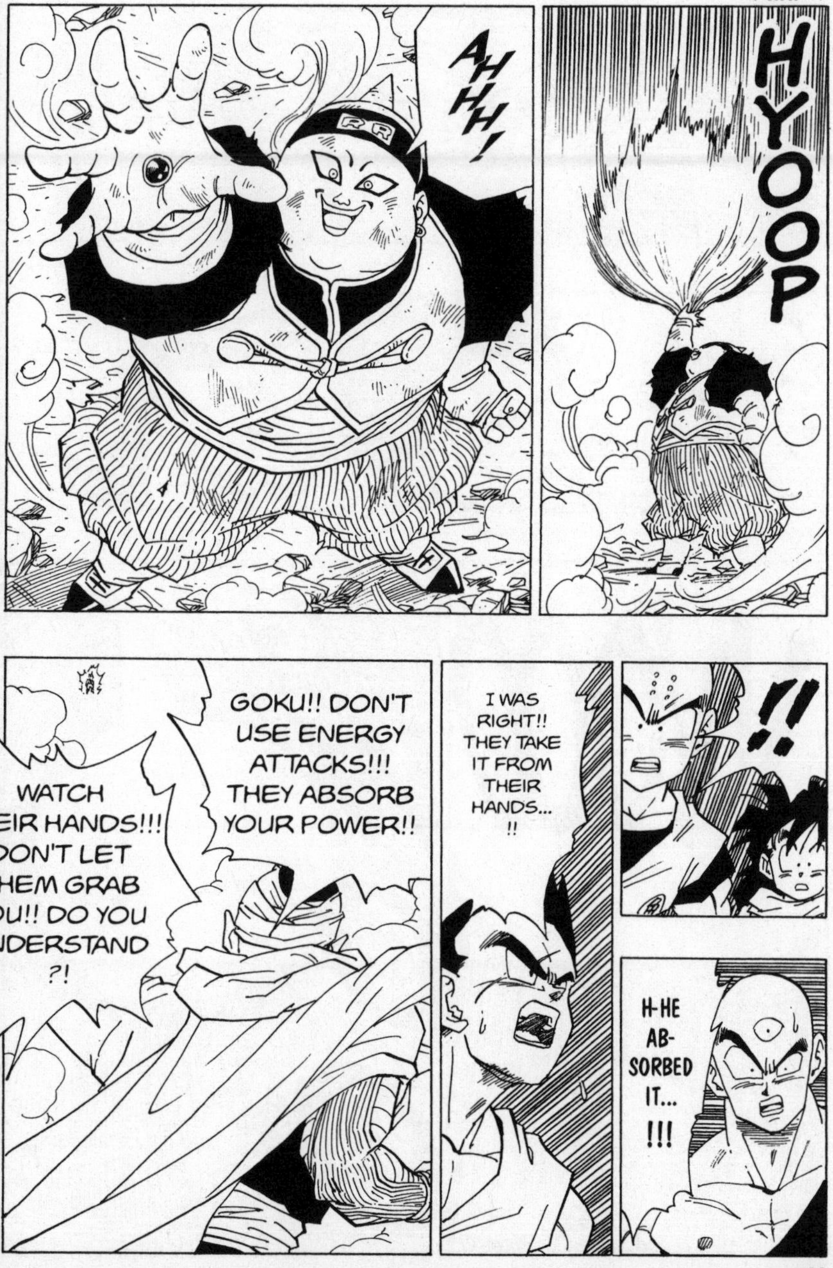
HYOOP
AHHH!
!!
H-HE AB-SORBED IT... !!!
I WAS RIGHT!! THEY TAKE IT FROM THEIR HANDS... !!
GOKU!! DON'T USE ENERGY ATTACKS!!! THEY ABSORB YOUR POWER!!
WATCH EIR HANDS!!! DON'T LET HEM GRAB DU!! DO YOU NDERSTAND ?!

READ THIS WAY

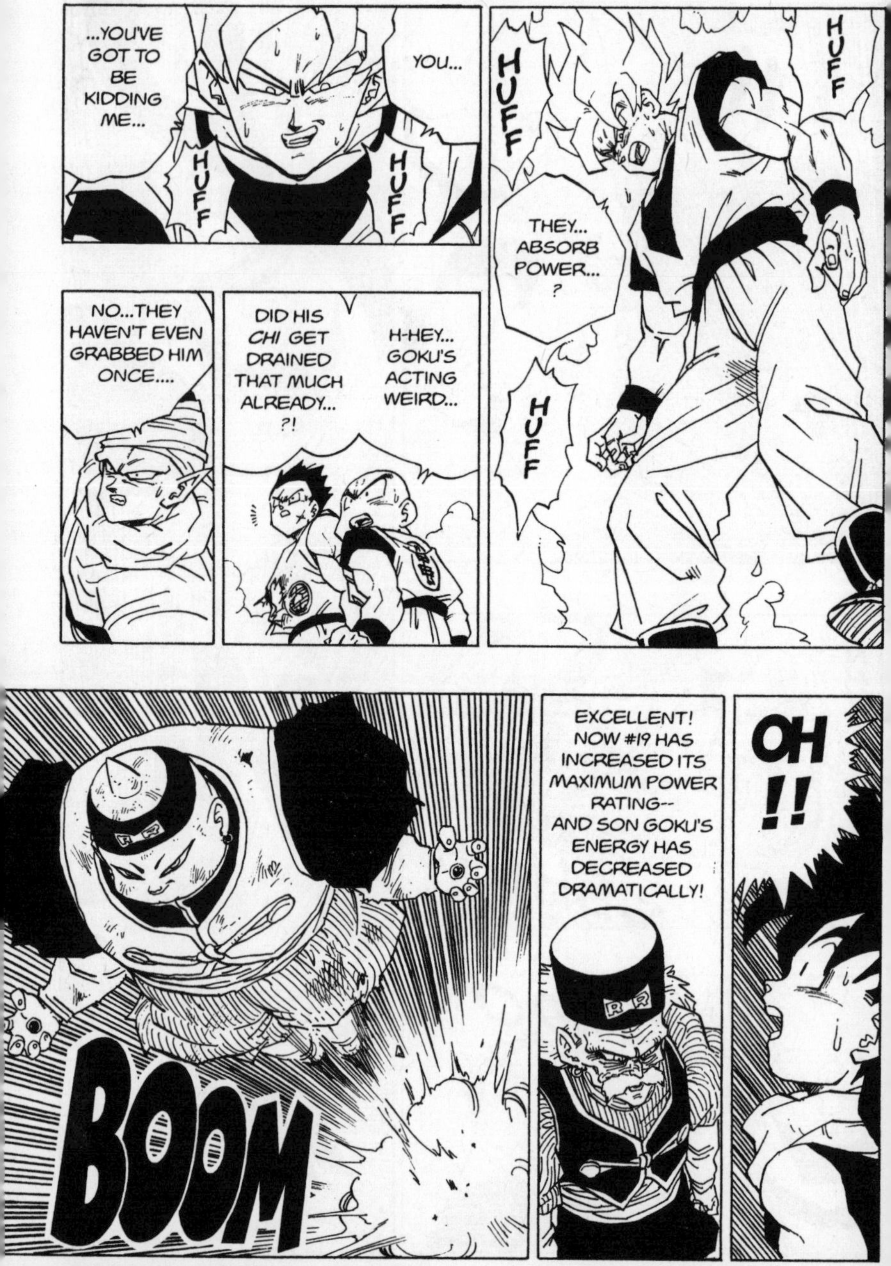
HUFF
HUFF
THEY... ABSORB POWER... ?
HUFF
YOU...
...YOU'VE GOT TO BE KIDDING ME...
HUFF
HUFF
H-HEY... GOKU'S ACTING WEIRD...
DID HIS CHI GET DRAINED THAT MUCH ALREADY... ?!
NO...THEY HAVEN'T EVEN GRABBED HIM ONCE....
OH !!
EXCELLENT! NOW #19 HAS INCREASED ITS MAXIMUM POWER RATING-- AND SON GOKU'S ENERGY HAS DECREASED DRAMATICALLY!
BOOM

NEXT: Goku Loses?!

## DBZ: 148 • One Down...

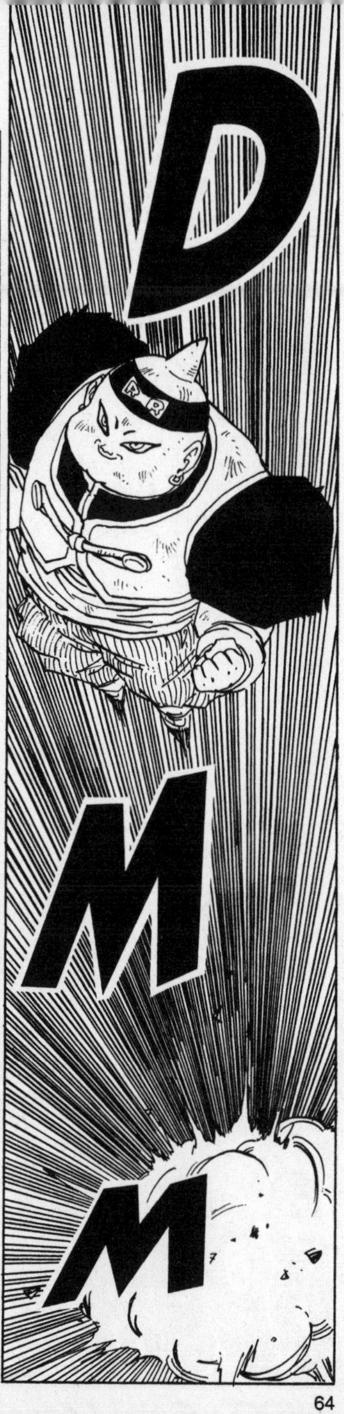
D
M
M

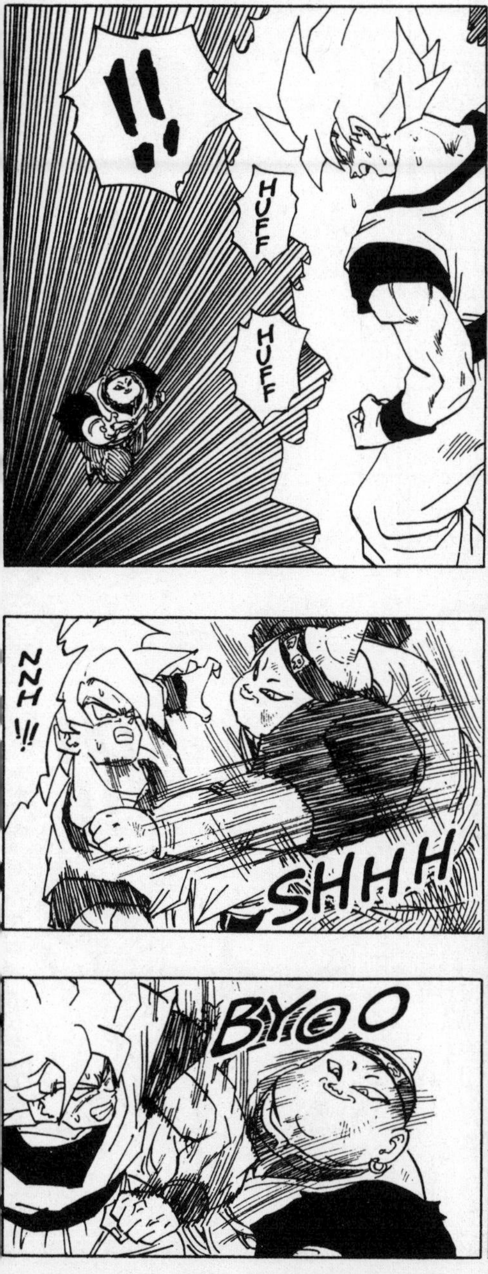
!!
HUFF
HUFF
NNH !!!
SHHH
BYOO

READ THIS WAY

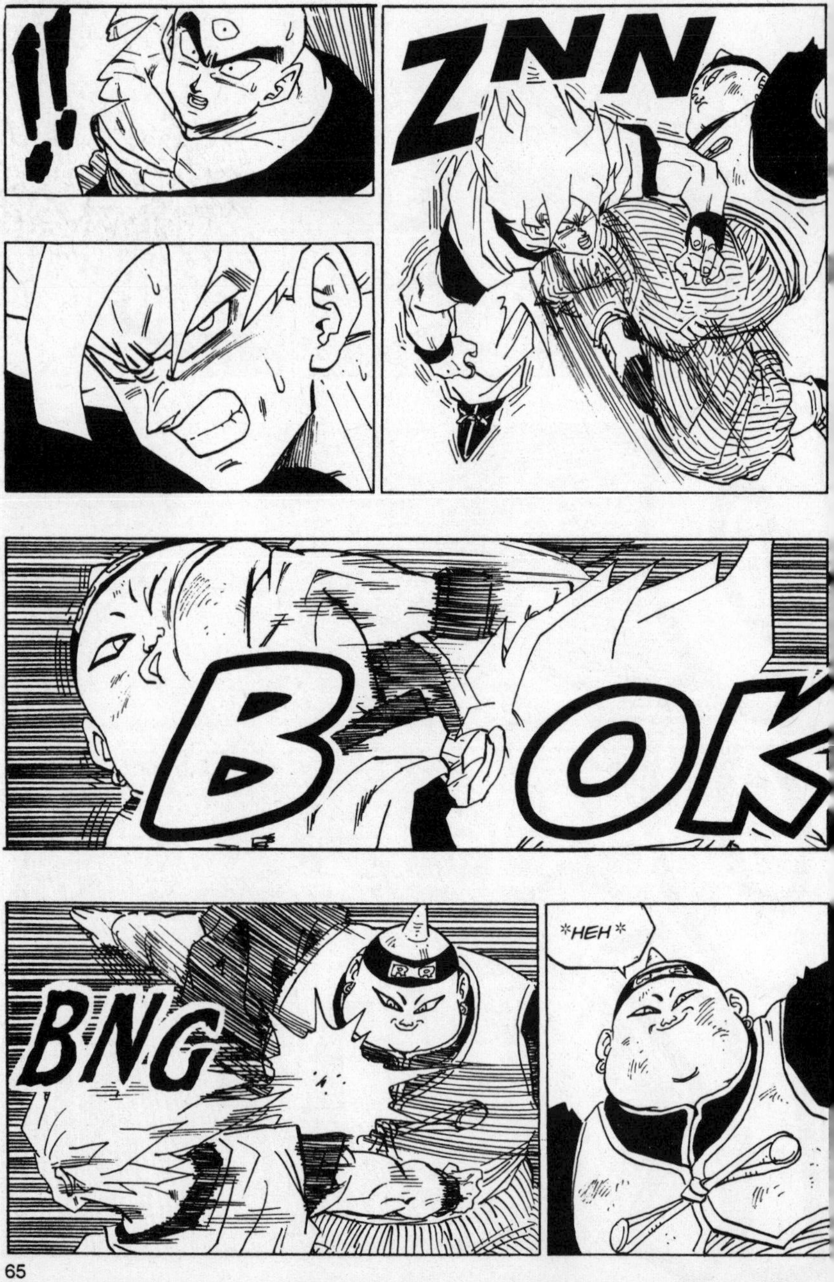
ZNN
!!
BOK
*HEH*
BNG

READ THIS WAY

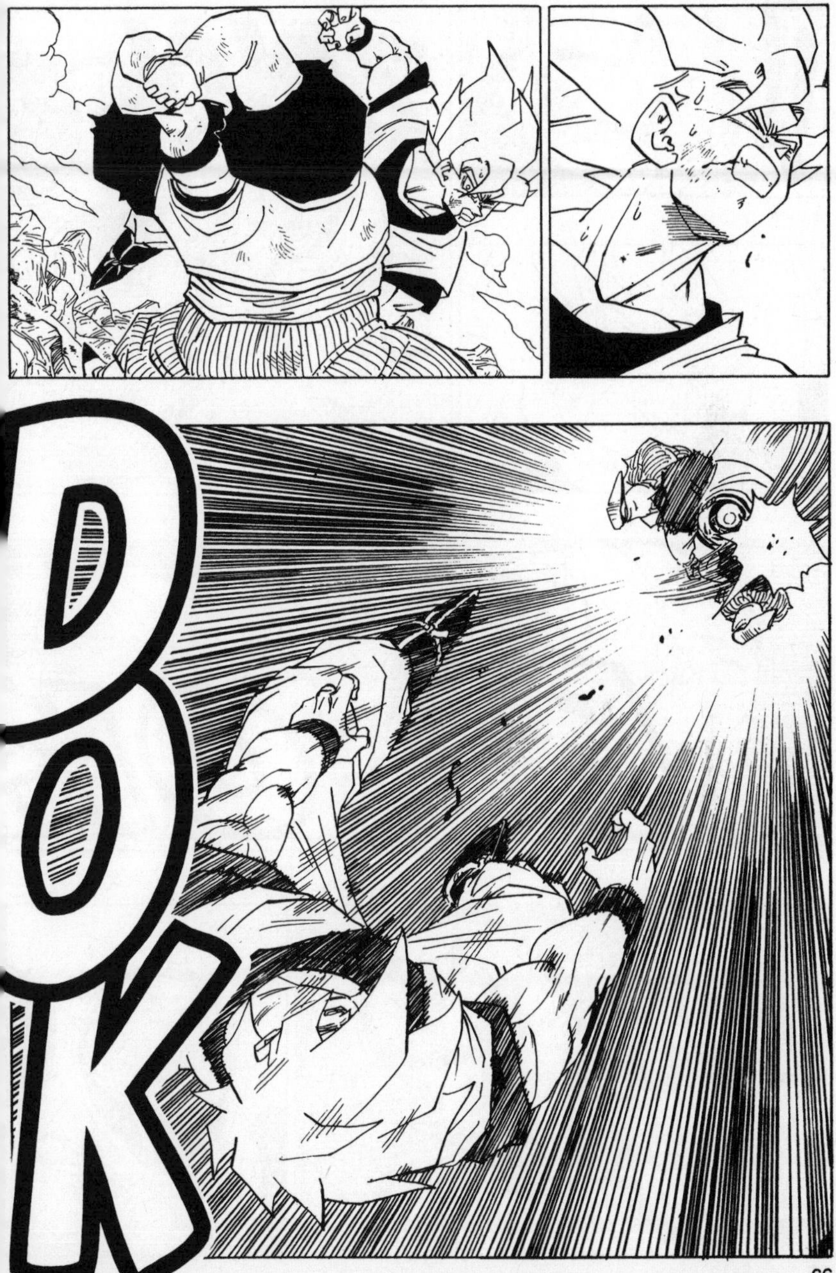
DOK

READ THIS WAY

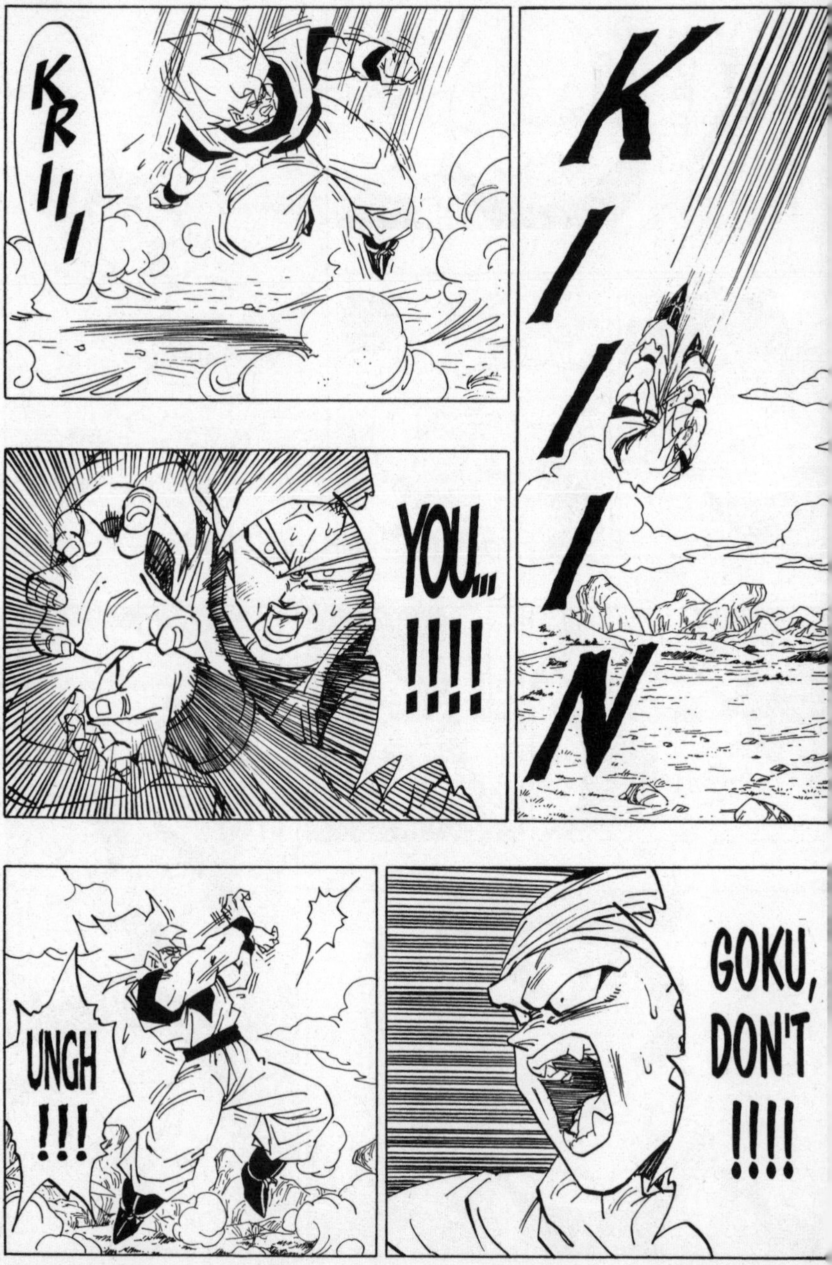
KIIIN
KRIII
YOU... !!!!
GOKU, DON'T !!!!
UNGH !!!

READ THIS WAY

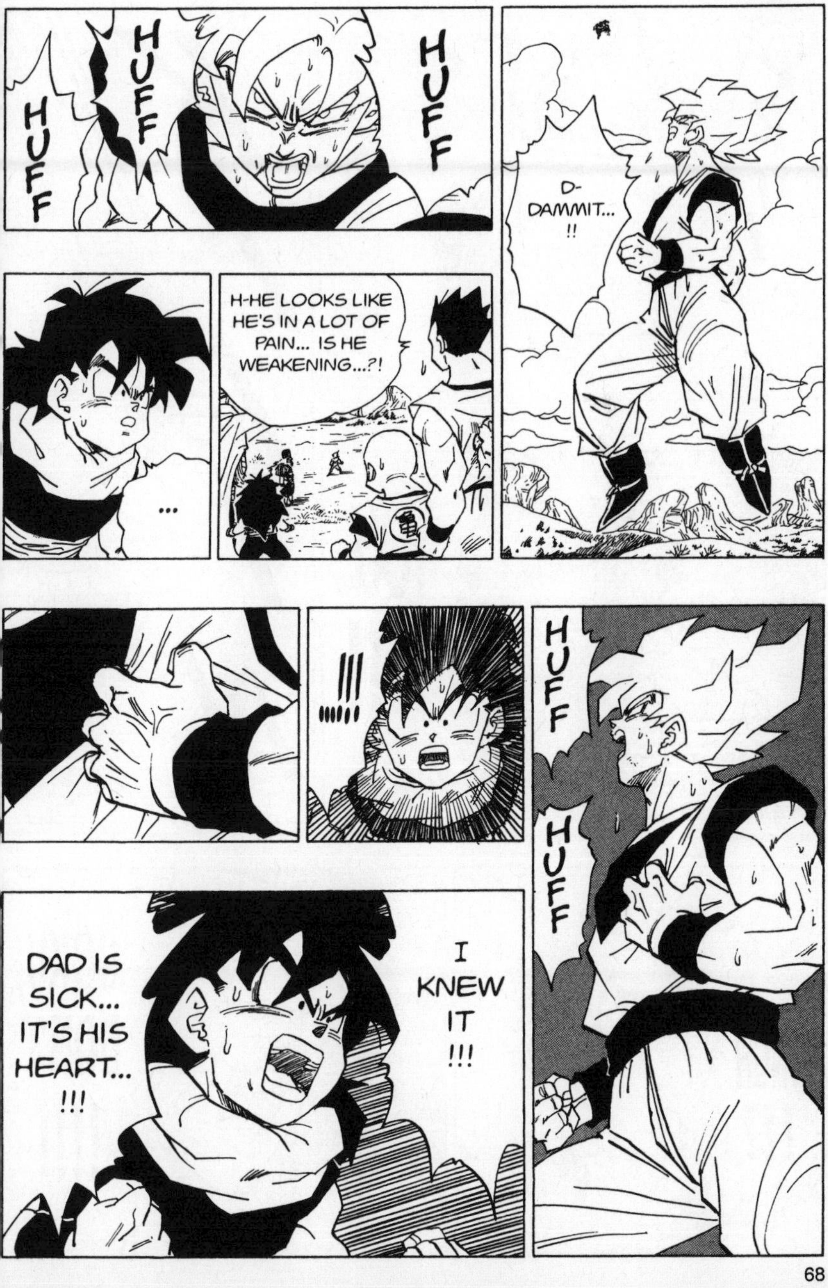
D-DAMMIT... !!
HUFF HUFF HUFF
H-HE LOOKS LIKE HE'S IN A LOT OF PAIN... IS HE WEAKENING...?!
...
HUFF HUFF
!!!
I KNEW IT !!!
DAD IS SICK... IT'S HIS HEART... !!!

READ THIS WAY

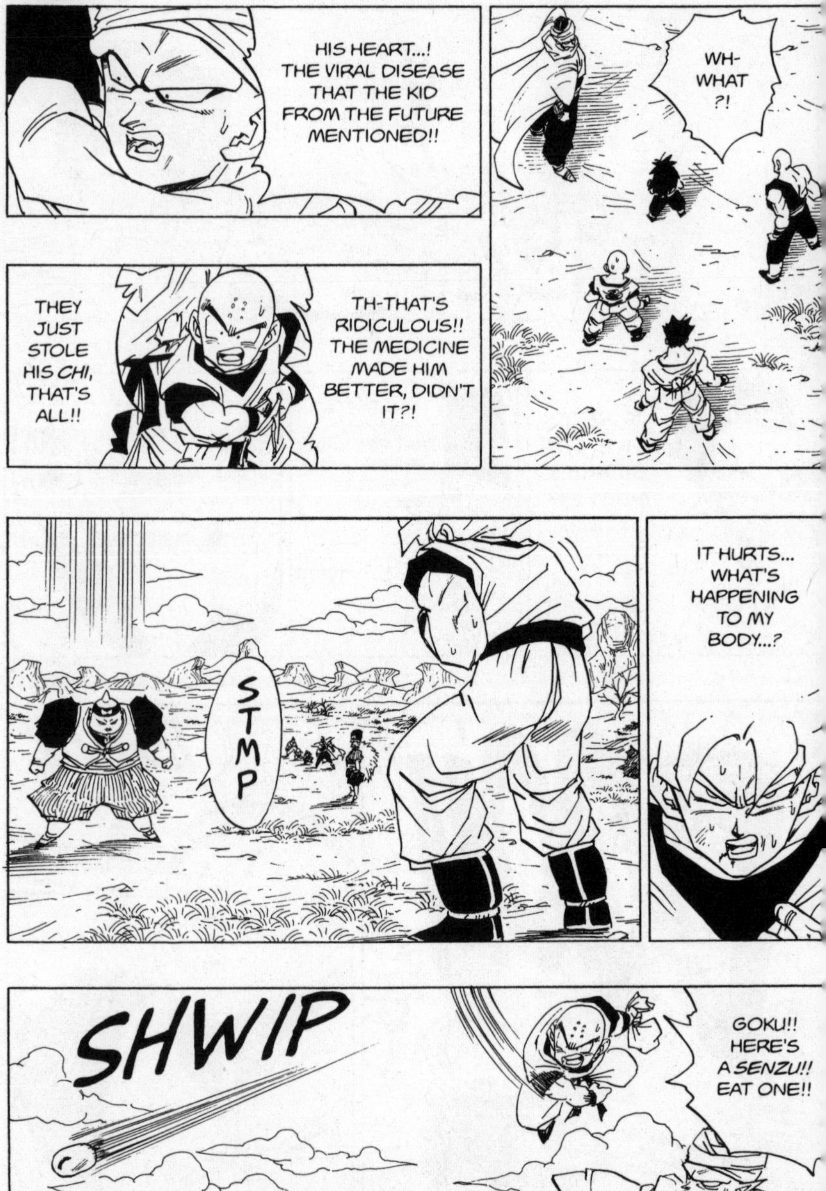

WH- WHAT ?!
HIS HEART...! THE VIRAL DISEASE THAT THE KID FROM THE FUTURE MENTIONED!!
TH-THAT'S RIDICULOUS!! THE MEDICINE MADE HIM BETTER, DIDN'T IT?!
THEY JUST STOLE HIS *CHI*, THAT'S ALL!!
IT HURTS... WHAT'S HAPPENING TO MY BODY...?
STMP
GOKU!! HERE'S A *SENZU*!! EAT ONE!!
SHWIP

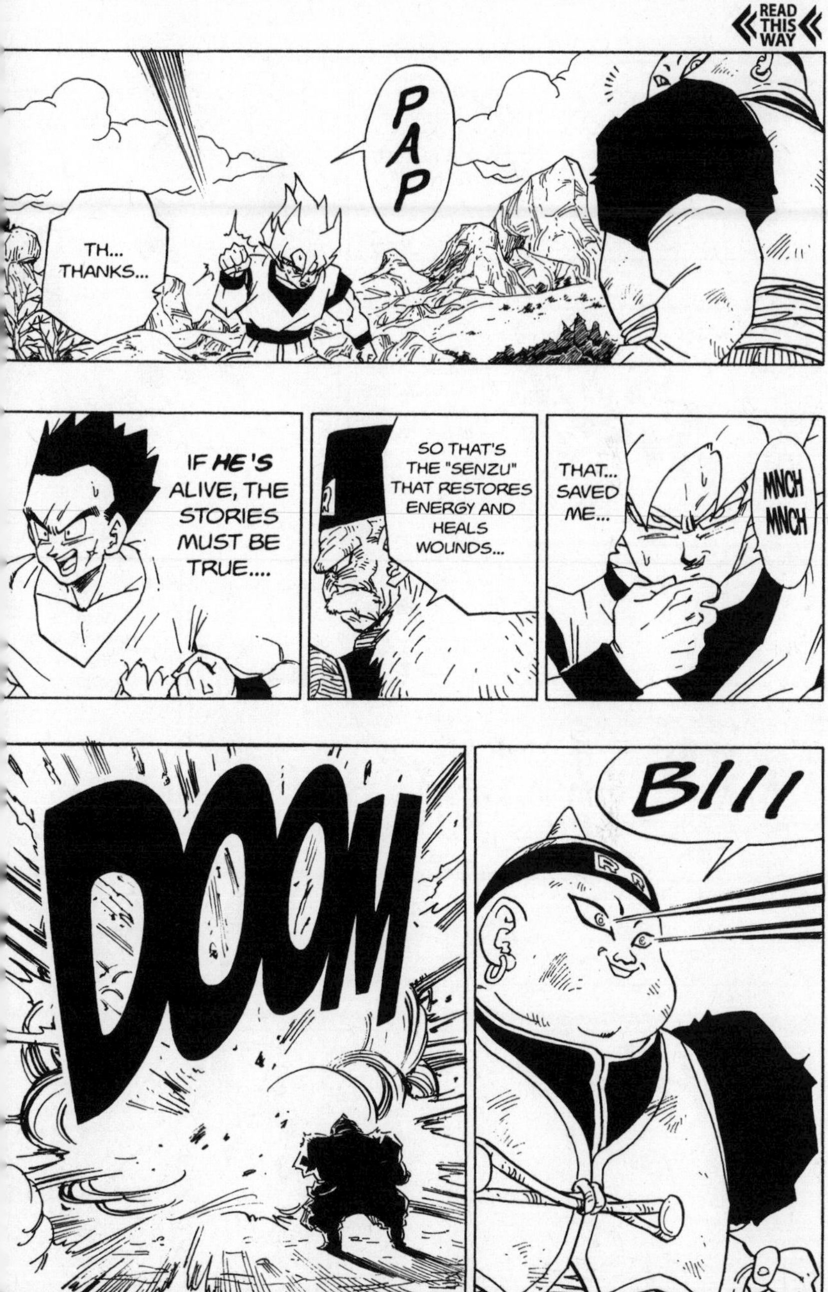
READ THIS WAY
PAP
TH... THANKS...
MNCH MNCH
THAT... SAVED ME...
SO THAT'S THE "SENZU" THAT RESTORES ENERGY AND HEALS WOUNDS...
IF HE'S ALIVE, THE STORIES MUST BE TRUE....
BIII
DOOM

READ THIS WAY

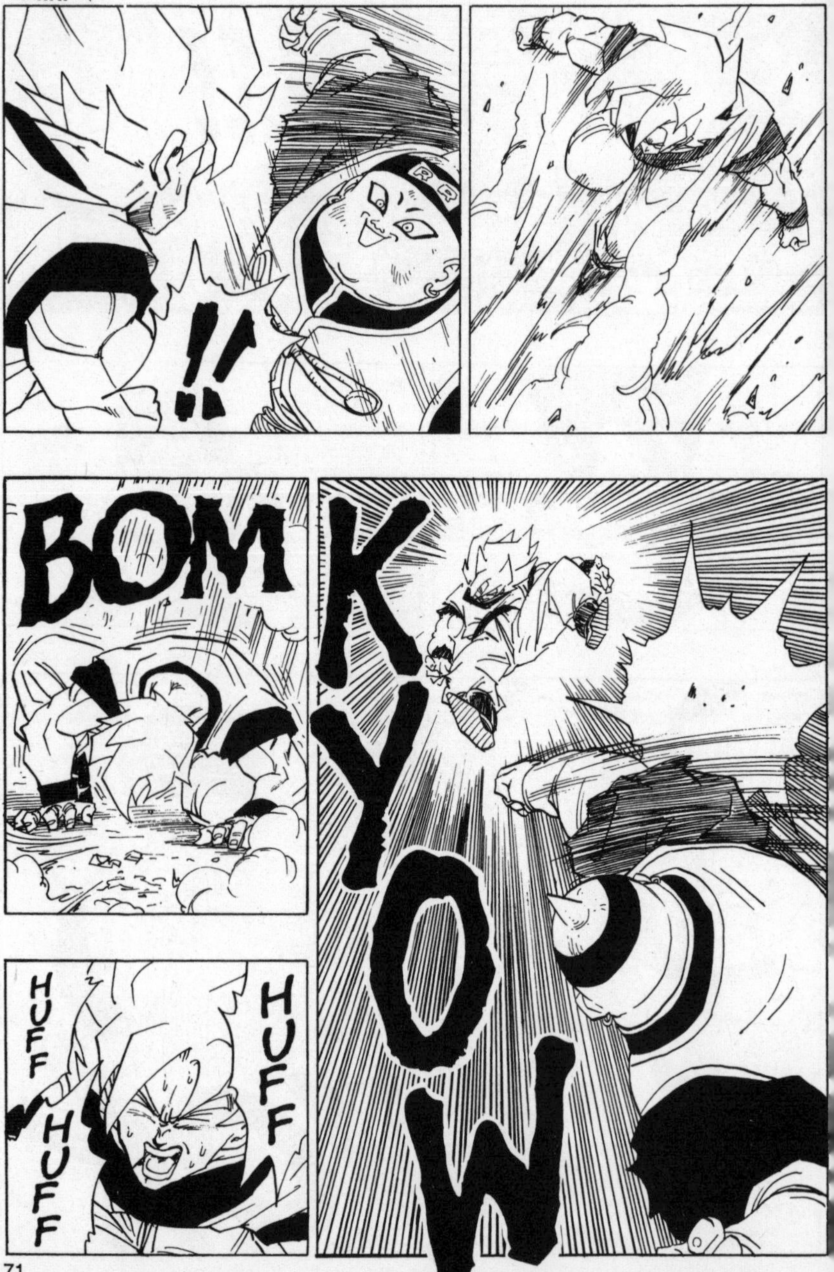
!!
KYOW
BOM
HUFF HUFF
HUFF HUFF

READ THIS WAY

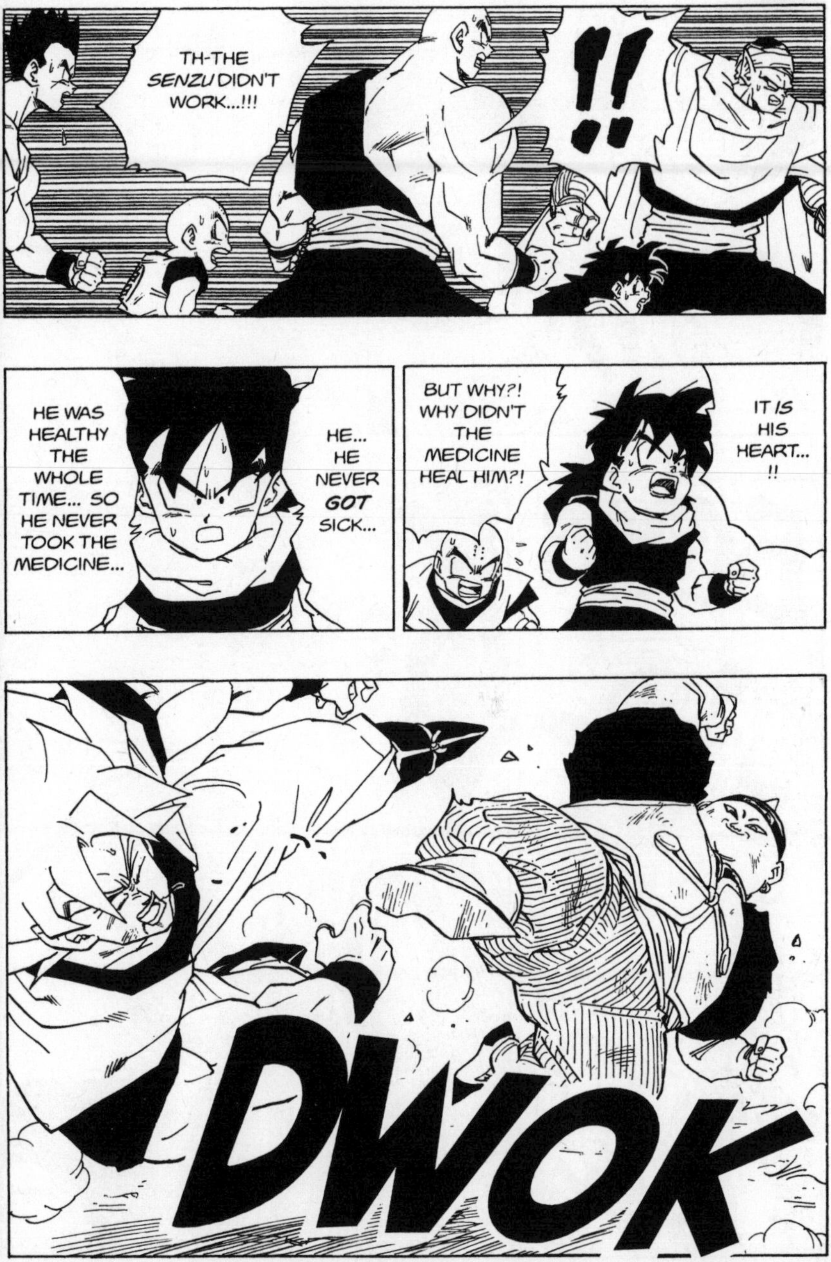
!!
TH-THE SENZU DIDN'T WORK...!!!
IT IS HIS HEART... !!
BUT WHY?! WHY DIDN'T THE MEDICINE HEAL HIM?!
HE... HE NEVER GOT SICK...
HE WAS HEALTHY THE WHOLE TIME... SO HE NEVER TOOK THE MEDICINE...
DWOK

READ THIS WAY

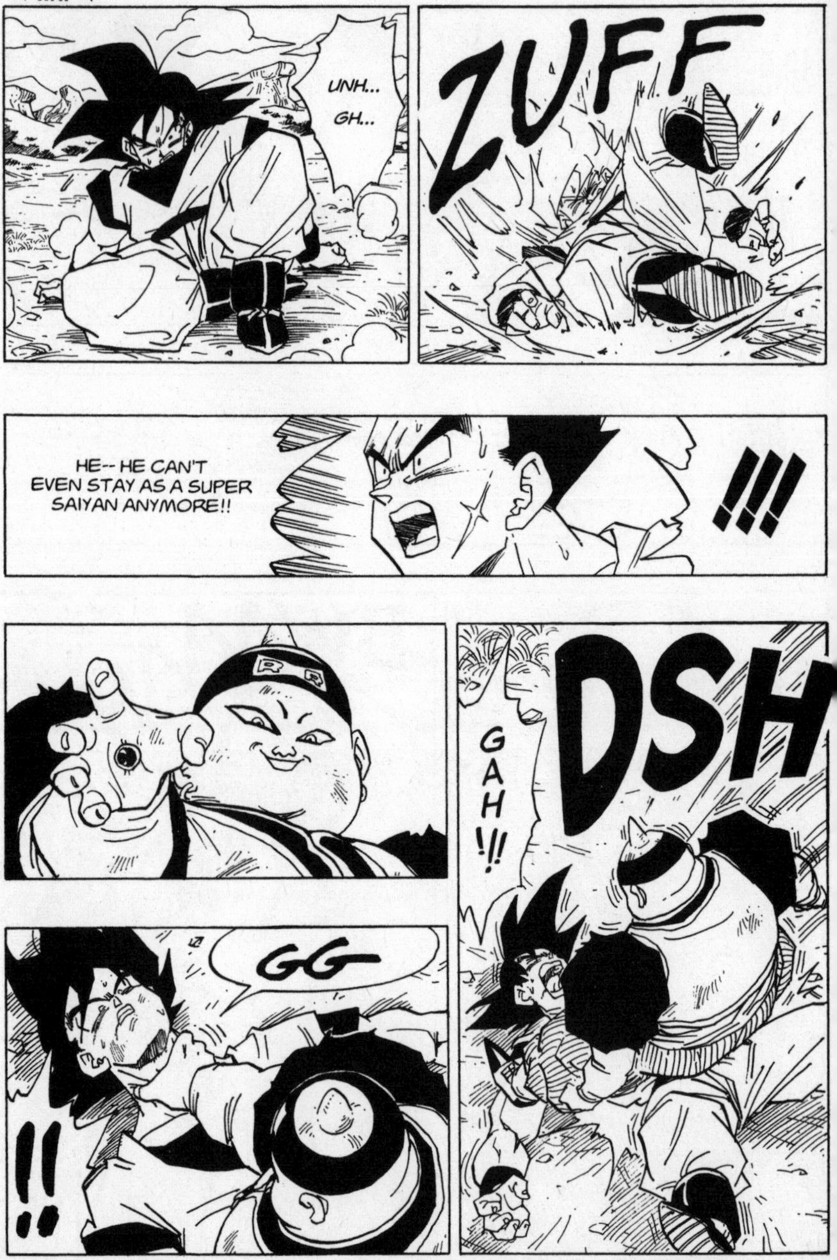

ZUFF
UNH... GH...
HE-- HE CAN'T EVEN STAY AS A SUPER SAIYAN ANYMORE!!
!!!
DSH
GAH!!!
GG
!!

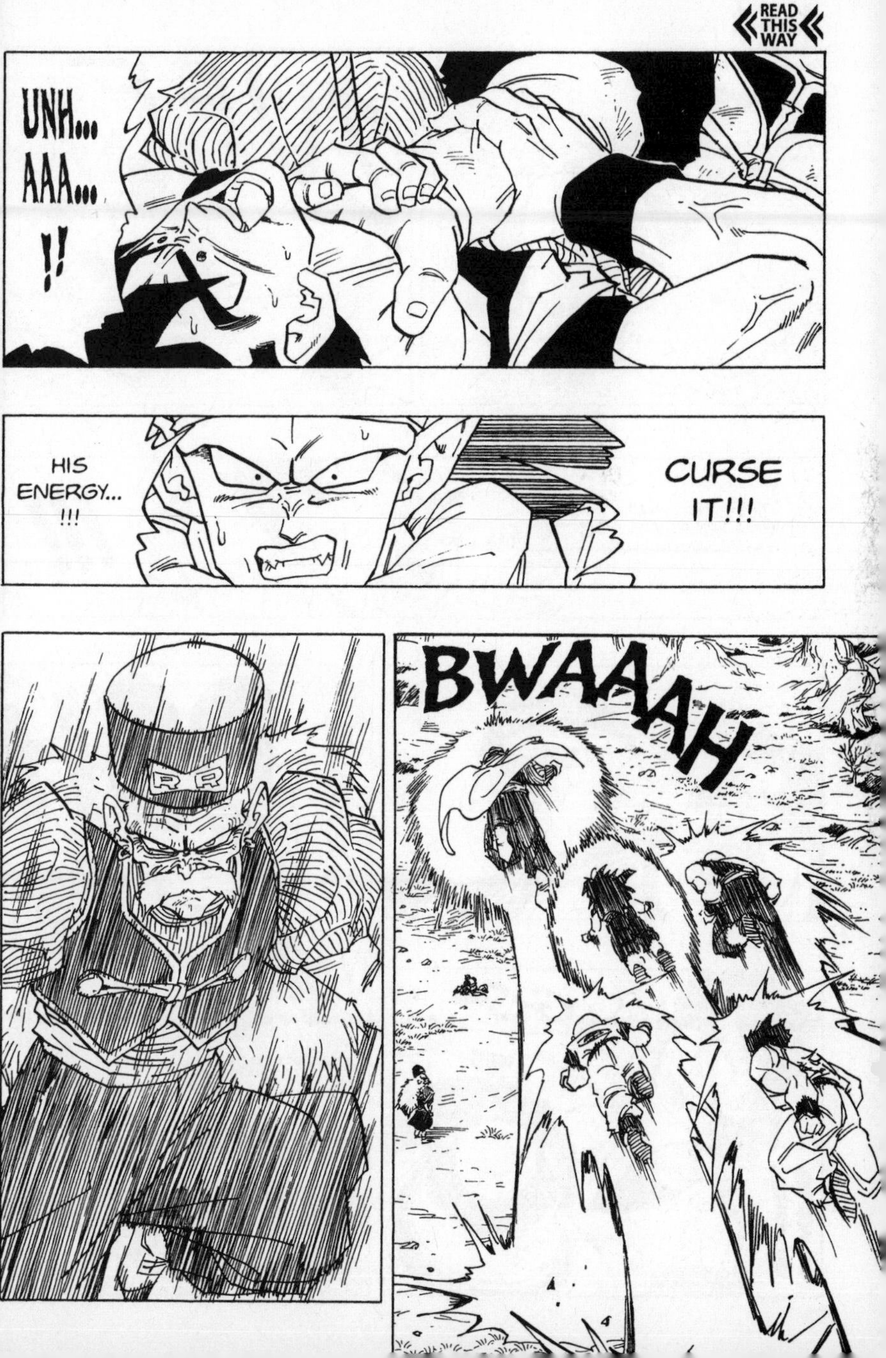
READ THIS WAY
UNH... AAA... !!
CURSE IT!!!
HIS ENERGY... !!!
BWAAAAH

READ THIS WAY

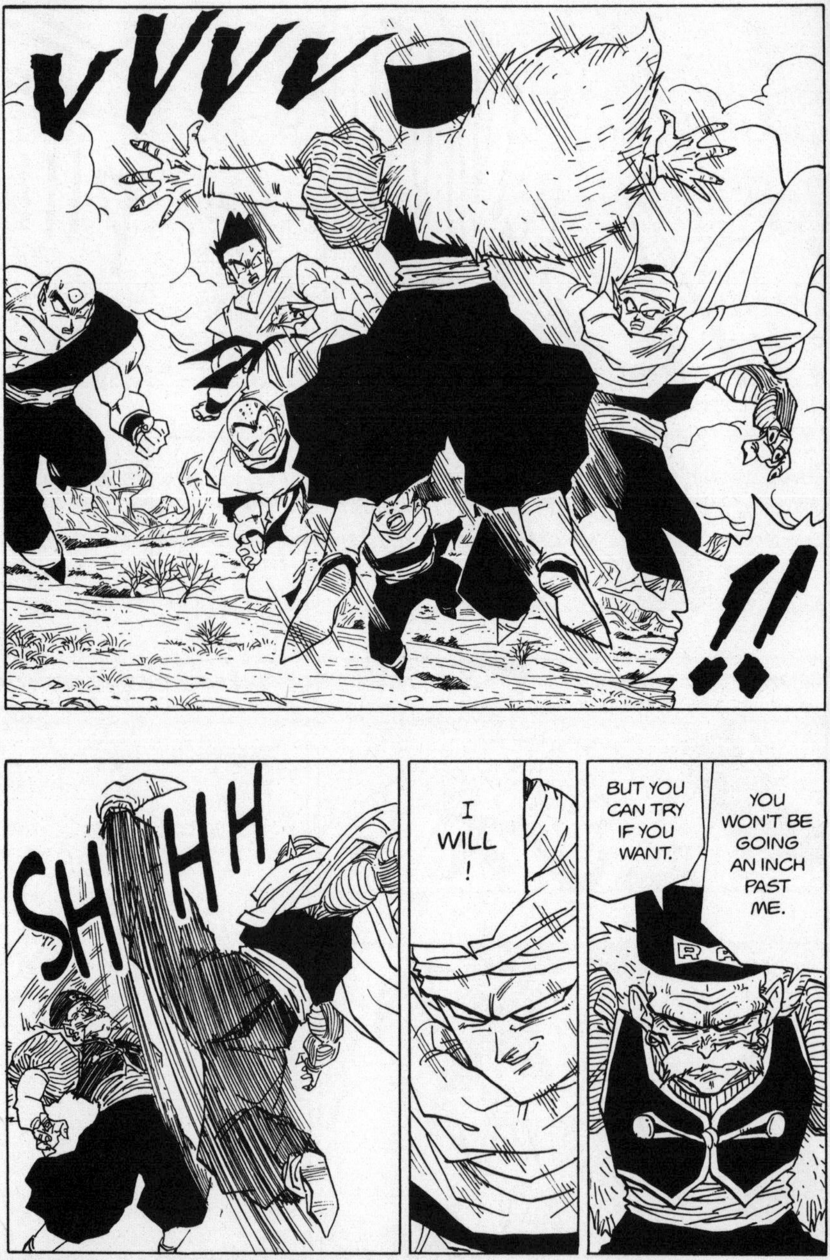
VVVV
!!
YOU WON'T BE GOING AN INCH PAST ME.
BUT YOU CAN TRY IF YOU WANT.
I WILL!
SHHHH

READ THIS WAY

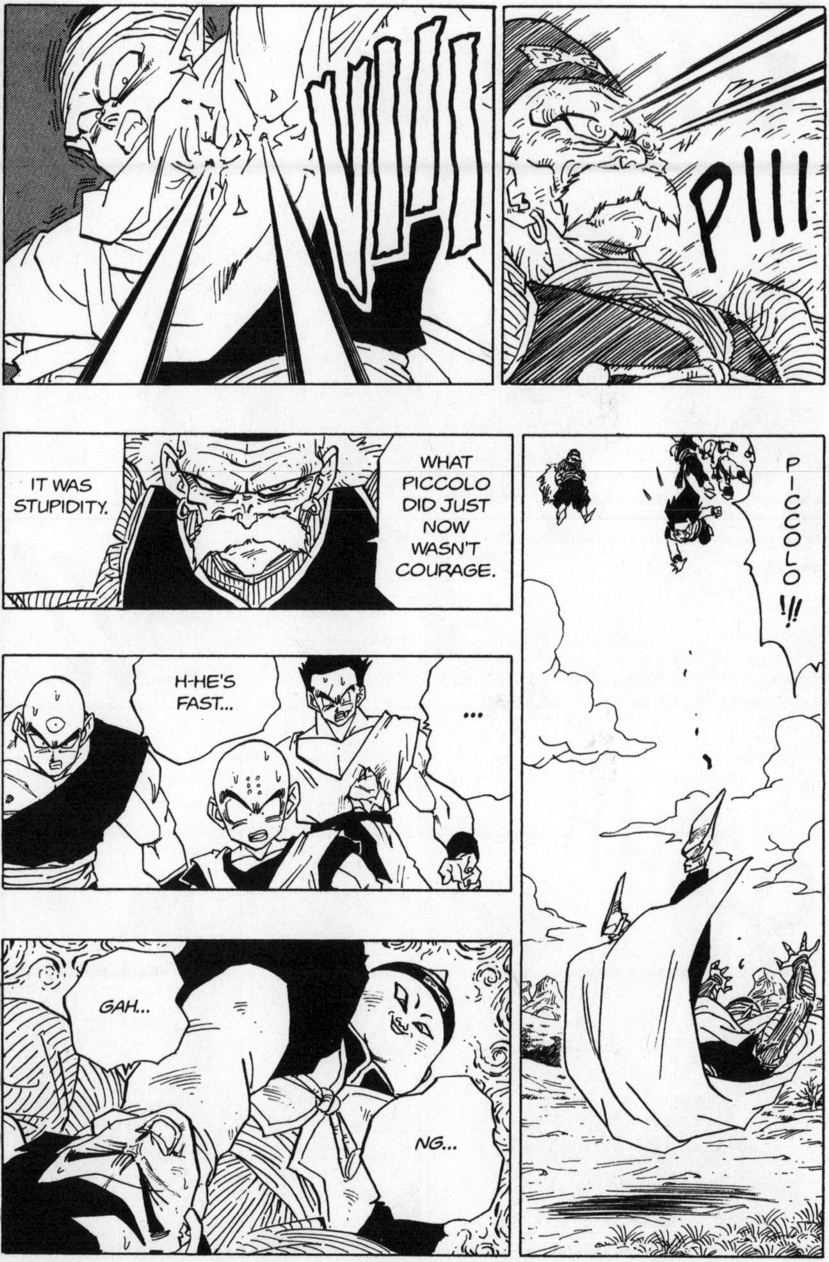
PIII
VIIII
PICCOLO !!!
WHAT PICCOLO DID JUST NOW WASN'T COURAGE.
IT WAS STUPIDITY.
...
H-HE'S FAST...
GAH...
NG...

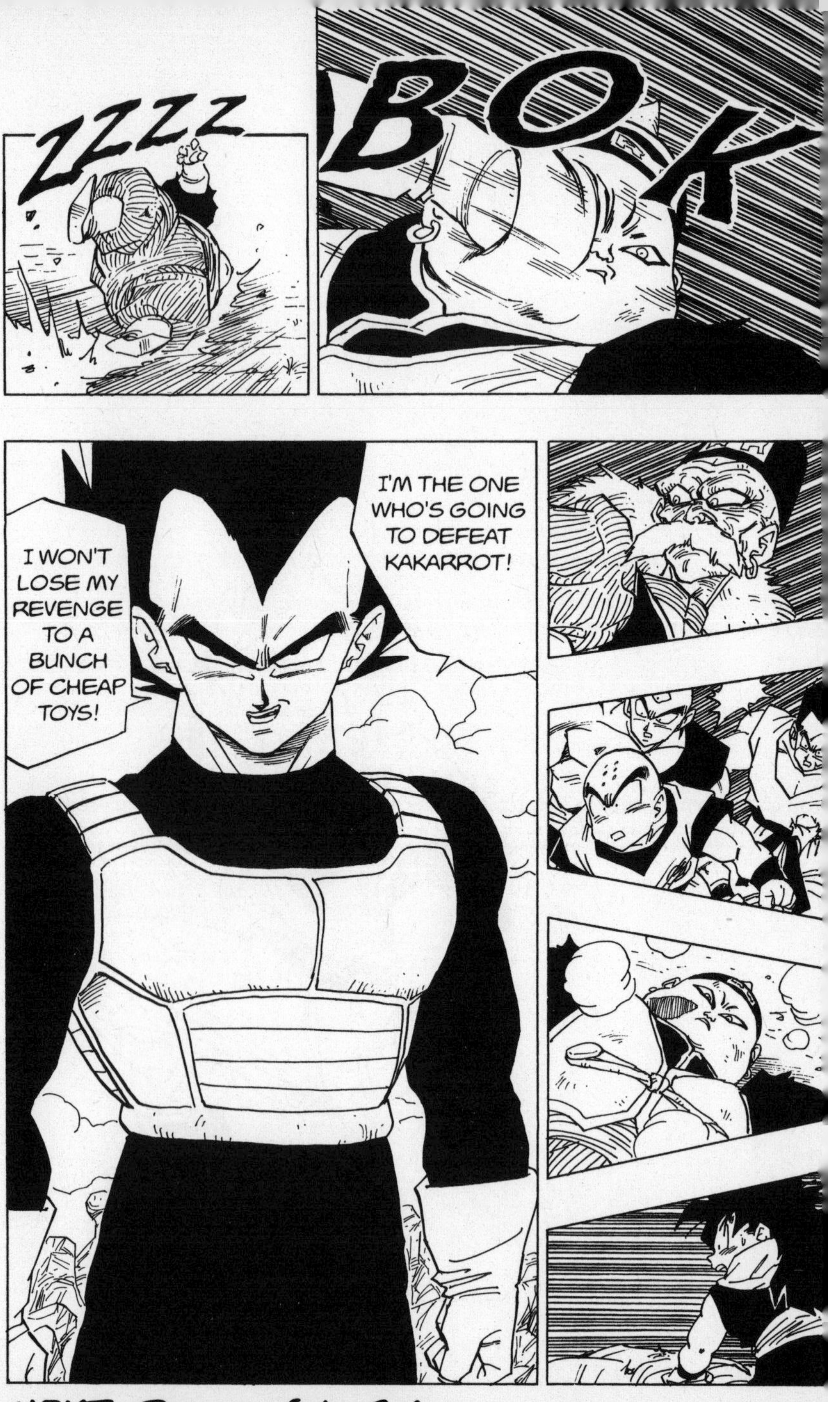
BOK
ZZZZ
I'M THE ONE WHO'S GOING TO DEFEAT KAKARROT!
I WON'T LOSE MY REVENGE TO A BUNCH OF CHEAP TOYS!

NEXT: Return of the Saiyan

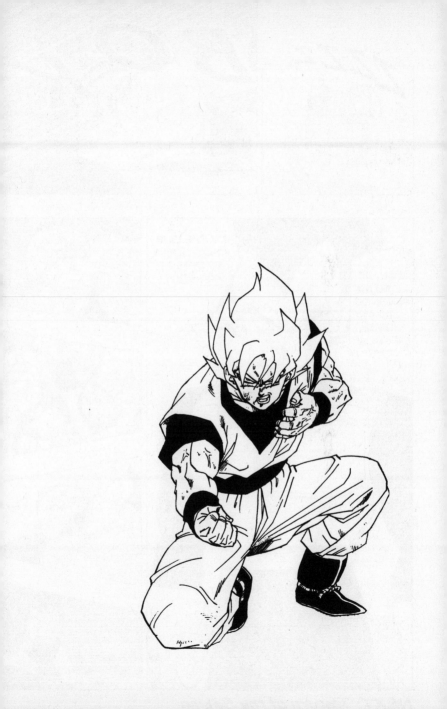

READ THIS WAY

# DBZ:149
# Vegeta Returns!!!

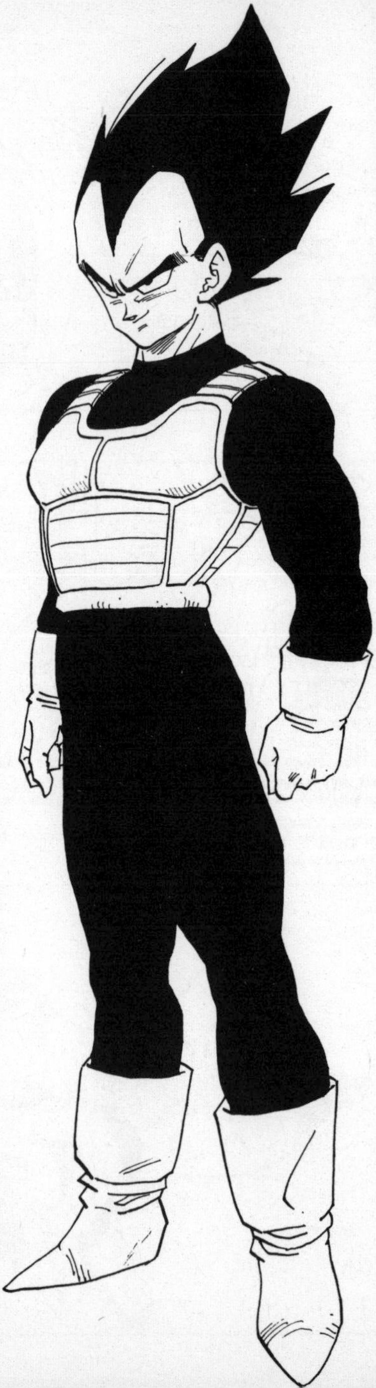

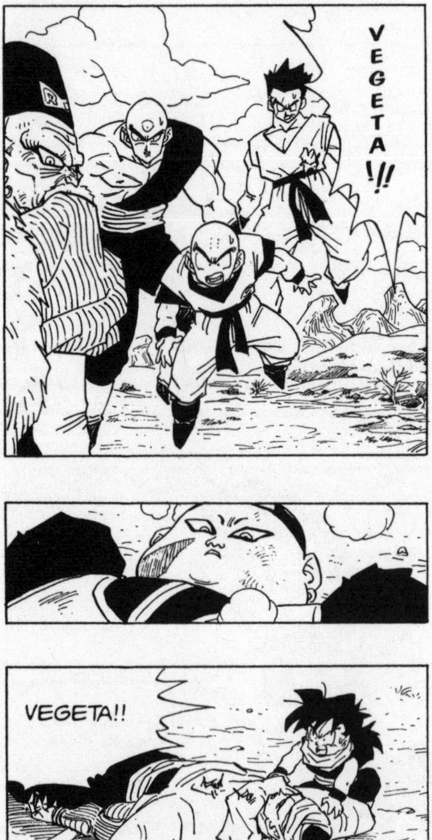
VEGETA!!!
VEGETA!!

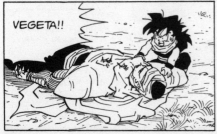

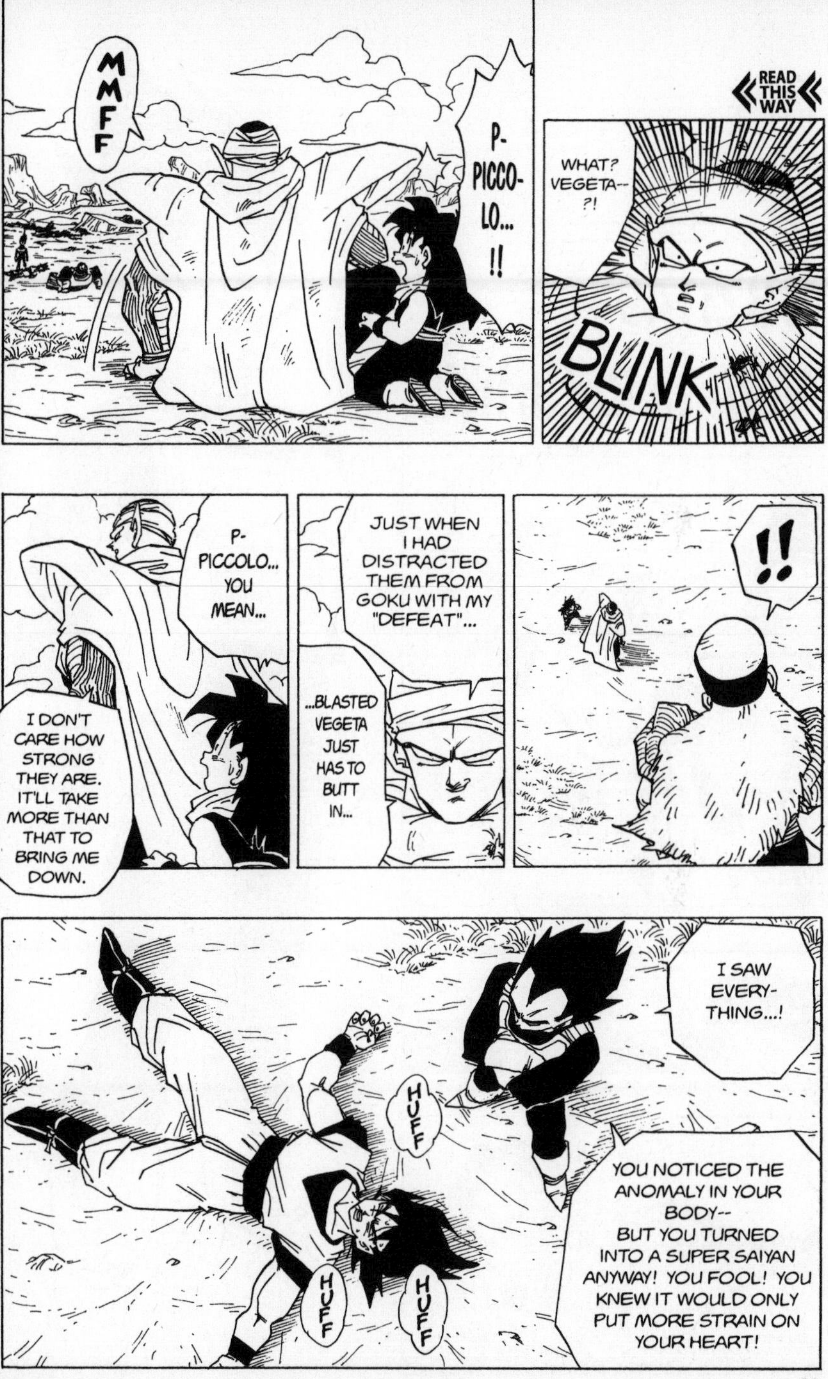
READ THIS WAY
WHAT? VEGETA-- ?!
BLINK
P- PICCOLO... !!
MMFF
!!
JUST WHEN I HAD DISTRACTED THEM FROM GOKU WITH MY "DEFEAT"...
...BLASTED VEGETA JUST HAS TO BUTT IN...
P- PICCOLO... YOU MEAN...
I DON'T CARE HOW STRONG THEY ARE. IT'LL TAKE MORE THAN THAT TO BRING ME DOWN.
I SAW EVERYTHING...!
YOU NOTICED THE ANOMALY IN YOUR BODY-- BUT YOU TURNED INTO A SUPER SAIYAN ANYWAY! YOU FOOL! YOU KNEW IT WOULD ONLY PUT MORE STRAIN ON YOUR HEART!
HUFF
HUFF
HUFF

READ THIS WAY

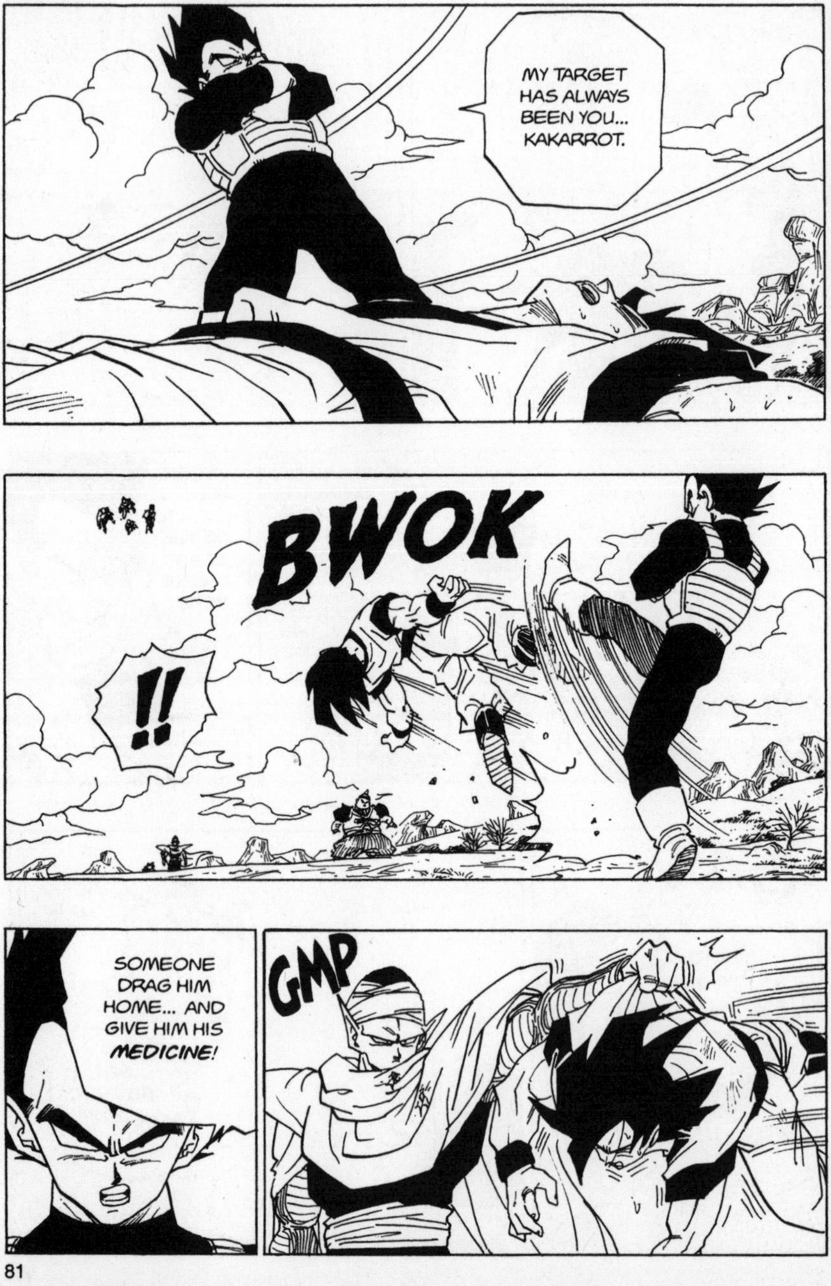

MY TARGET HAS ALWAYS BEEN YOU... KAKARROT.
BWOK
!!
GMP
SOMEONE DRAG HIM HOME... AND GIVE HIM HIS *MEDICINE!*

READ THIS WAY

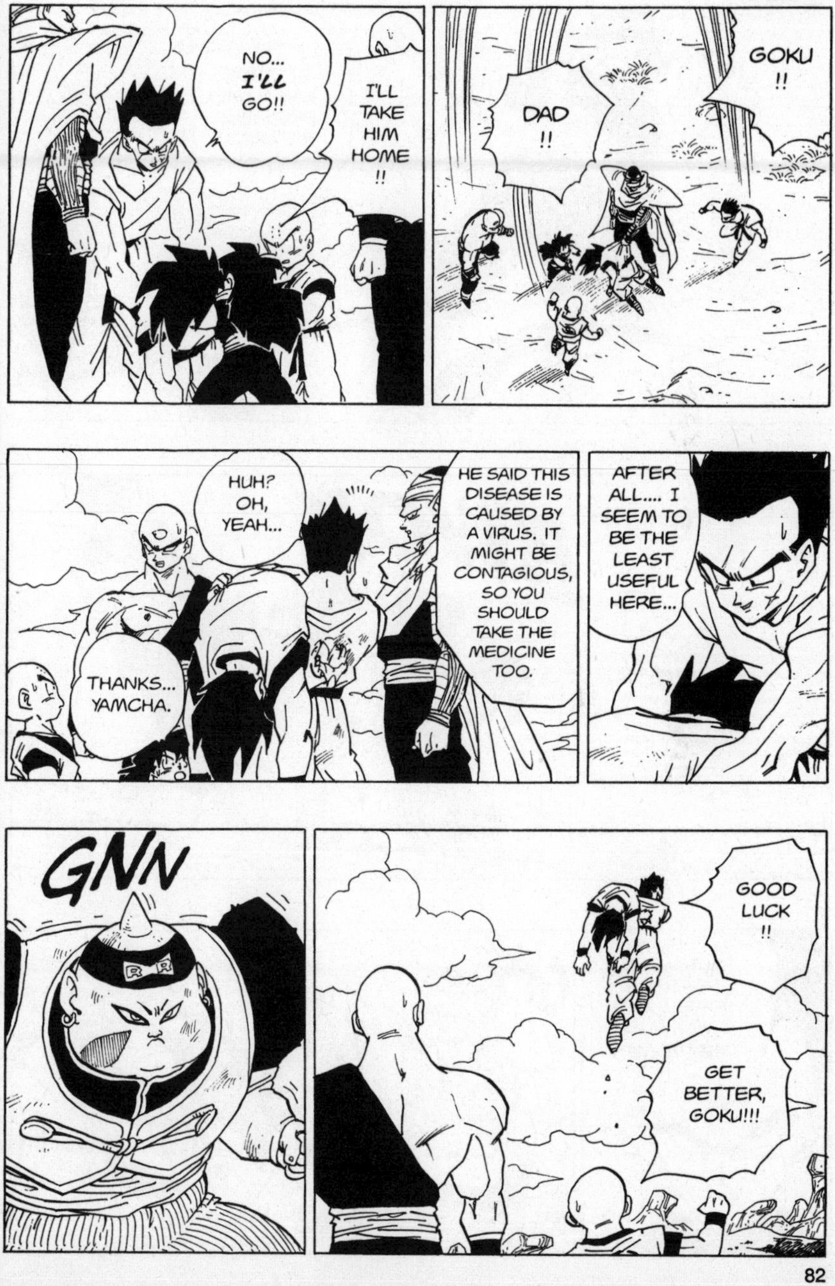
GOKU !!
DAD !!
I'LL TAKE HIM HOME !!
NO... I'LL GO!!
AFTER ALL.... I SEEM TO BE THE LEAST USEFUL HERE...
HE SAID THIS DISEASE IS CAUSED BY A VIRUS. IT MIGHT BE CONTAGIOUS, SO YOU SHOULD TAKE THE MEDICINE TOO.
HUH? OH, YEAH...
THANKS... YAMCHA.
GOOD LUCK !!
GET BETTER, GOKU!!!
GNN

READ THIS WAY

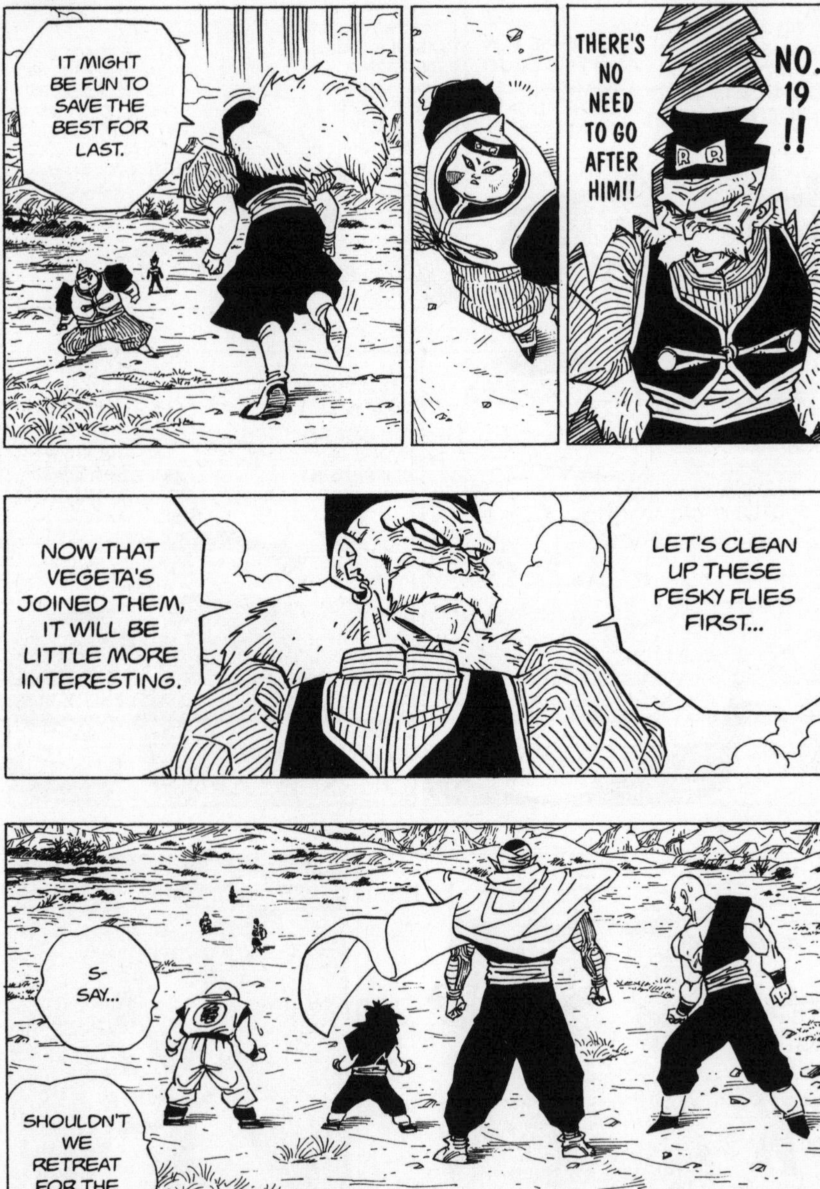
NO. 19 !!
THERE'S NO NEED TO GO AFTER HIM!!
IT MIGHT BE FUN TO SAVE THE BEST FOR LAST.
LET'S CLEAN UP THESE PESKY FLIES FIRST...
NOW THAT VEGETA'S JOINED THEM, IT WILL BE LITTLE MORE INTERESTING.
S- SAY...
SHOULDN'T WE RETREAT FOR THE TIME BEING?

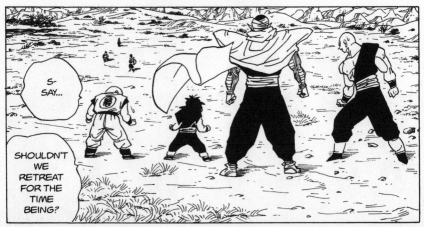

READ THIS WAY

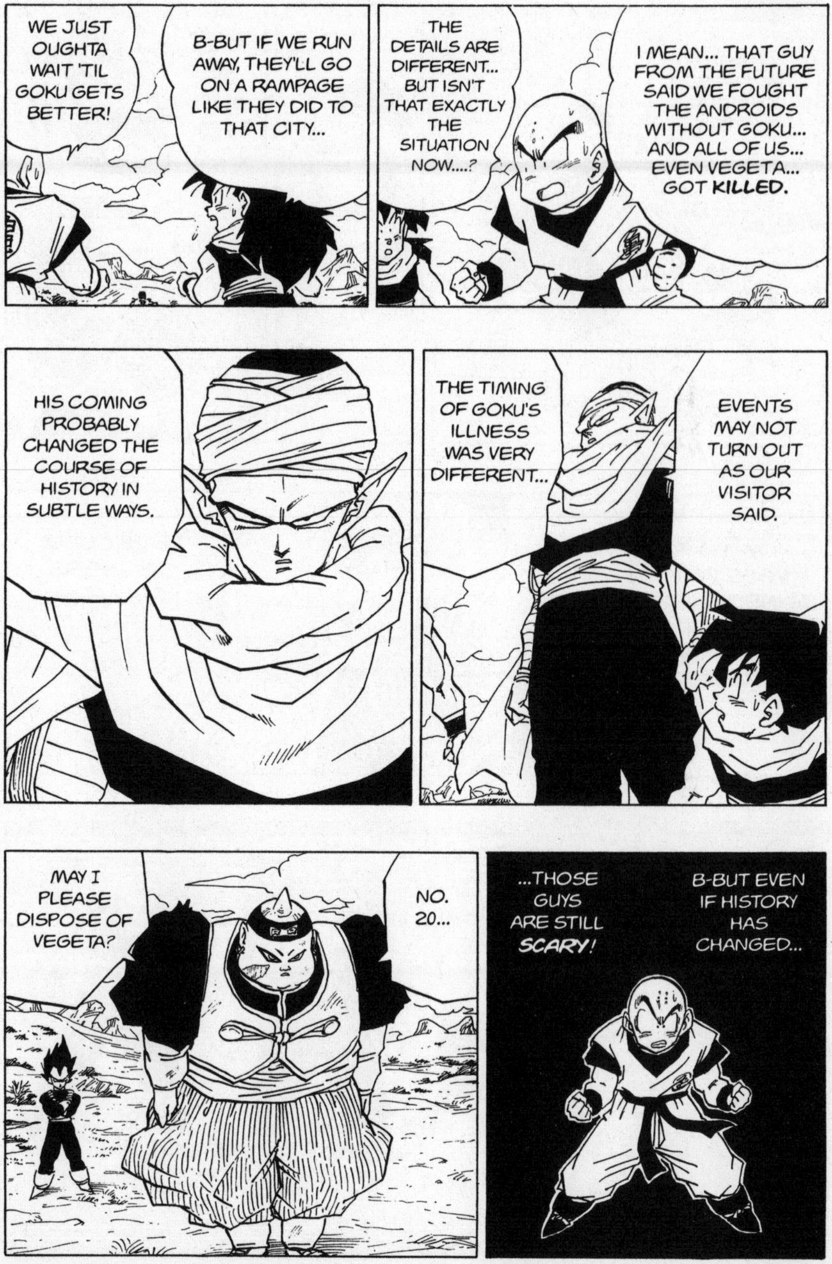
I MEAN... THAT GUY FROM THE FUTURE SAID WE FOUGHT THE ANDROIDS WITHOUT GOKU... AND ALL OF US... EVEN VEGETA... GOT **KILLED.**
THE DETAILS ARE DIFFERENT... BUT ISN'T THAT EXACTLY THE SITUATION NOW....?
B-BUT IF WE RUN AWAY, THEY'LL GO ON A RAMPAGE LIKE THEY DID TO THAT CITY...
WE JUST OUGHTA WAIT 'TIL GOKU GETS BETTER!
EVENTS MAY NOT TURN OUT AS OUR VISITOR SAID.
THE TIMING OF GOKU'S ILLNESS WAS VERY DIFFERENT...
HIS COMING PROBABLY CHANGED THE COURSE OF HISTORY IN SUBTLE WAYS.
B-BUT EVEN IF HISTORY HAS CHANGED...
...THOSE GUYS ARE STILL ***SCARY!***
NO. 20...
MAY I PLEASE DISPOSE OF VEGETA?

READ THIS WAY

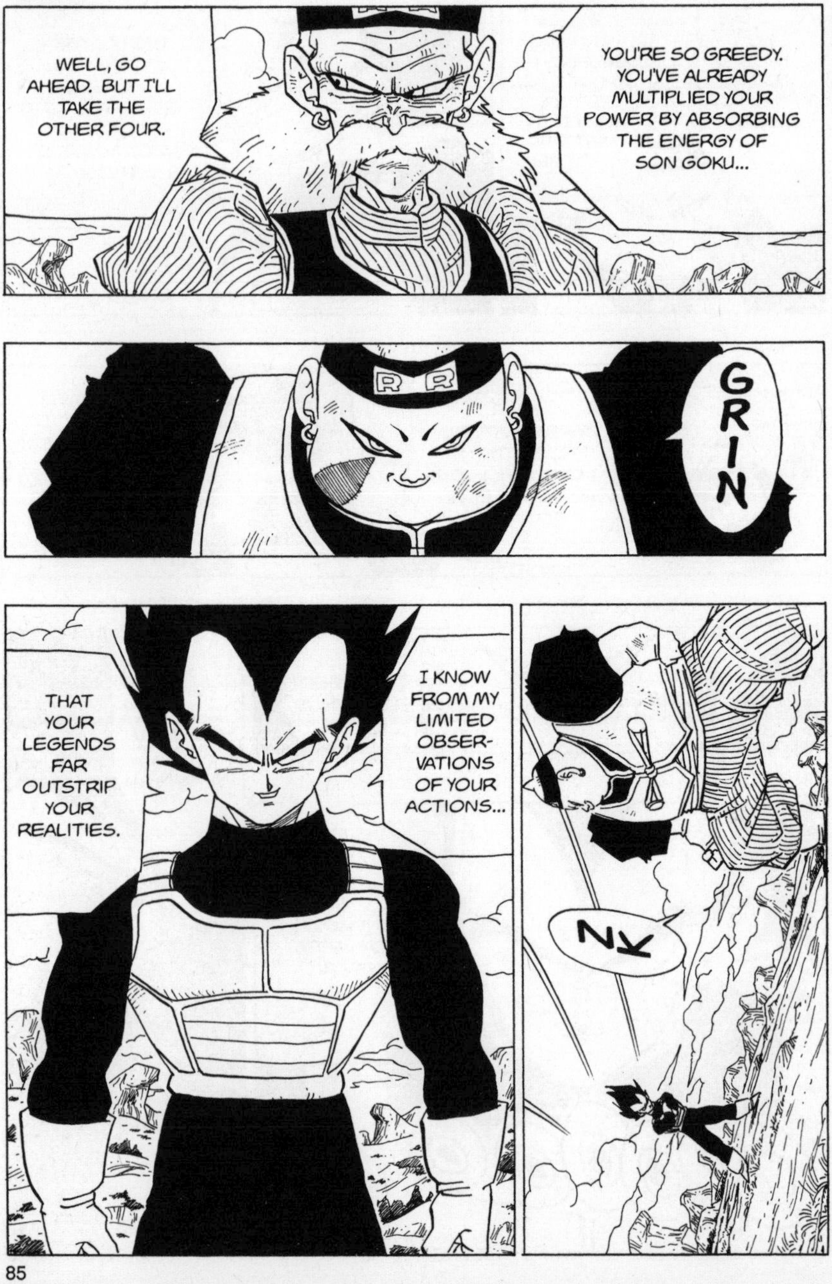

YOU'RE SO GREEDY. YOU'VE ALREADY MULTIPLIED YOUR POWER BY ABSORBING THE ENERGY OF SON GOKU...
WELL, GO AHEAD. BUT I'LL TAKE THE OTHER FOUR.
GRIN
I KNOW FROM MY LIMITED OBSER-VATIONS OF YOUR ACTIONS...
THAT YOUR LEGENDS FAR OUTSTRIP YOUR REALITIES.

READ THIS WAY

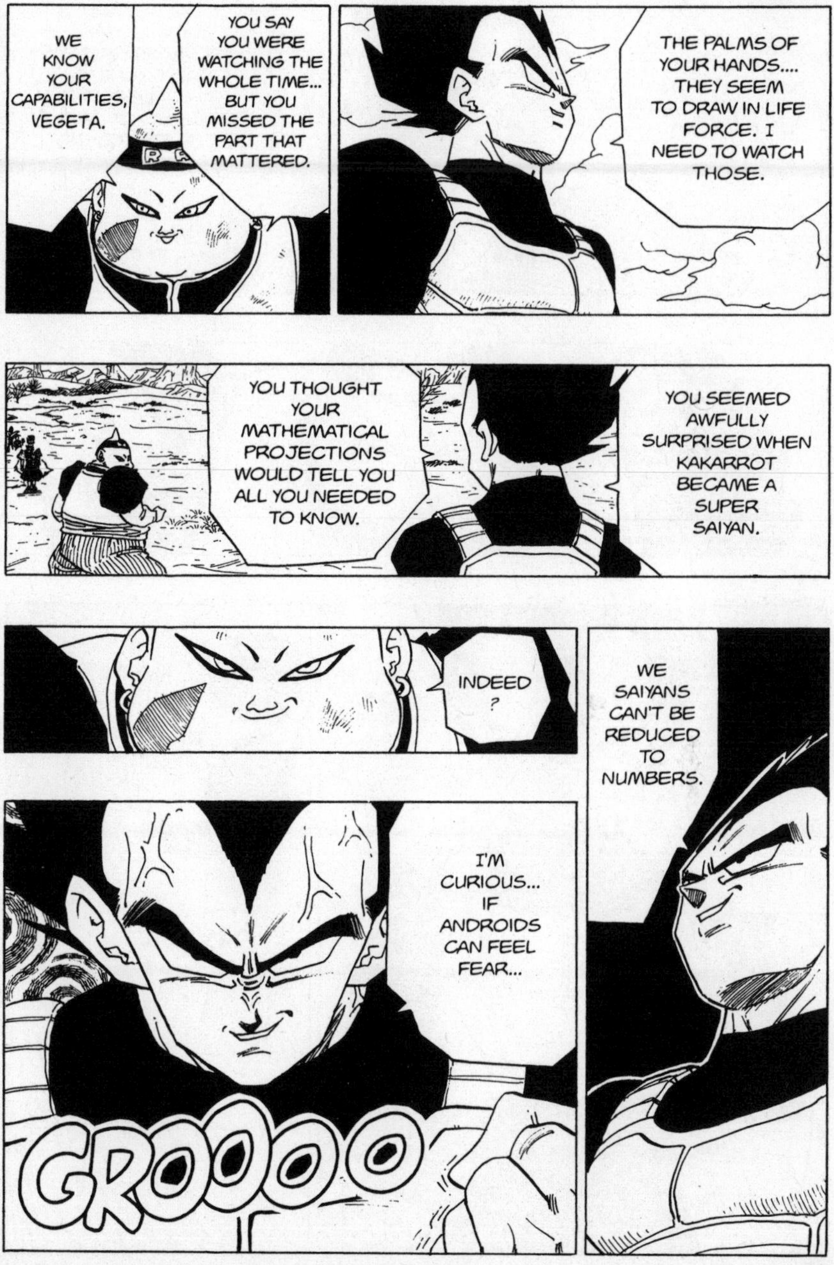

THE PALMS OF YOUR HANDS.... THEY SEEM TO DRAW IN LIFE FORCE. I NEED TO WATCH THOSE.
YOU SAY YOU WERE WATCHING THE WHOLE TIME... BUT YOU MISSED THE PART THAT MATTERED.
WE KNOW YOUR CAPABILITIES, VEGETA.
YOU SEEMED AWFULLY SURPRISED WHEN KAKARROT BECAME A SUPER SAIYAN.
YOU THOUGHT YOUR MATHEMATICAL PROJECTIONS WOULD TELL YOU ALL YOU NEEDED TO KNOW.
WE SAIYANS CAN'T BE REDUCED TO NUMBERS.
INDEED ?
I'M CURIOUS... IF ANDROIDS CAN FEEL FEAR...
GROOOOO

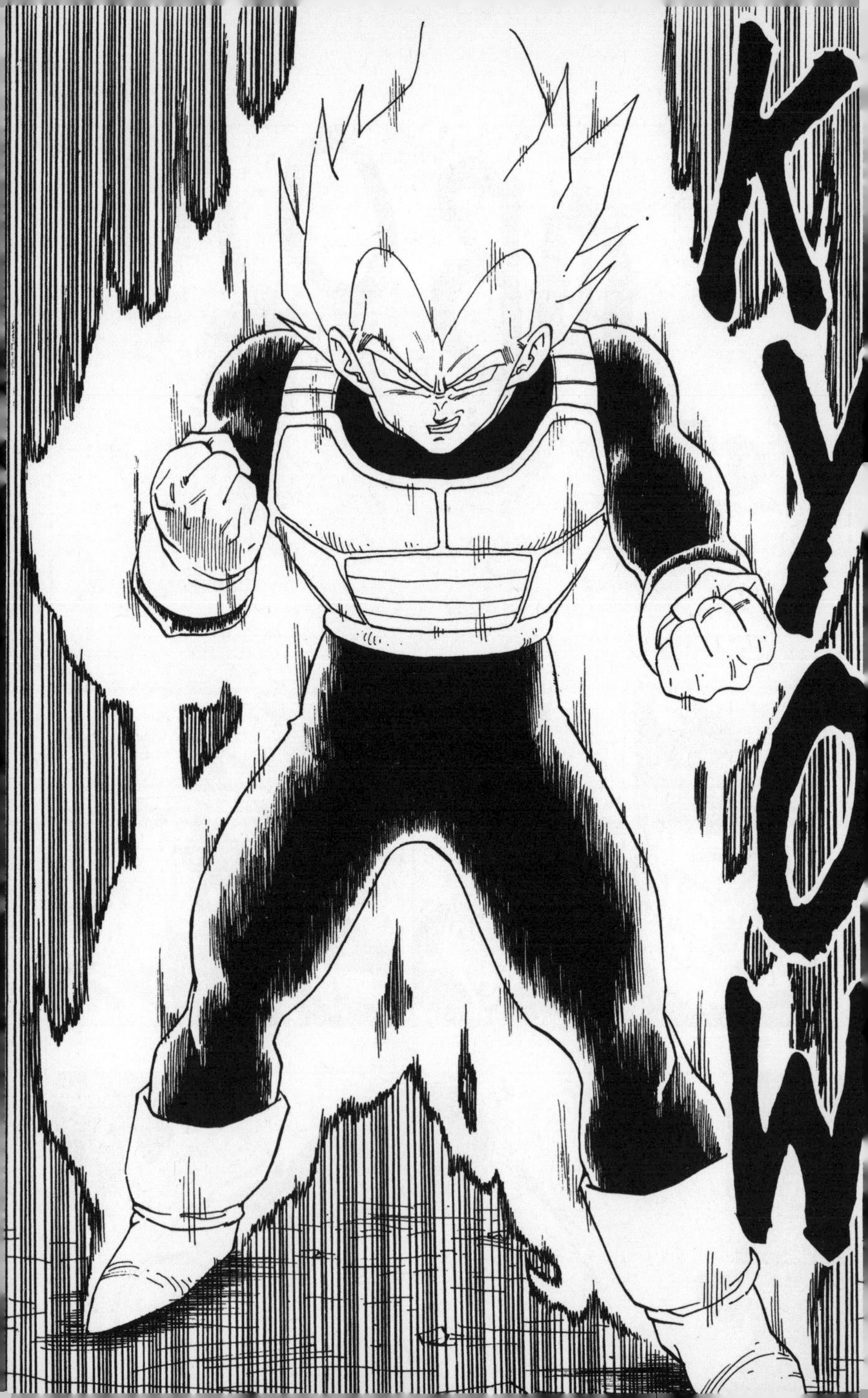
KYOW

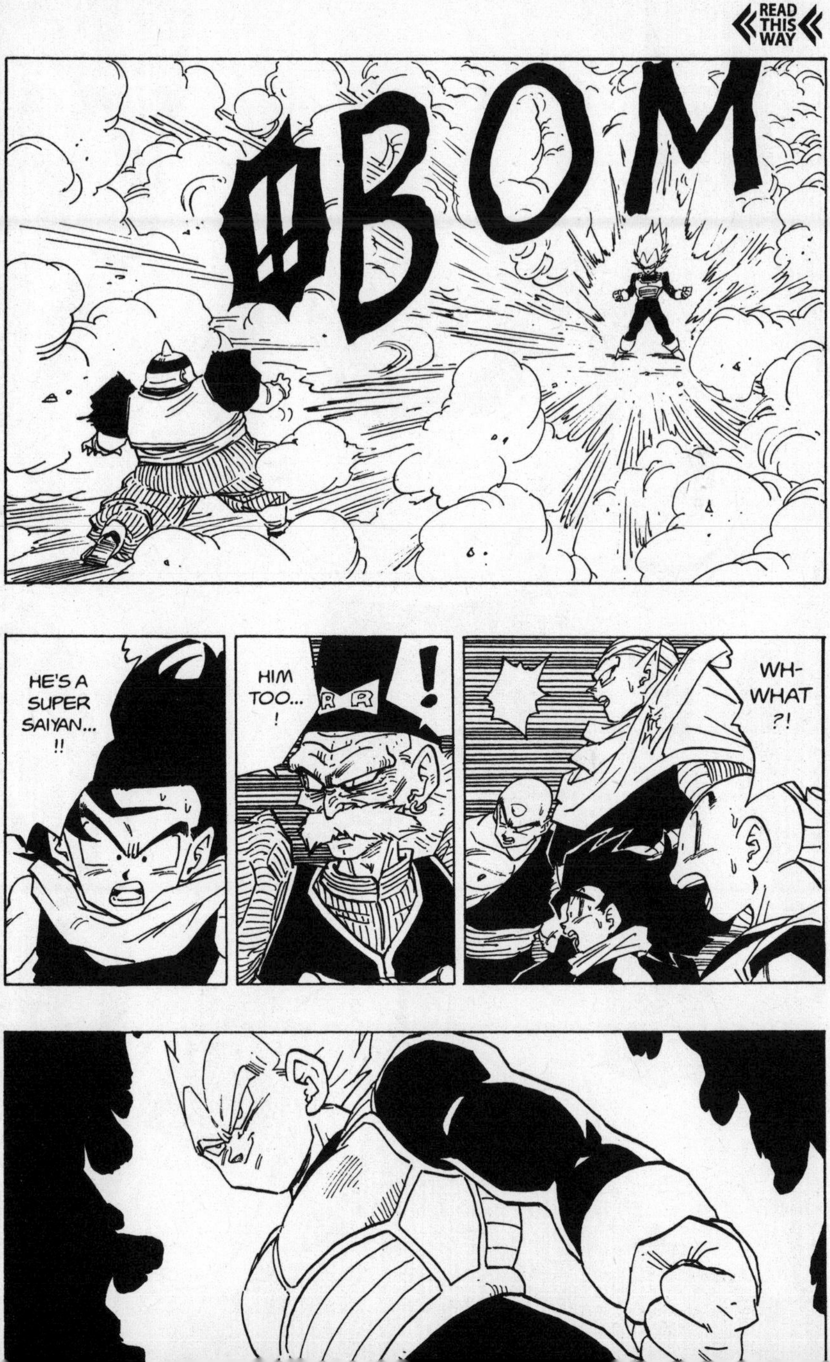
READ THIS WAY
BOM
WH-WHAT ?!
HIM TOO... !
!
HE'S A SUPER SAIYAN... !!

READ THIS WAY

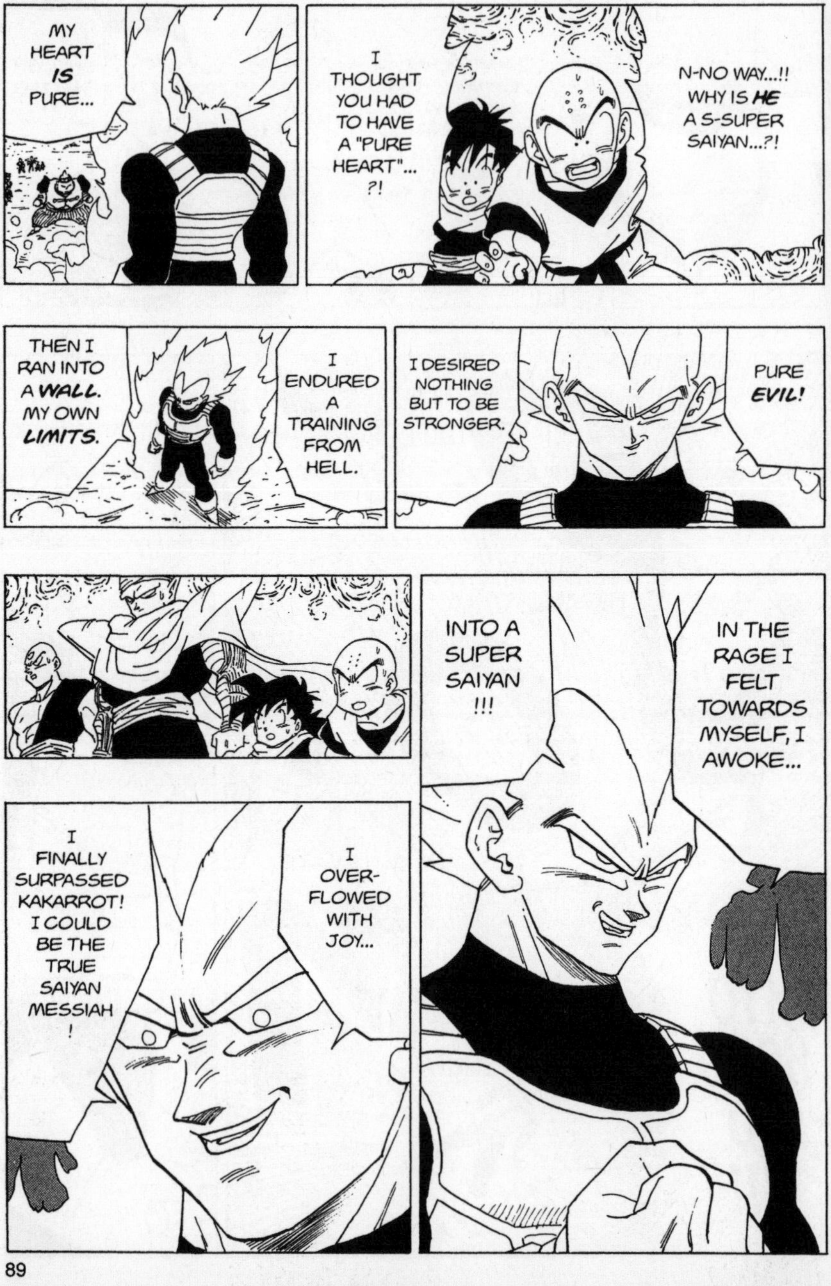
N-NO WAY...!! WHY IS **HE** A S-SUPER SAIYAN...?!
I THOUGHT YOU HAD TO HAVE A "PURE HEART"...?!
MY HEART **IS** PURE...
PURE **EVIL!**
I DESIRED NOTHING BUT TO BE STRONGER.
I ENDURED A TRAINING FROM HELL.
THEN I RAN INTO A **WALL**. MY OWN **LIMITS**.
IN THE RAGE I FELT TOWARDS MYSELF, I AWOKE...
INTO A SUPER SAIYAN!!!
I OVERFLOWED WITH JOY...
I FINALLY SURPASSED KAKARROT! I COULD BE THE TRUE SAIYAN MESSIAH!

READ THIS WAY

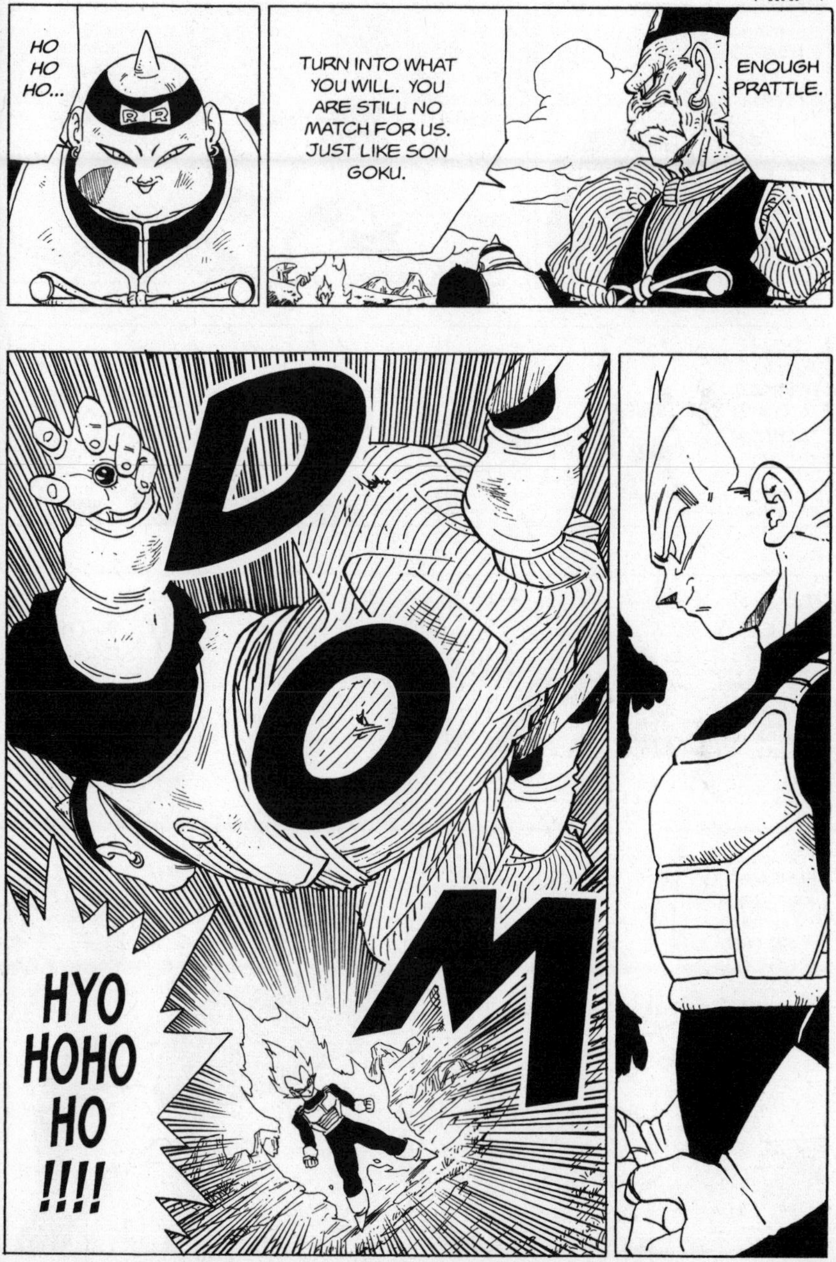

ENOUGH PRATTLE.
TURN INTO WHAT YOU WILL. YOU ARE STILL NO MATCH FOR US. JUST LIKE SON GOKU.
HO HO HO...
DOM
HYO HOHO HO!!!!

READ THIS WAY

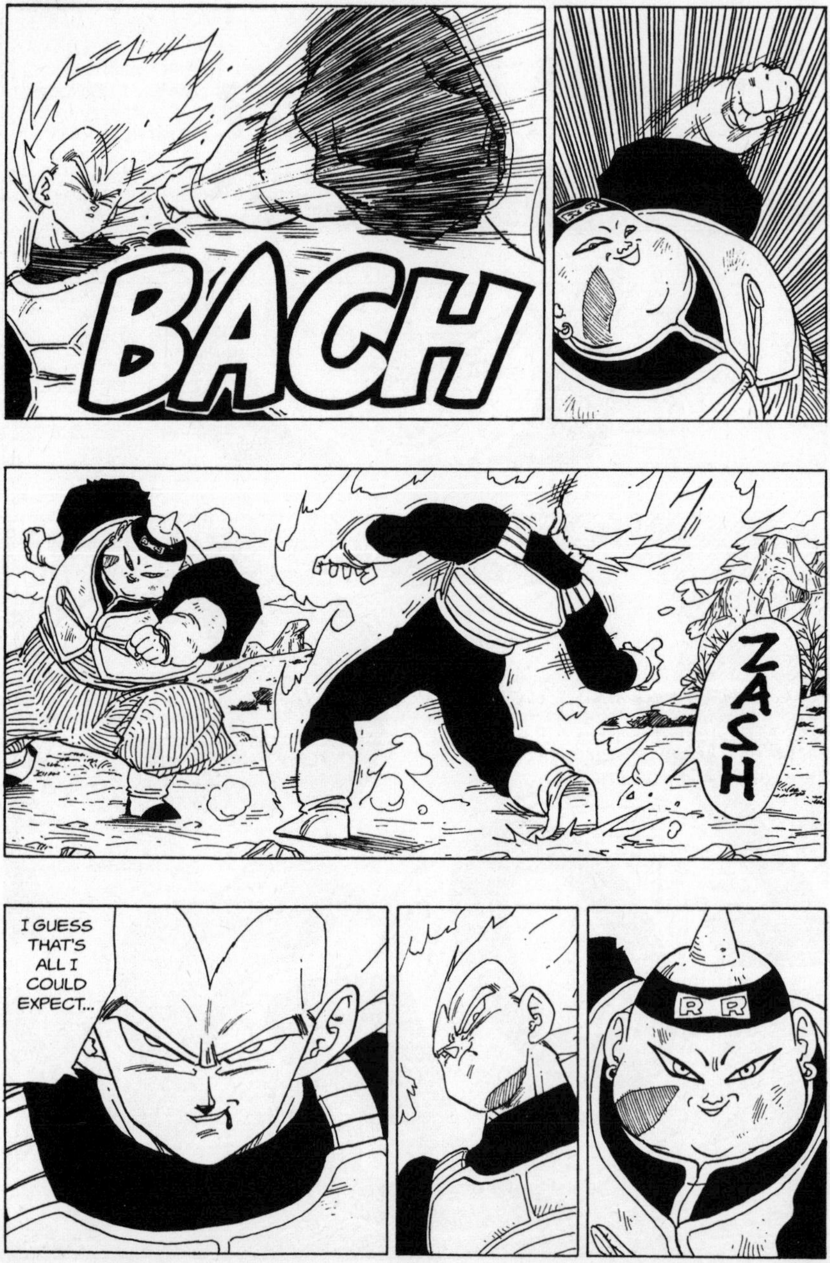
BACH
ZASH
I GUESS THAT'S ALL I COULD EXPECT...

READ THIS WAY

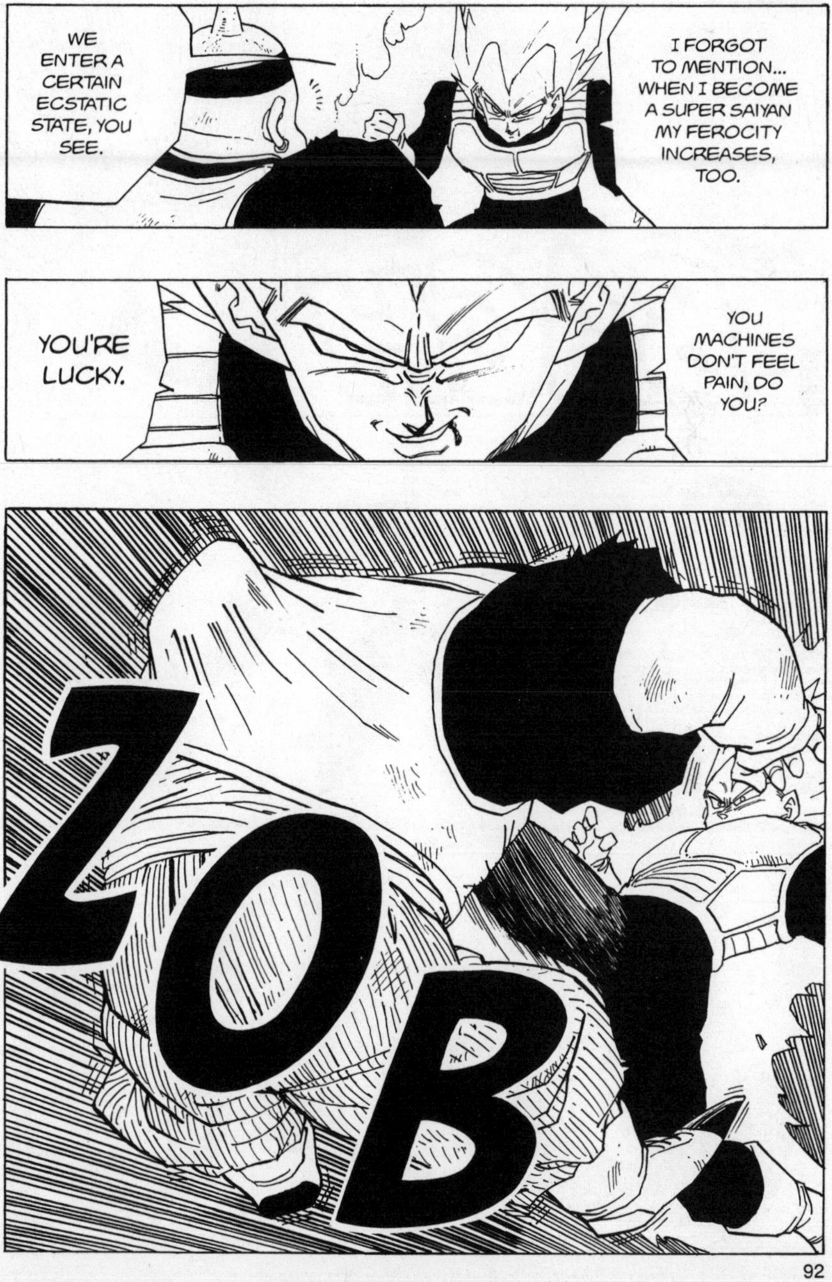
I FORGOT TO MENTION... WHEN I BECOME A SUPER SAIYAN MY FEROCITY INCREASES, TOO.
WE ENTER A CERTAIN ECSTATIC STATE, YOU SEE.
YOU MACHINES DON'T FEEL PAIN, DO YOU?
YOU'RE LUCKY.
ZOB

READ THIS WAY

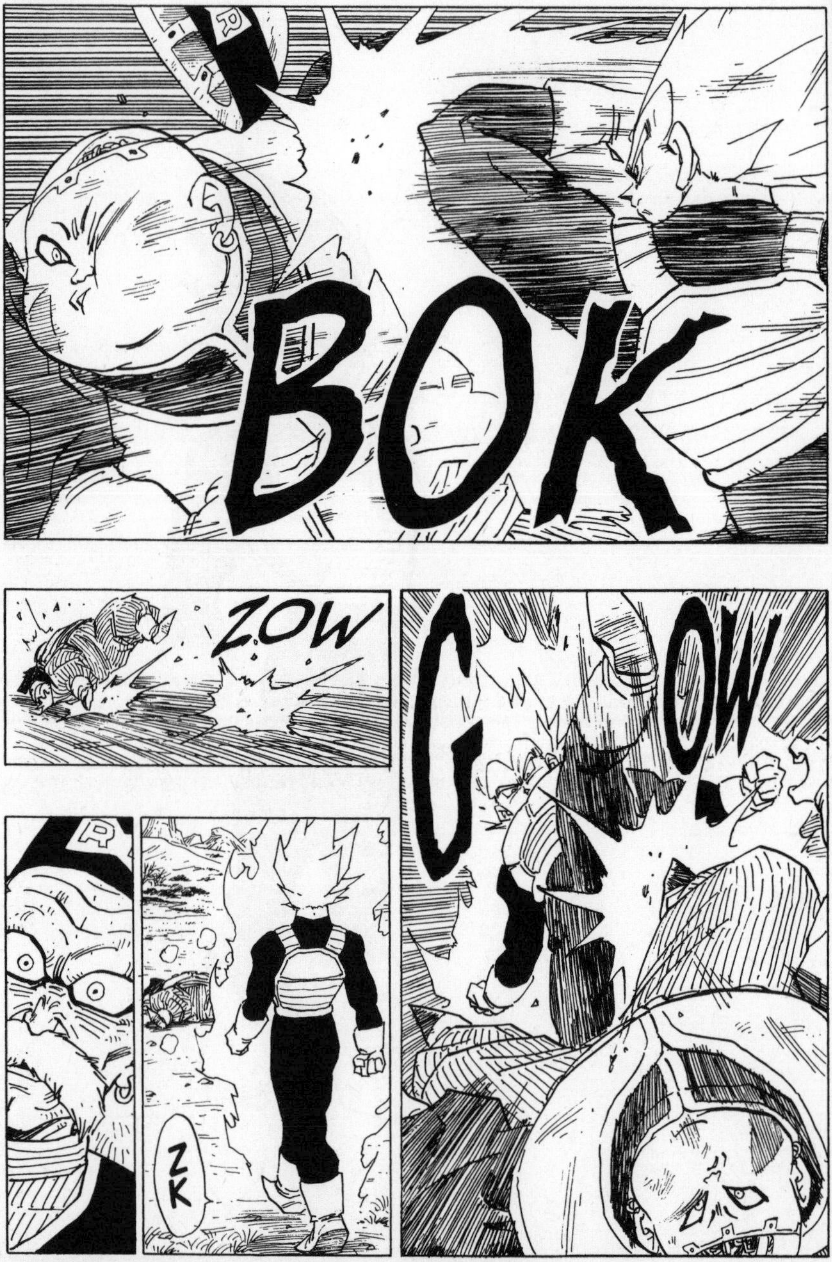
BOK
GOW
ZOW
ZK

NEXT: The Limit of the Machines

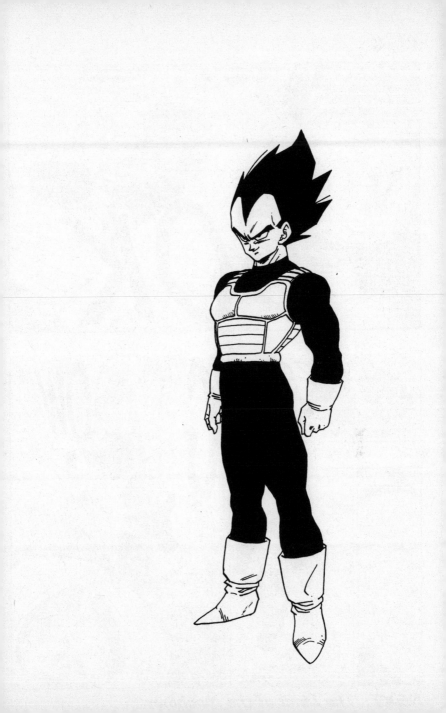

# DBZ:150
# The Androids Unhinged

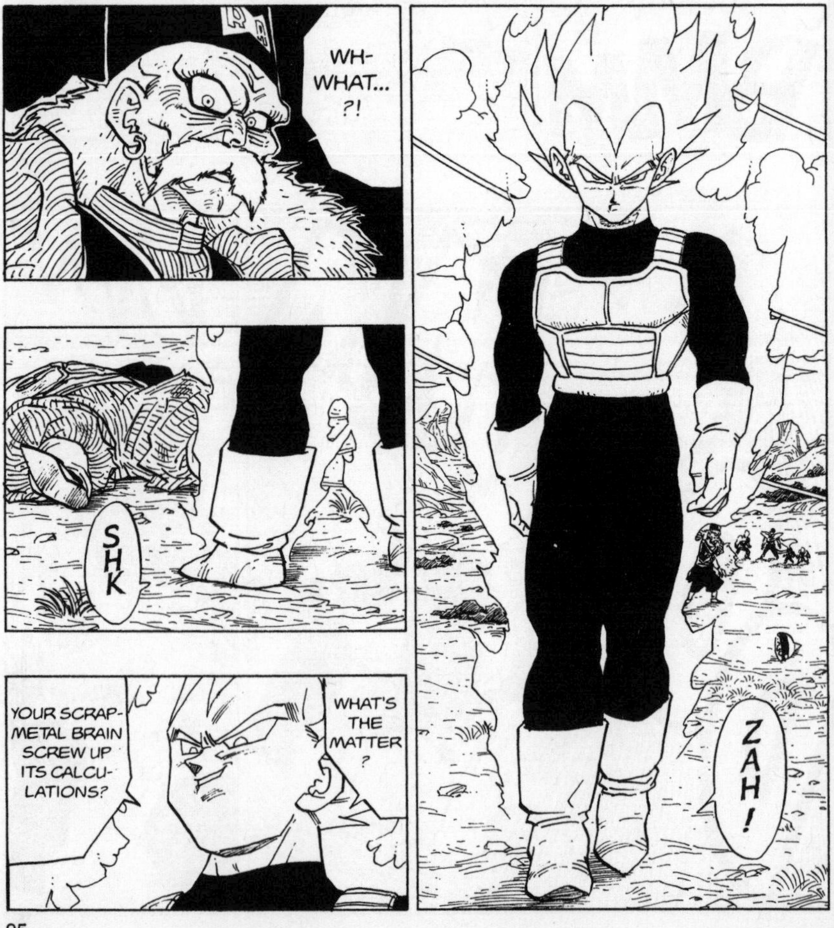
ZAH!
WH- WHAT...?!
SHK
WHAT'S THE MATTER?
YOUR SCRAP-METAL BRAIN SCREW UP ITS CALCULATIONS?

READ THIS WAY

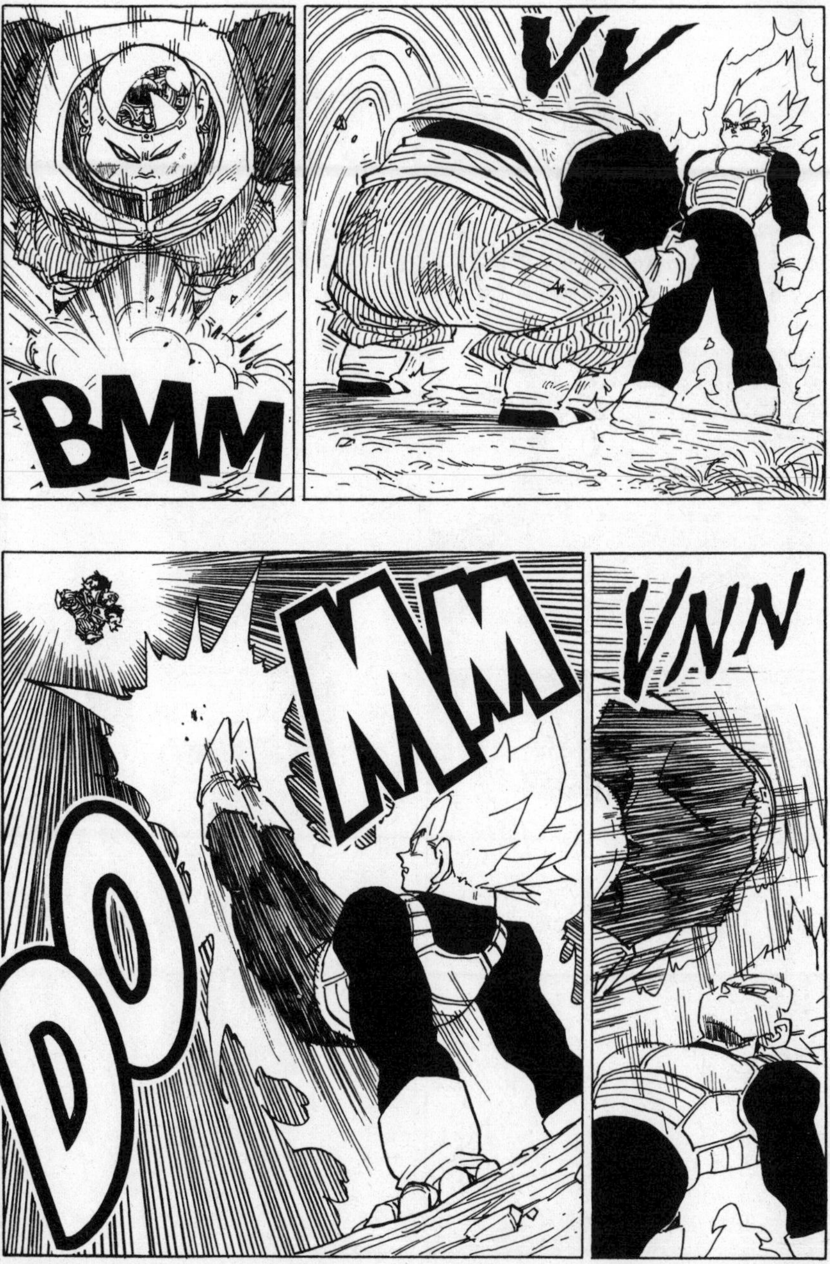
VV
BMM
VNN
DO
MM

READ THIS WAY

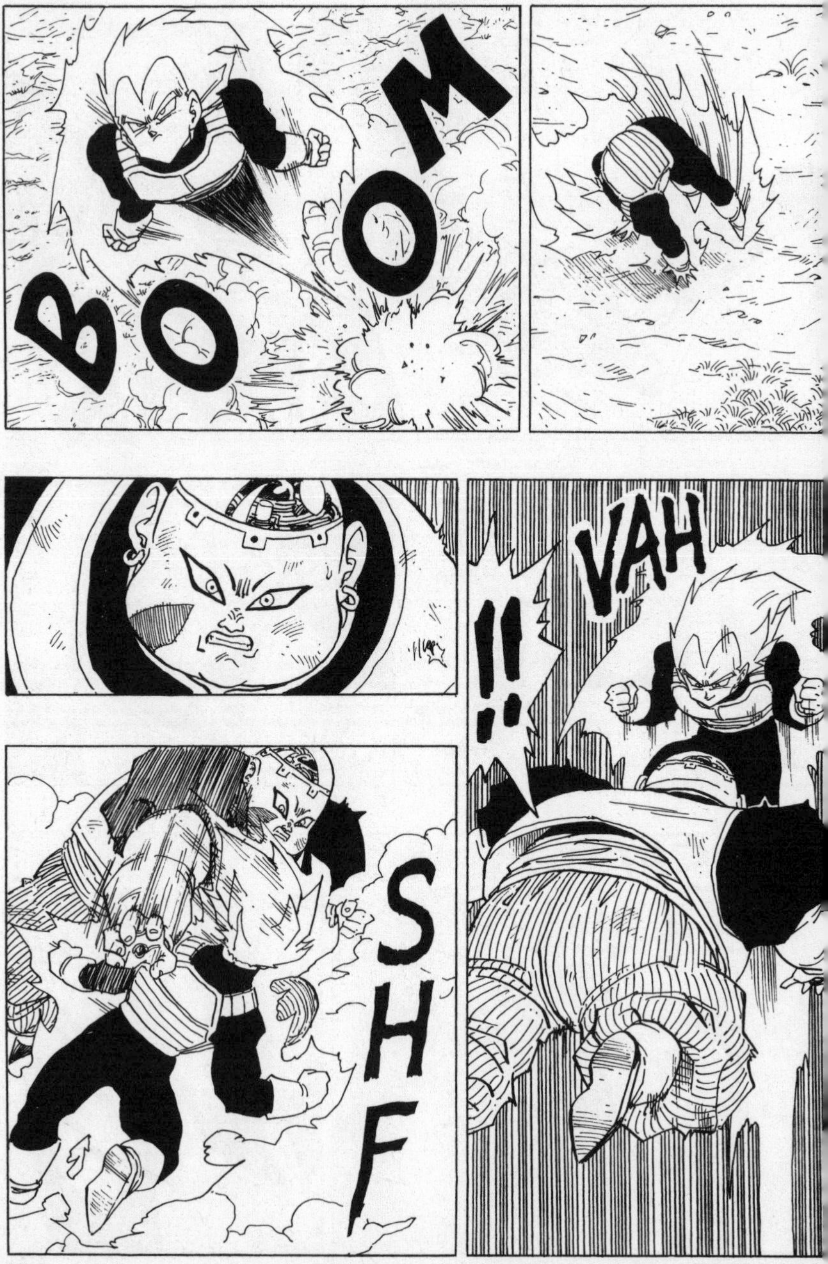
BOOM
VAH
!!
SHF

READ THIS WAY

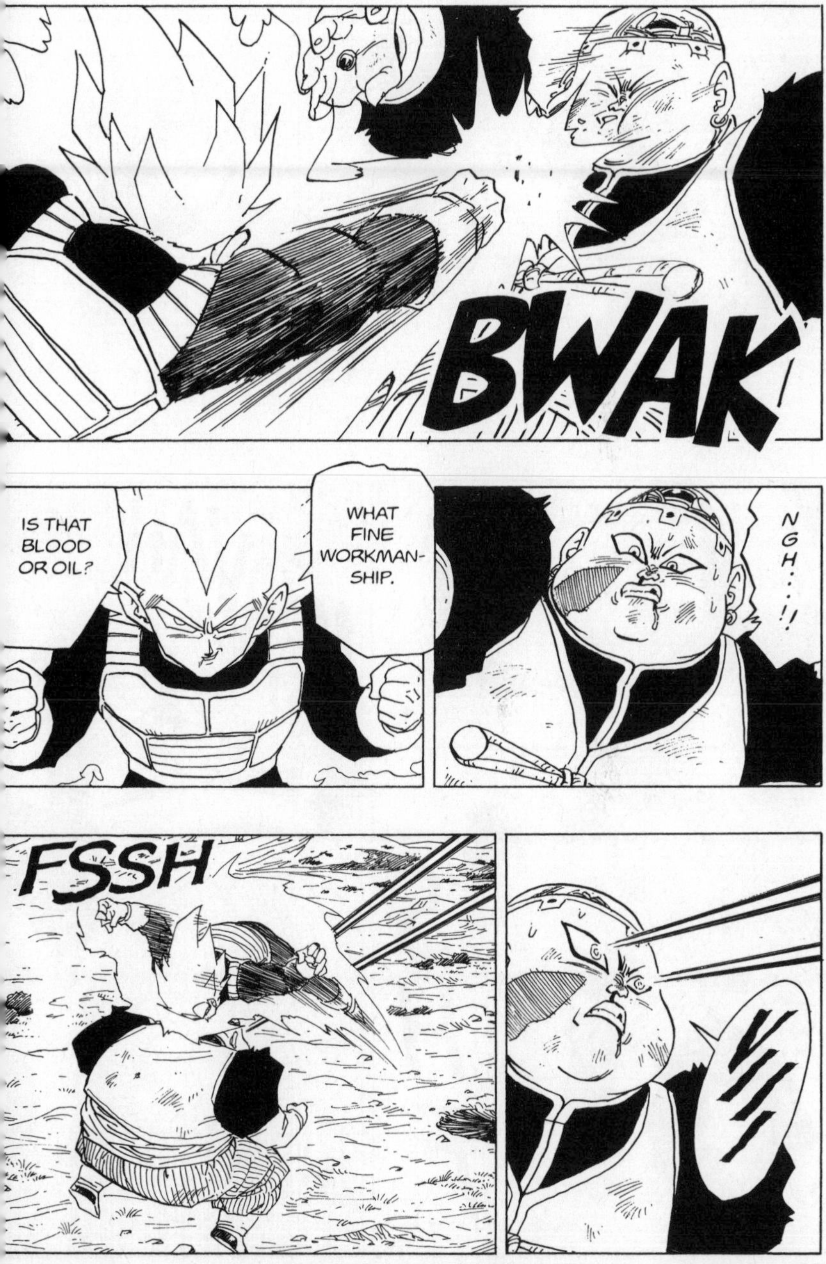
BWAK
NGH...!!
WHAT FINE WORKMAN-SHIP.
IS THAT BLOOD OR OIL?
FSSH

READ THIS WAY

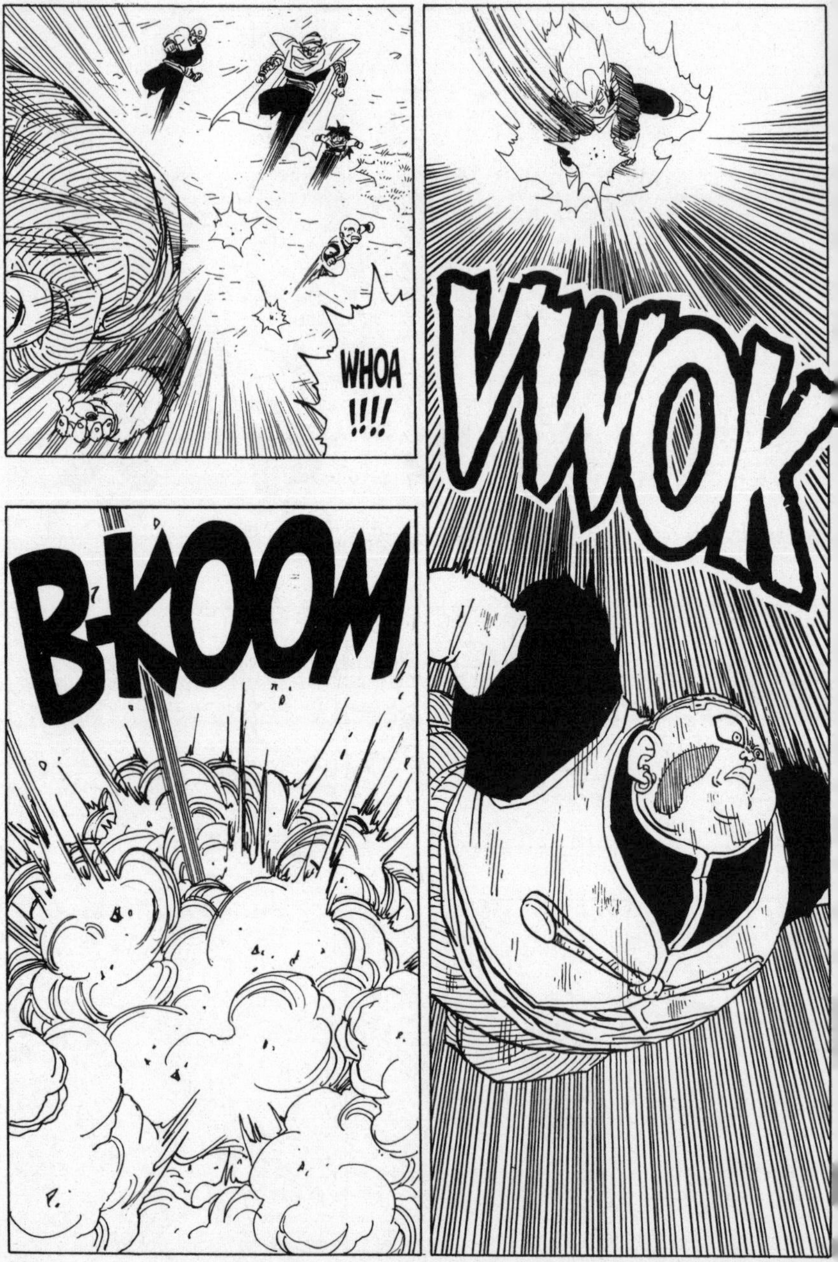
VWOK
WHOA !!!!
B-KOOM

READ THIS WAY

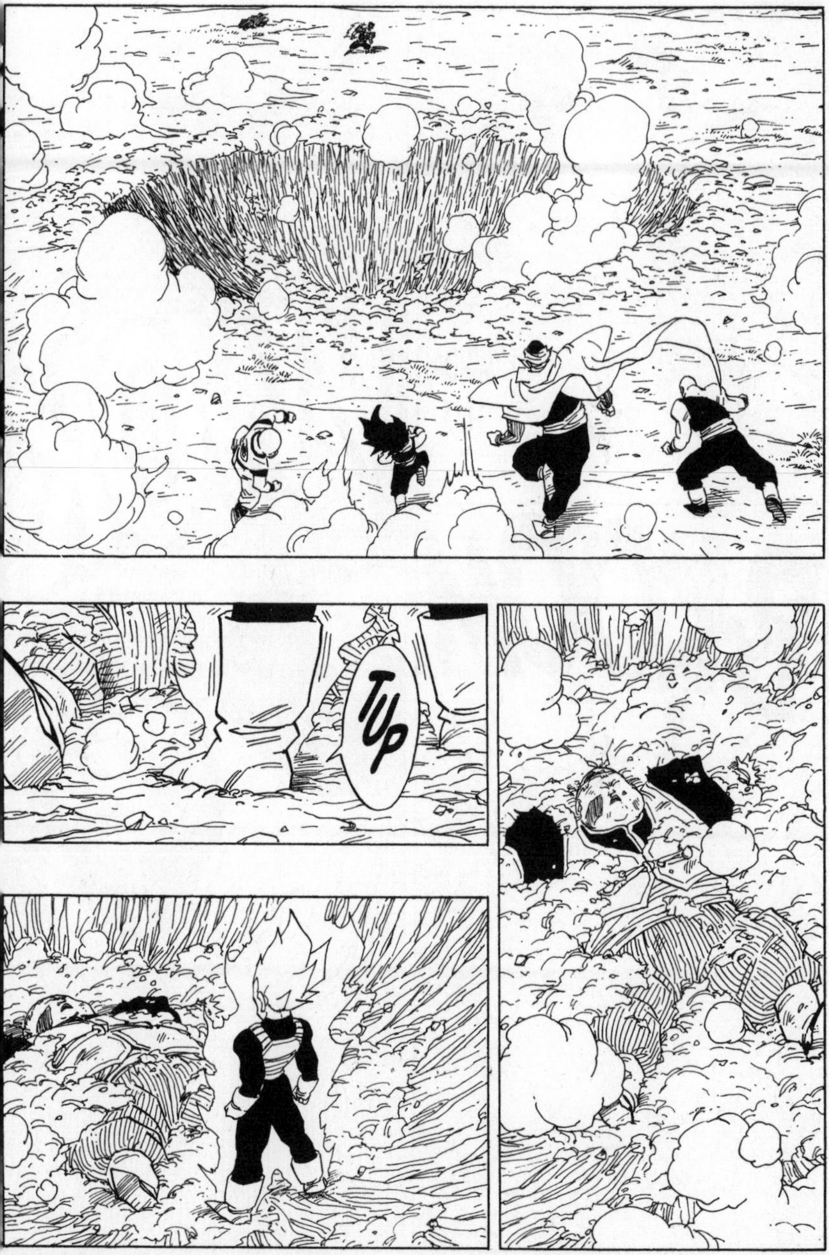
TUP

READ THIS WAY

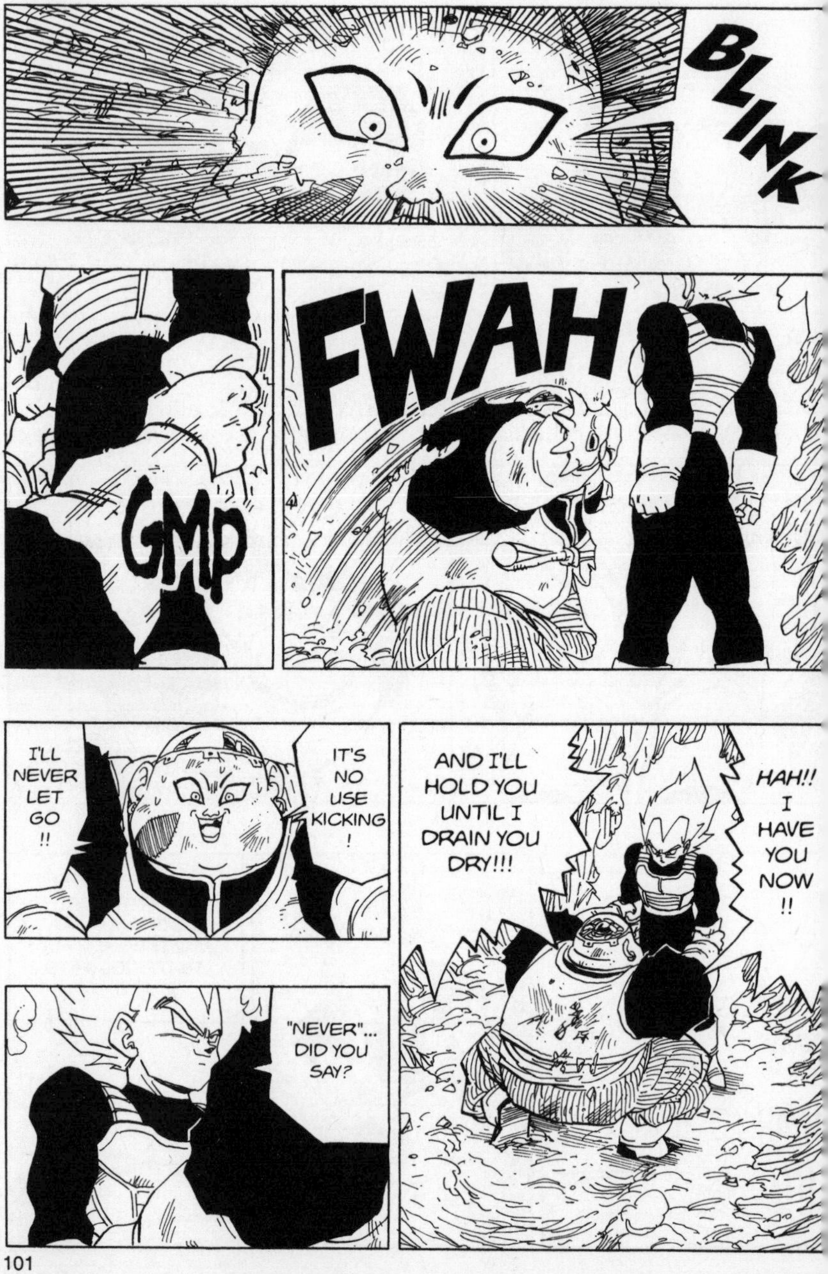

BLINK
FWAH
GMP
HAH!! I HAVE YOU NOW!!
AND I'LL HOLD YOU UNTIL I DRAIN YOU DRY!!!
IT'S NO USE KICKING!
I'LL NEVER LET GO!!
"NEVER"... DID YOU SAY?

READ THIS WAY

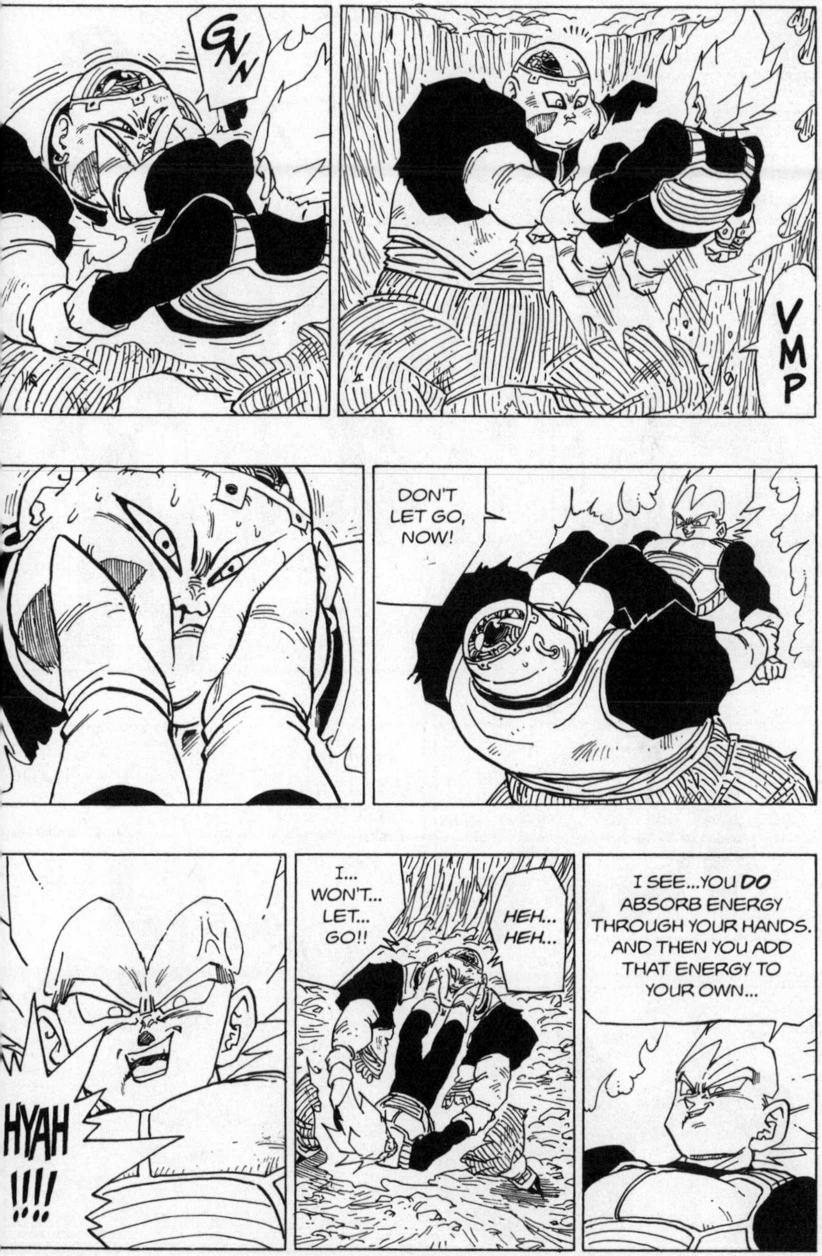
VMP
GNN
DON'T LET GO, NOW!
I SEE...YOU **DO** ABSORB ENERGY THROUGH YOUR HANDS. AND THEN YOU ADD THAT ENERGY TO YOUR OWN...
HEH... HEH...
I... WON'T... LET... GO!!
HYAH !!!!

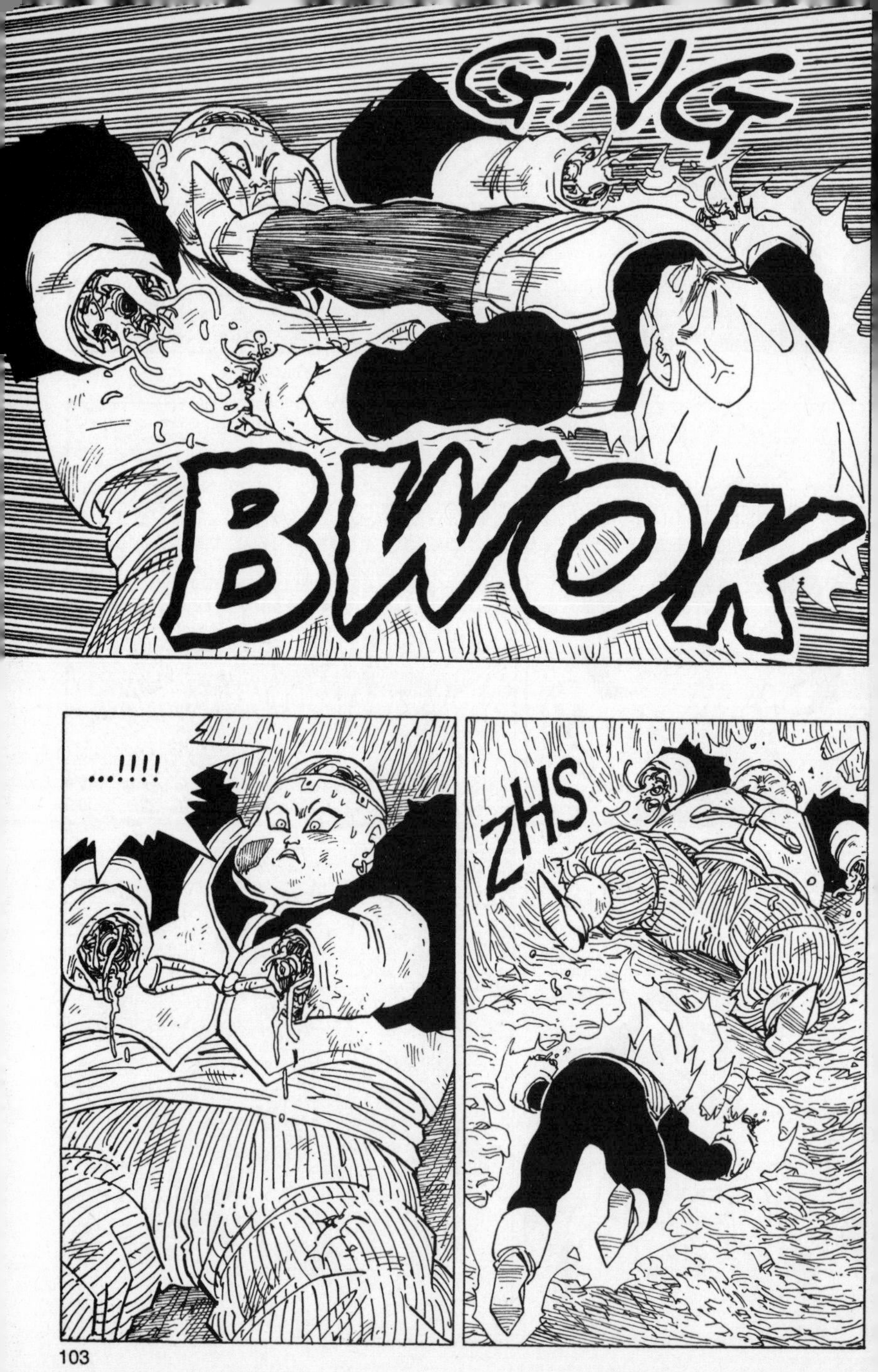
GNG
BWOK
ZHS
...!!!!

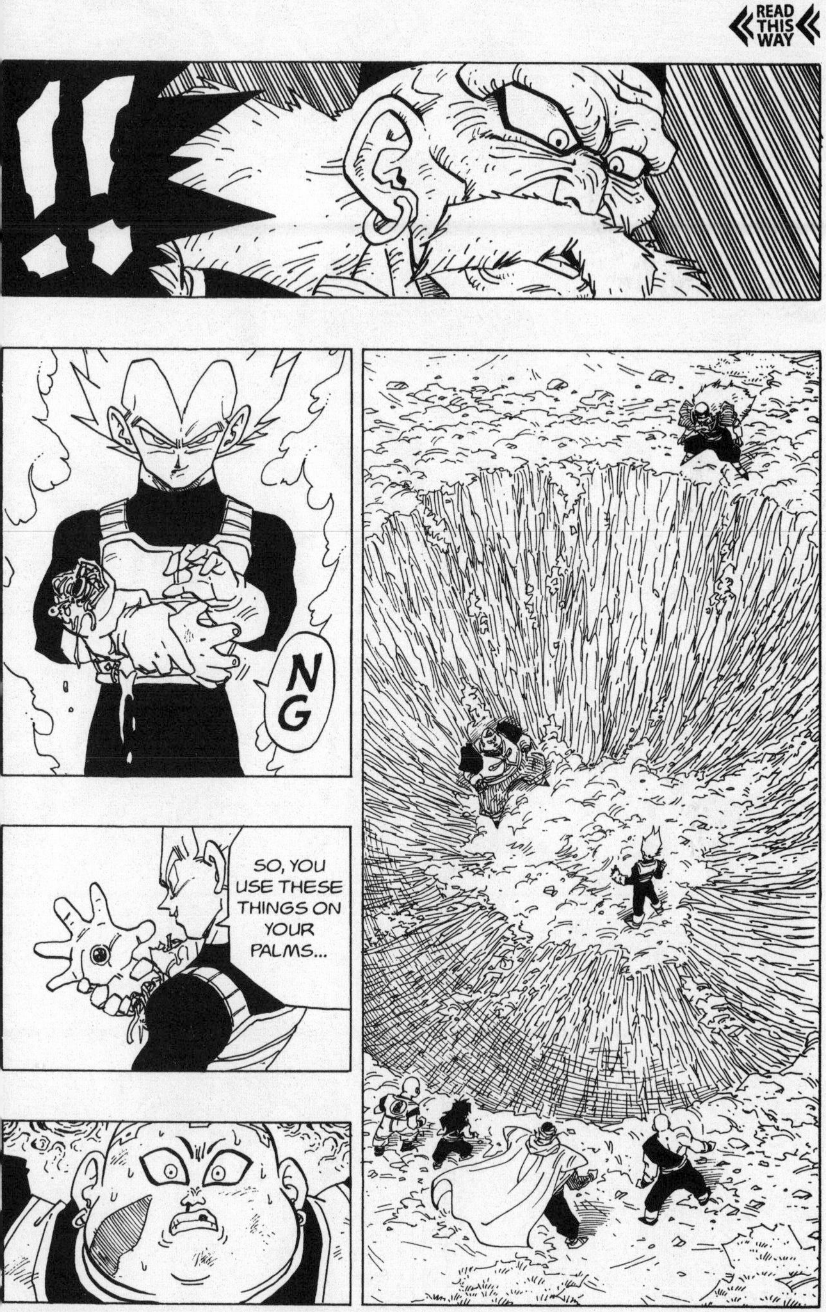
READ THIS WAY
!!
NG
SO, YOU USE THESE THINGS ON YOUR PALMS...

READ THIS WAY

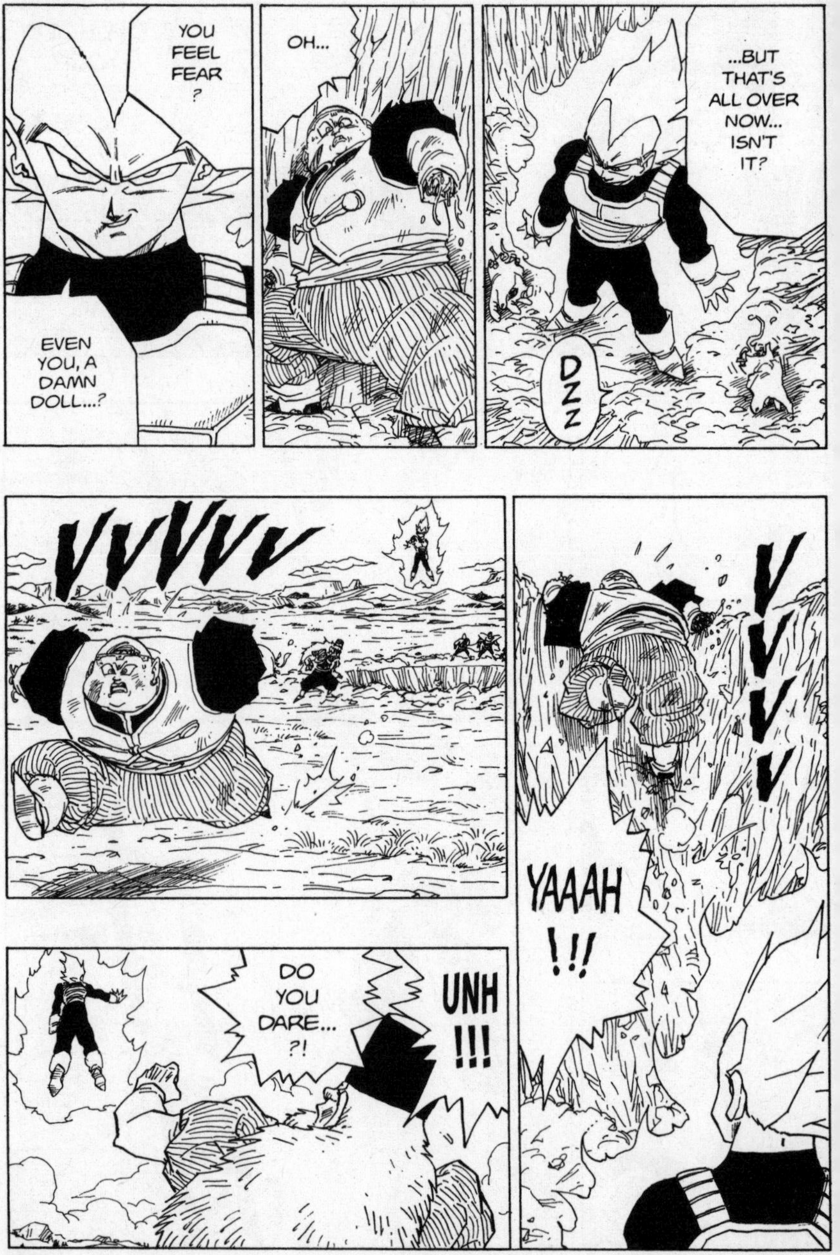
...BUT THAT'S ALL OVER NOW... ISN'T IT?
DZZ
OH...
YOU FEEL FEAR?
EVEN YOU, A DAMN DOLL...?
VVVV
YAAAH!!!
VVVVVV
UNH!!!
DO YOU DARE...?!

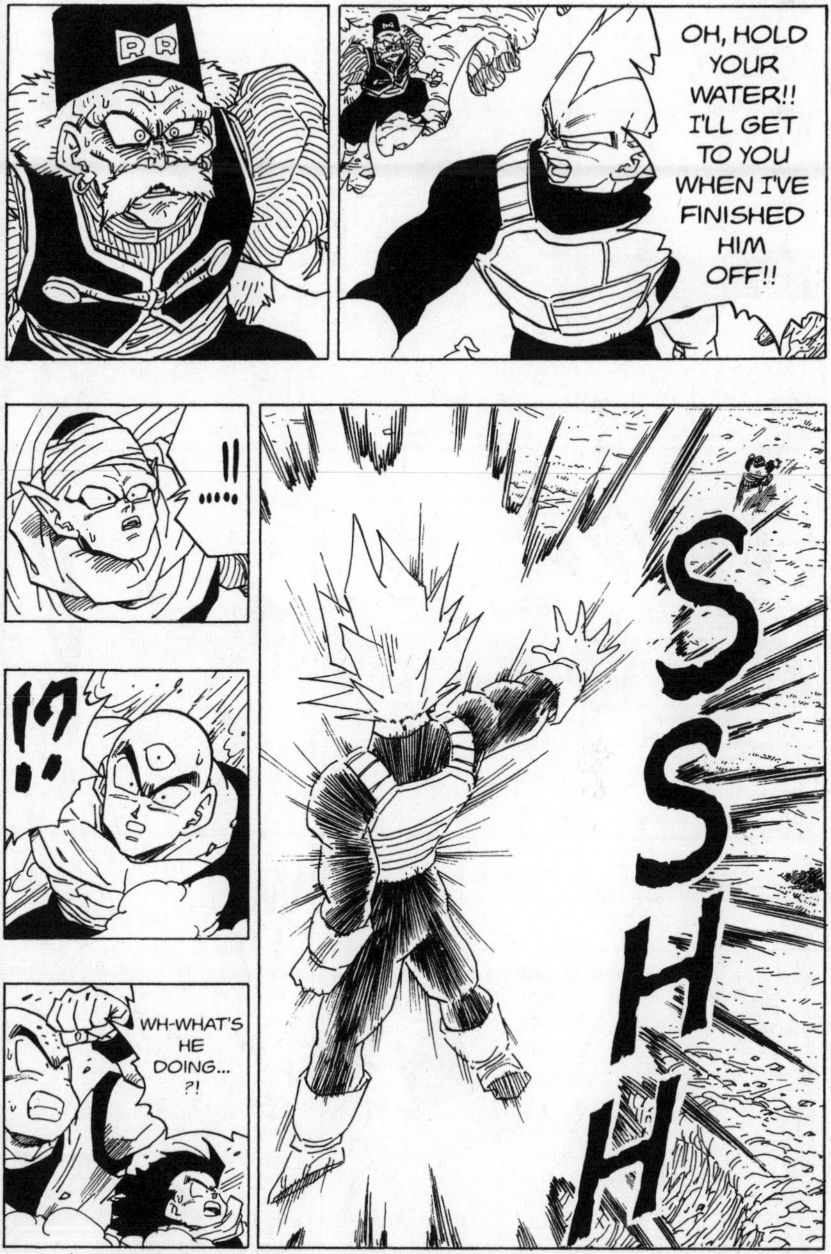
READ THIS WAY
OH, HOLD YOUR WATER!! I'LL GET TO YOU WHEN I'VE FINISHED HIM OFF!!
SSHHH
....!!
!?
WH-WHAT'S HE DOING...?!

READ THIS WAY

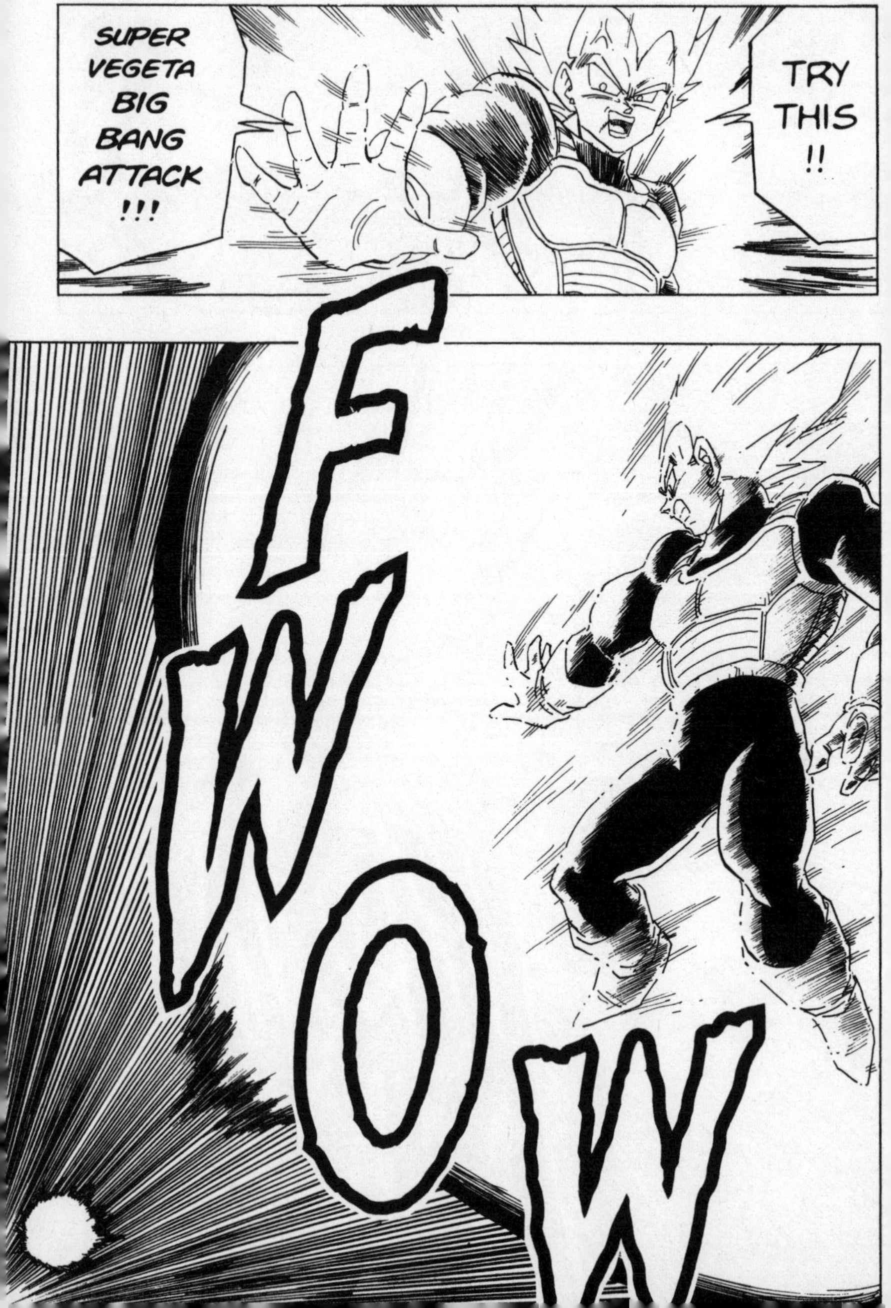
TRY THIS !!
SUPER VEGETA BIG BANG ATTACK !!!
FWOOW

READ THIS WAY

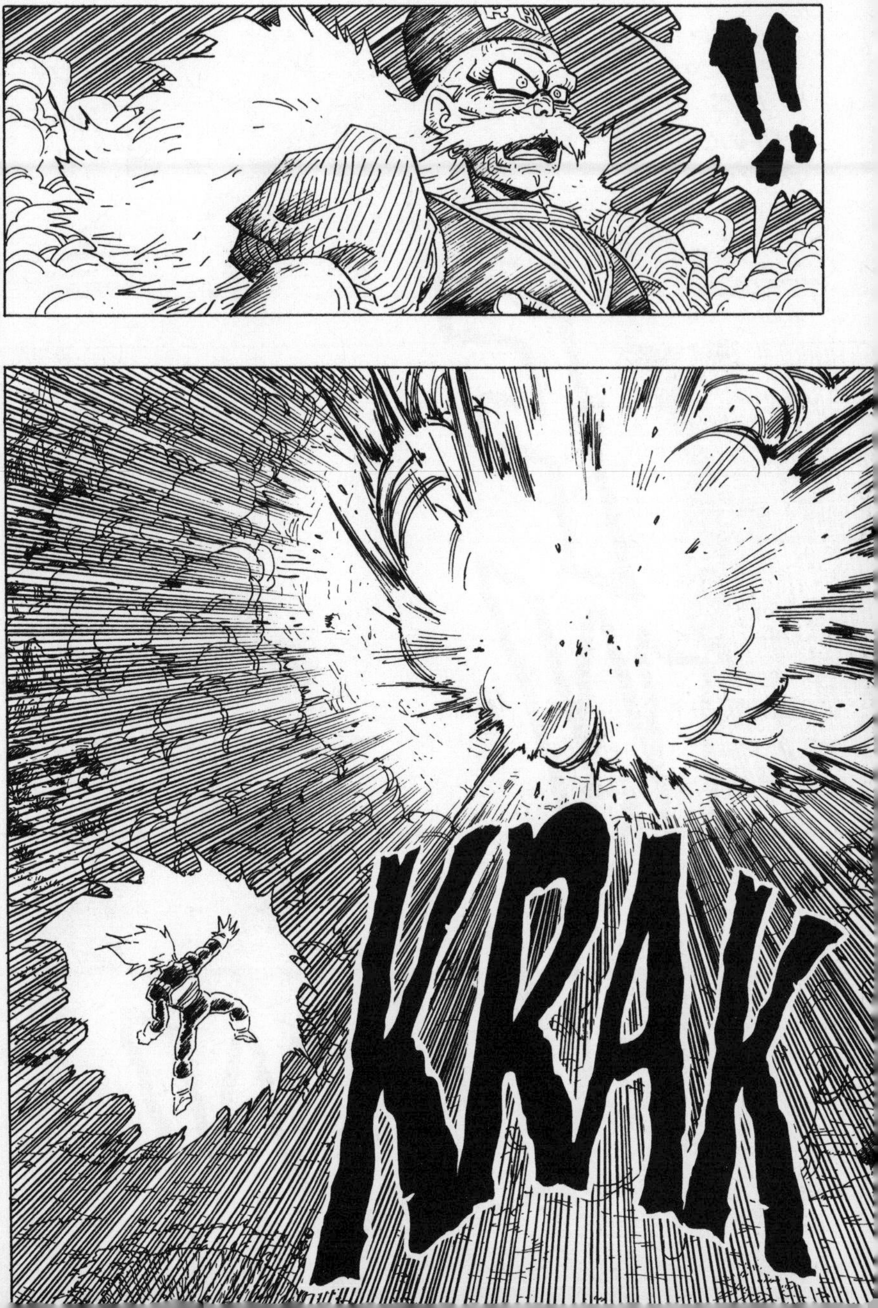
!!
KRAK

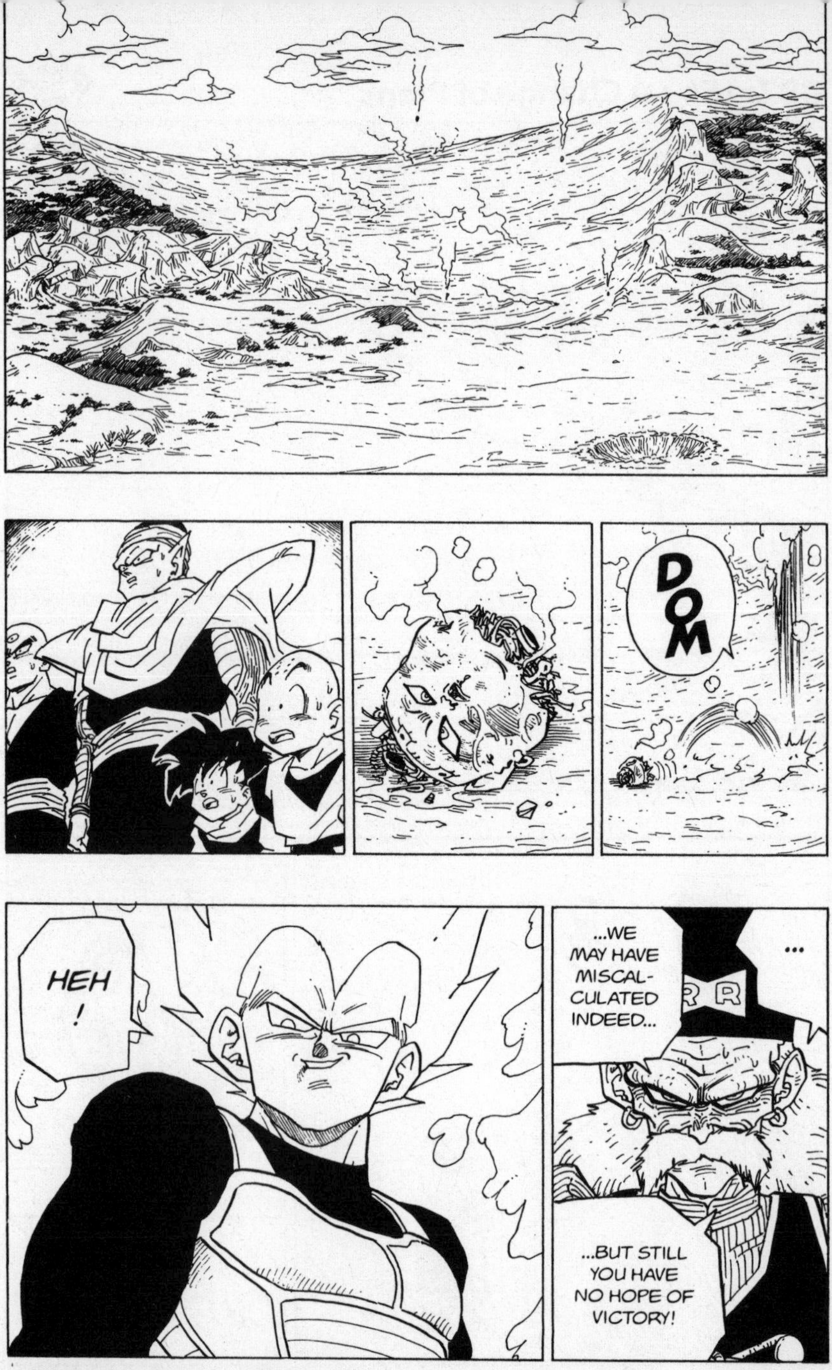
DOM
...WE MAY HAVE MISCAL-CULATED INDEED...
...BUT STILL YOU HAVE NO HOPE OF VICTORY!
...
HEH !

NEXT: Android Fear!

# DBZ: 151 • A Change of Plans

READ THIS WAY

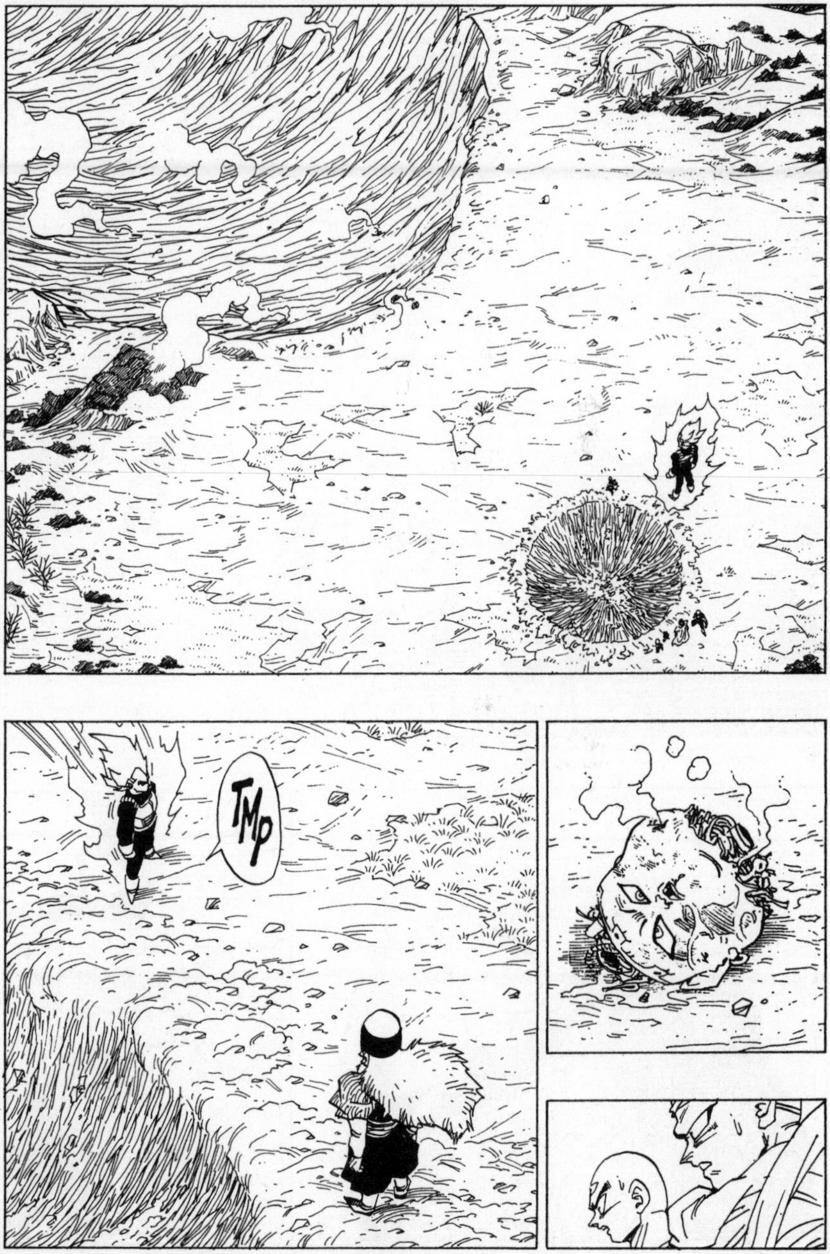
TMP

READ THIS WAY

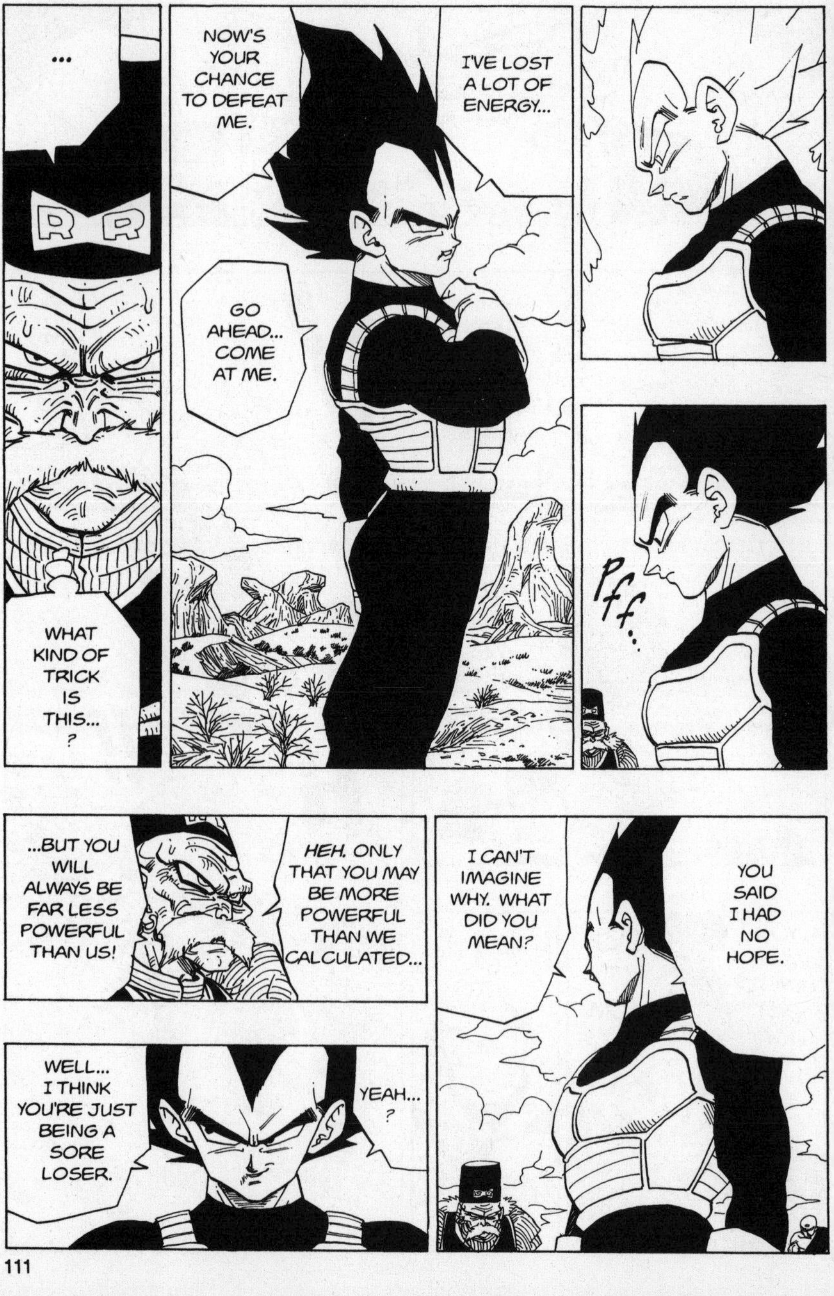
Pff...
I'VE LOST A LOT OF ENERGY...
NOW'S YOUR CHANCE TO DEFEAT ME.
GO AHEAD... COME AT ME.
...
WHAT KIND OF TRICK IS THIS... ?
YOU SAID I HAD NO HOPE.
I CAN'T IMAGINE WHY. WHAT DID YOU MEAN?
HEH. ONLY THAT YOU MAY BE MORE POWERFUL THAN WE CALCULATED...
...BUT YOU WILL ALWAYS BE FAR LESS POWERFUL THAN US!
YEAH... ?
WELL... I THINK YOU'RE JUST BEING A SORE LOSER.

READ THIS WAY

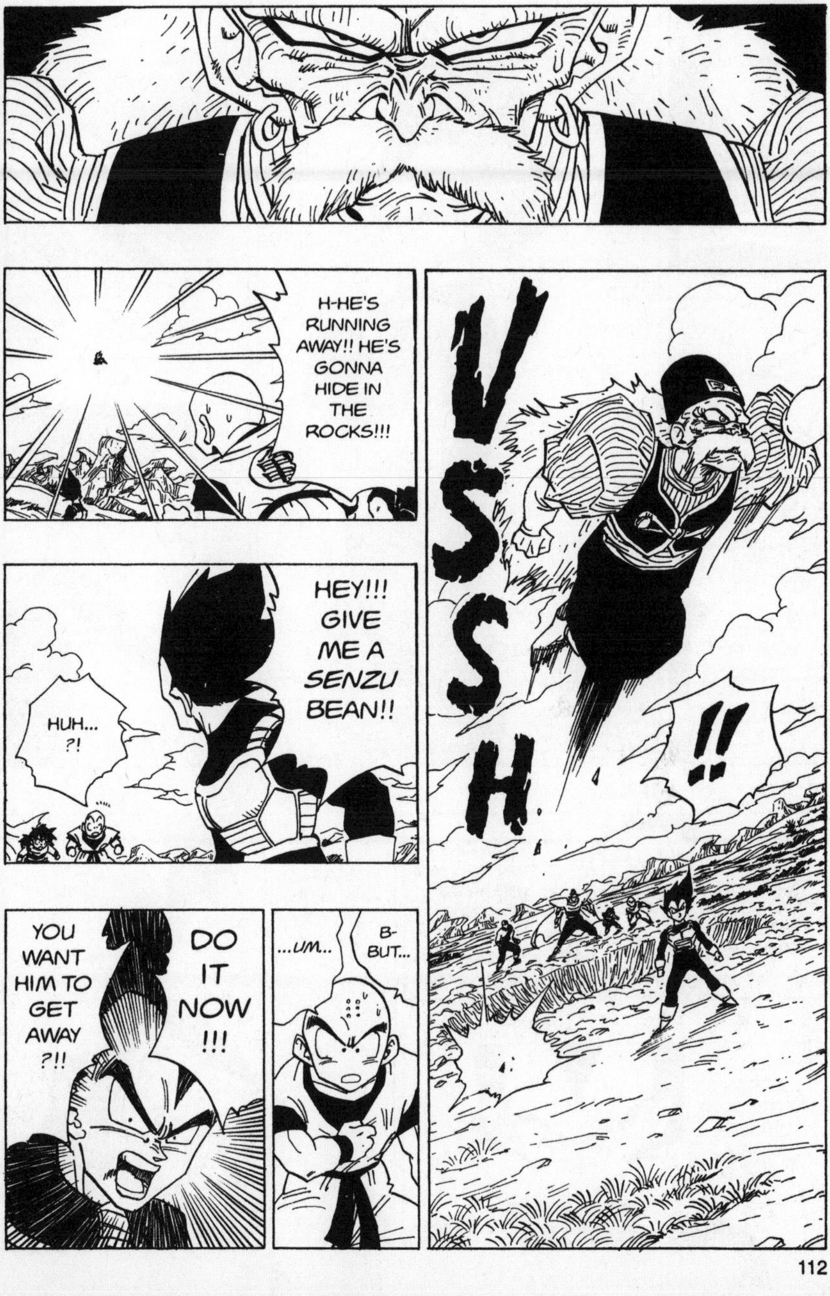
VSSH
!!
H-HE'S RUNNING AWAY!! HE'S GONNA HIDE IN THE ROCKS!!!
HEY!!! GIVE ME A SENZU BEAN!!
HUH... ?!
B-BUT...
...UM...
DO IT NOW !!!
YOU WANT HIM TO GET AWAY ?!!

READ THIS WAY

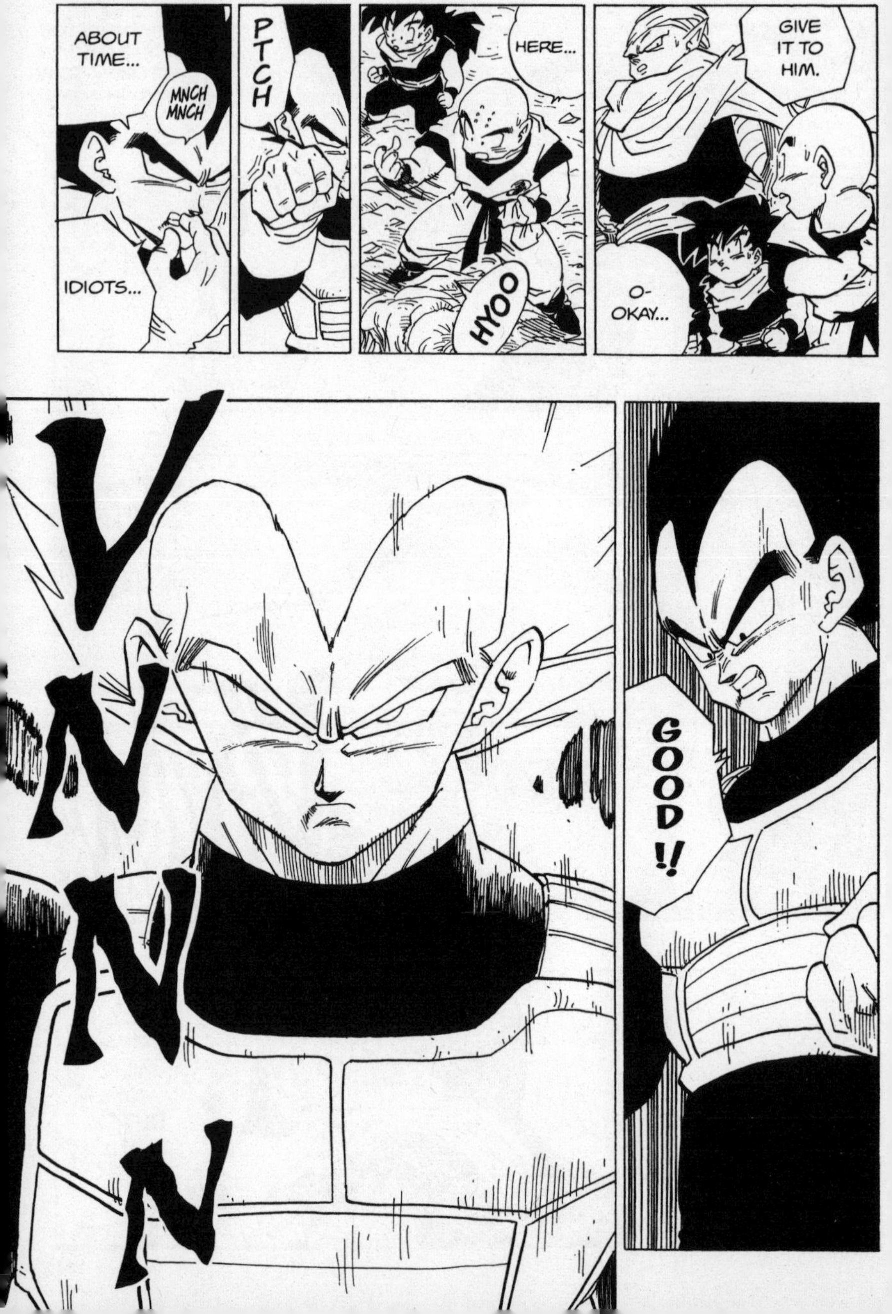

GIVE IT TO HIM.
O- OKAY...
HERE...
HYOO
PTCH
ABOUT TIME...
MNCH MNCH
IDIOTS...
GOOD!!
VNNN

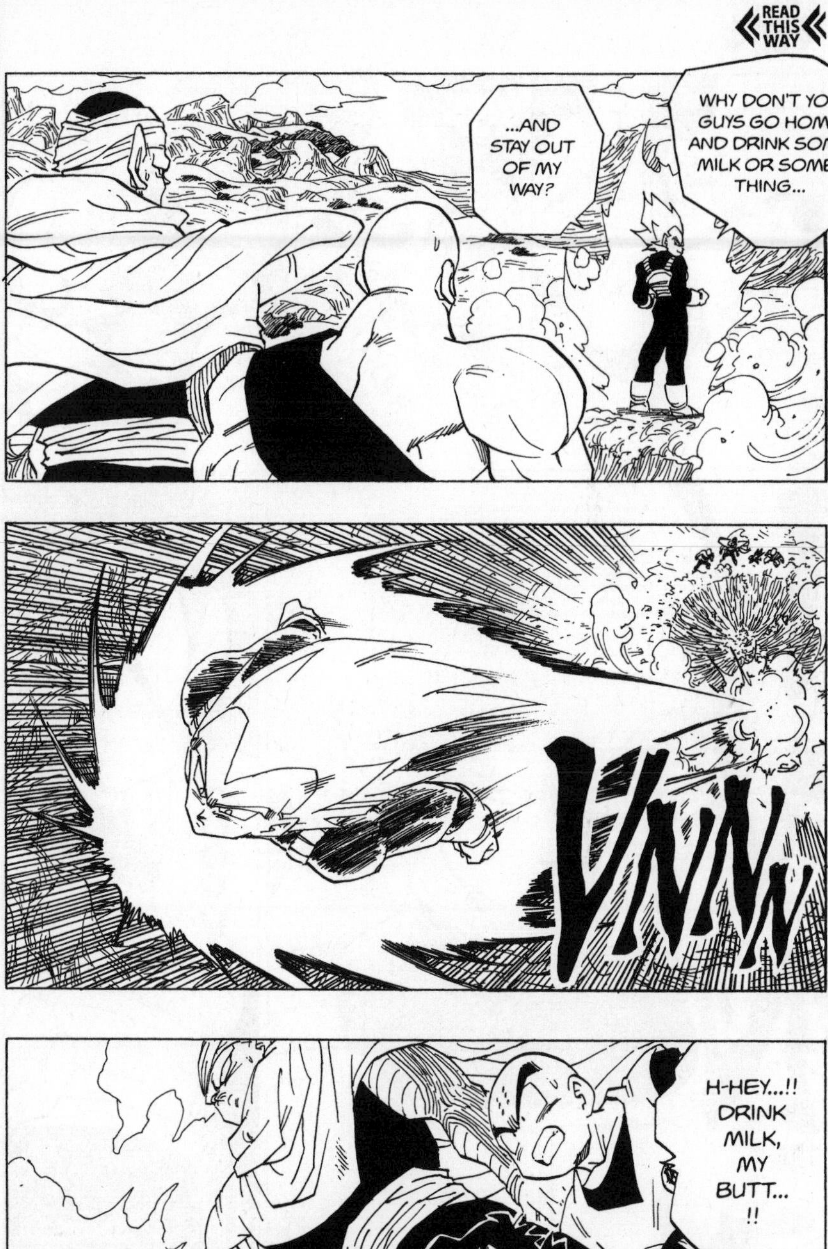
READ THIS WAY
WHY DON'T YOU GUYS GO HOME AND DRINK SOME MILK OR SOME- THING...
...AND STAY OUT OF MY WAY?
VNNN
H-HEY...!! DRINK MILK, MY BUTT... !!

READ THIS WAY

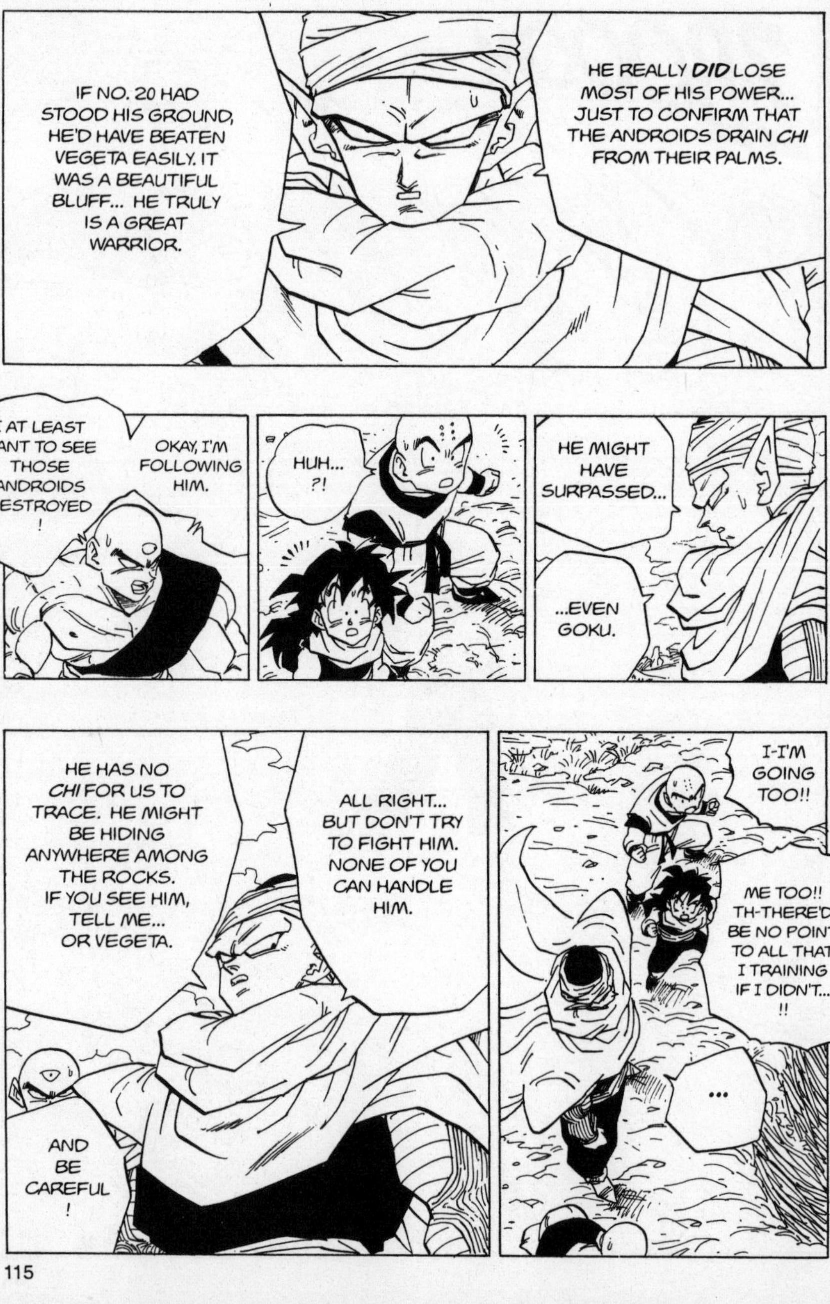

HE REALLY *DID* LOSE MOST OF HIS POWER... JUST TO CONFIRM THAT THE ANDROIDS DRAIN *CHI* FROM THEIR PALMS.
IF NO. 20 HAD STOOD HIS GROUND, HE'D HAVE BEATEN VEGETA EASILY. IT WAS A BEAUTIFUL BLUFF... HE TRULY IS A GREAT WARRIOR.
HE MIGHT HAVE SURPASSED...
...EVEN GOKU.
HUH... ?!
OKAY, I'M FOLLOWING HIM.
I AT LEAST WANT TO SEE THOSE ANDROIDS DESTROYED!
I-I'M GOING TOO!!
ME TOO!! TH-THERE'D BE NO POINT TO ALL THAT I TRAINING IF I DIDN'T...!!
...
ALL RIGHT... BUT DON'T TRY TO FIGHT HIM. NONE OF YOU CAN HANDLE HIM.
HE HAS NO *CHI* FOR US TO TRACE. HE MIGHT BE HIDING ANYWHERE AMONG THE ROCKS. IF YOU SEE HIM, TELL ME... OR VEGETA.
AND BE CAREFUL!

READ THIS WAY

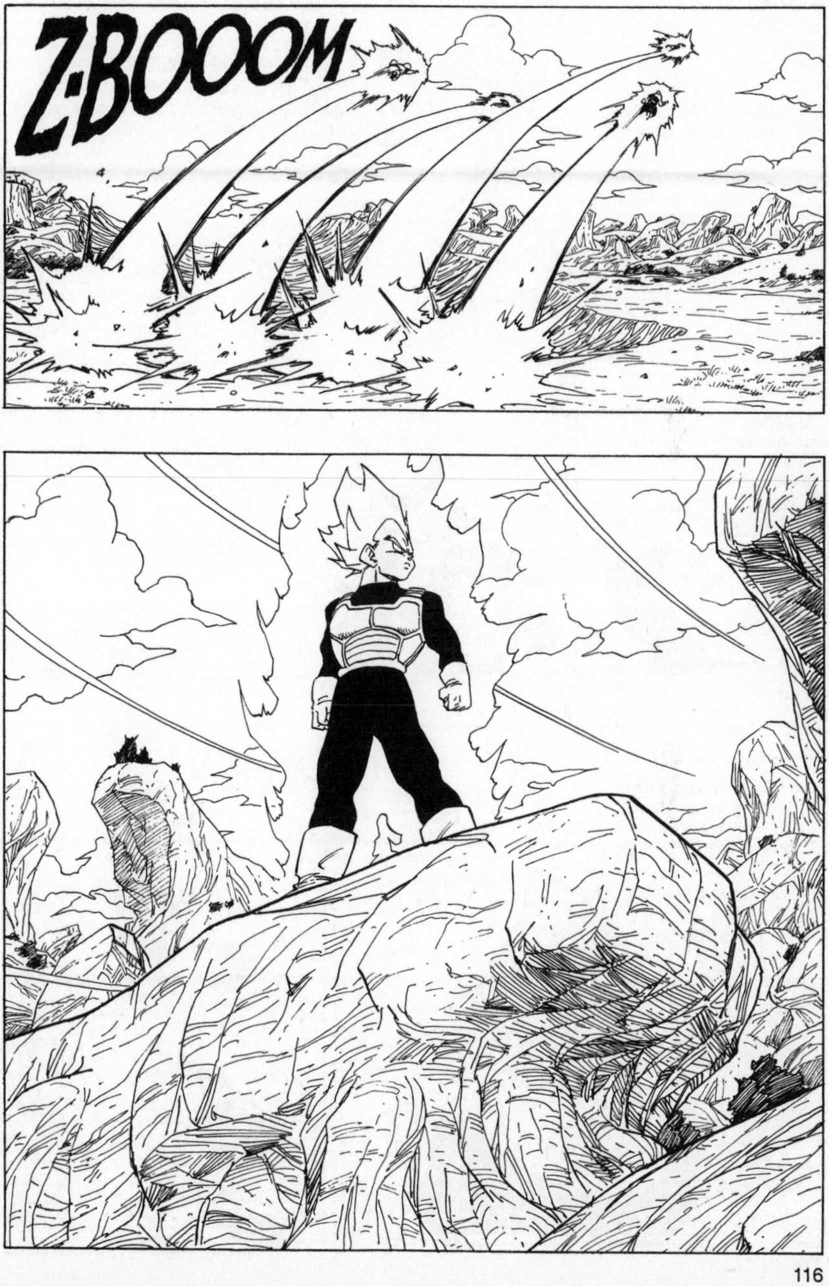
Z-BOOOM

READ THIS WAY

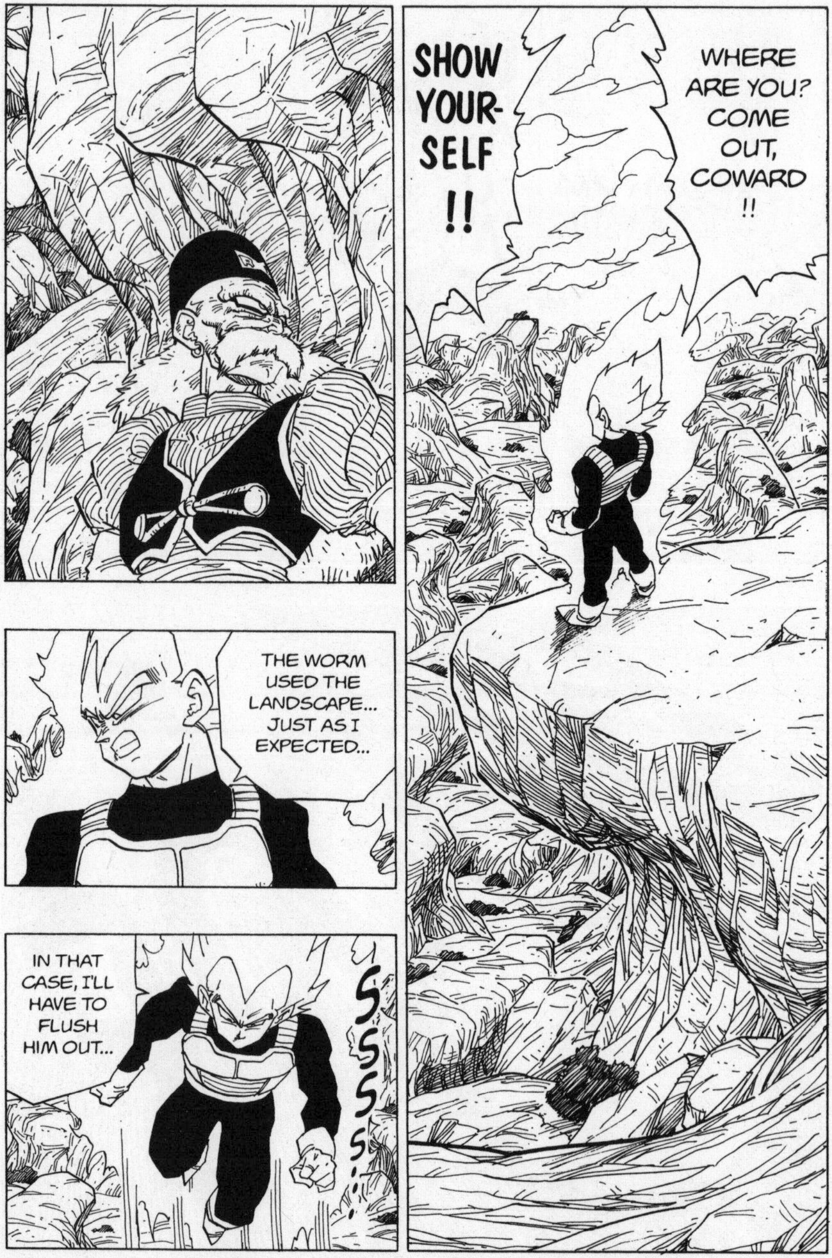

WHERE ARE YOU? COME OUT, COWARD!!
SHOW YOURSELF!!
THE WORM USED THE LANDSCAPE... JUST AS I EXPECTED...
IN THAT CASE, I'LL HAVE TO FLUSH HIM OUT...
SSSS...

READ THIS WAY

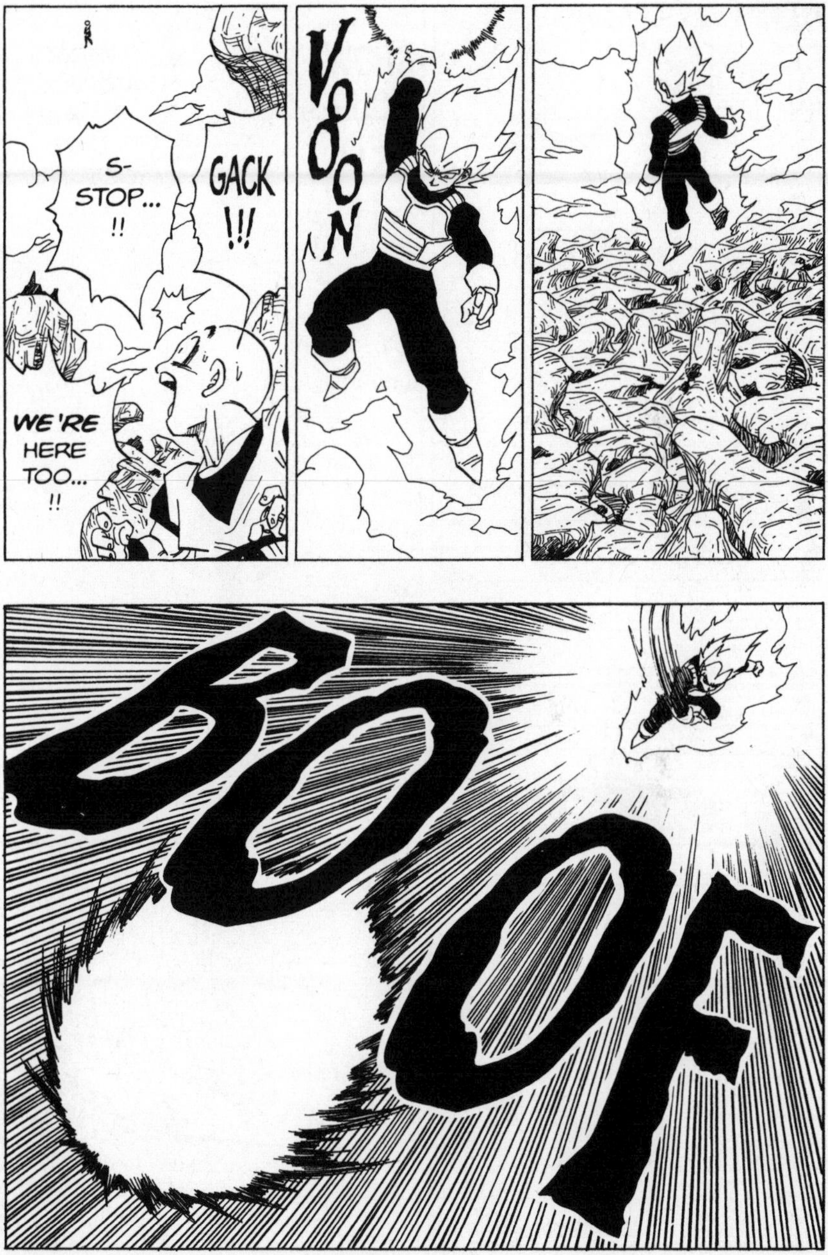
VOOON
GACK!!!
S-STOP...!!
WE'RE HERE TOO...!!
BOOF

READ THIS WAY

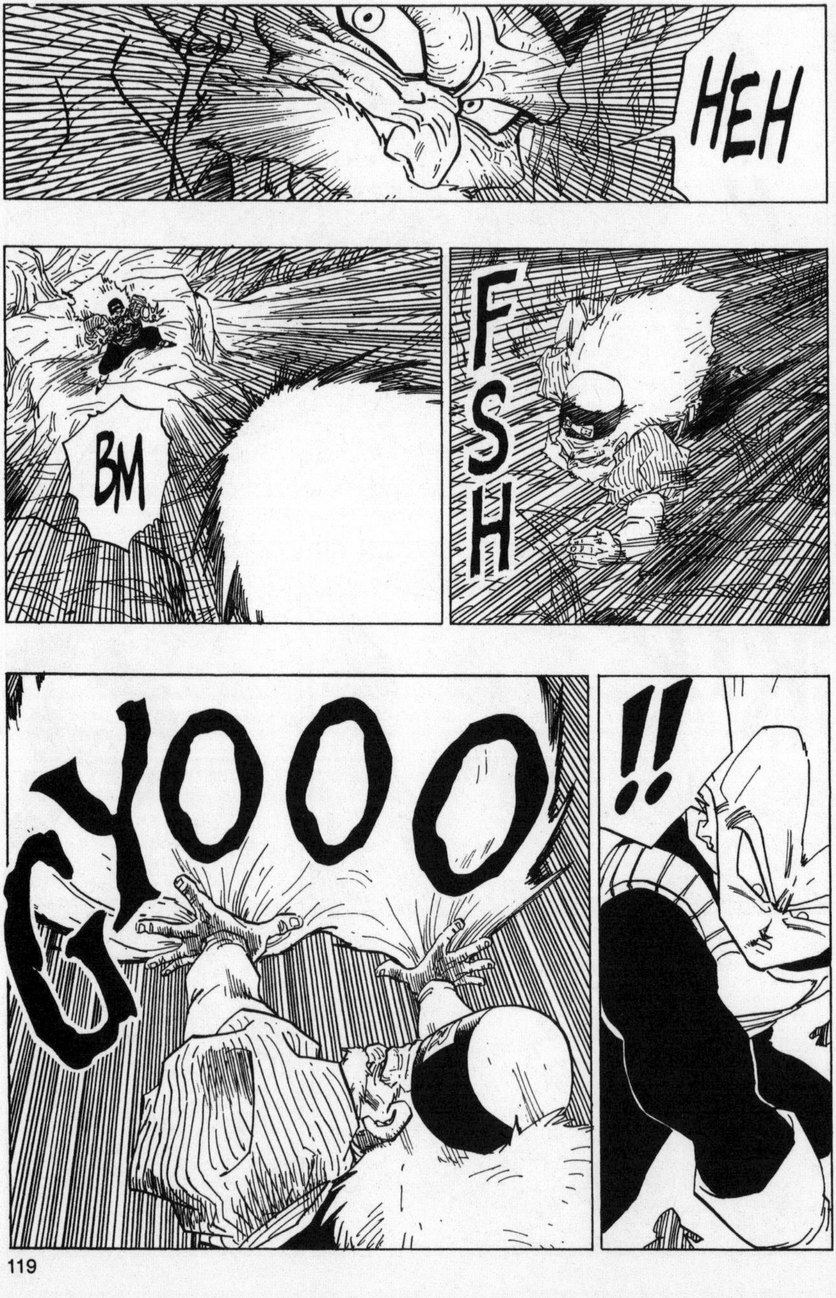
HEH
FSH
BM
!!
GYOOO

READ THIS WAY

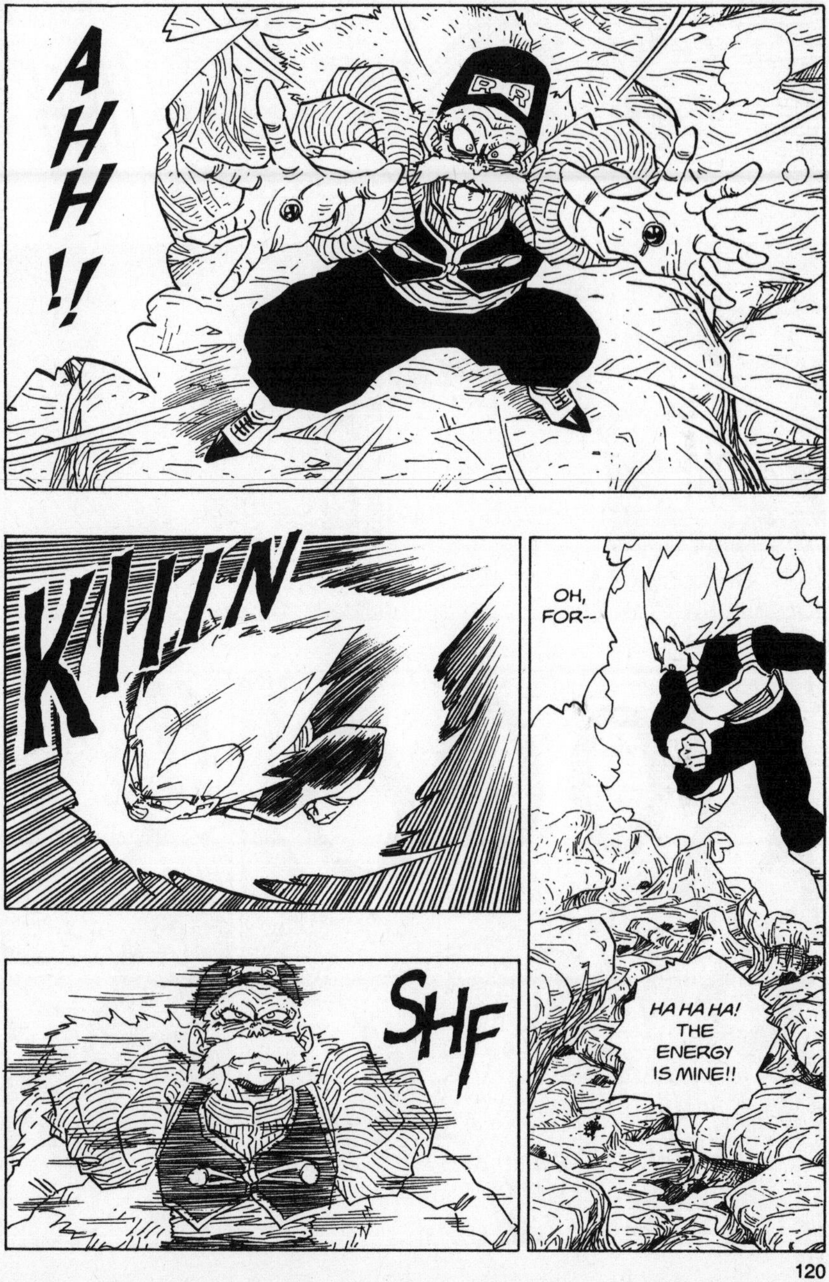
AHH!!
OH, FOR--
HA HA HA! THE ENERGY IS MINE!!
KIIIN
SHF

READ THIS WAY

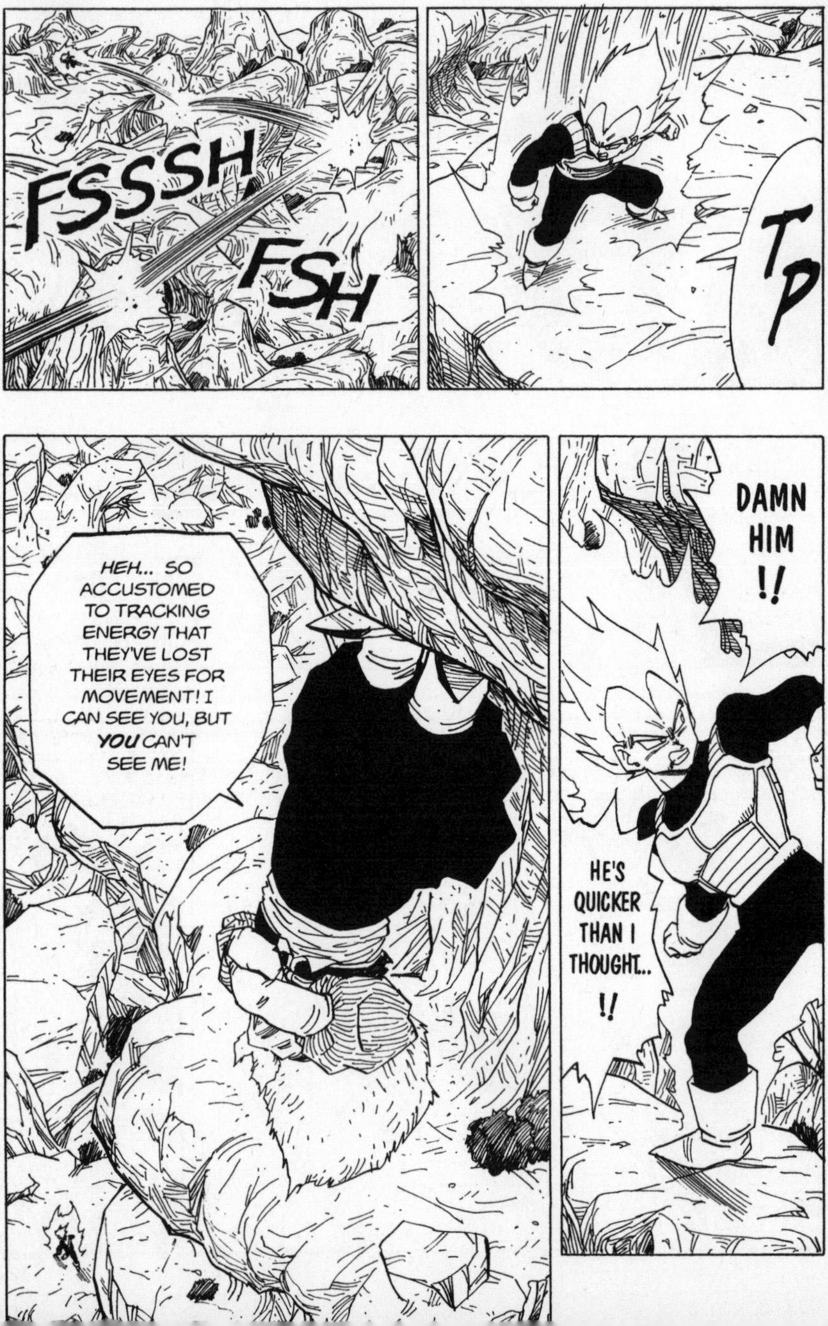
TP
FSSSH
FSH
DAMN HIM!!
HE'S QUICKER THAN I THOUGHT...
!!
HEH... SO ACCUSTOMED TO TRACKING ENERGY THAT THEY'VE LOST THEIR EYES FOR MOVEMENT! I CAN SEE YOU, BUT YOU CAN'T SEE ME!

READ THIS WAY

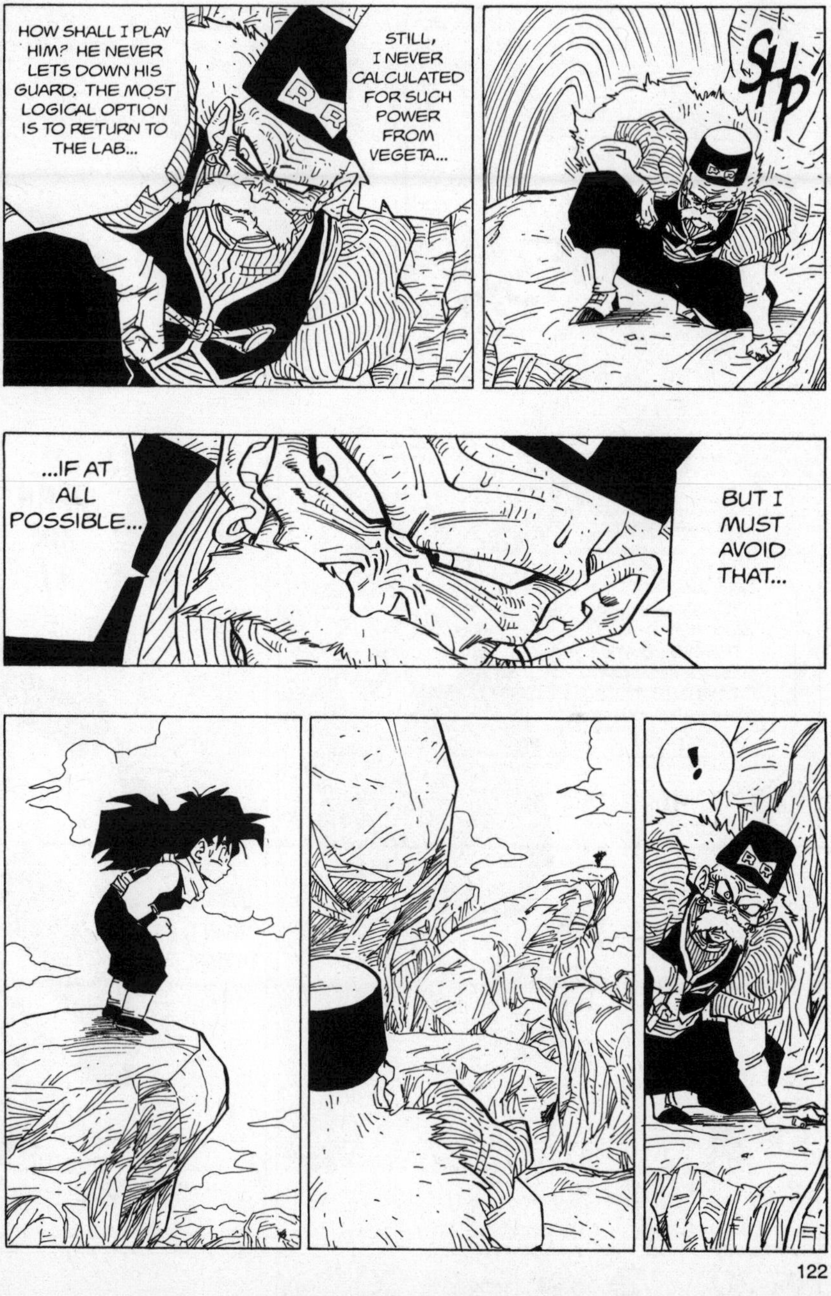
SHP
STILL, I NEVER CALCULATED FOR SUCH POWER FROM VEGETA...
HOW SHALL I PLAY HIM? HE NEVER LETS DOWN HIS GUARD. THE MOST LOGICAL OPTION IS TO RETURN TO THE LAB...
BUT I MUST AVOID THAT...
...IF AT ALL POSSIBLE...
!

READ THIS WAY

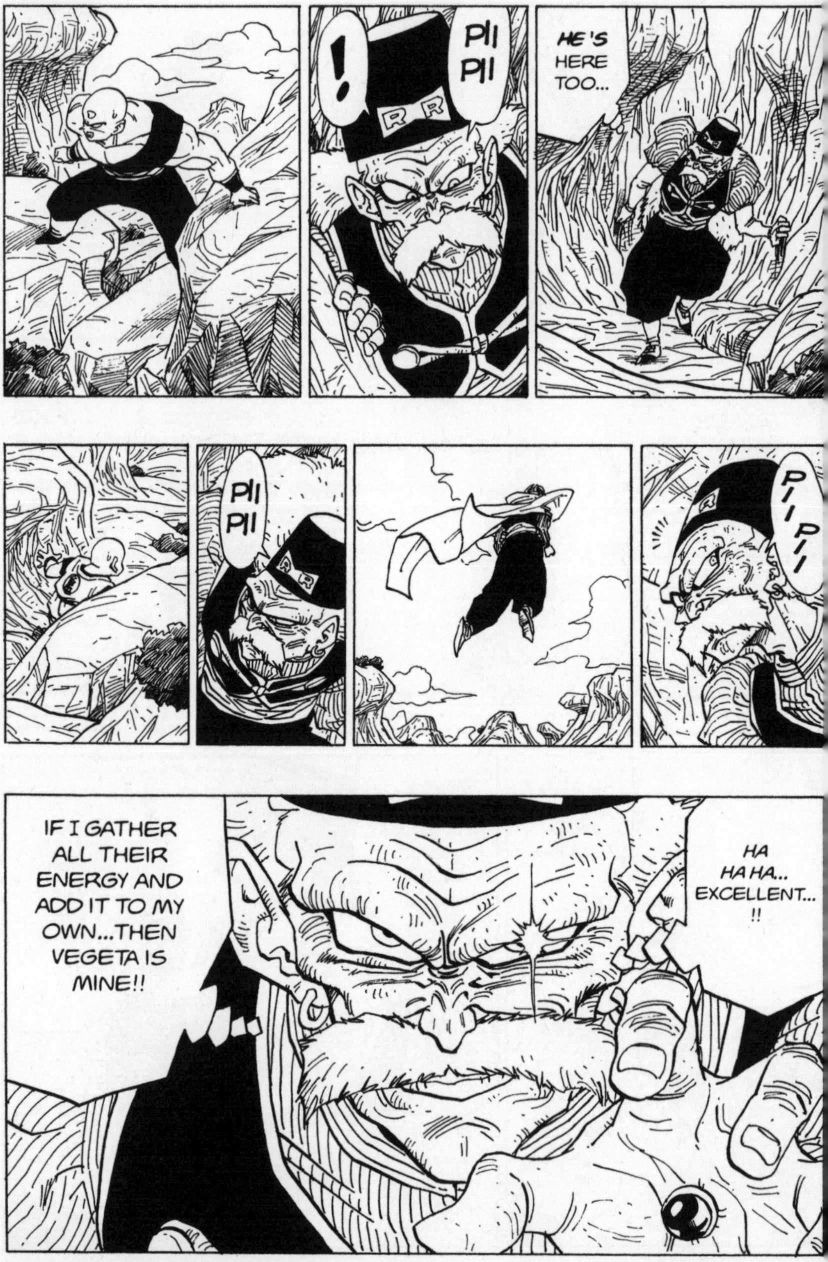
HE'S HERE TOO...
PII PII
!
PII PII
PII PII
HA HA HA... EXCELLENT... !!
IF I GATHER ALL THEIR ENERGY AND ADD IT TO MY OWN...THEN VEGETA IS MINE!!

**NEXT: Hide and Seek**

# DBZ: 152 • Trunks Returns!

READ THIS WAY

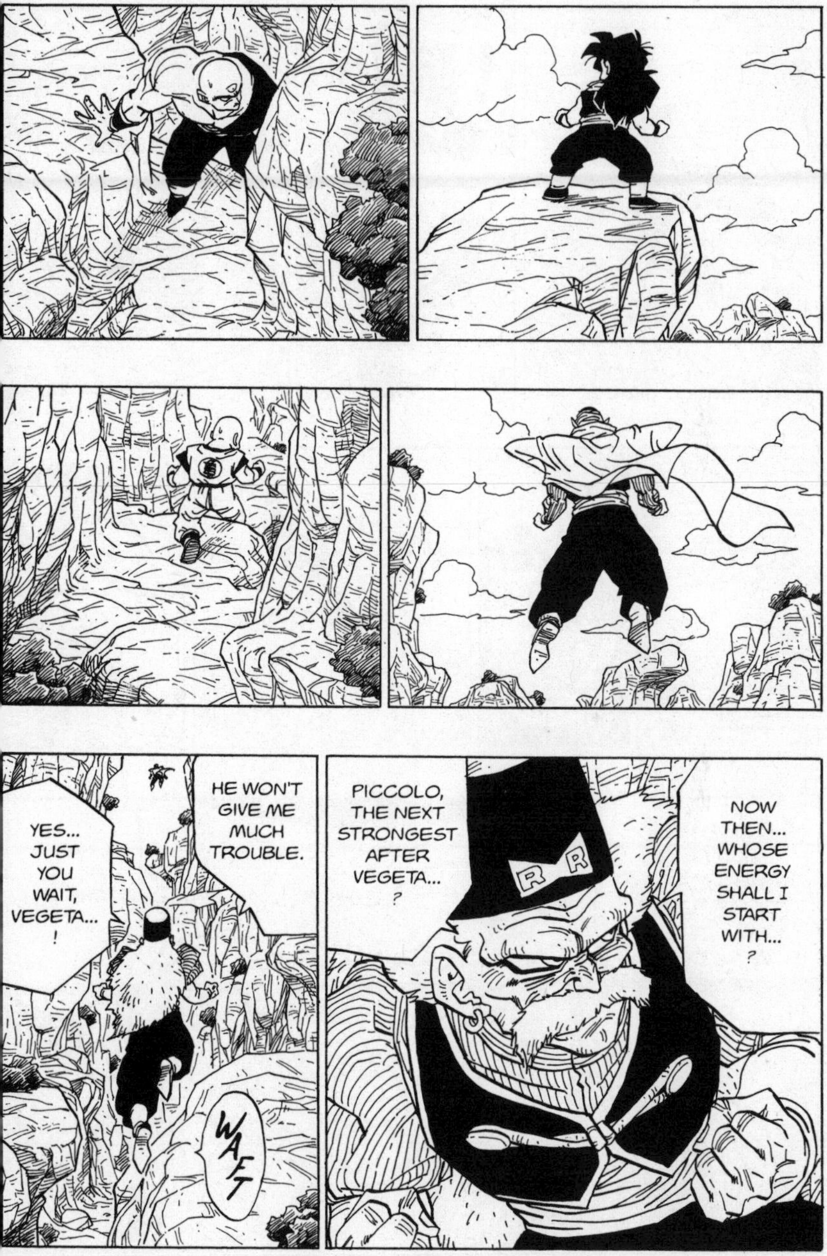
NOW THEN... WHOSE ENERGY SHALL I START WITH... ?
PICCOLO, THE NEXT STRONGEST AFTER VEGETA... ?
HE WON'T GIVE ME MUCH TROUBLE.
YES... JUST YOU WAIT, VEGETA... !
WAFT

READ THIS WAY

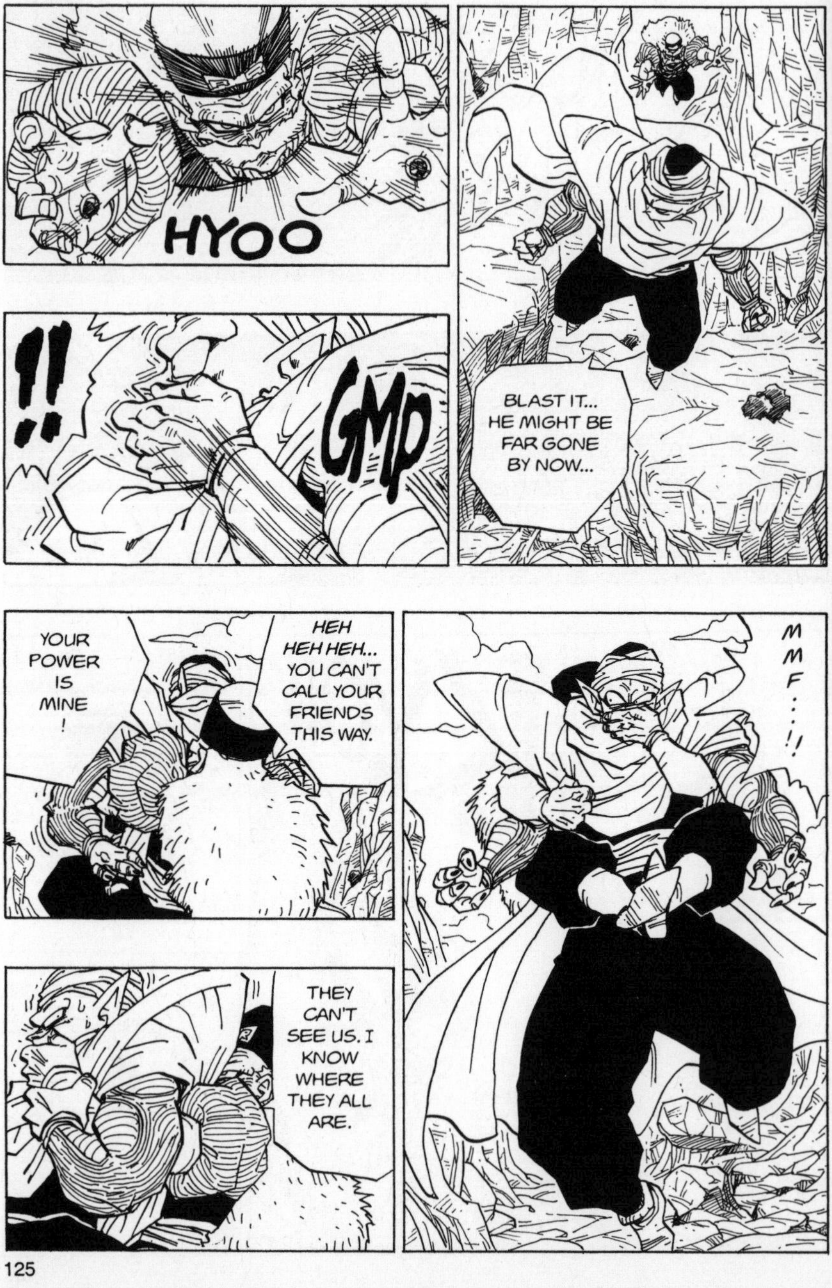

BLAST IT... HE MIGHT BE FAR GONE BY NOW...
HYOO
GMP
!!
MMF...!!
HEH HEH HEH... YOU CAN'T CALL YOUR FRIENDS THIS WAY.
YOUR POWER IS MINE!
THEY CAN'T SEE US. I KNOW WHERE THEY ALL ARE.

READ THIS WAY

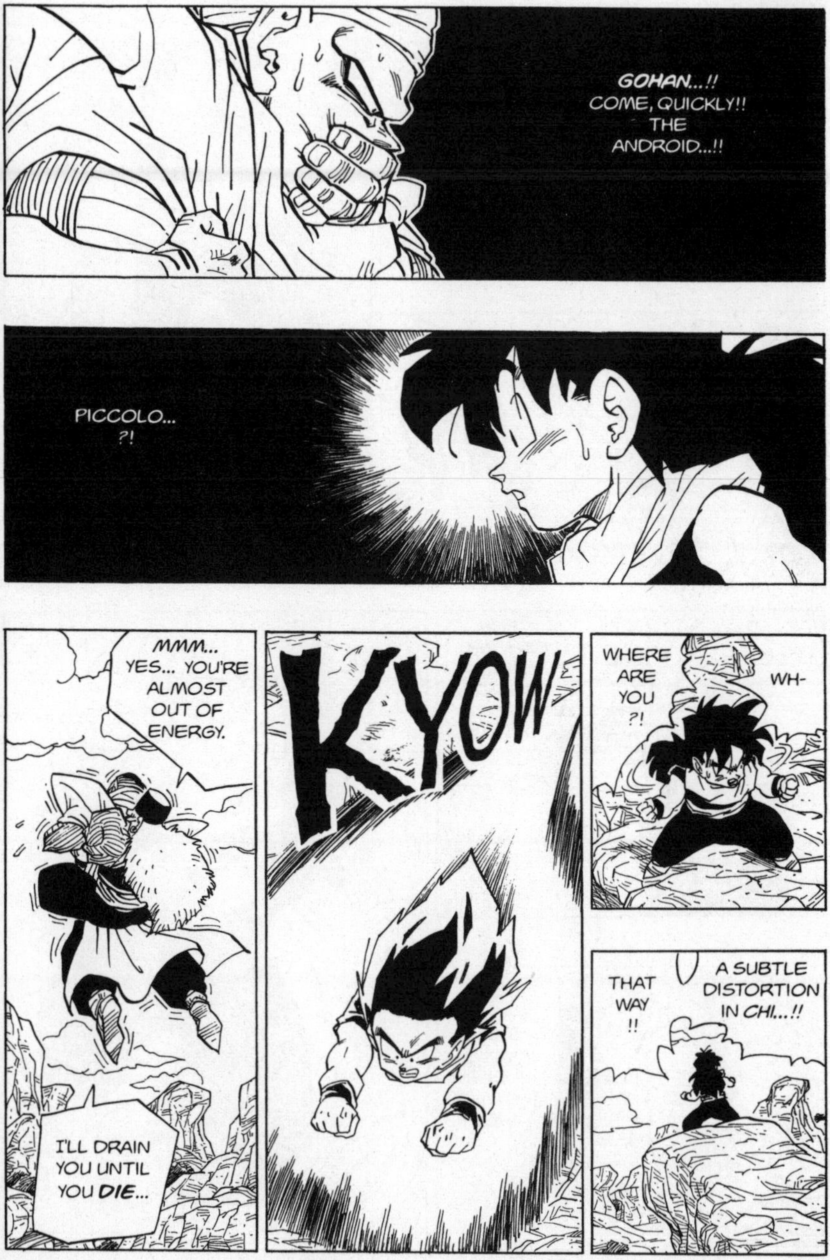

GOHAN...!! COME, QUICKLY!! THE ANDROID...!!
PICCOLO... ?!
WH-
WHERE ARE YOU ?!
A SUBTLE DISTORTION IN CHI...!!
THAT WAY !!
KYOW
MMM... YES... YOU'RE ALMOST OUT OF ENERGY.
I'LL DRAIN YOU UNTIL YOU DIE...

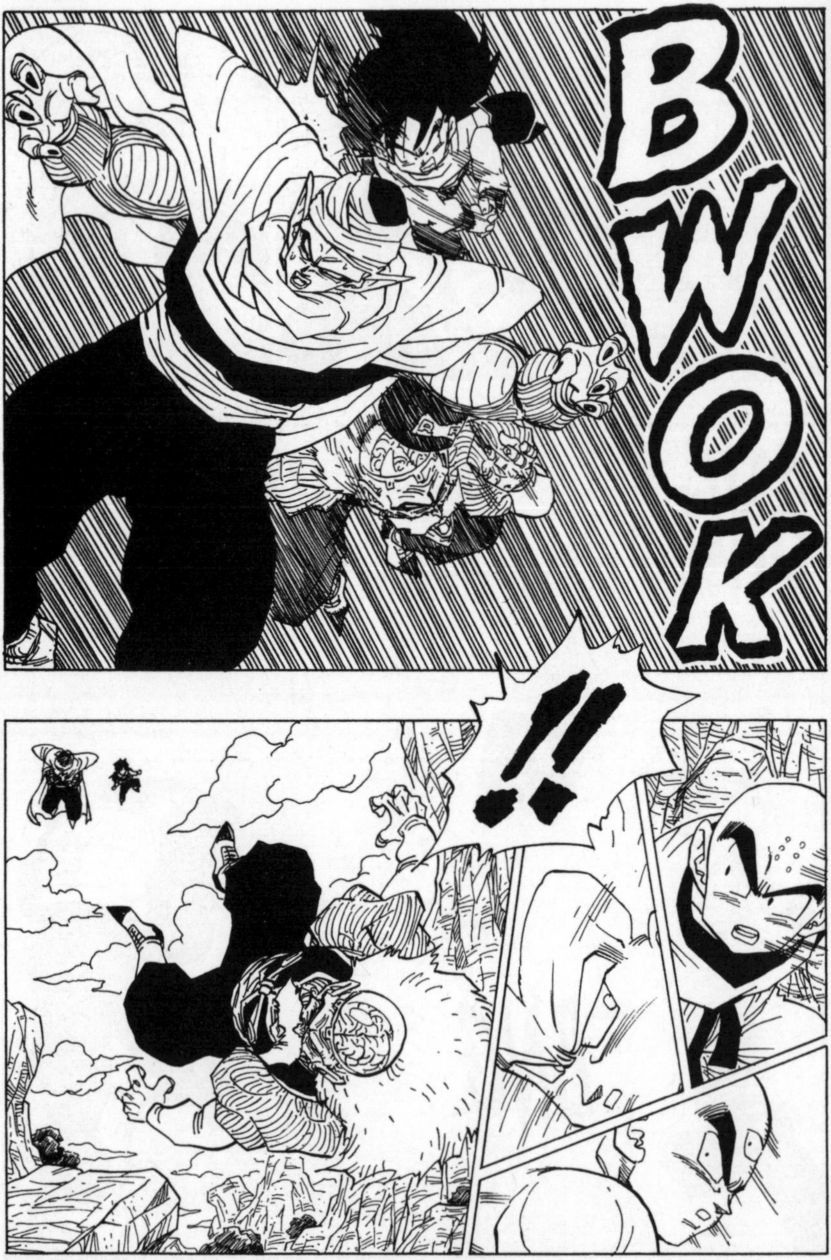
BWOK
!!

READ THIS WAY

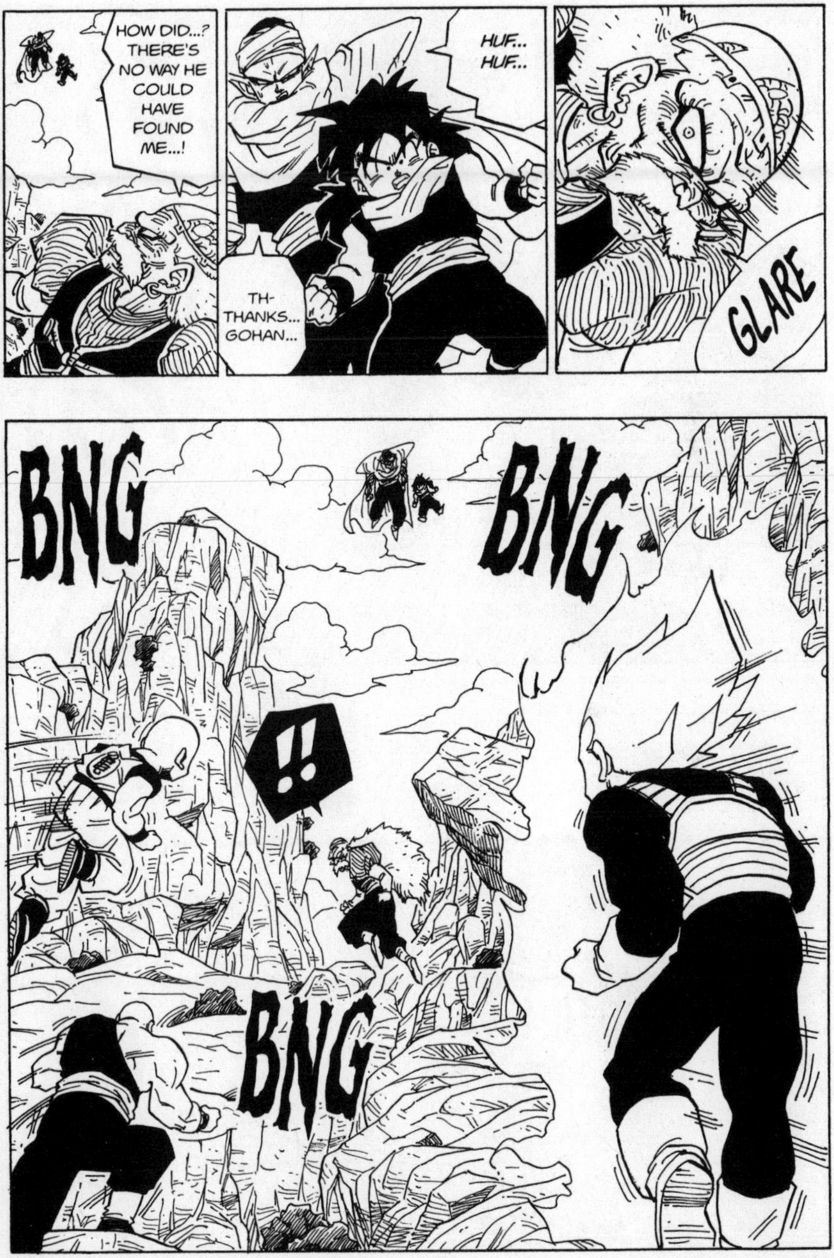
GLARE
HUF... HUF...
TH- THANKS... GOHAN...
HOW DID...? THERE'S NO WAY HE COULD HAVE FOUND ME...!
BNG
BNG
!!
BNG

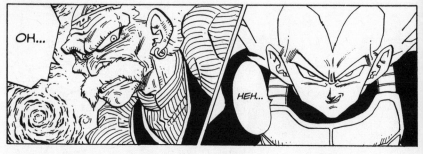

OH...

HEH...

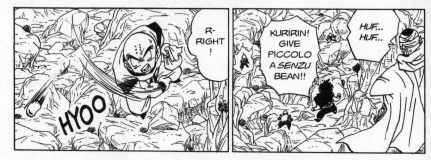

R-RIGHT!

KURIRIN! GIVE PICCOLO A SENZU BEAN!!

HUF... HUF...

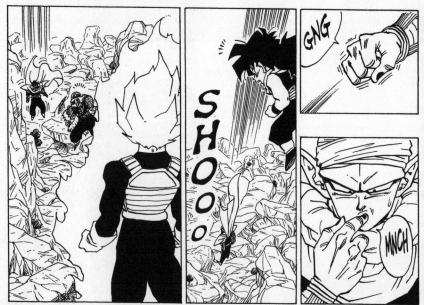

SHOOO

GNG

MNCH

READ THIS WAY

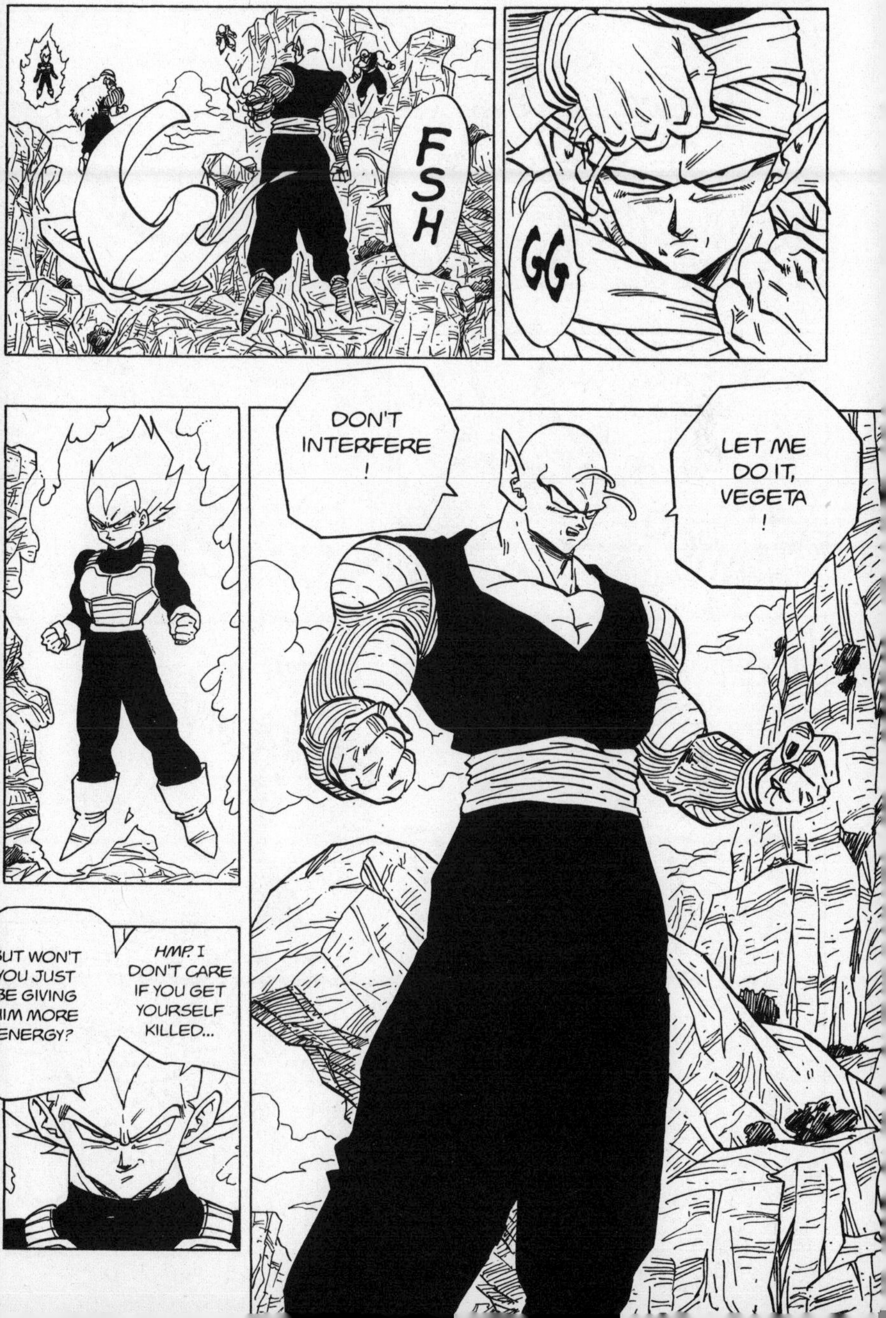
GG
FSH
LET ME DO IT, VEGETA!
DON'T INTERFERE!
HMP. I DON'T CARE IF YOU GET YOURSELF KILLED...
BUT WON'T YOU JUST BE GIVING HIM MORE ENERGY?

READ THIS WAY

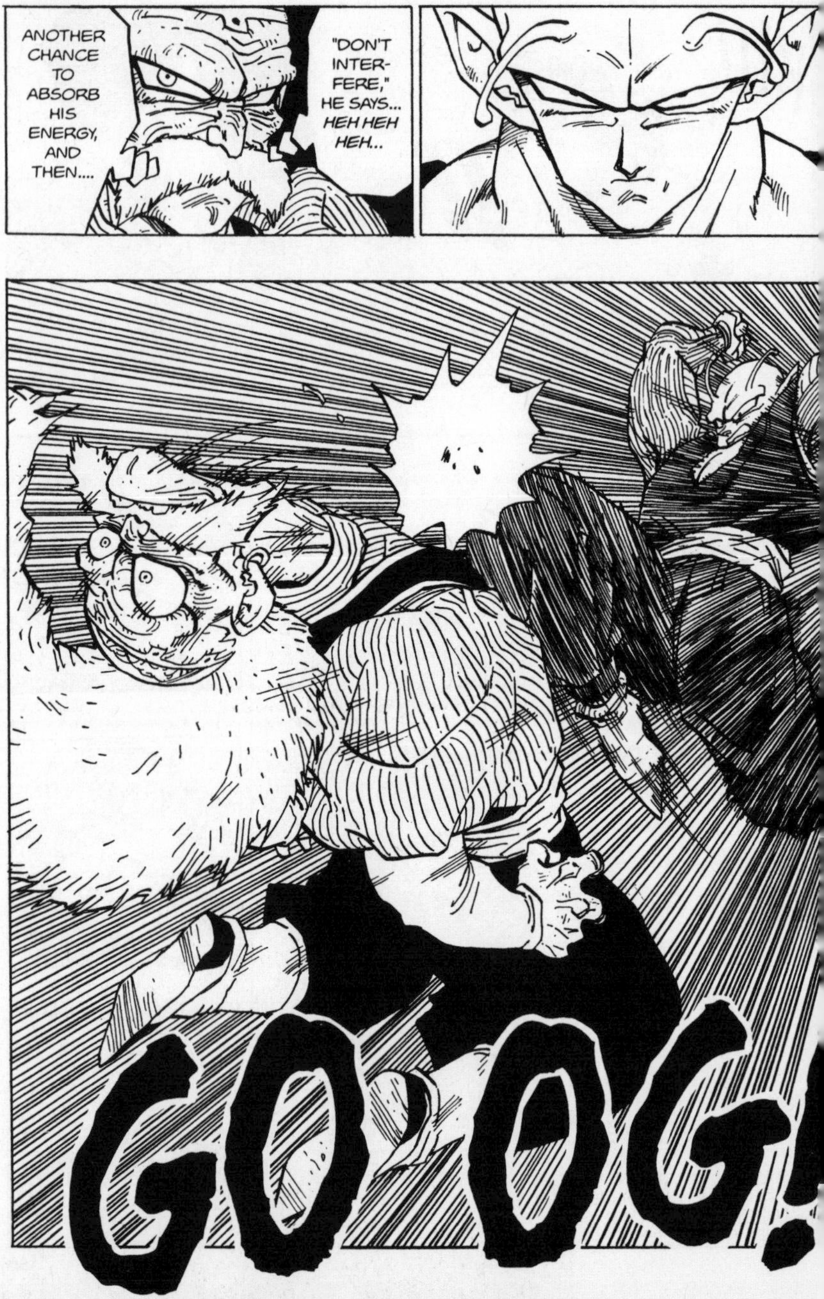
"DON'T INTERFERE," HE SAYS... HEH HEH HEH...
ANOTHER CHANCE TO ABSORB HIS ENERGY, AND THEN....
GOOG!

READ THIS WAY

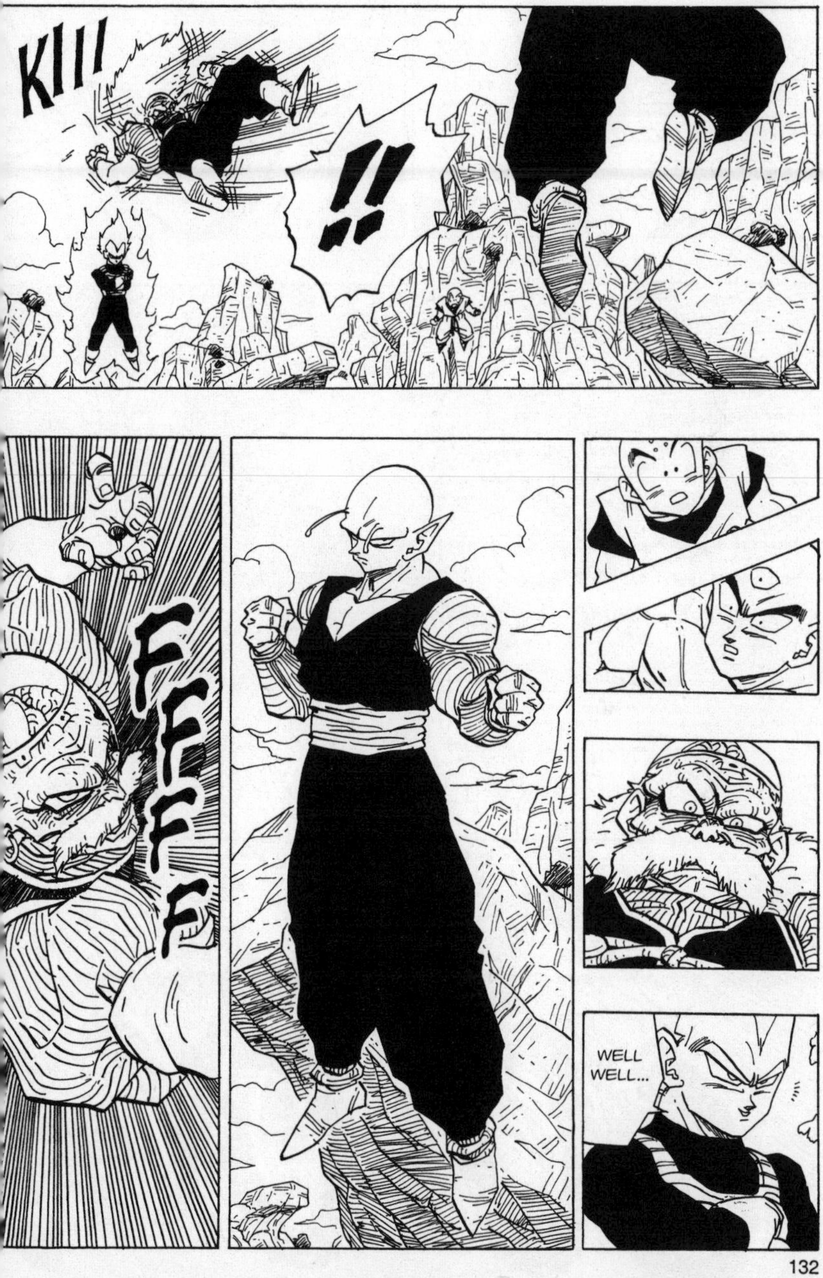
!!
KIII
WELL WELL...
FFFF

READ THIS WAY

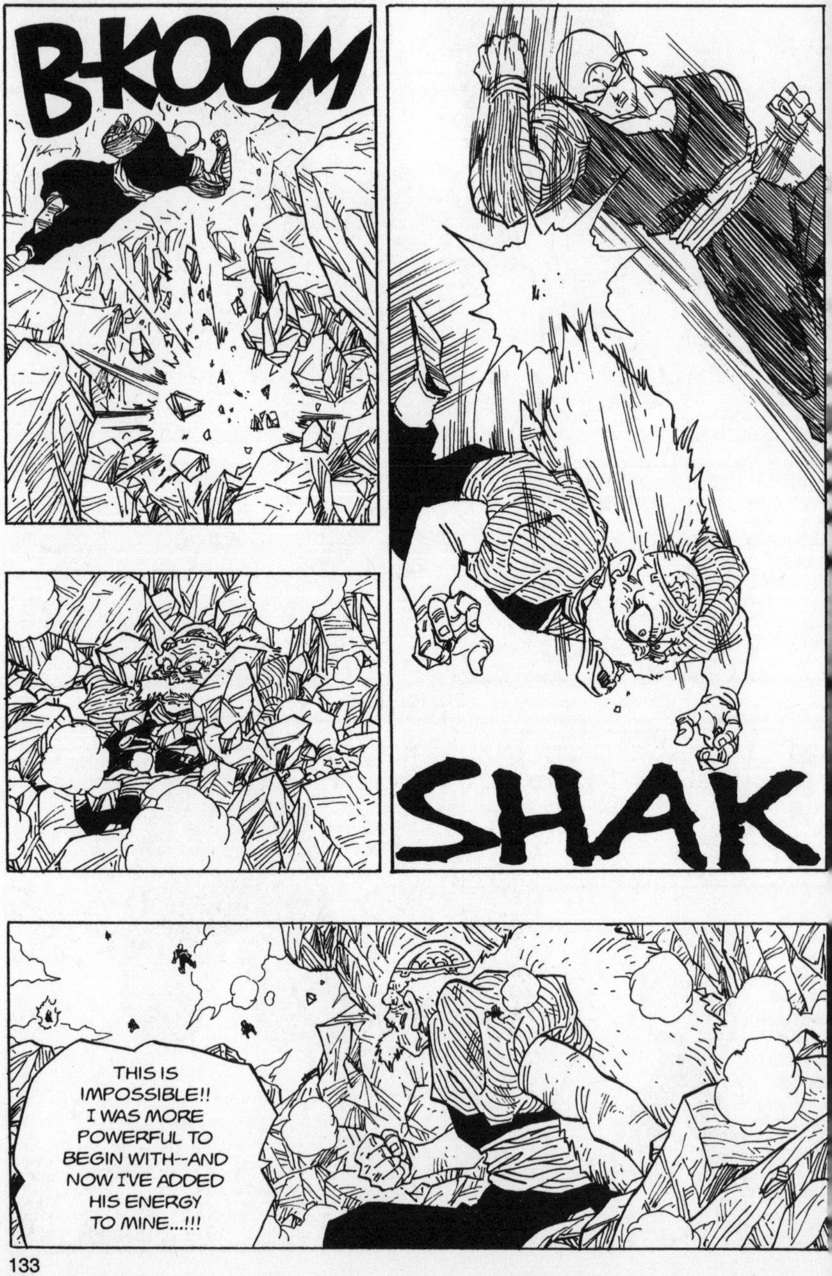
SHAK
B-KOOM
THIS IS IMPOSSIBLE!! I WAS MORE POWERFUL TO BEGIN WITH--AND NOW I'VE ADDED HIS ENERGY TO MINE...!!!

READ THIS WAY

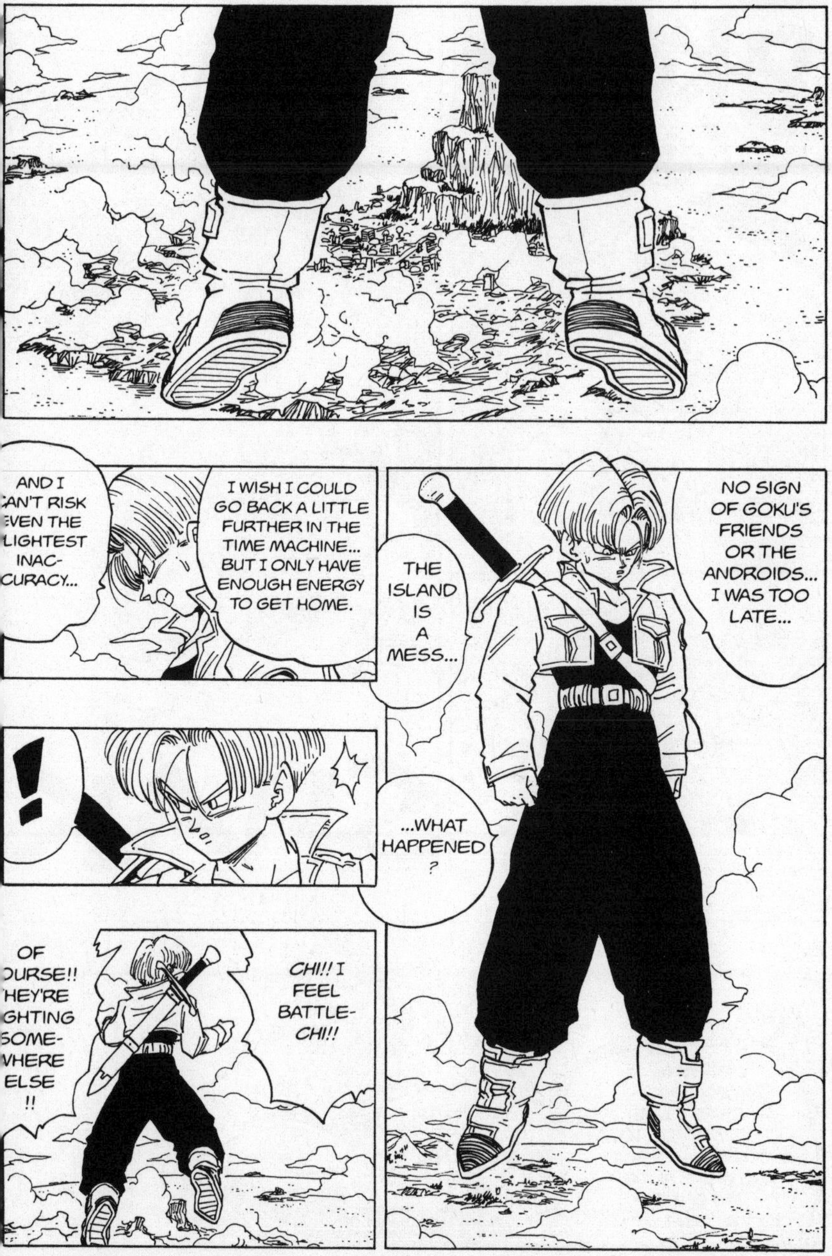

NO SIGN OF GOKU'S FRIENDS OR THE ANDROIDS... I WAS TOO LATE...
THE ISLAND IS A MESS...
...WHAT HAPPENED ?
I WISH I COULD GO BACK A LITTLE FURTHER IN THE TIME MACHINE... BUT I ONLY HAVE ENOUGH ENERGY TO GET HOME.
AND I CAN'T RISK EVEN THE LIGHTEST INAC-CURACY...
!
CHI!! I FEEL BATTLE-CHI!!
OF COURSE!! THEY'RE FIGHTING SOME-WHERE ELSE !!

READ THIS WAY

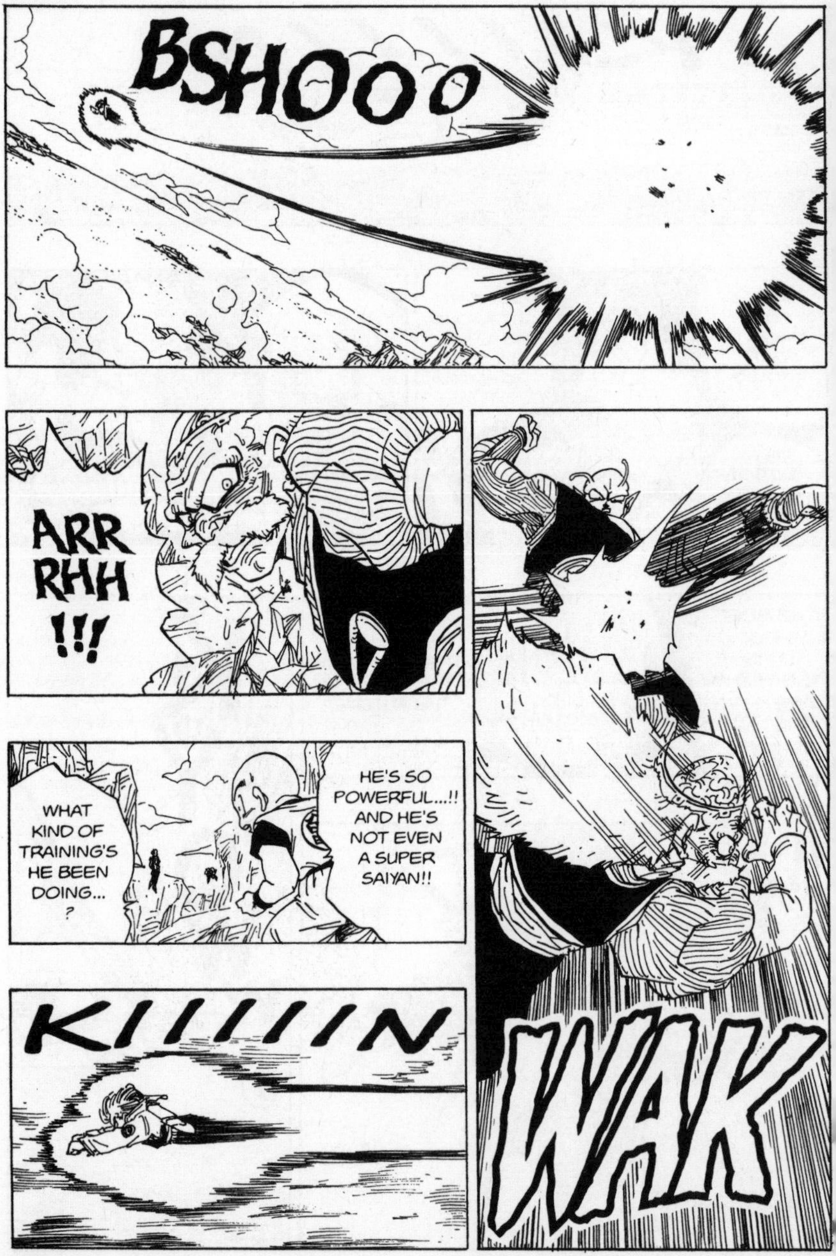
BSHOOO
WAK
ARR RHH !!!
HE'S SO POWERFUL...!! AND HE'S NOT EVEN A SUPER SAIYAN!!
WHAT KIND OF TRAINING'S HE BEEN DOING... ?
KIIIIN

READ THIS WAY

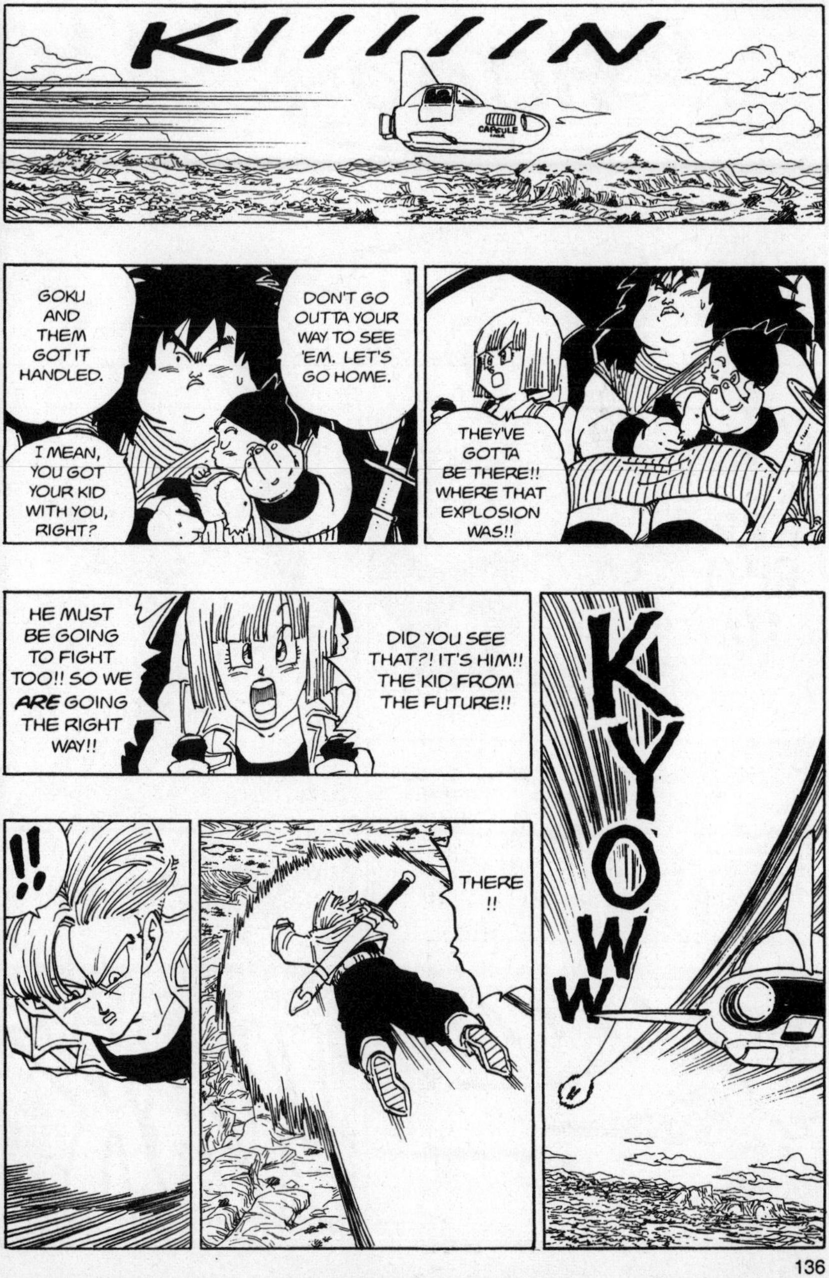
KIIIIIN
THEY'VE GOTTA BE THERE!! WHERE THAT EXPLOSION WAS!!
DON'T GO OUTTA YOUR WAY TO SEE 'EM. LET'S GO HOME.
GOKU AND THEM GOT IT HANDLED.
I MEAN, YOU GOT YOUR KID WITH YOU, RIGHT?
KYOWW
DID YOU SEE THAT?! IT'S HIM!! THE KID FROM THE FUTURE!!
HE MUST BE GOING TO FIGHT TOO!! SO WE *ARE* GOING THE RIGHT WAY!!
THERE!!
!!

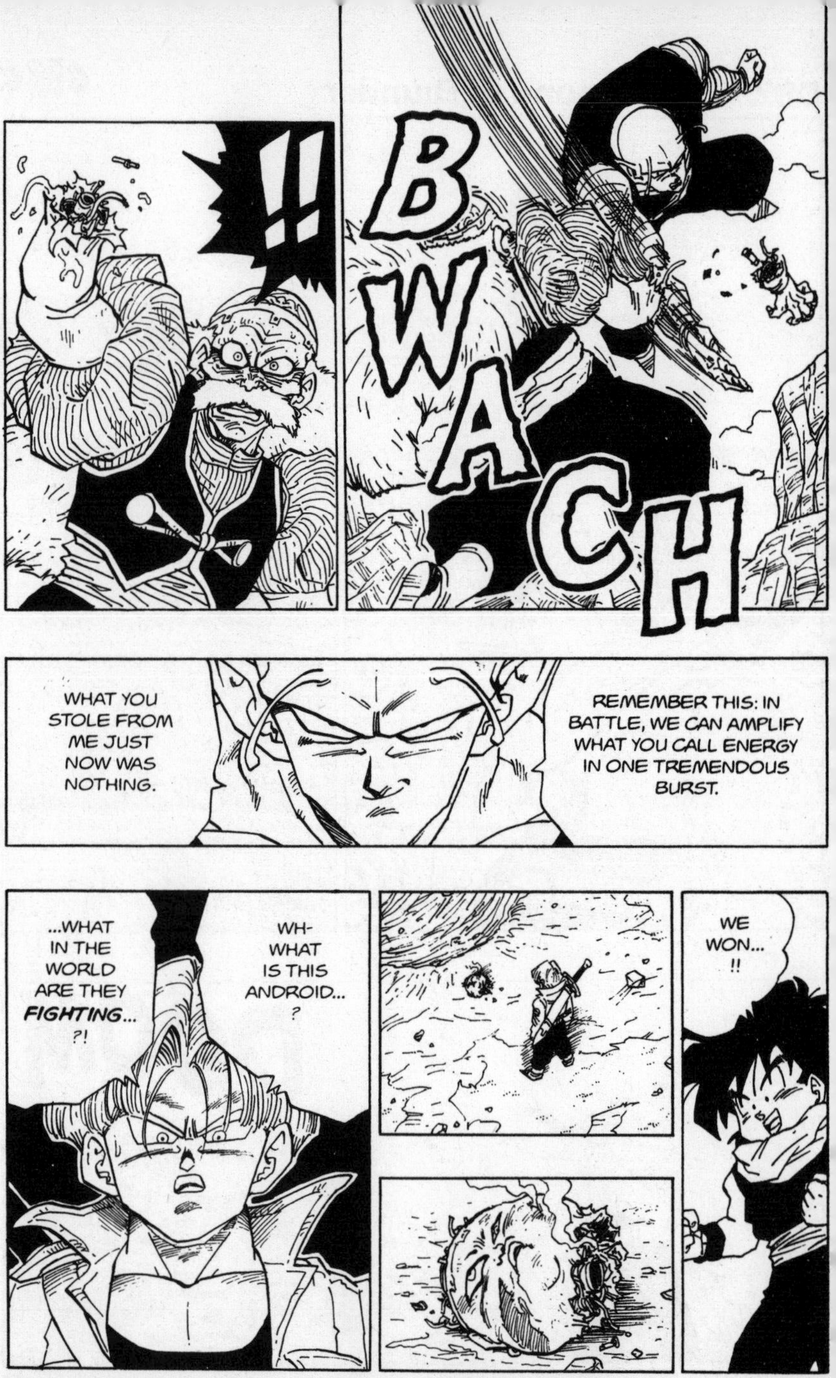
BWACH
!!
REMEMBER THIS: IN BATTLE, WE CAN AMPLIFY WHAT YOU CALL ENERGY IN ONE TREMENDOUS BURST.
WHAT YOU STOLE FROM ME JUST NOW WAS NOTHING.
WE WON... !!
WH- WHAT IS THIS ANDROID... ?
...WHAT IN THE WORLD ARE THEY *FIGHTING*... ?!

**NEXT: The Future Gone Wrong???**

# DBZ: 153 • A Sound of Thunder

READ THIS WAY

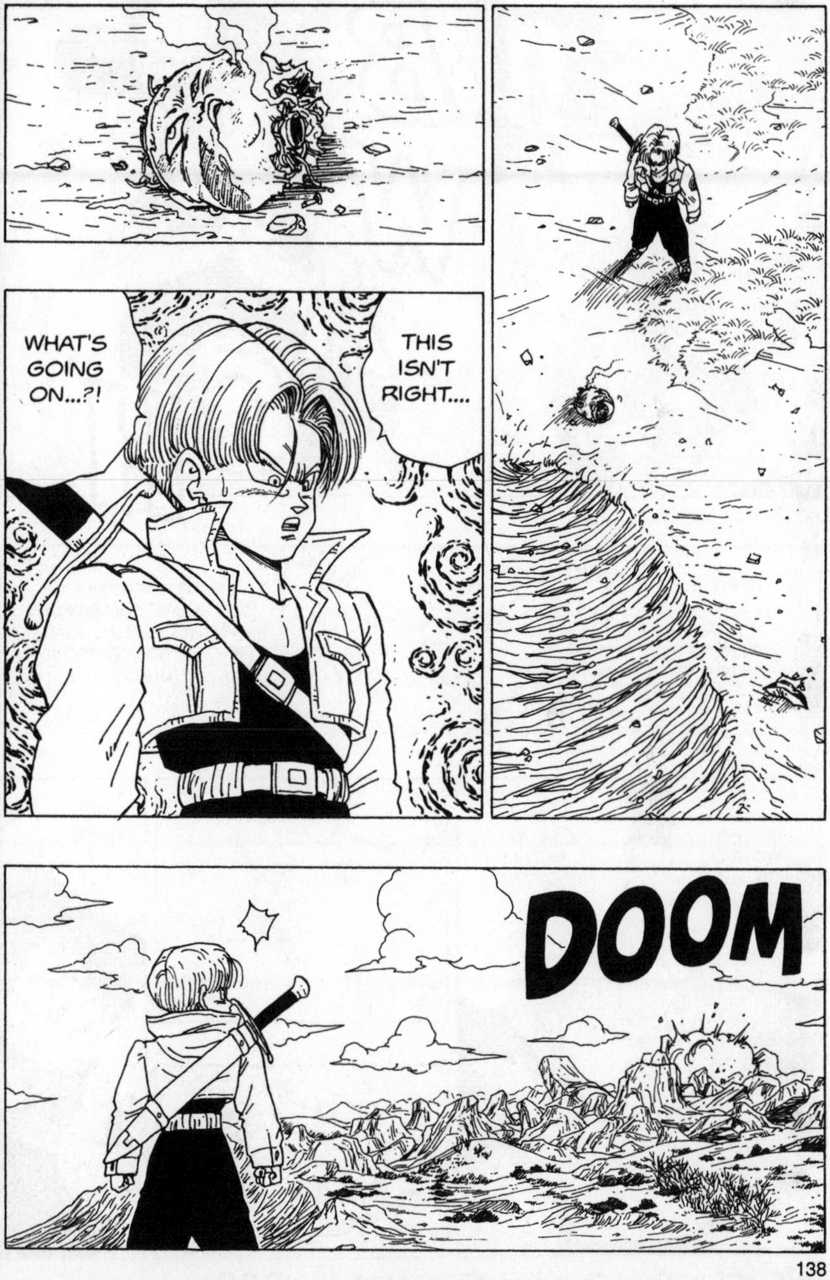
THIS ISN'T RIGHT....
WHAT'S GOING ON...?!
DOOM

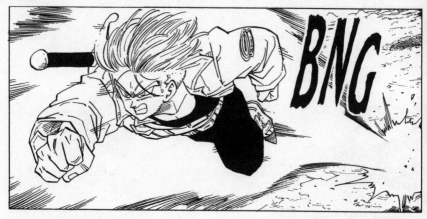

BNG

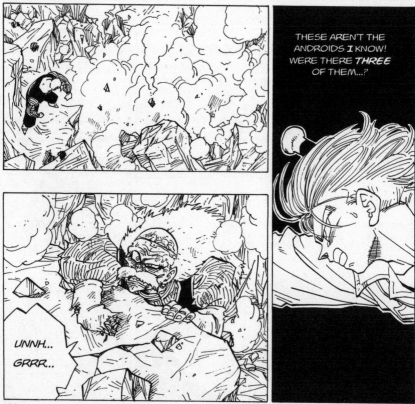

THESE AREN'T THE
ANDROIDS *I* KNOW!
WERE THERE *THREE*
OF THEM...?

UNNH...
GRRR...

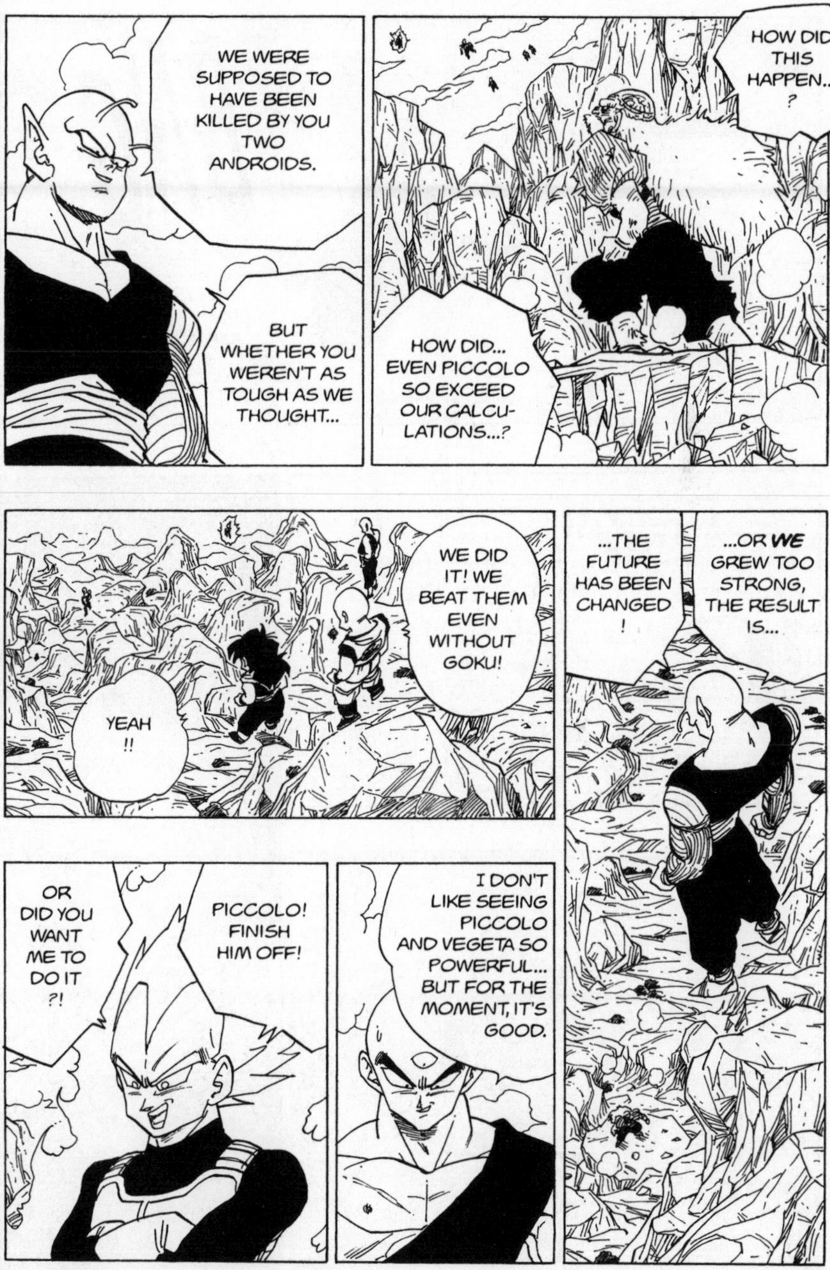
HOW DID THIS HAPPEN... ?
HOW DID... EVEN PICCOLO SO EXCEED OUR CALCULATIONS...?
WE WERE SUPPOSED TO HAVE BEEN KILLED BY YOU TWO ANDROIDS.
BUT WHETHER YOU WEREN'T AS TOUGH AS WE THOUGHT...
...OR *WE* GREW TOO STRONG, THE RESULT IS...
...THE FUTURE HAS BEEN CHANGED !
WE DID IT! WE BEAT THEM EVEN WITHOUT GOKU!
YEAH !!
I DON'T LIKE SEEING PICCOLO AND VEGETA SO POWERFUL... BUT FOR THE MOMENT, IT'S GOOD.
PICCOLO! FINISH HIM OFF!
OR DID YOU WANT ME TO DO IT ?!

READ THIS WAY

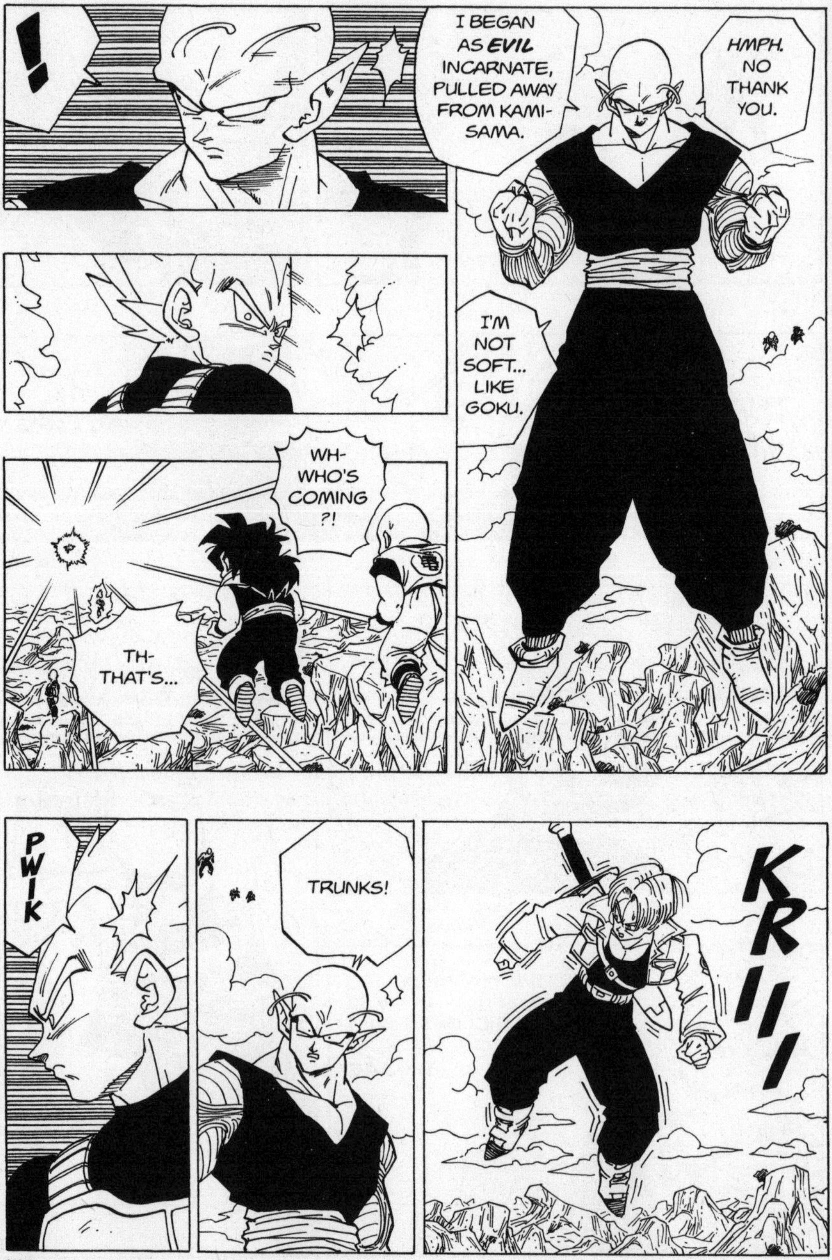
HMPH. NO THANK YOU.
I BEGAN AS EVIL INCARNATE, PULLED AWAY FROM KAMI-SAMA.
I'M NOT SOFT... LIKE GOKU.
!
WH- WHO'S COMING ?!
TH- THAT'S...
KRIII
TRUNKS!
PWIK

READ THIS WAY

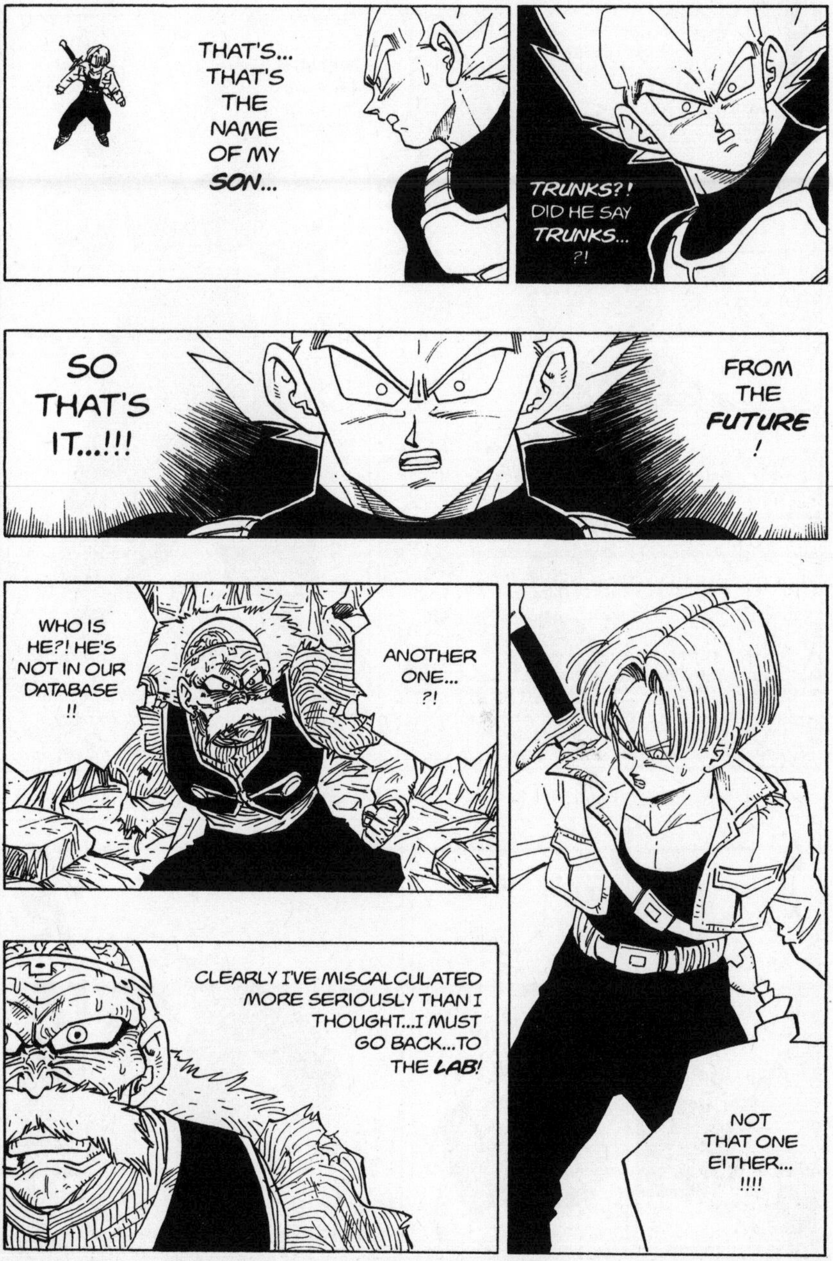

TRUNKS?! DID HE SAY TRUNKS...?!
THAT'S... THAT'S THE NAME OF MY SON...
FROM THE FUTURE!
SO THAT'S IT...!!!
NOT THAT ONE EITHER...!!!!
ANOTHER ONE...?!
WHO IS HE?! HE'S NOT IN OUR DATABASE!!
CLEARLY I'VE MISCALCULATED MORE SERIOUSLY THAN I THOUGHT...I MUST GO BACK...TO THE LAB!

READ THIS WAY

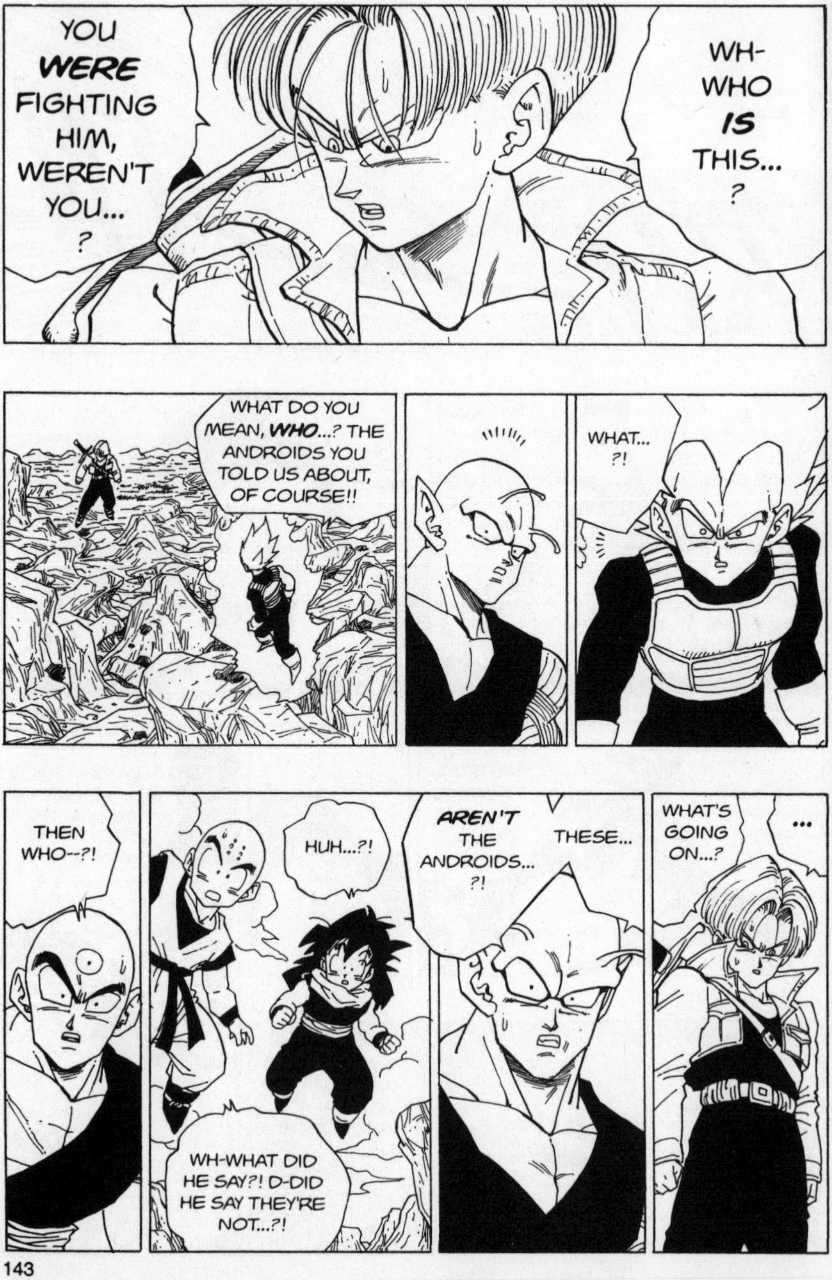
WH-WHO IS THIS...?
YOU WERE FIGHTING HIM, WEREN'T YOU...?
WHAT...?!
WHAT DO YOU MEAN, WHO...? THE ANDROIDS YOU TOLD US ABOUT, OF COURSE!!
...
WHAT'S GOING ON...?
THESE...
AREN'T THE ANDROIDS...?!
HUH...?!
WH-WHAT DID HE SAY?! D-DID HE SAY THEY'RE NOT...?!
THEN WHO--?!

READ THIS WAY

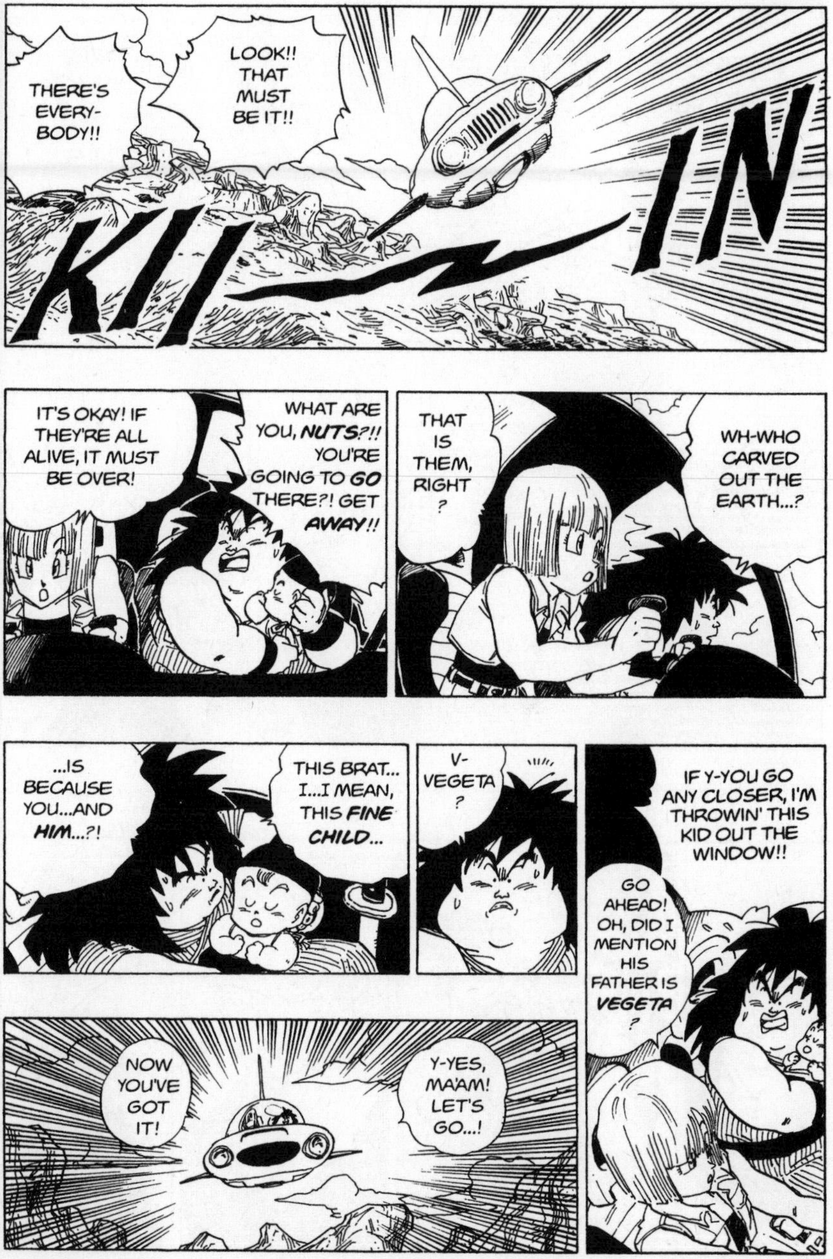

LOOK!! THAT MUST BE IT!!
THERE'S EVERY-BODY!!
KII—IN
WH-WHO CARVED OUT THE EARTH...?
THAT IS THEM, RIGHT?
WHAT ARE YOU, NUTS?!! YOU'RE GOING TO GO THERE?! GET AWAY!!
IT'S OKAY! IF THEY'RE ALL ALIVE, IT MUST BE OVER!
IF Y-YOU GO ANY CLOSER, I'M THROWIN' THIS KID OUT THE WINDOW!!
GO AHEAD! OH, DID I MENTION HIS FATHER IS VEGETA?
V-VEGETA?
THIS BRAT... I...I MEAN, THIS FINE CHILD...
...IS BECAUSE YOU...AND HIM...?!
Y-YES, MA'AM! LET'S GO...!
NOW YOU'VE GOT IT!

READ THIS WAY

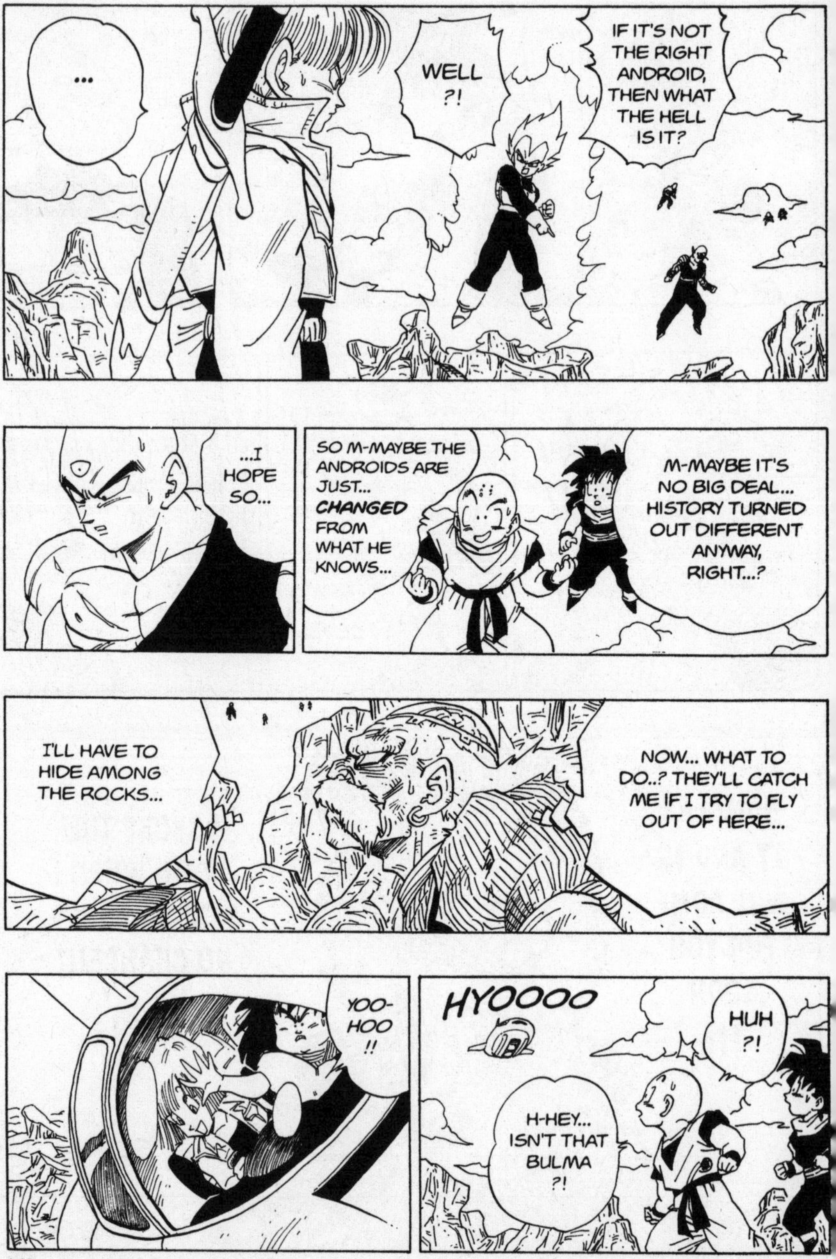

IF IT'S NOT THE RIGHT ANDROID, THEN WHAT THE HELL IS IT?
WELL ?!
...
M-MAYBE IT'S NO BIG DEAL... HISTORY TURNED OUT DIFFERENT ANYWAY, RIGHT...?
SO M-MAYBE THE ANDROIDS ARE JUST... **CHANGED** FROM WHAT HE KNOWS...
...I HOPE SO...
NOW... WHAT TO DO..? THEY'LL CATCH ME IF I TRY TO FLY OUT OF HERE...
I'LL HAVE TO HIDE AMONG THE ROCKS...
HYOOOO
HUH ?!
H-HEY... ISN'T THAT BULMA ?!
YOO-HOO !!

READ THIS WAY

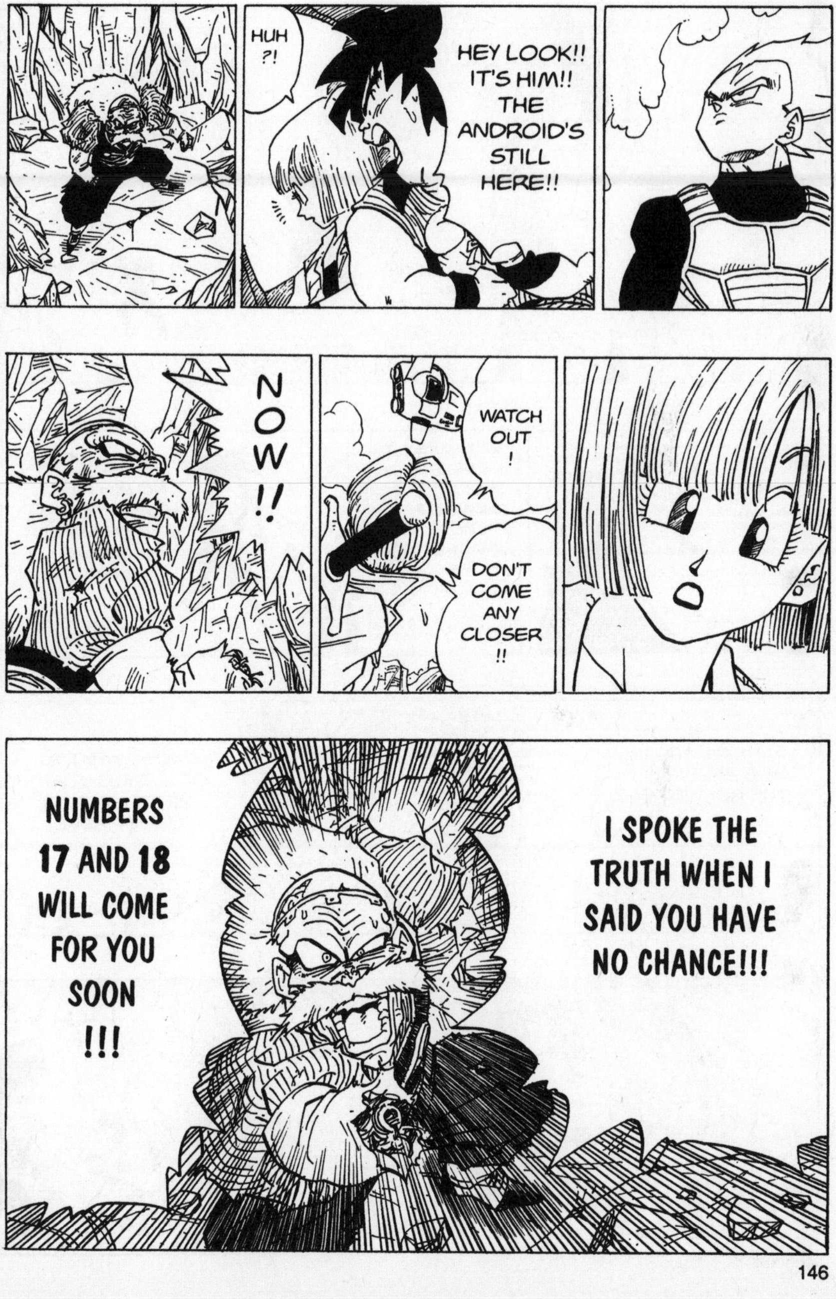

HEY LOOK!! IT'S HIM!! THE ANDROID'S STILL HERE!!
HUH ?!
WATCH OUT !
DON'T COME ANY CLOSER !!
NOW!!
I SPOKE THE TRUTH WHEN I SAID YOU HAVE NO CHANCE!!!
NUMBERS 17 AND 18 WILL COME FOR YOU SOON !!!

READ THIS WAY

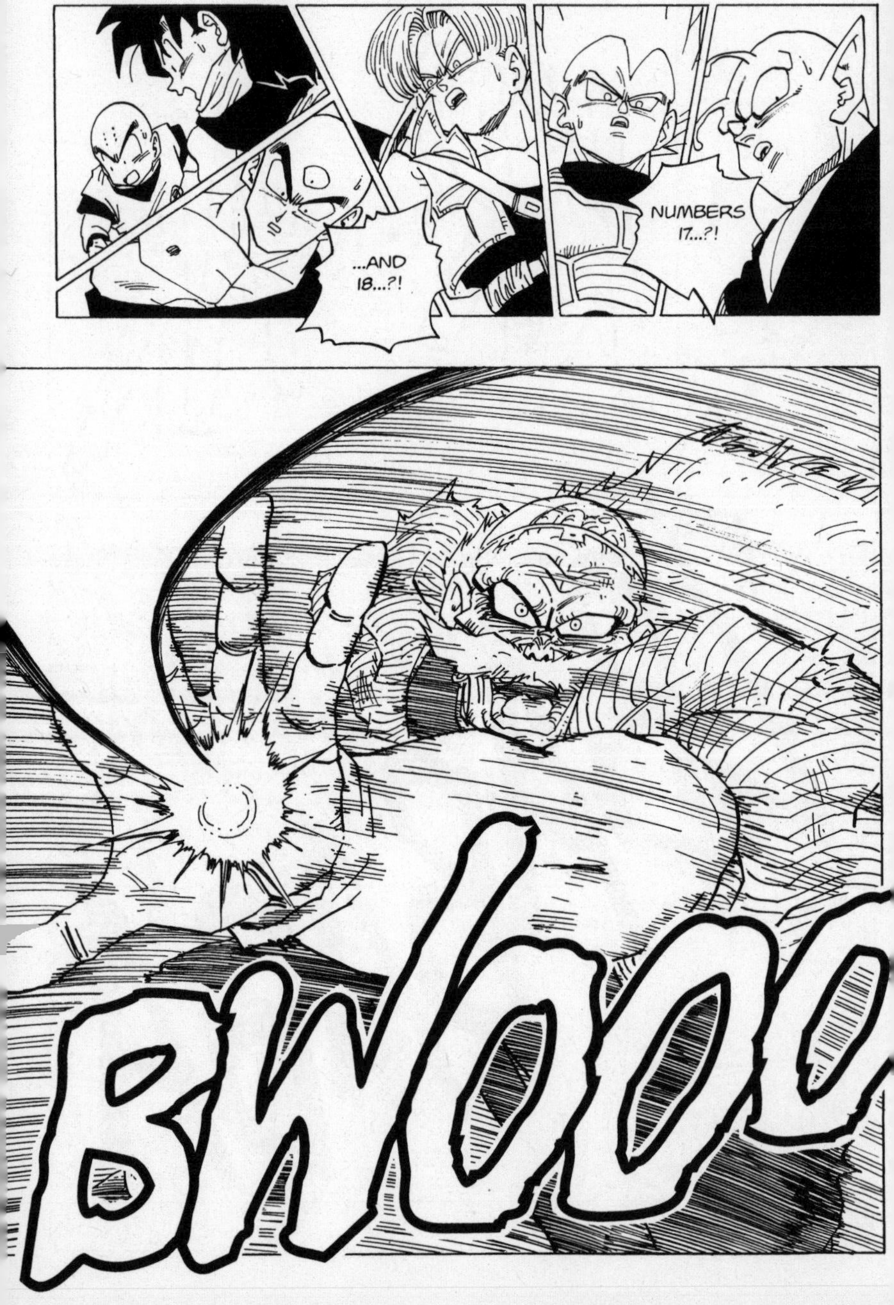
NUMBERS 17...?!
...AND 18...?!
BWOOO

READ THIS WAY

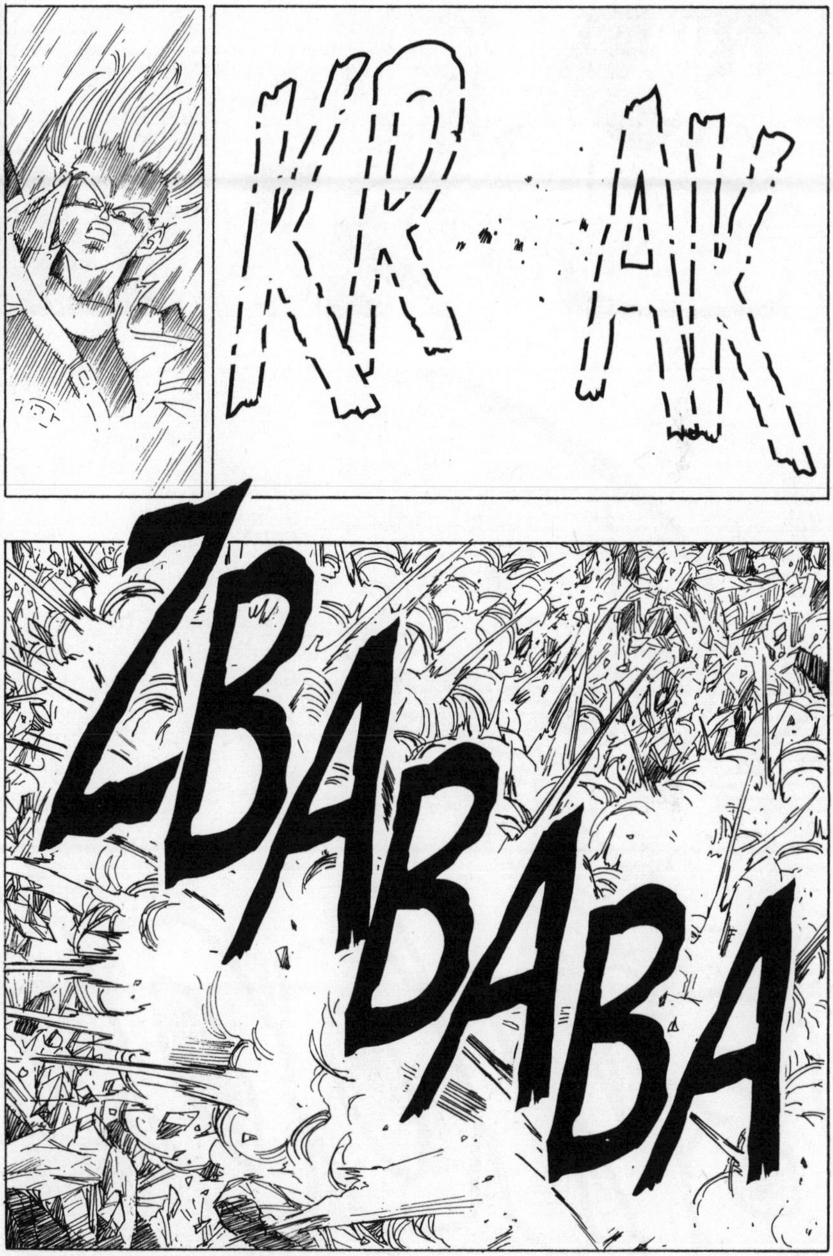
KRAK
ZBABABABA

READ THIS WAY

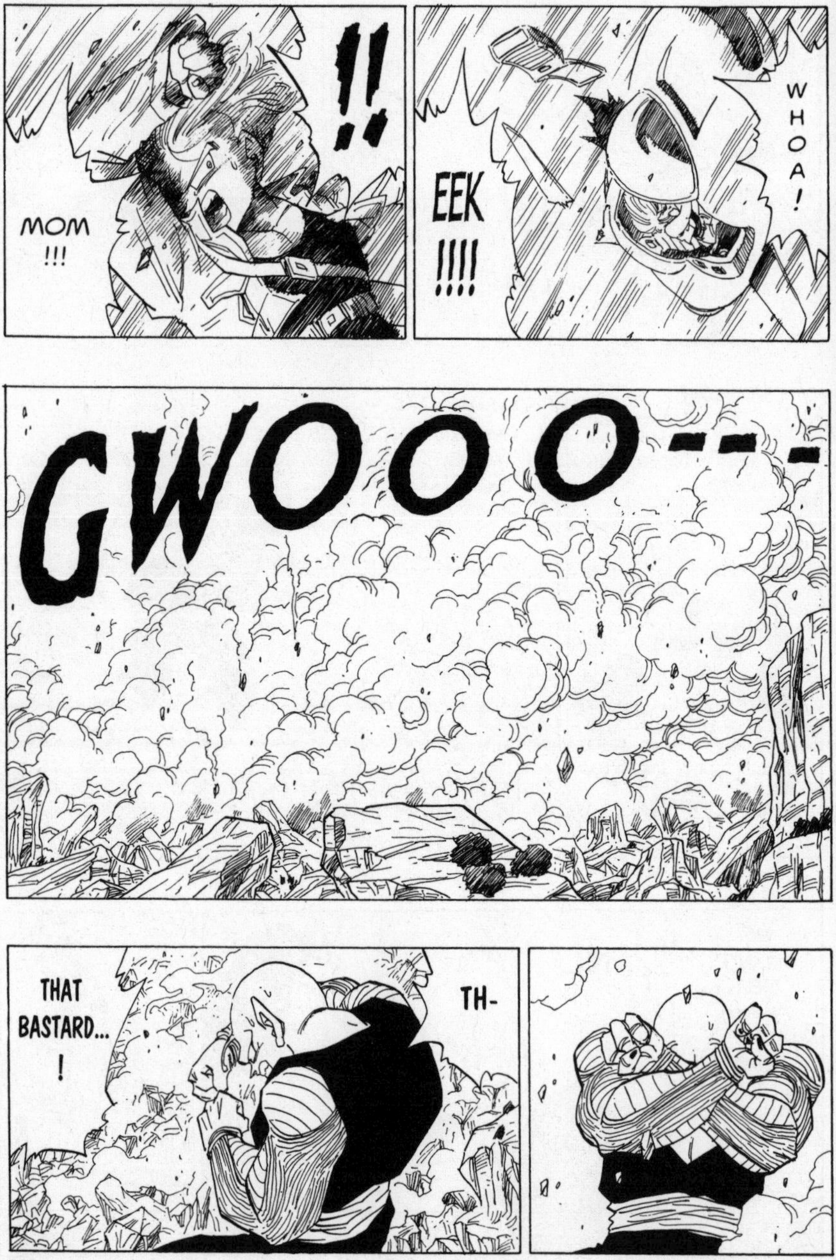

WHOA!
EEK!!!!
!!
MOM!!!
GWOOO---
TH-
THAT BASTARD...!

READ THIS WAY

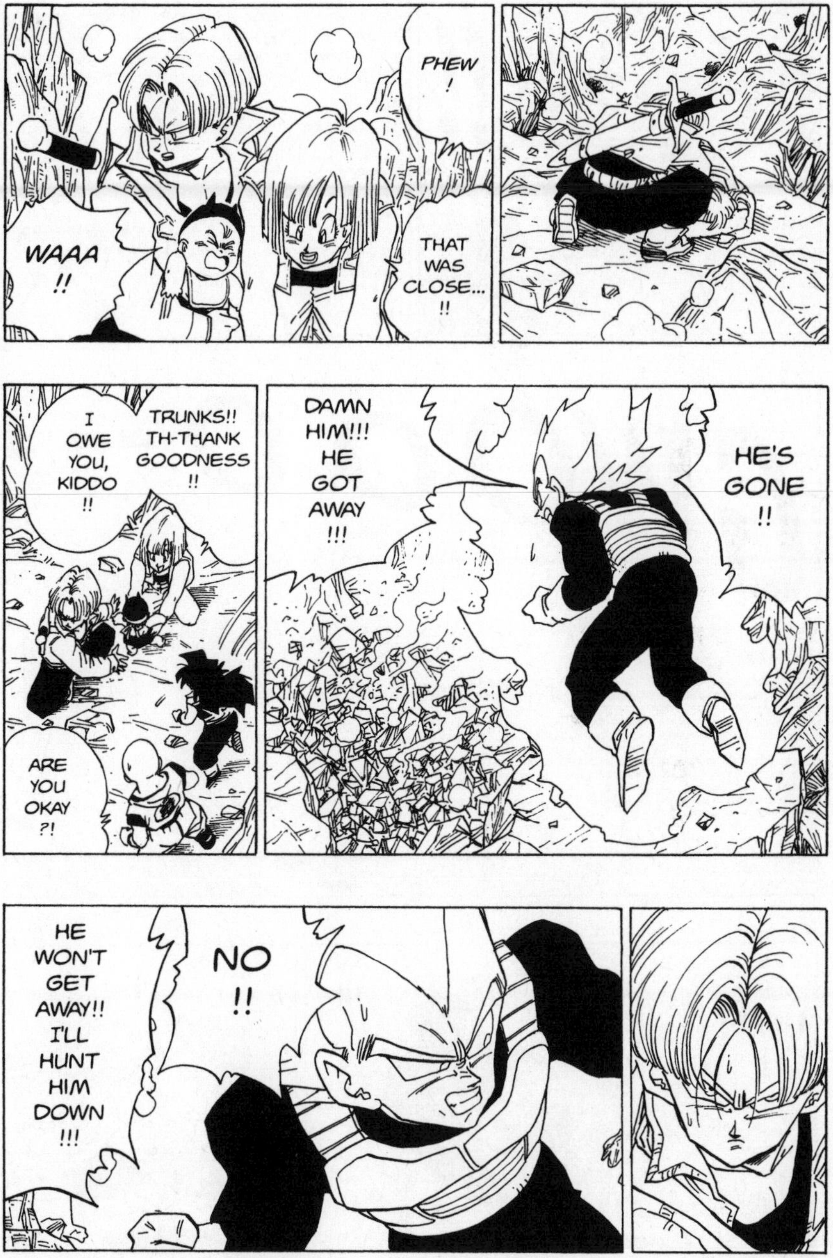
PHEW!
THAT WAS CLOSE...!!
WAAA!!
HE'S GONE!!
DAMN HIM!!! HE GOT AWAY!!!
TRUNKS!! TH-THANK GOODNESS!!
I OWE YOU, KIDDO!!
ARE YOU OKAY?!
NO!!
HE WON'T GET AWAY!! I'LL HUNT HIM DOWN!!!

READ THIS WAY

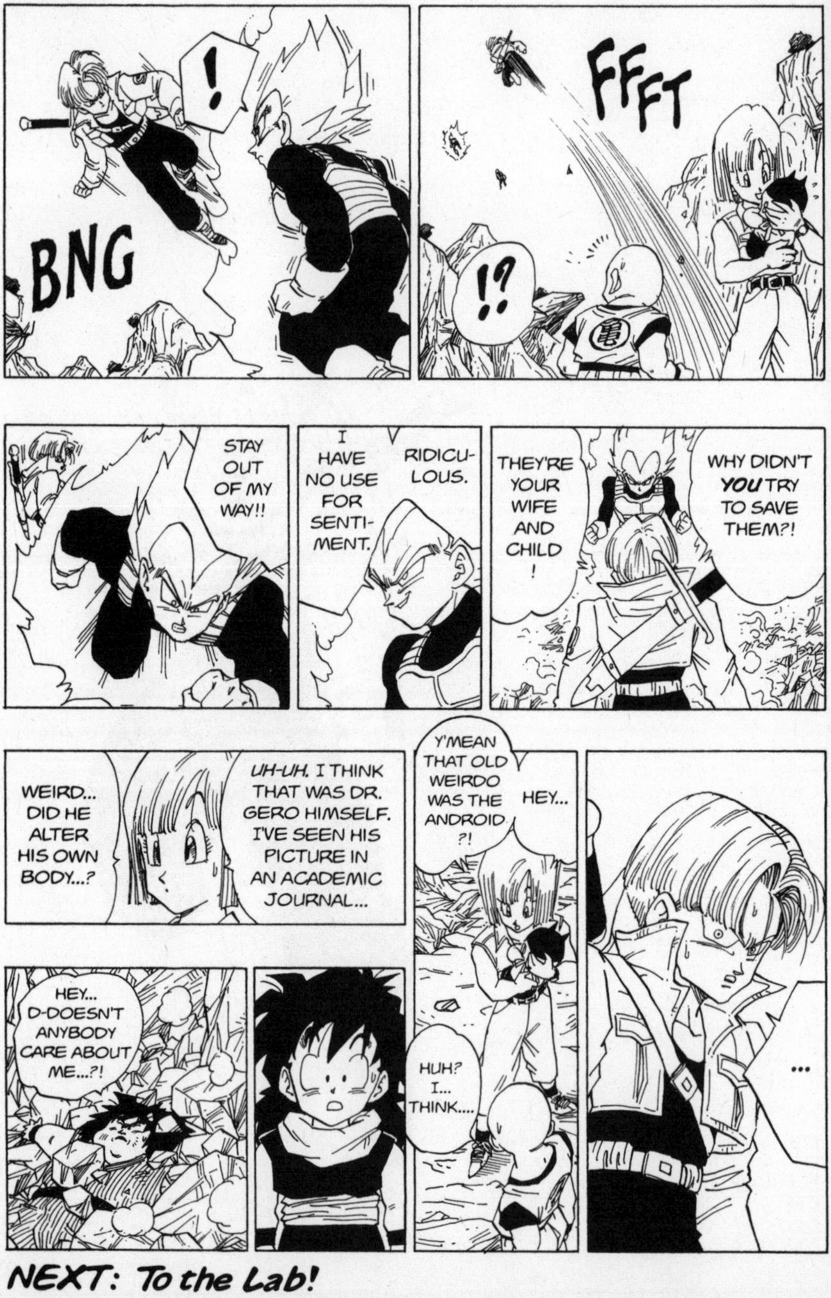
FFFT
!?
!
BNG
WHY DIDN'T YOU TRY TO SAVE THEM?!
THEY'RE YOUR WIFE AND CHILD!
RIDICULOUS.
I HAVE NO USE FOR SENTIMENT.
STAY OUT OF MY WAY!!
...
HEY...
Y'MEAN THAT OLD WEIRDO WAS THE ANDROID?!
HUH? I... THINK....
UH-UH. I THINK THAT WAS DR. GERO HIMSELF. I'VE SEEN HIS PICTURE IN AN ACADEMIC JOURNAL...
WEIRD... DID HE ALTER HIS OWN BODY...?
HEY... D-DOESN'T ANYBODY CARE ABOUT ME...?!

***NEXT*: *To the Lab!***

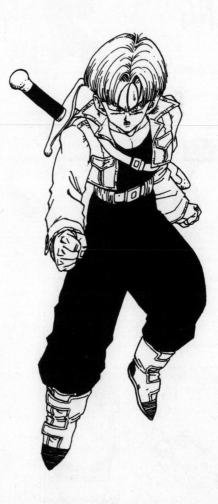

# DBZ:154 • Dr. Gero's Laboratory

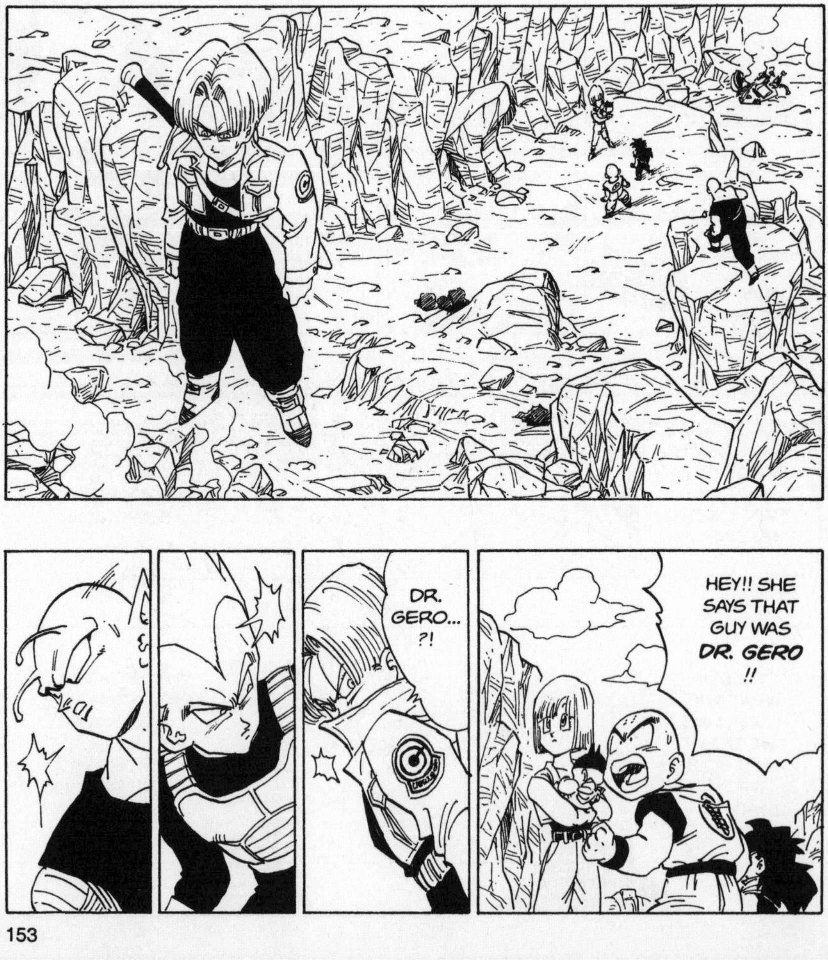
HEY!! SHE SAYS THAT GUY WAS **DR. GERO** !!
DR. GERO... ?!

READ THIS WAY

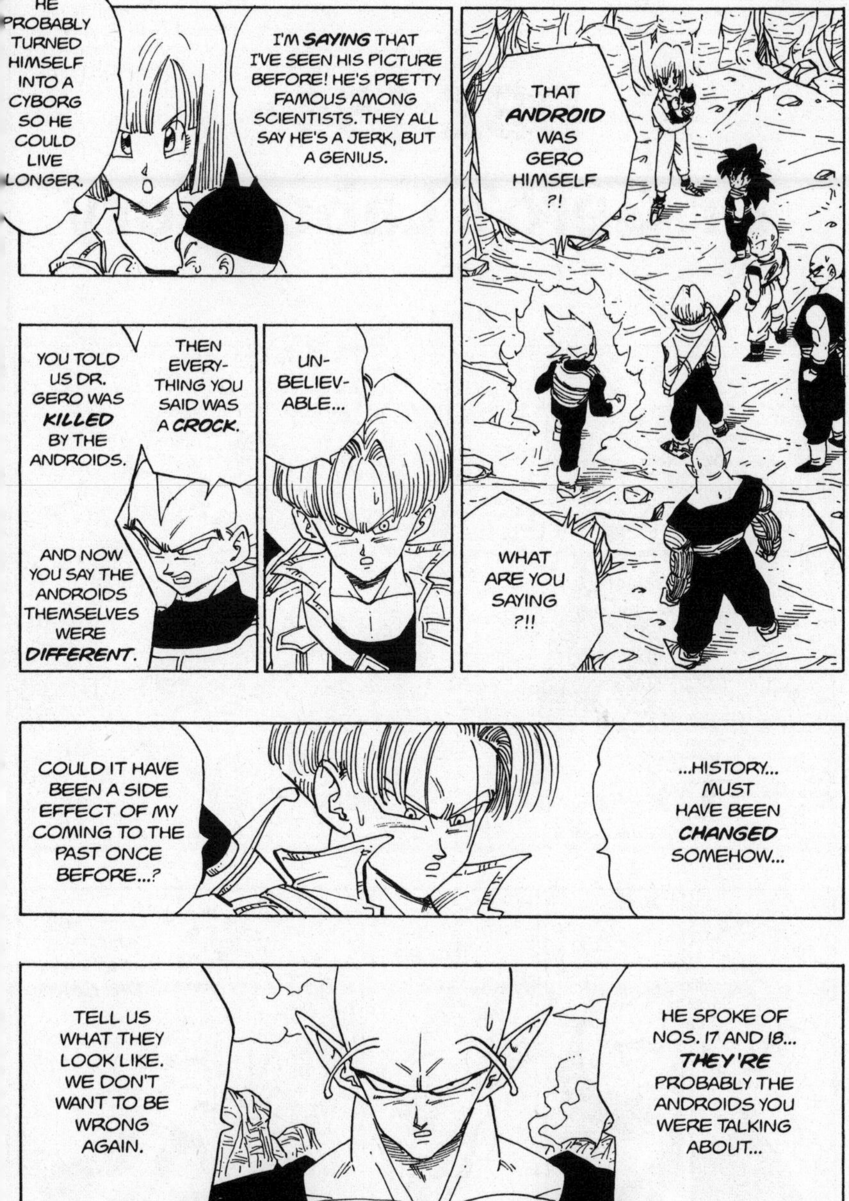
THAT ANDROID WAS GERO HIMSELF ?!
WHAT ARE YOU SAYING ?!!
I'M SAYING THAT I'VE SEEN HIS PICTURE BEFORE! HE'S PRETTY FAMOUS AMONG SCIENTISTS. THEY ALL SAY HE'S A JERK, BUT A GENIUS.
HE PROBABLY TURNED HIMSELF INTO A CYBORG SO HE COULD LIVE LONGER.
UN-BELIEV-ABLE...
THEN EVERY-THING YOU SAID WAS A CROCK.
YOU TOLD US DR. GERO WAS KILLED BY THE ANDROIDS.
AND NOW YOU SAY THE ANDROIDS THEMSELVES WERE DIFFERENT.
...HISTORY... MUST HAVE BEEN CHANGED SOMEHOW...
COULD IT HAVE BEEN A SIDE EFFECT OF MY COMING TO THE PAST ONCE BEFORE...?
HE SPOKE OF NOS. 17 AND 18... THEY'RE PROBABLY THE ANDROIDS YOU WERE TALKING ABOUT...
TELL US WHAT THEY LOOK LIKE. WE DON'T WANT TO BE WRONG AGAIN.

READ THIS WAY

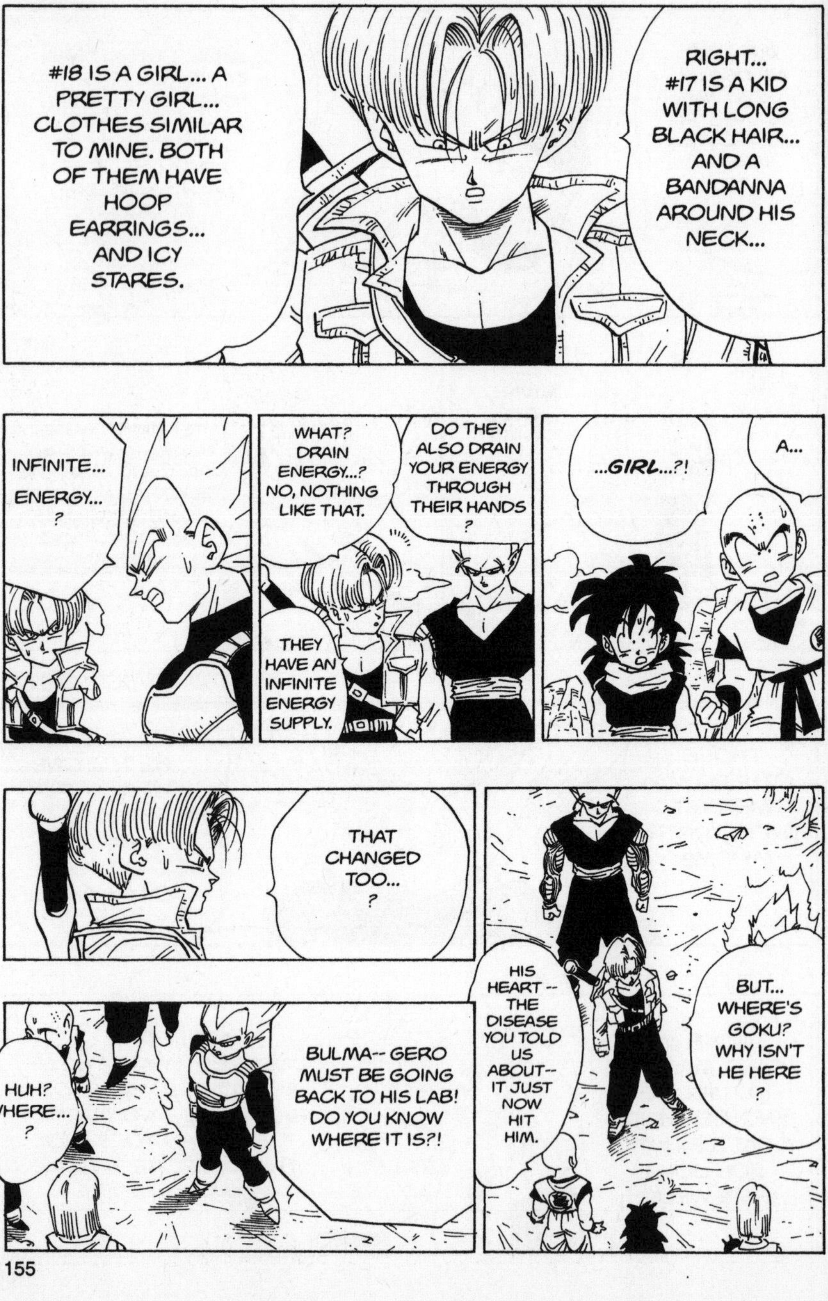
RIGHT... #17 IS A KID WITH LONG BLACK HAIR... AND A BANDANNA AROUND HIS NECK...
#18 IS A GIRL... A PRETTY GIRL... CLOTHES SIMILAR TO MINE. BOTH OF THEM HAVE HOOP EARRINGS... AND ICY STARES.
A...
...GIRL...?!
DO THEY ALSO DRAIN YOUR ENERGY THROUGH THEIR HANDS ?
WHAT? DRAIN ENERGY...? NO, NOTHING LIKE THAT.
THEY HAVE AN INFINITE ENERGY SUPPLY.
INFINITE... ENERGY... ?
BUT... WHERE'S GOKU? WHY ISN'T HE HERE ?
HIS HEART -- THE DISEASE YOU TOLD US ABOUT-- IT JUST NOW HIT HIM.
THAT CHANGED TOO... ?
BULMA-- GERO MUST BE GOING BACK TO HIS LAB! DO YOU KNOW WHERE IT IS?!
HUH? WHERE... ?

READ THIS WAY

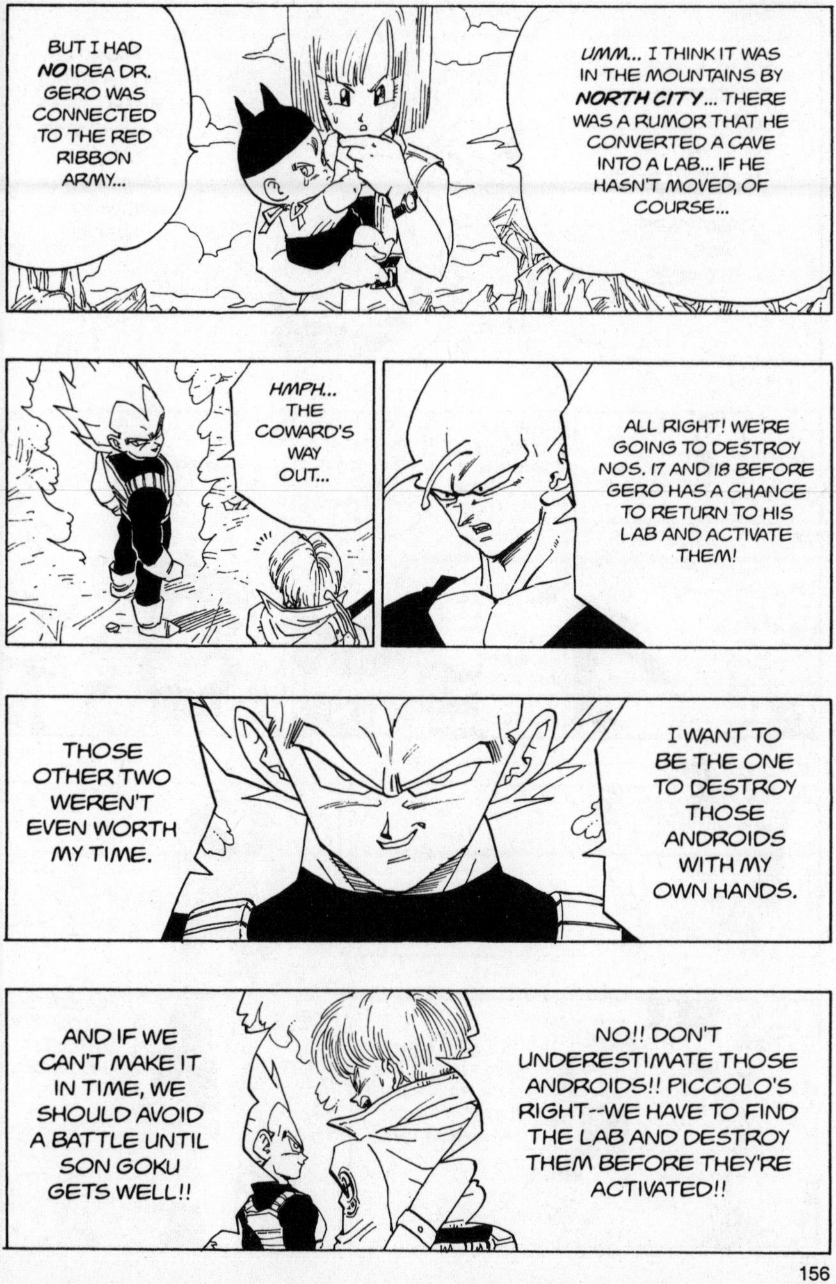
UMM... I THINK IT WAS IN THE MOUNTAINS BY NORTH CITY... THERE WAS A RUMOR THAT HE CONVERTED A CAVE INTO A LAB... IF HE HASN'T MOVED, OF COURSE...
BUT I HAD NO IDEA DR. GERO WAS CONNECTED TO THE RED RIBBON ARMY...
ALL RIGHT! WE'RE GOING TO DESTROY NOS. 17 AND 18 BEFORE GERO HAS A CHANCE TO RETURN TO HIS LAB AND ACTIVATE THEM!
HMPH... THE COWARD'S WAY OUT...
I WANT TO BE THE ONE TO DESTROY THOSE ANDROIDS WITH MY OWN HANDS.
THOSE OTHER TWO WEREN'T EVEN WORTH MY TIME.
NO!! DON'T UNDERESTIMATE THOSE ANDROIDS!! PICCOLO'S RIGHT--WE HAVE TO FIND THE LAB AND DESTROY THEM BEFORE THEY'RE ACTIVATED!!
AND IF WE CAN'T MAKE IT IN TIME, WE SHOULD AVOID A BATTLE UNTIL SON GOKU GETS WELL!!

READ THIS WAY

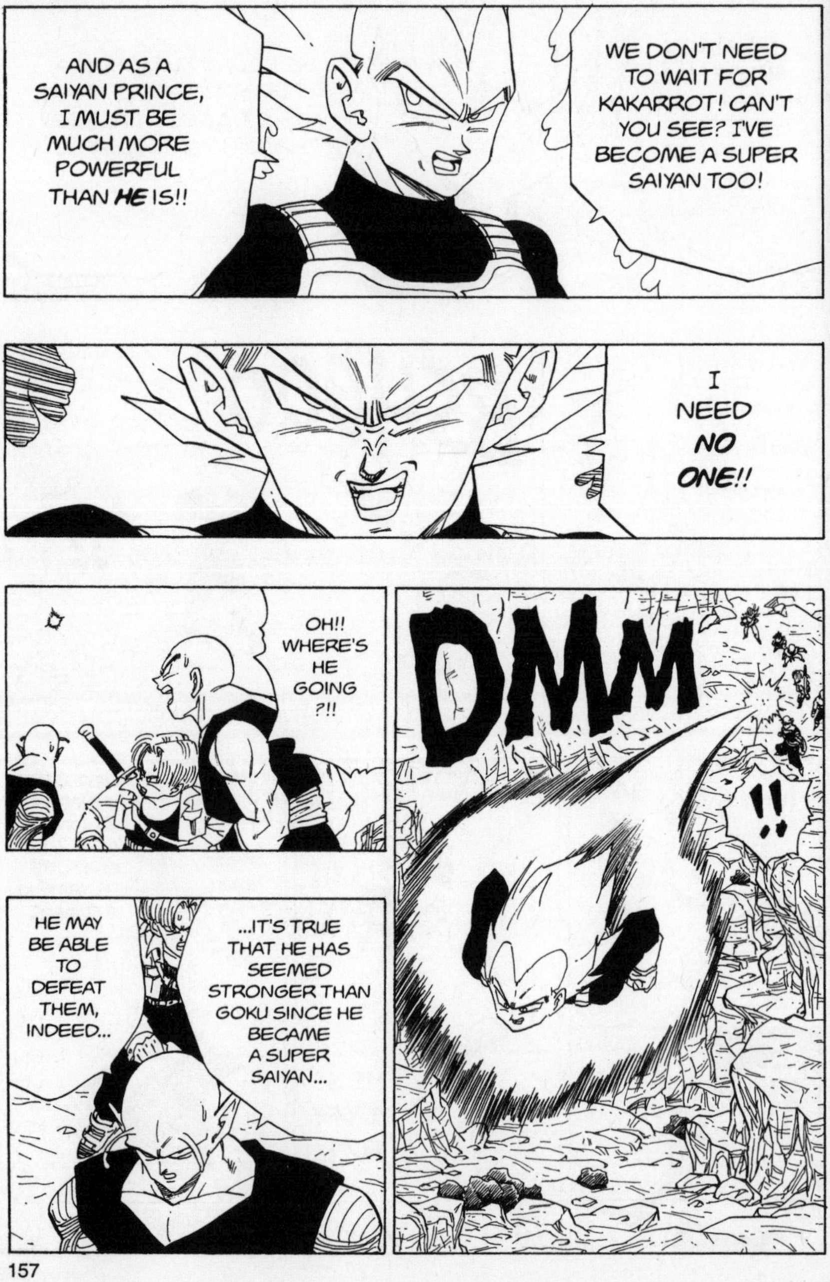

WE DON'T NEED TO WAIT FOR KAKARROT! CAN'T YOU SEE? I'VE BECOME A SUPER SAIYAN TOO!
AND AS A SAIYAN PRINCE, I MUST BE MUCH MORE POWERFUL THAN HE IS!!
I NEED NO ONE!!
DMM
!!
OH!! WHERE'S HE GOING?!!
...IT'S TRUE THAT HE HAS SEEMED STRONGER THAN GOKU SINCE HE BECAME A SUPER SAIYAN...
HE MAY BE ABLE TO DEFEAT THEM, INDEED...

READ THIS WAY

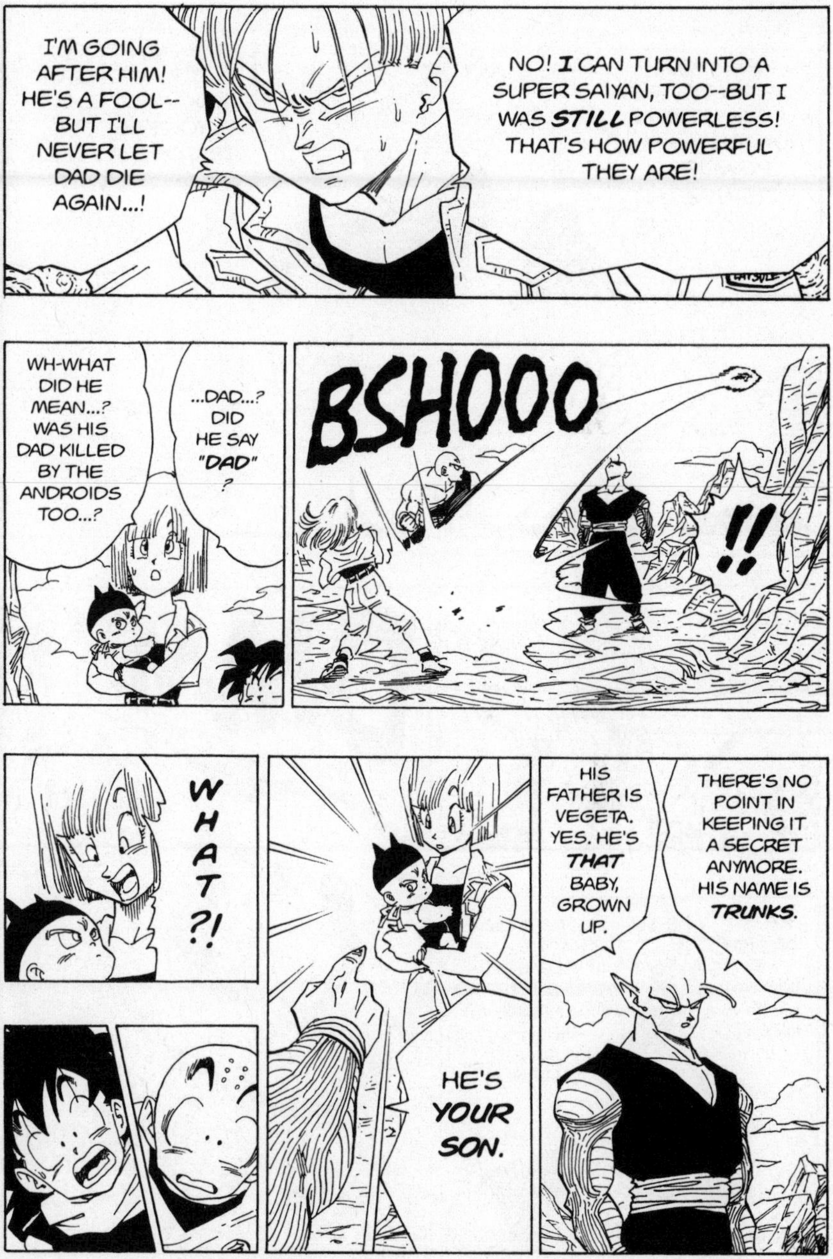

NO! I CAN TURN INTO A SUPER SAIYAN, TOO--BUT I WAS STILL POWERLESS! THAT'S HOW POWERFUL THEY ARE!
I'M GOING AFTER HIM! HE'S A FOOL-- BUT I'LL NEVER LET DAD DIE AGAIN...!
BSHOOO
!!
...DAD...? DID HE SAY "DAD"?
WH-WHAT DID HE MEAN...? WAS HIS DAD KILLED BY THE ANDROIDS TOO...?
THERE'S NO POINT IN KEEPING IT A SECRET ANYMORE. HIS NAME IS TRUNKS.
HIS FATHER IS VEGETA. YES. HE'S THAT BABY, GROWN UP.
HE'S YOUR SON.
WHAT?!

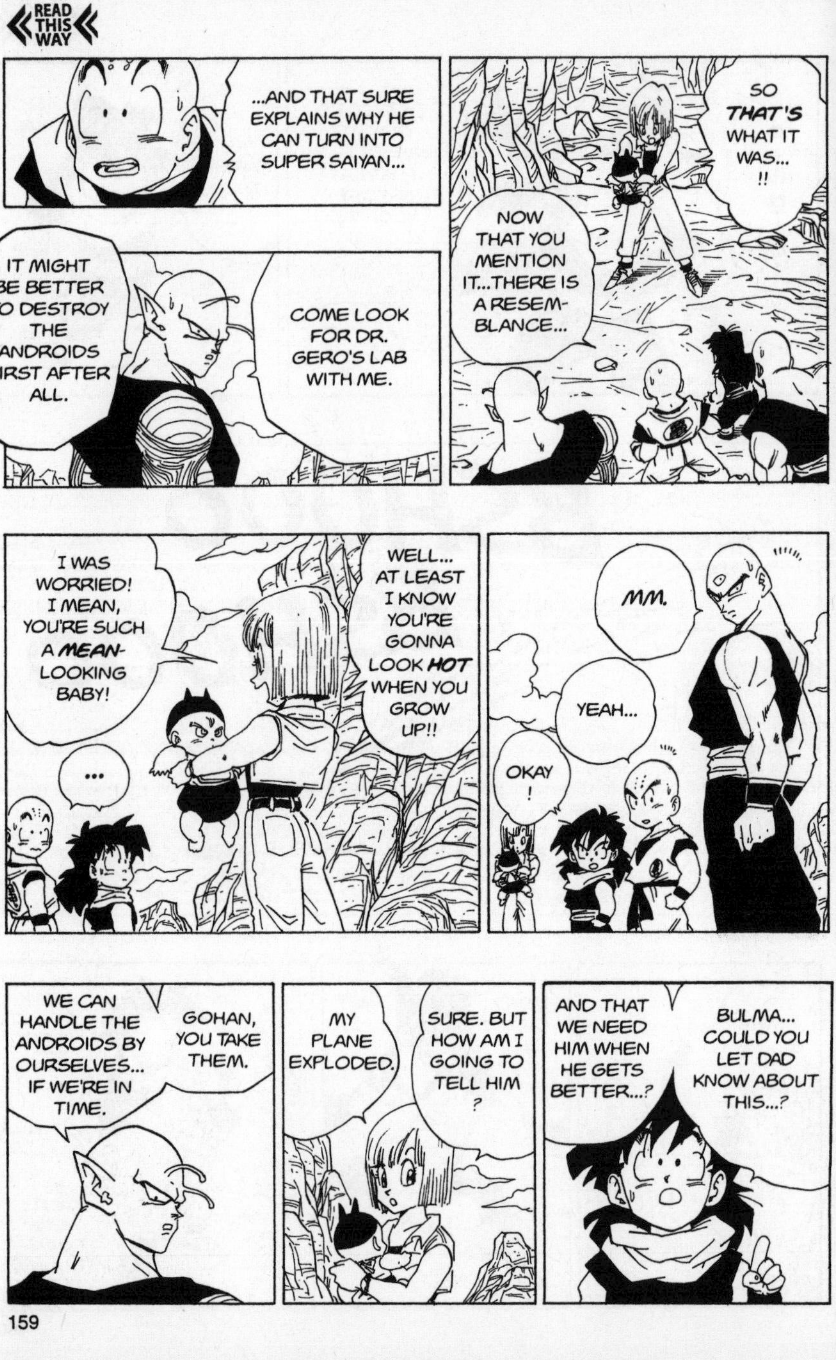
READ THIS WAY
SO THAT'S WHAT IT WAS... !!
NOW THAT YOU MENTION IT...THERE IS A RESEMBLANCE...
...AND THAT SURE EXPLAINS WHY HE CAN TURN INTO SUPER SAIYAN...
IT MIGHT BE BETTER TO DESTROY THE ANDROIDS FIRST AFTER ALL.
COME LOOK FOR DR. GERO'S LAB WITH ME.
MM.
YEAH...
OKAY!
WELL... AT LEAST I KNOW YOU'RE GONNA LOOK HOT WHEN YOU GROW UP!!
I WAS WORRIED! I MEAN, YOU'RE SUCH A MEAN-LOOKING BABY!
...
BULMA... COULD YOU LET DAD KNOW ABOUT THIS...?
AND THAT WE NEED HIM WHEN HE GETS BETTER...?
SURE. BUT HOW AM I GOING TO TELL HIM?
MY PLANE EXPLODED.
GOHAN, YOU TAKE THEM.
WE CAN HANDLE THE ANDROIDS BY OURSELVES... IF WE'RE IN TIME.

READ THIS WAY

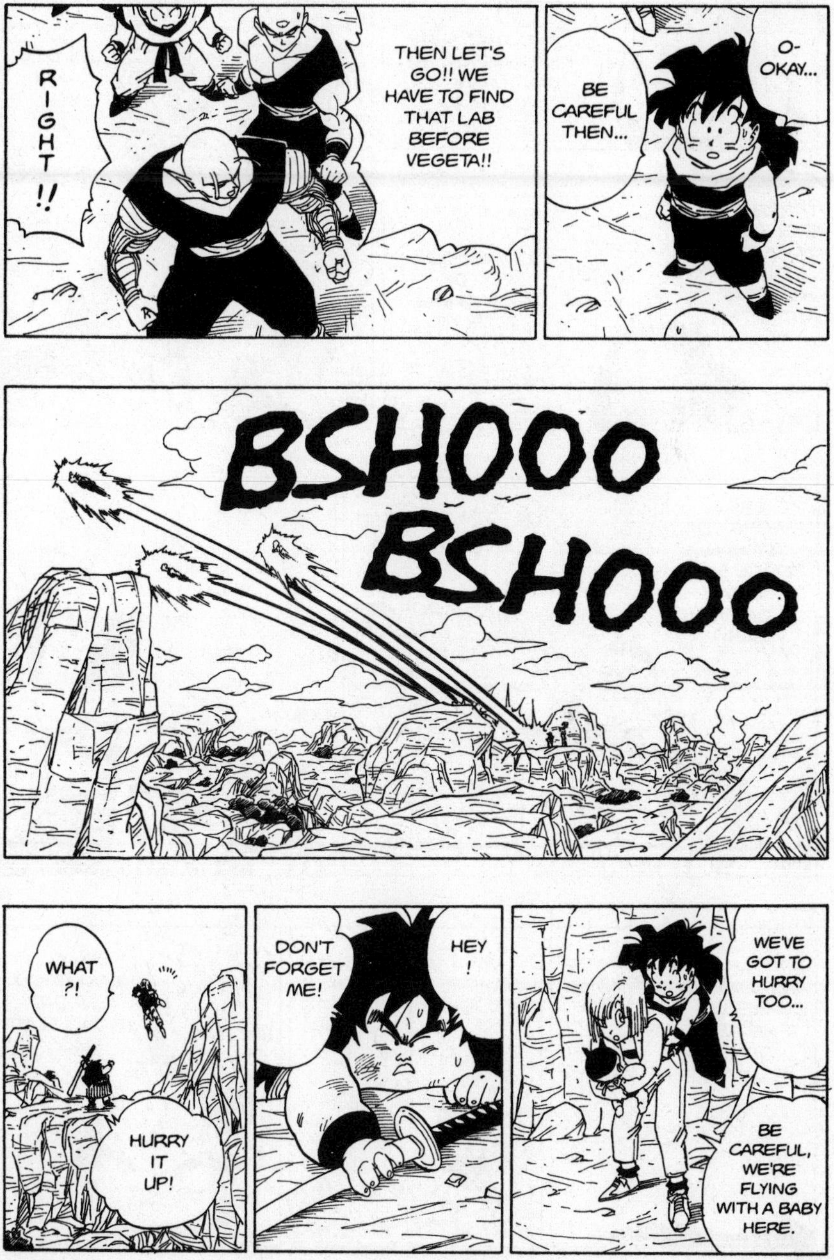
O-OKAY...
BE CAREFUL THEN...
THEN LET'S GO!! WE HAVE TO FIND THAT LAB BEFORE VEGETA!!
RIGHT!!
BSHOOO
BSHOOO
WE'VE GOT TO HURRY TOO...
BE CAREFUL, WE'RE FLYING WITH A BABY HERE.
HEY!
DON'T FORGET ME!
WHAT?!
HURRY IT UP!

READ THIS WAY

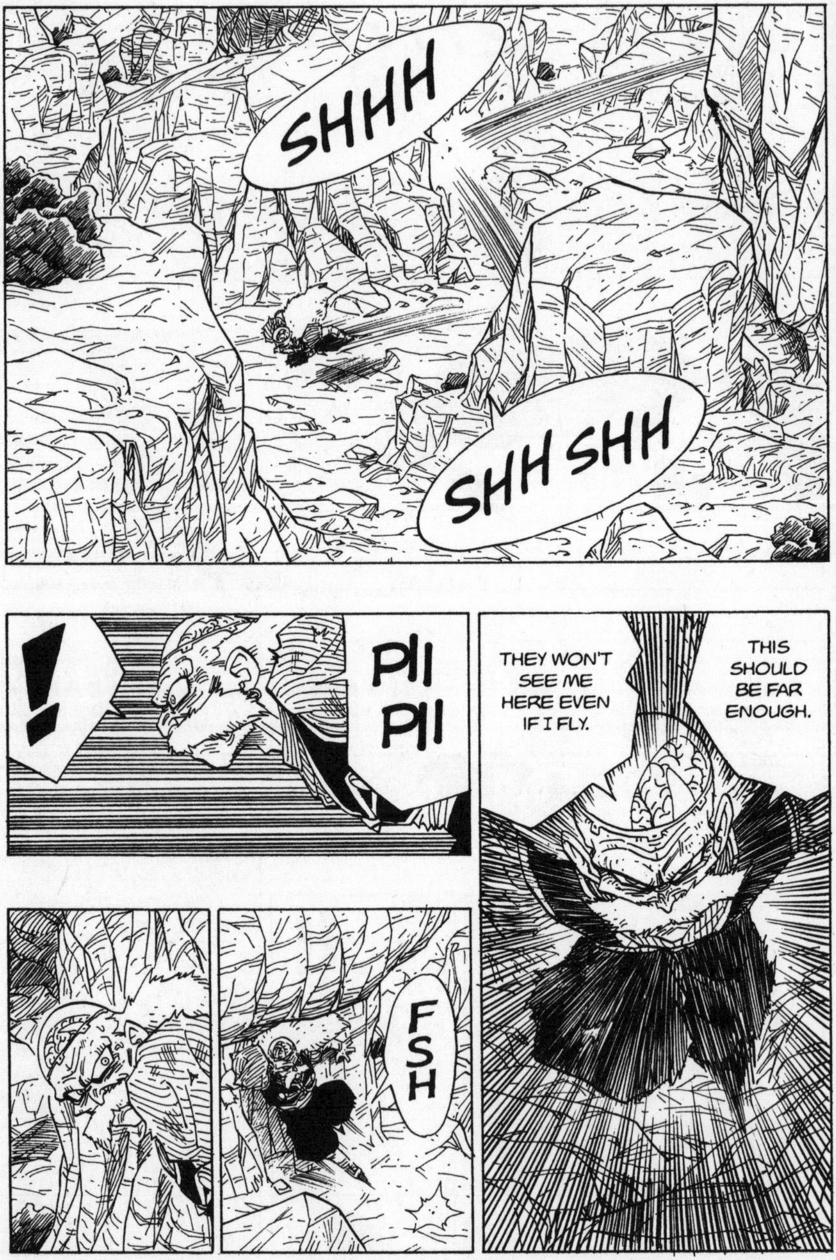
SHHH
SHH SHH
THIS SHOULD BE FAR ENOUGH.
THEY WON'T SEE ME HERE EVEN IF I FLY.
PII PII
!
FSH

READ THIS WAY

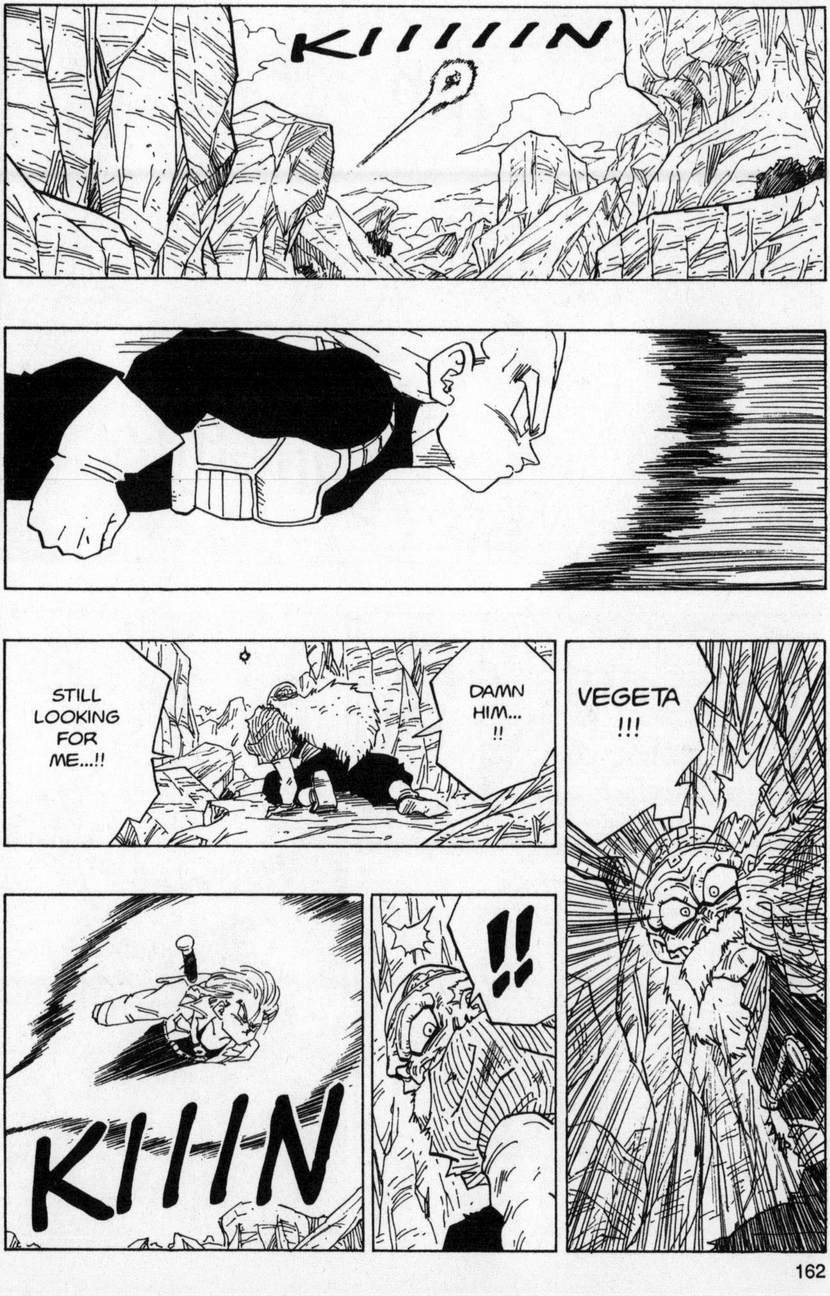

KIIIIIN
VEGETA !!!
DAMN HIM... !!
STILL LOOKING FOR ME...!!
!!
KIIIN

READ THIS WAY

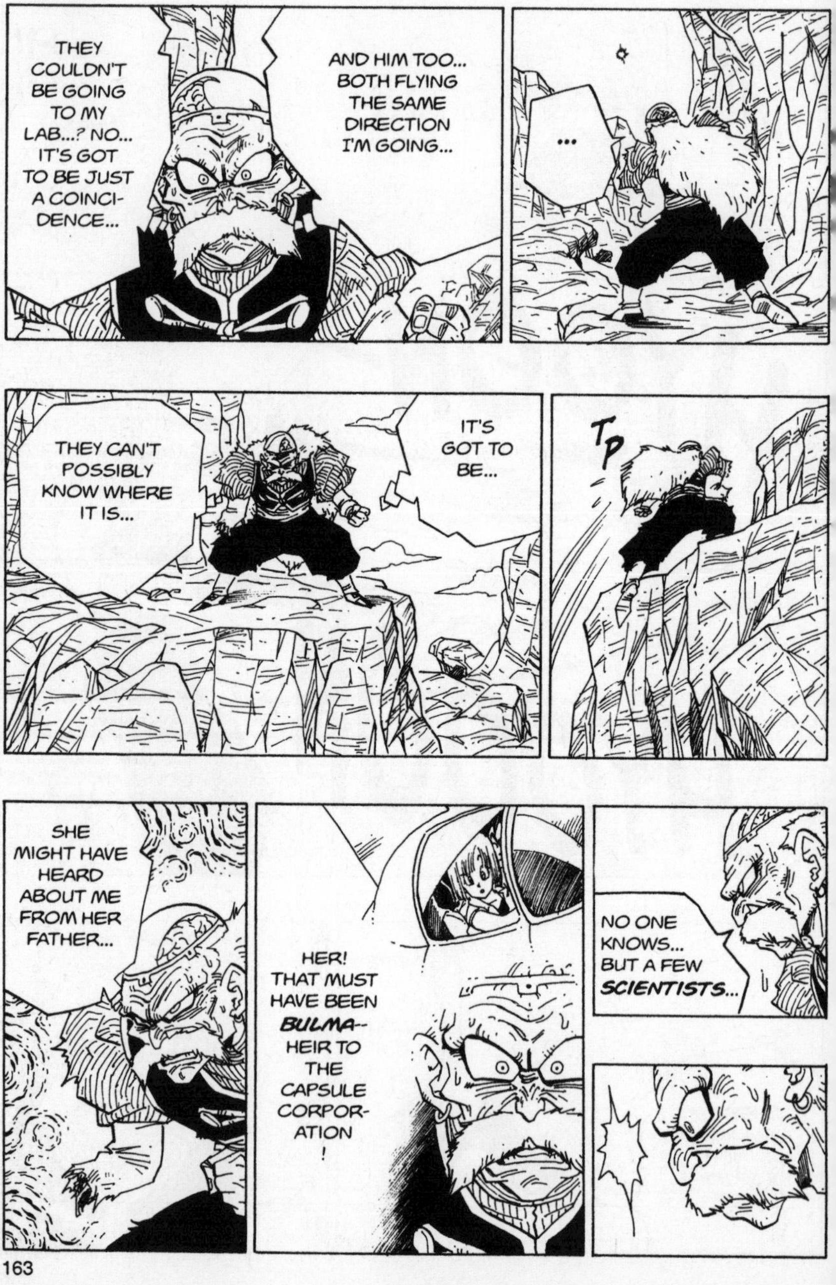
...
AND HIM TOO... BOTH FLYING THE SAME DIRECTION I'M GOING...
THEY COULDN'T BE GOING TO MY LAB...? NO... IT'S GOT TO BE JUST A COINCIDENCE...
TP
IT'S GOT TO BE...
THEY CAN'T POSSIBLY KNOW WHERE IT IS...
NO ONE KNOWS... BUT A FEW SCIENTISTS...
HER! THAT MUST HAVE BEEN BULMA-- HEIR TO THE CAPSULE CORPORATION!
SHE MIGHT HAVE HEARD ABOUT ME FROM HER FATHER...

READ THIS WAY

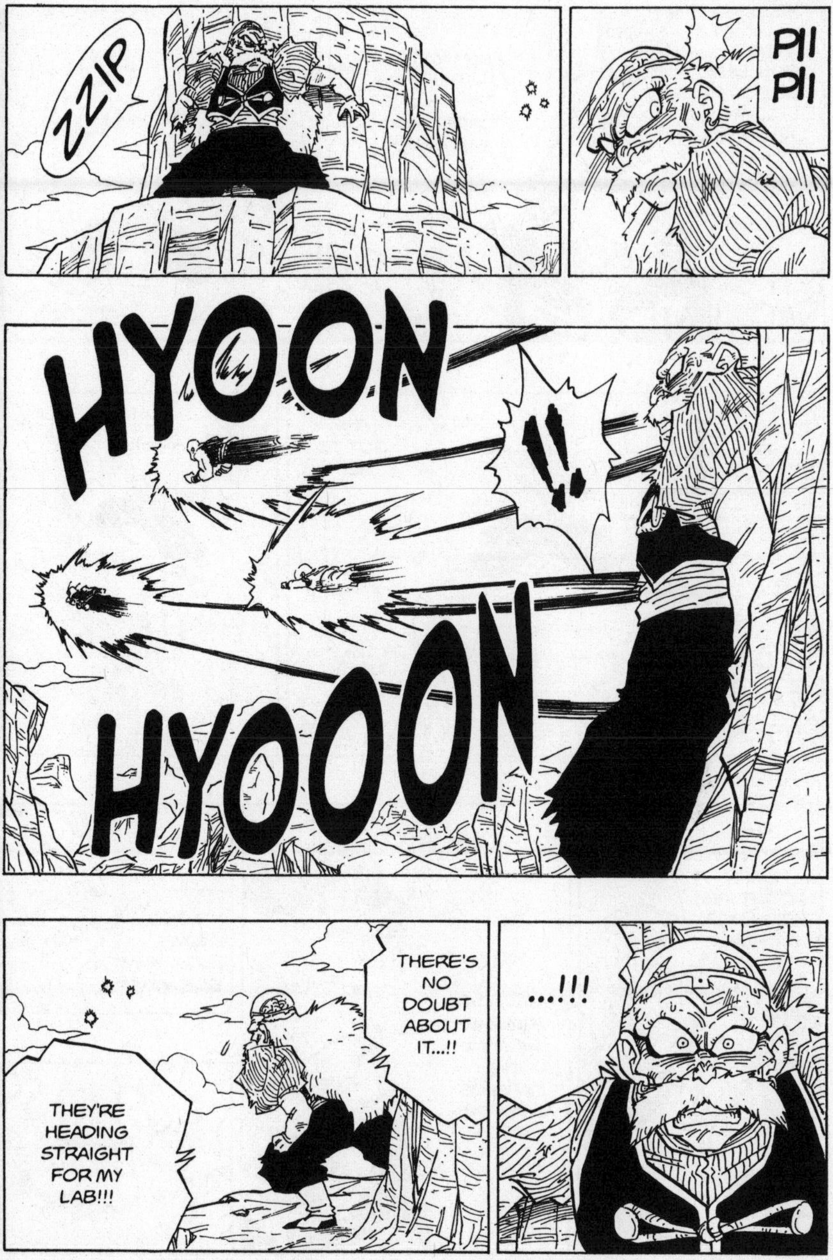

PII PII
ZZIP
HYOON
!!
HYOOON
...!!!
THERE'S NO DOUBT ABOUT IT...!!
THEY'RE HEADING STRAIGHT FOR MY LAB!!!

READ THIS WAY

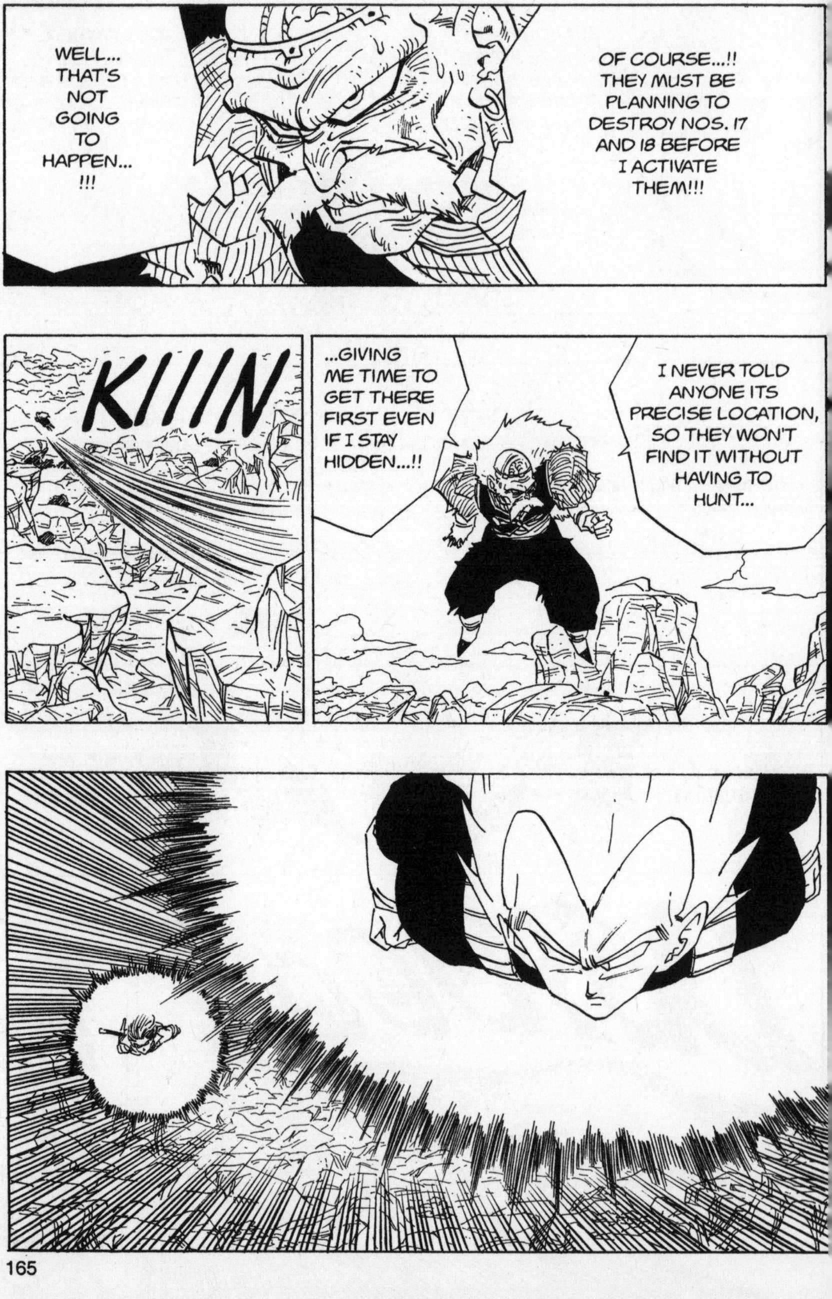
OF COURSE...!! THEY MUST BE PLANNING TO DESTROY NOS. 17 AND 18 BEFORE I ACTIVATE THEM!!!
WELL... THAT'S NOT GOING TO HAPPEN... !!!
I NEVER TOLD ANYONE ITS PRECISE LOCATION, SO THEY WON'T FIND IT WITHOUT HAVING TO HUNT...
...GIVING ME TIME TO GET THERE FIRST EVEN IF I STAY HIDDEN...!!
KIIIN

READ THIS WAY

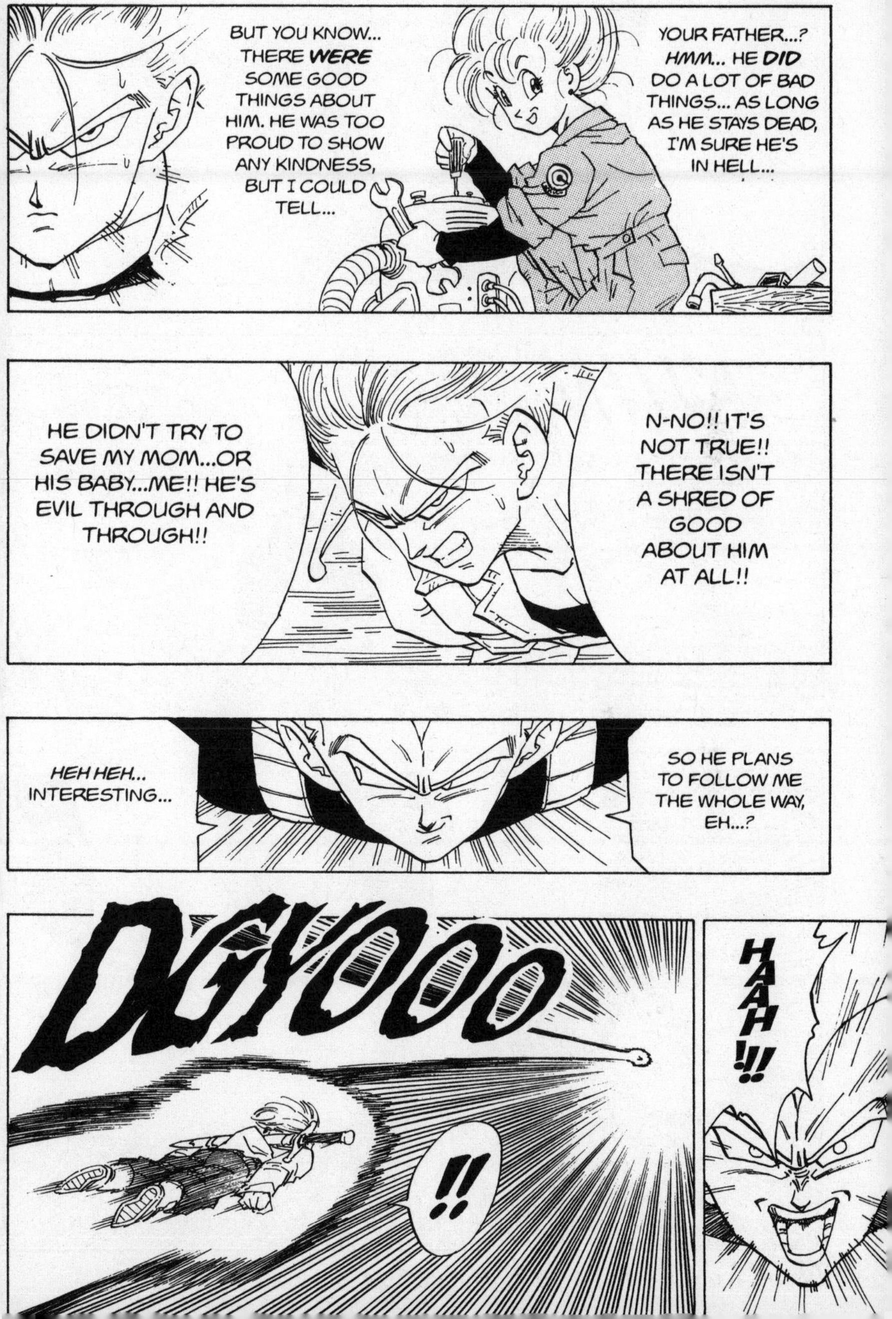
YOUR FATHER...? HMM... HE DID DO A LOT OF BAD THINGS... AS LONG AS HE STAYS DEAD, I'M SURE HE'S IN HELL...
BUT YOU KNOW... THERE WERE SOME GOOD THINGS ABOUT HIM. HE WAS TOO PROUD TO SHOW ANY KINDNESS, BUT I COULD TELL...
N-NO!! IT'S NOT TRUE!! THERE ISN'T A SHRED OF GOOD ABOUT HIM AT ALL!!
HE DIDN'T TRY TO SAVE MY MOM...OR HIS BABY...ME!! HE'S EVIL THROUGH AND THROUGH!!
SO HE PLANS TO FOLLOW ME THE WHOLE WAY, EH...?
HEH HEH... INTERESTING...
HAAH!!!
DGYOOO
!!

READ THIS WAY

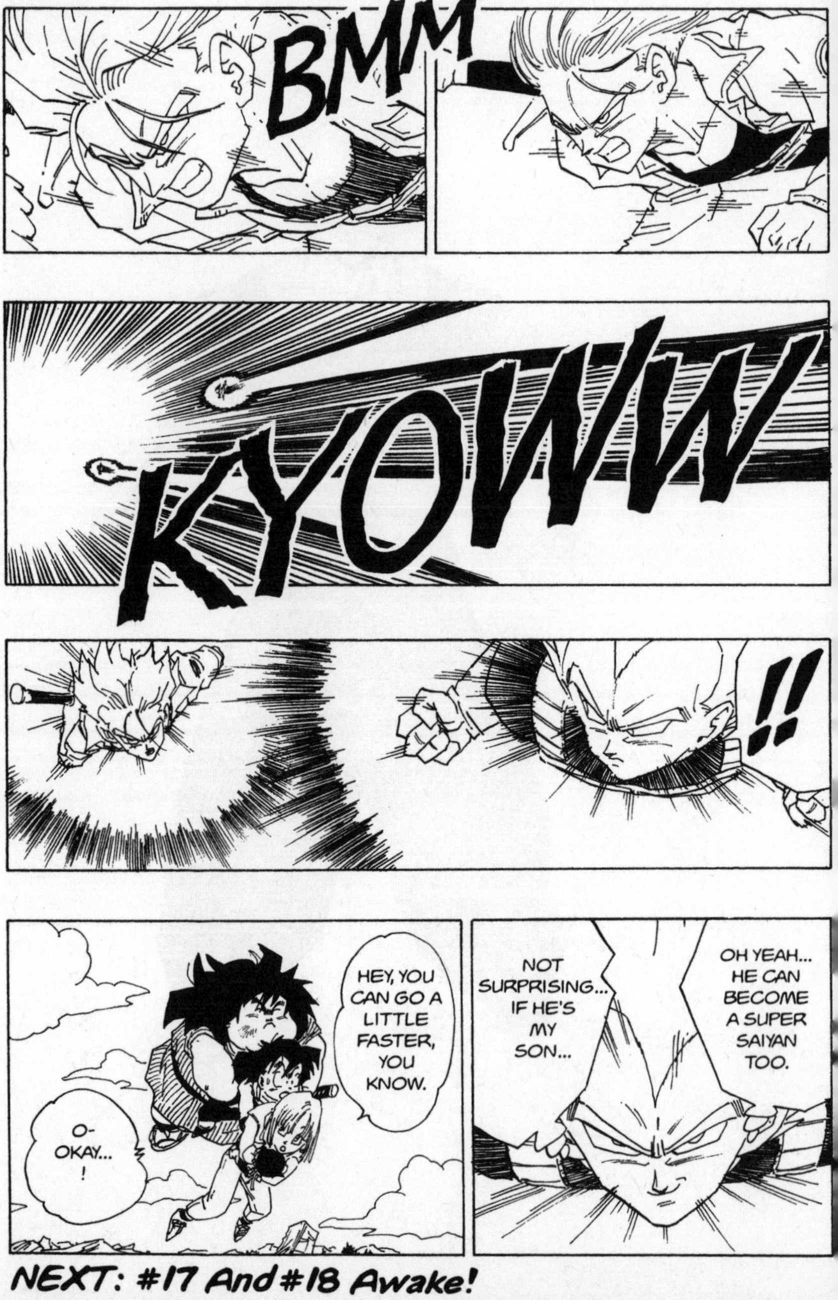
BMM
KYOWW
!!
OH YEAH... HE CAN BECOME A SUPER SAIYAN TOO.
NOT SURPRISING... IF HE'S MY SON...
HEY, YOU CAN GO A LITTLE FASTER, YOU KNOW.
O-OKAY...!

NEXT: #17 And #18 Awake!

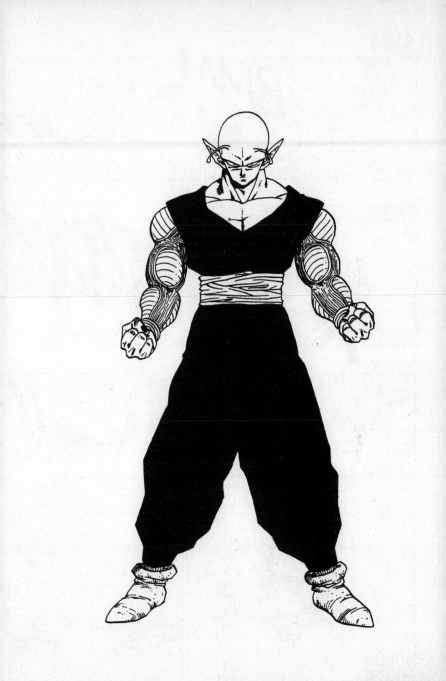

# DBZ:155 • The Androids Awake!

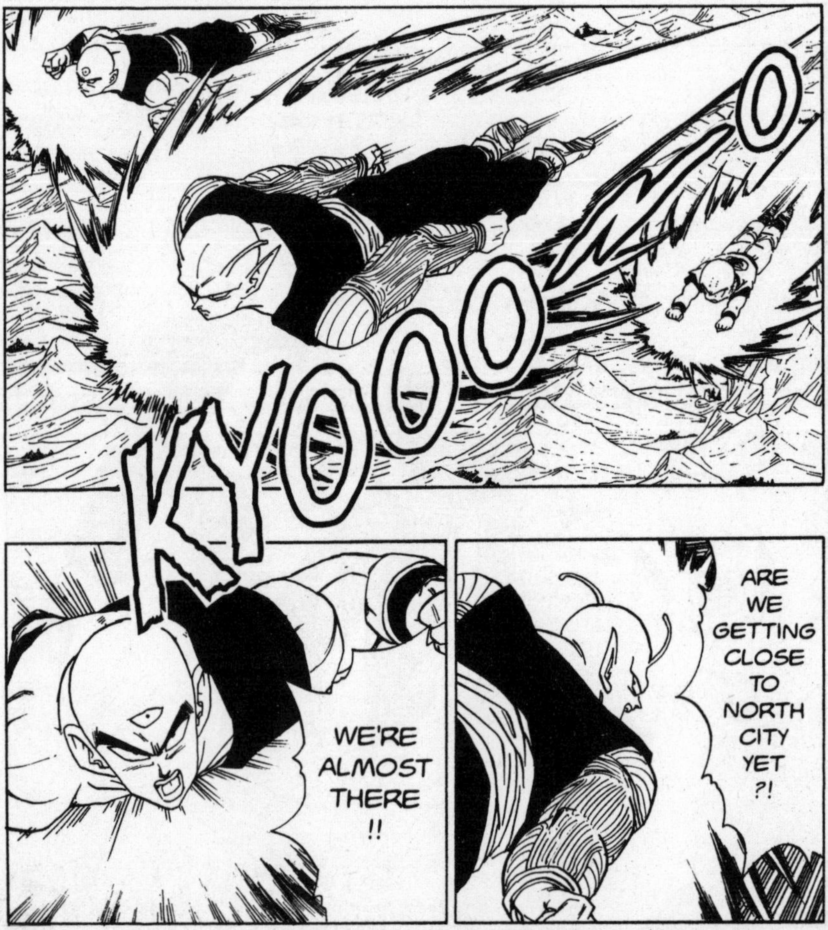
KYOOOOOO
ARE WE GETTING CLOSE TO NORTH CITY YET ?!
WE'RE ALMOST THERE !!

READ THIS WAY

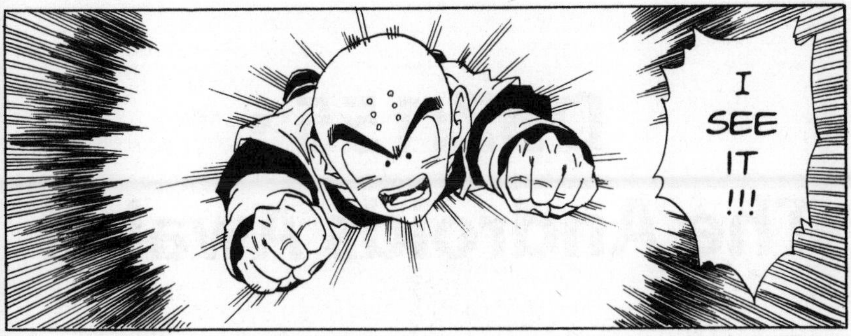
I SEE IT !!!

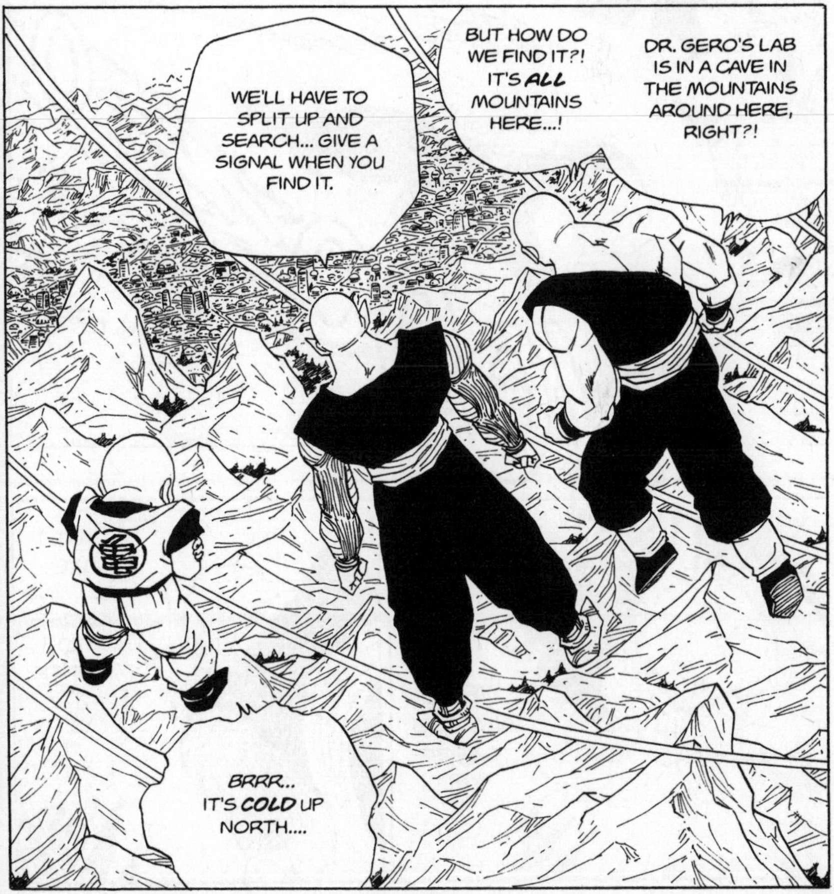
DR. GERO'S LAB IS IN A CAVE IN THE MOUNTAINS AROUND HERE, RIGHT?!
BUT HOW DO WE FIND IT?! IT'S ALL MOUNTAINS HERE...!
WE'LL HAVE TO SPLIT UP AND SEARCH... GIVE A SIGNAL WHEN YOU FIND IT.
BRRR... IT'S COLD UP NORTH....

READ THIS WAY

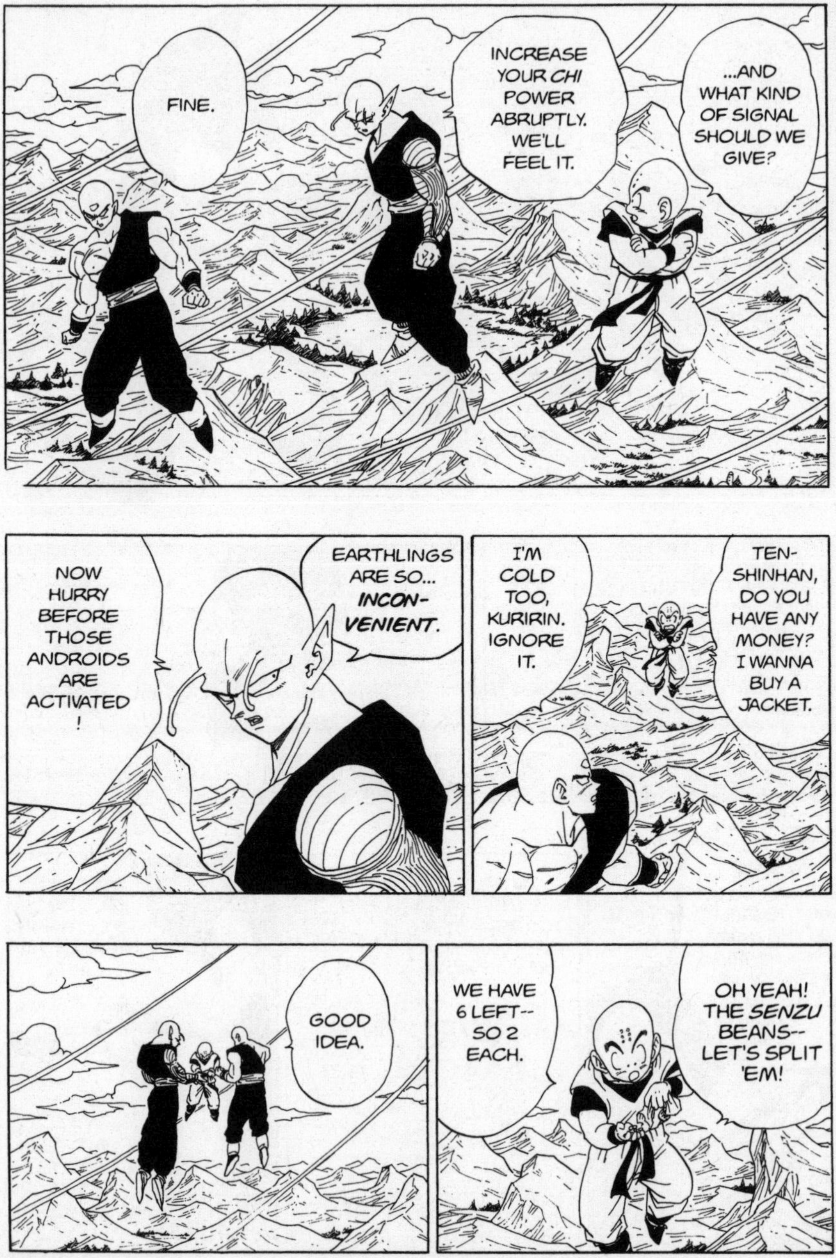
...AND WHAT KIND OF SIGNAL SHOULD WE GIVE?
INCREASE YOUR *CHI* POWER ABRUPTLY. WE'LL FEEL IT.
FINE.
TEN-SHINHAN, DO YOU HAVE ANY MONEY? I WANNA BUY A JACKET.
I'M COLD TOO, KURIRIN. IGNORE IT.
EARTHLINGS ARE SO... ***INCON-VENIENT***.
NOW HURRY BEFORE THOSE ANDROIDS ARE ACTIVATED!
OH YEAH! THE *SENZU* BEANS-- LET'S SPLIT 'EM!
WE HAVE 6 LEFT-- SO 2 EACH.
GOOD IDEA.

READ THIS WAY

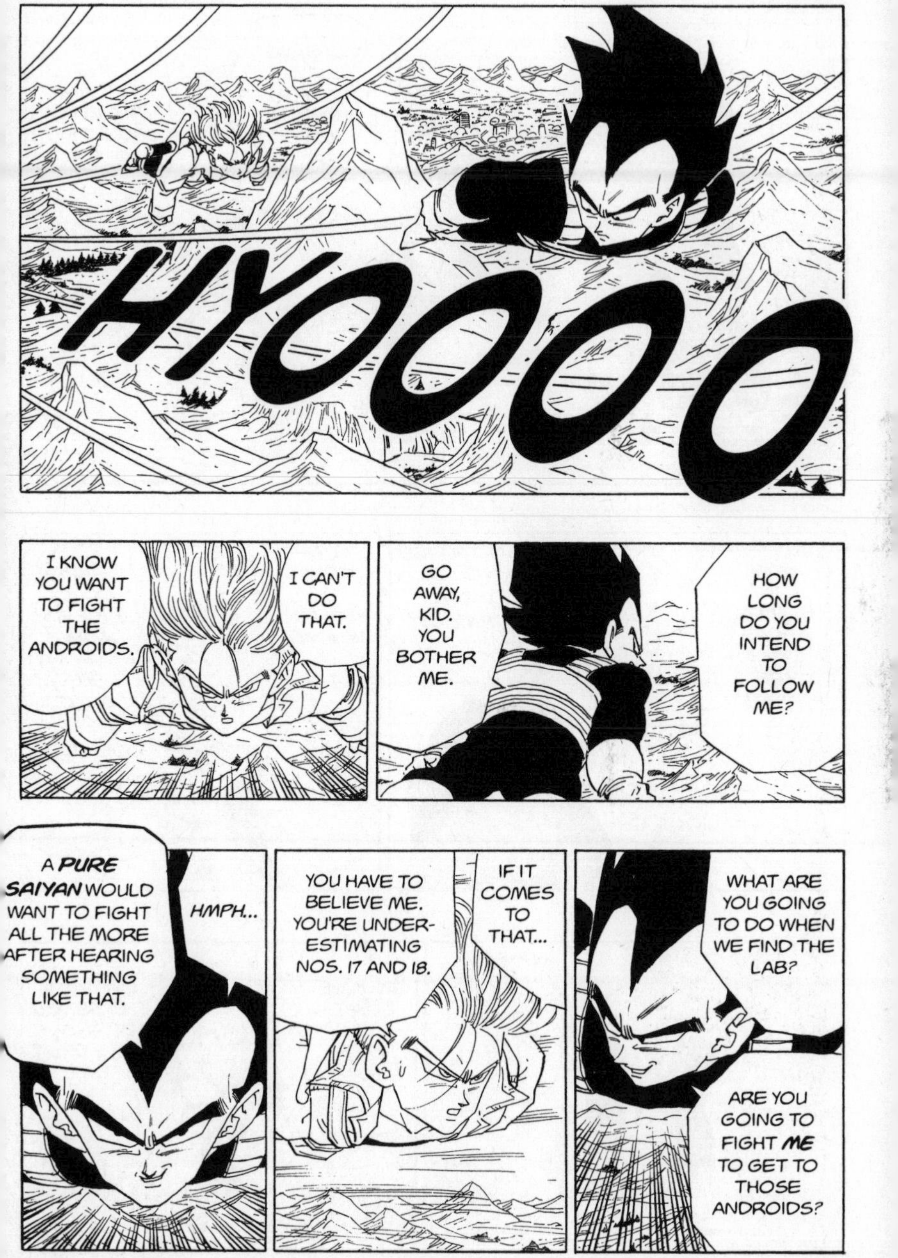
HYOOOO
HOW LONG DO YOU INTEND TO FOLLOW ME?
GO AWAY, KID. YOU BOTHER ME.
I CAN'T DO THAT.
I KNOW YOU WANT TO FIGHT THE ANDROIDS.
WHAT ARE YOU GOING TO DO WHEN WE FIND THE LAB?
ARE YOU GOING TO FIGHT ***ME*** TO GET TO THOSE ANDROIDS?
IF IT COMES TO THAT...
YOU HAVE TO BELIEVE ME. YOU'RE UNDER-ESTIMATING NOS. 17 AND 18.
HMPH...
A ***PURE SAIYAN*** WOULD WANT TO FIGHT ALL THE MORE AFTER HEARING SOMETHING LIKE THAT.

READ THIS WAY

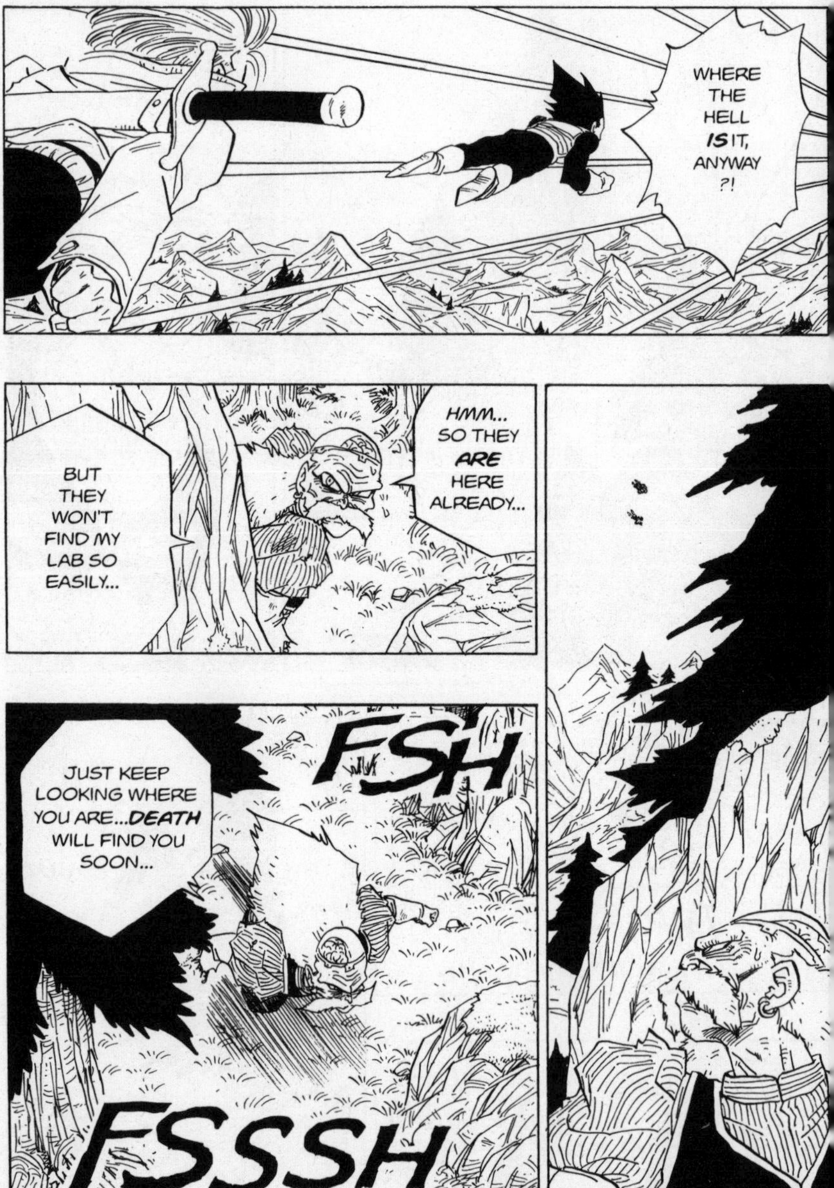
WHERE THE HELL IS IT, ANYWAY ?!
HMM... SO THEY ARE HERE ALREADY...
BUT THEY WON'T FIND MY LAB SO EASILY...
FSH
JUST KEEP LOOKING WHERE YOU ARE...DEATH WILL FIND YOU SOON...
FSSSH

READ THIS WAY

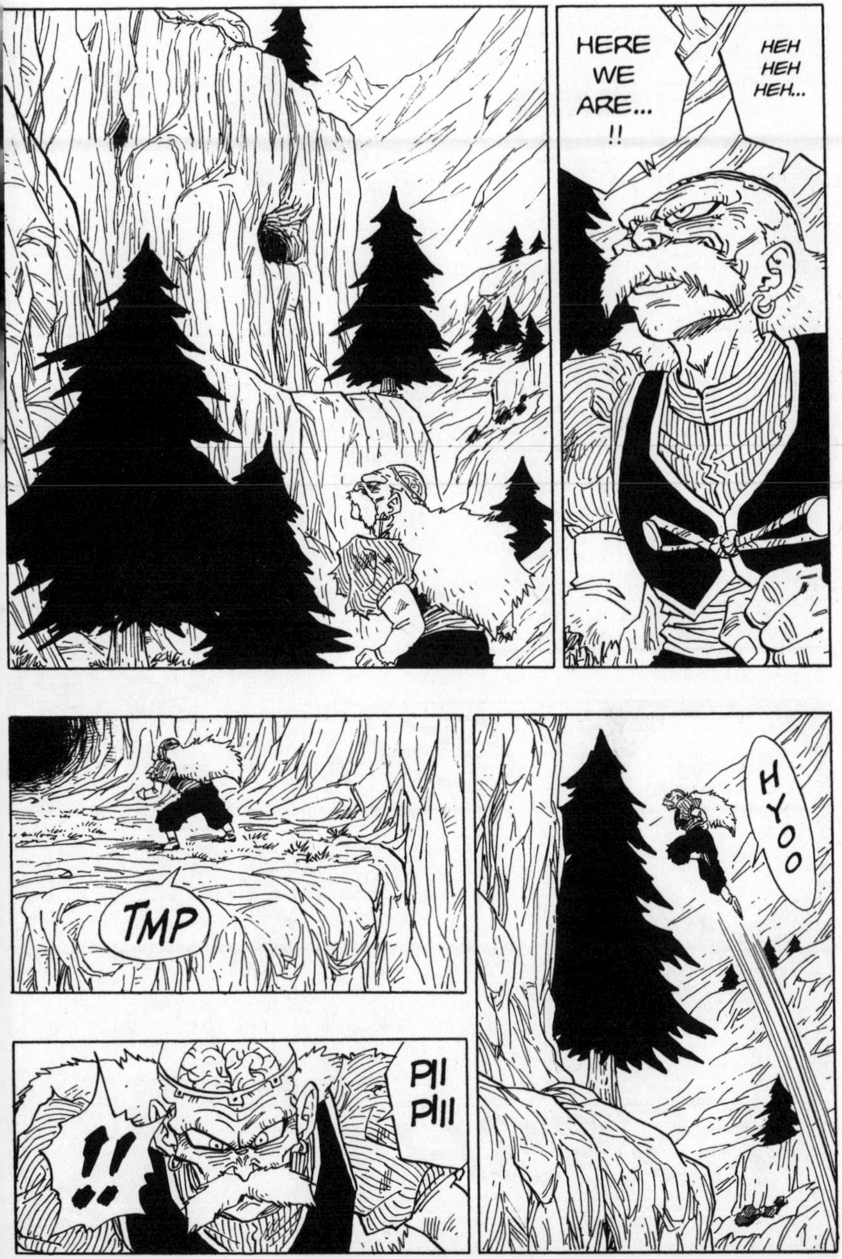
HEH HEH HEH...
HERE WE ARE... !!
HYOO
TMP
PII PIII
!!

READ THIS WAY

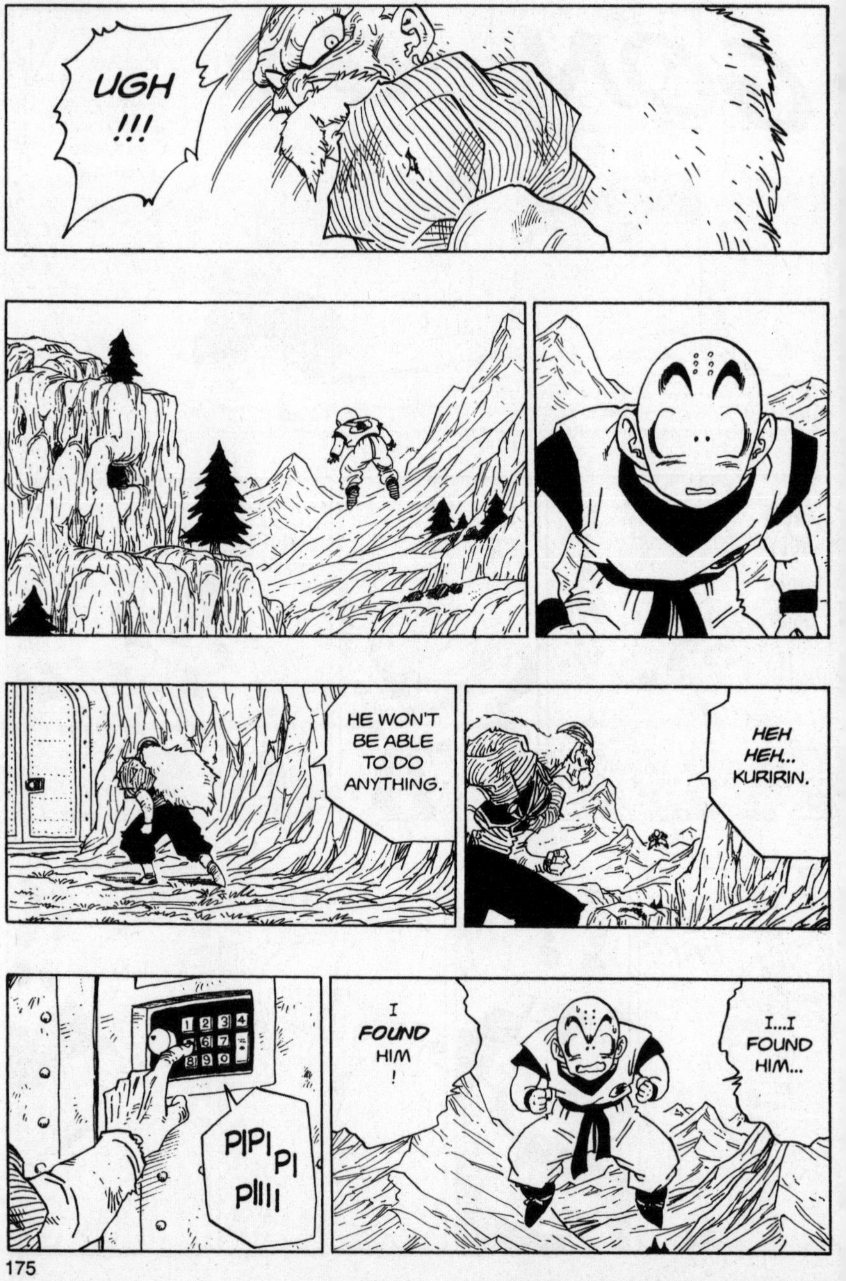
UGH !!!
HEH HEH... KURIRIN.
HE WON'T BE ABLE TO DO ANYTHING.
I...I FOUND HIM...
I FOUND HIM !
PIPI PI PIIII

READ THIS WAY

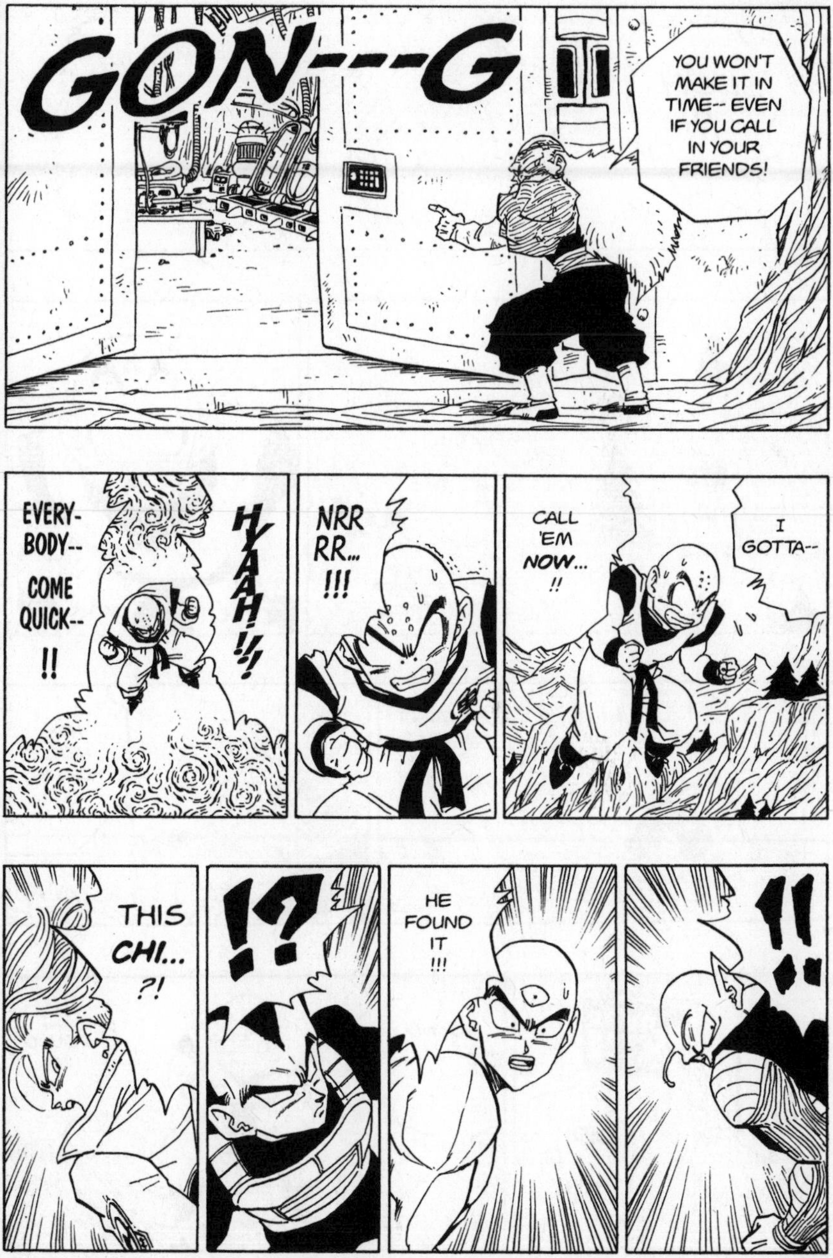

YOU WON'T MAKE IT IN TIME-- EVEN IF YOU CALL IN YOUR FRIENDS!
GON---G
I GOTTA--
CALL 'EM NOW... !!
NRR RR... !!!
HYAAAH!!!
EVERY-BODY-- COME QUICK-- !!
!!
HE FOUND IT !!!
!?
THIS CHI... ?!

READ THIS WAY

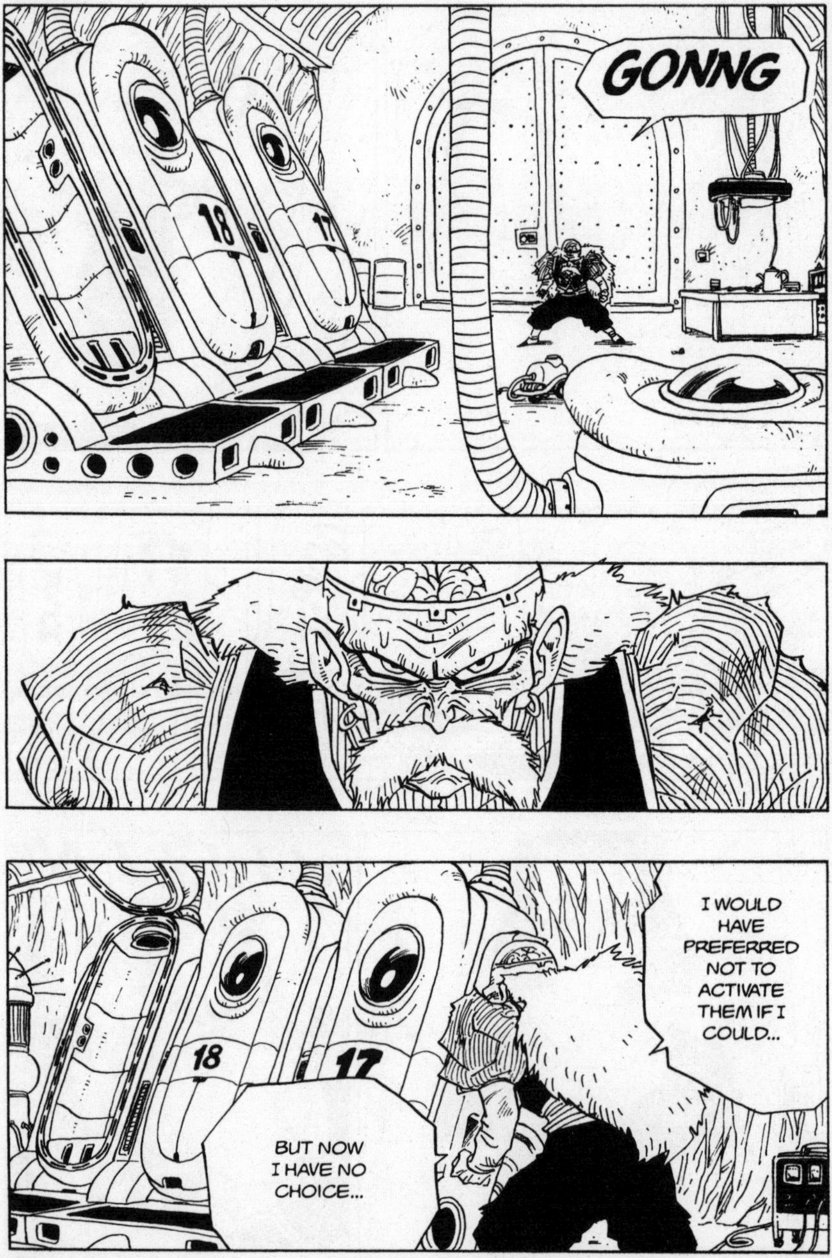
GONNG
I WOULD HAVE PREFERRED NOT TO ACTIVATE THEM IF I COULD...
BUT NOW I HAVE NO CHOICE...

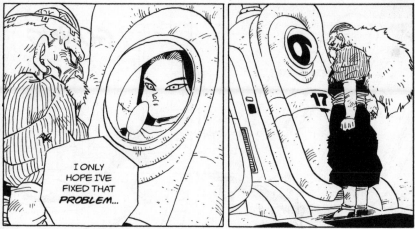

I ONLY HOPE I'VE FIXED THAT *PROBLEM*...

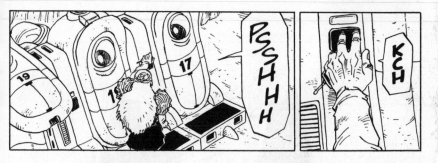

PSSHH

KCH

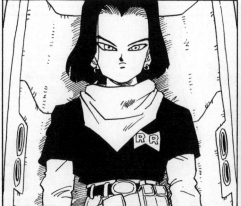

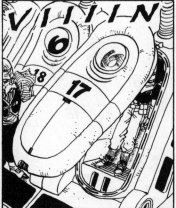

VIIIN

READ THIS WAY

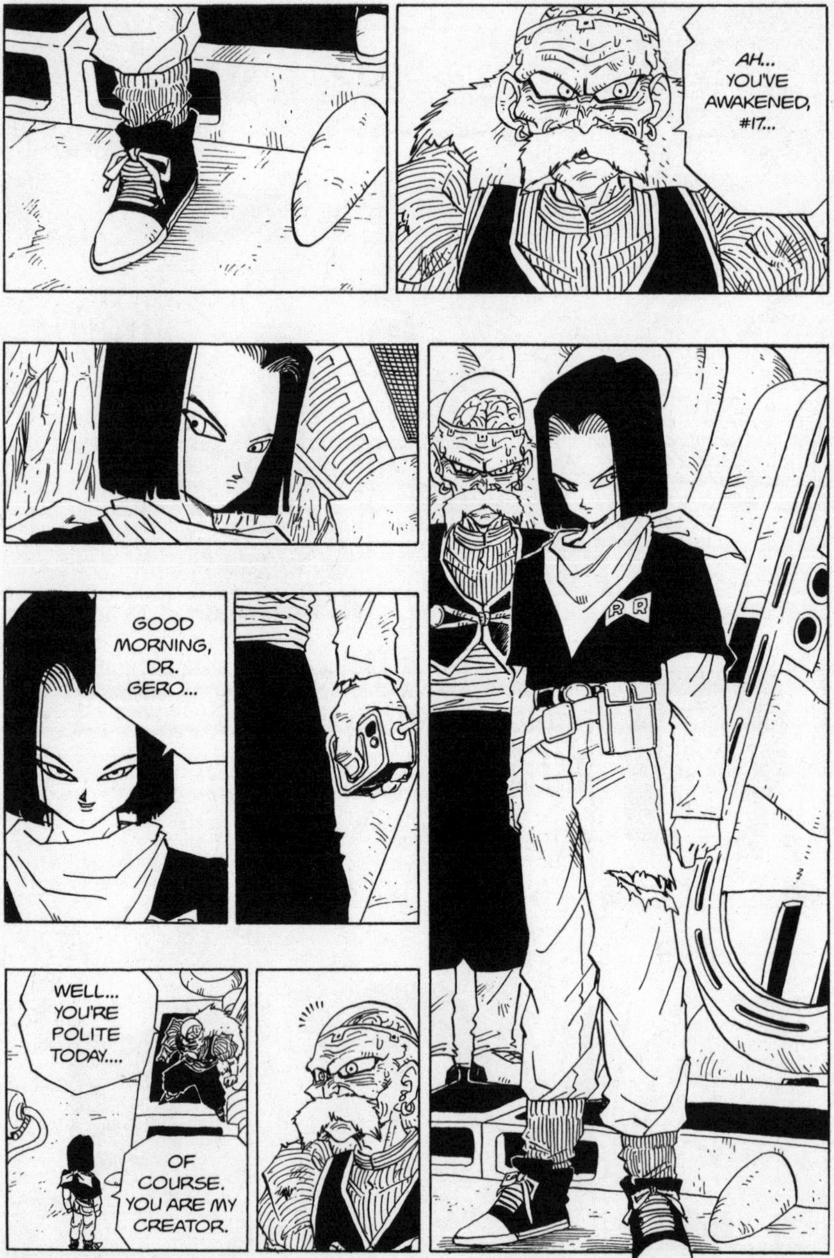
AH... YOU'VE AWAKENED, #17...
GOOD MORNING, DR. GERO...
WELL... YOU'RE POLITE TODAY....
OF COURSE. YOU ARE MY CREATOR.

READ THIS WAY

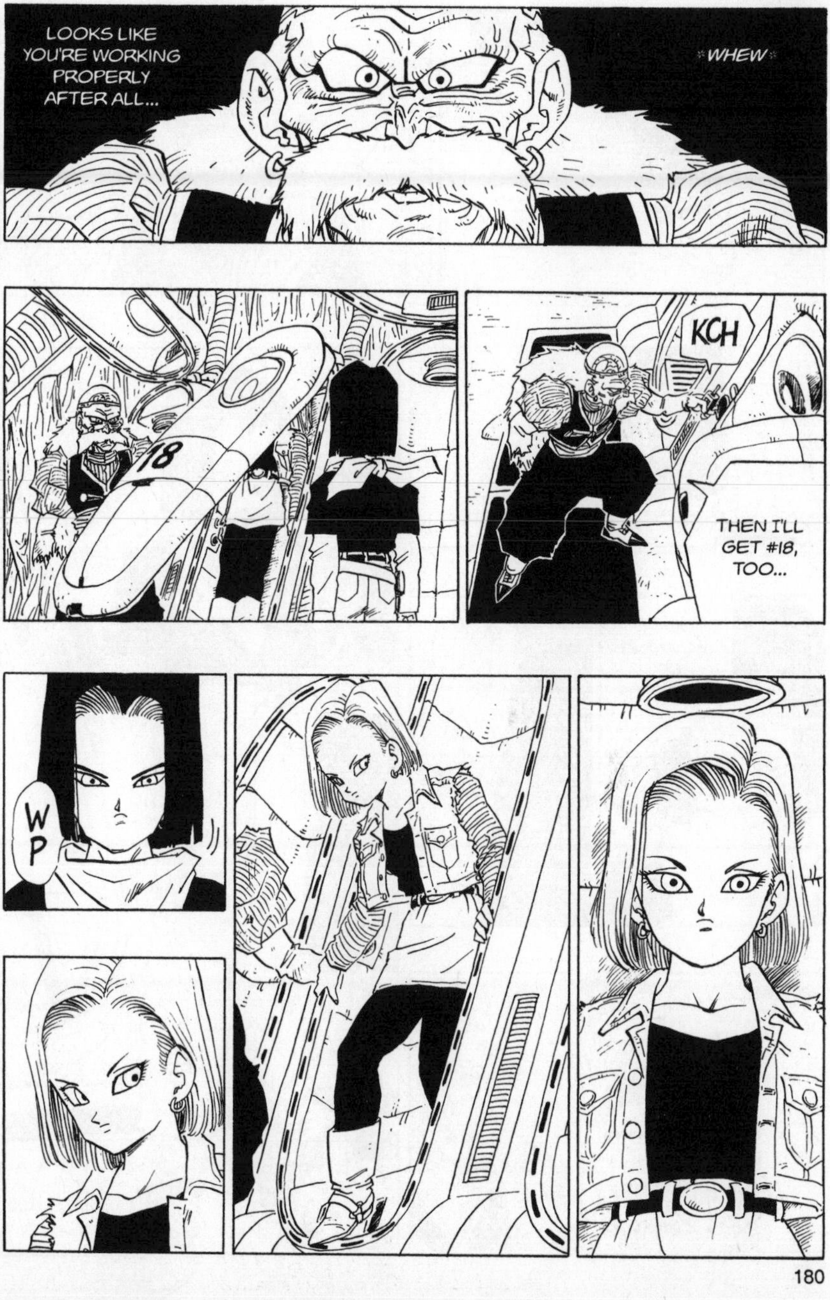
*WHEW*
LOOKS LIKE YOU'RE WORKING PROPERLY AFTER ALL...
KCH
THEN I'LL GET #18, TOO...
18
WP

READ THIS WAY

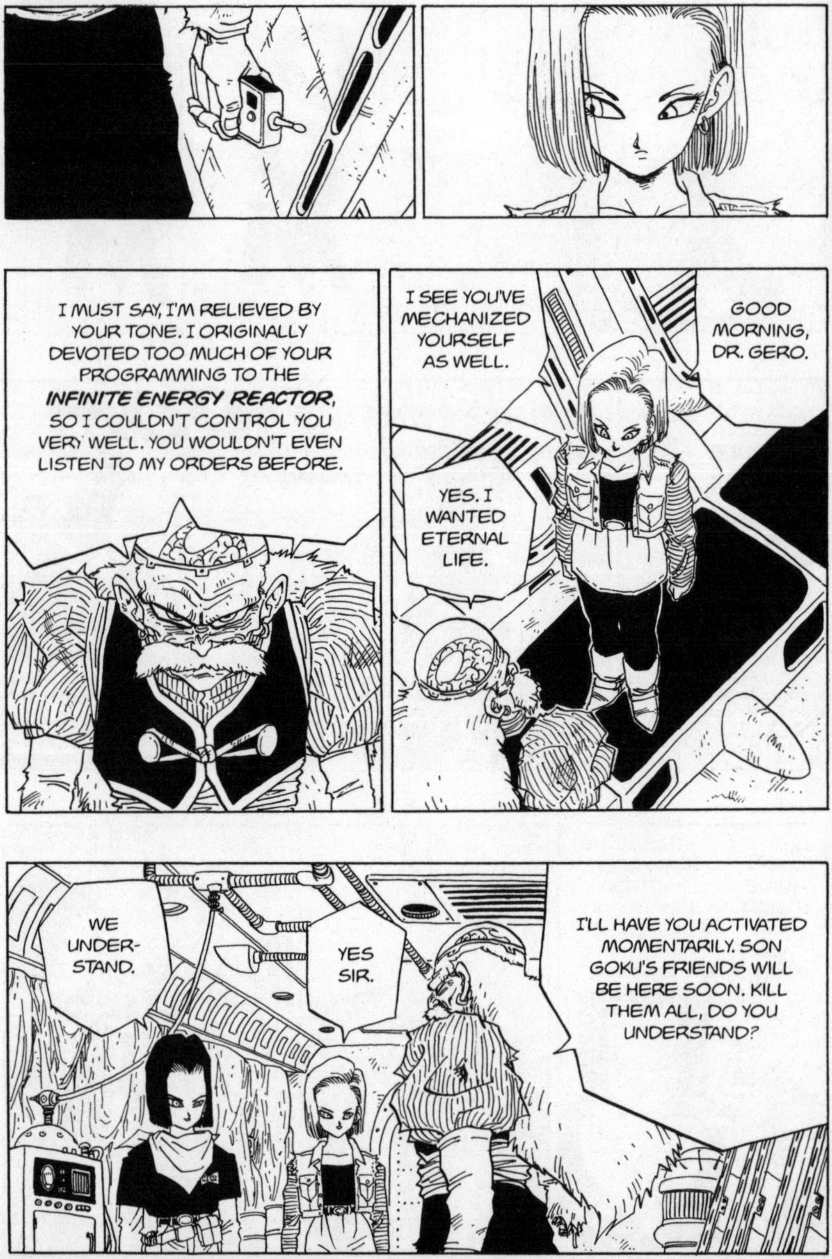
GOOD MORNING, DR. GERO.
I SEE YOU'VE MECHANIZED YOURSELF AS WELL.
YES. I WANTED ETERNAL LIFE.
I MUST SAY, I'M RELIEVED BY YOUR TONE. I ORIGINALLY DEVOTED TOO MUCH OF YOUR PROGRAMMING TO THE ***INFINITE ENERGY REACTOR***, SO I COULDN'T CONTROL YOU VERY WELL. YOU WOULDN'T EVEN LISTEN TO MY ORDERS BEFORE.
I'LL HAVE YOU ACTIVATED MOMENTARILY. SON GOKU'S FRIENDS WILL BE HERE SOON. KILL THEM ALL, DO YOU UNDERSTAND?
YES SIR.
WE UNDER-STAND.

READ THIS WAY

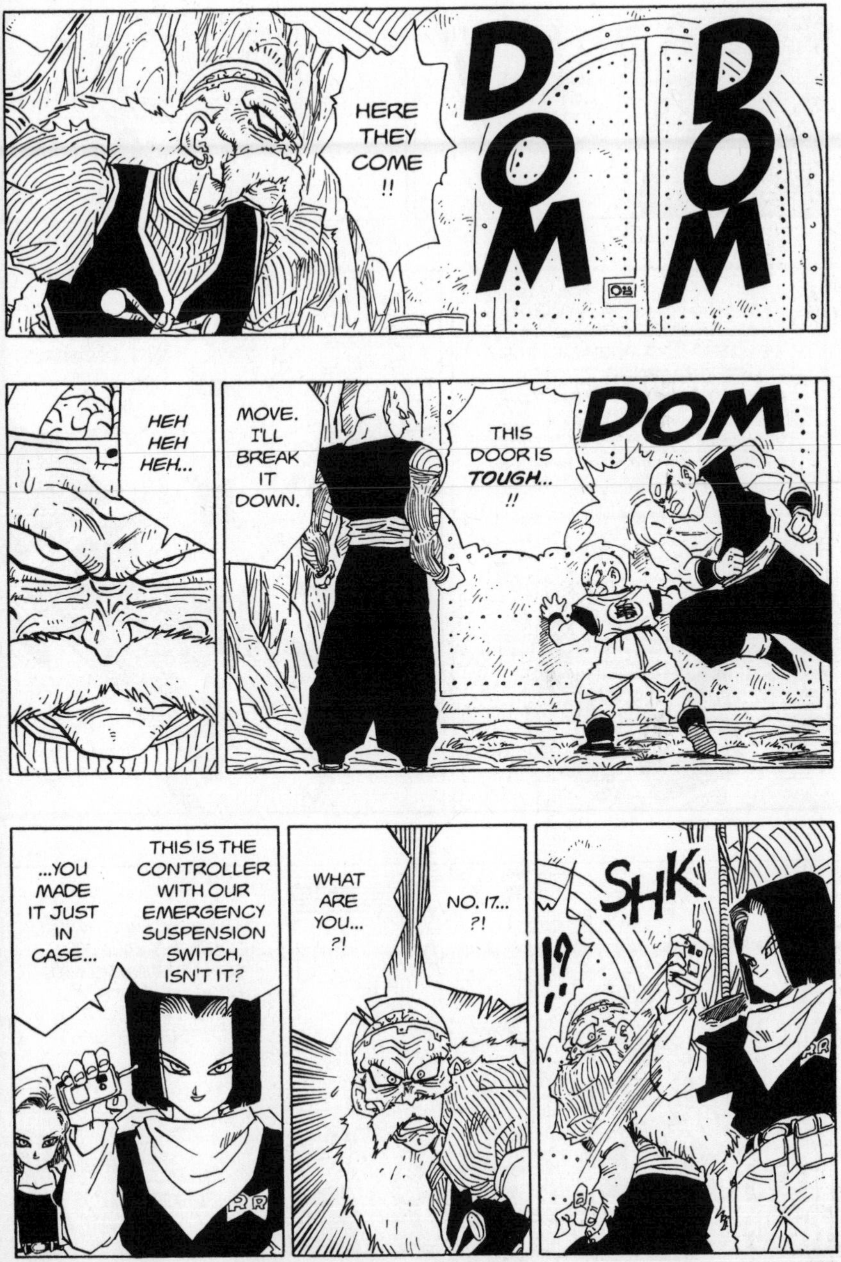
DOM DOM
HERE THEY COME !!
DOM
THIS DOOR IS TOUGH... !!
MOVE. I'LL BREAK IT DOWN.
HEH HEH HEH...
SHK
!?
NO. 17... ?!
WHAT ARE YOU... ?!
THIS IS THE CONTROLLER WITH OUR EMERGENCY SUSPENSION SWITCH, ISN'T IT?
...YOU MADE IT JUST IN CASE...

READ THIS WAY

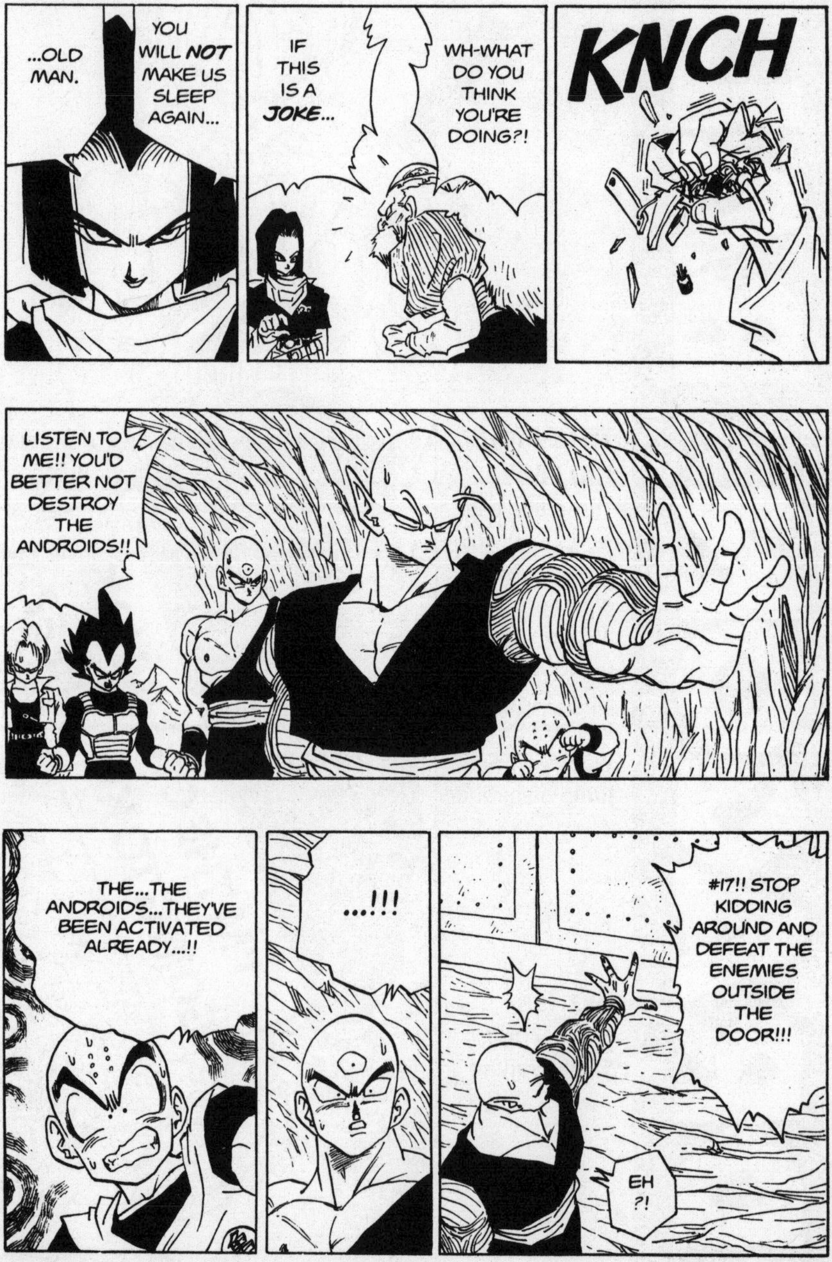
KNCH
WH-WHAT DO YOU THINK YOU'RE DOING?!
IF THIS IS A **JOKE**...
YOU WILL **NOT** MAKE US SLEEP AGAIN...
...OLD MAN.
LISTEN TO ME!! YOU'D BETTER NOT DESTROY THE ANDROIDS!!
#17!! STOP KIDDING AROUND AND DEFEAT THE ENEMIES OUTSIDE THE DOOR!!!
EH ?!
...!!!
THE...THE ANDROIDS...THEY'VE BEEN ACTIVATED ALREADY...!!

**NEXT: The Last Android**

DRAGON BALL

**TITLE PAGE GALLERY**

These title pages were used when these chapters of **Dragon Ball** were originally published in Japan from 1991 to 1992 in **Weekly Shonen Jump** magazine.

**DBZ:138 • The Second Super Saiyan**

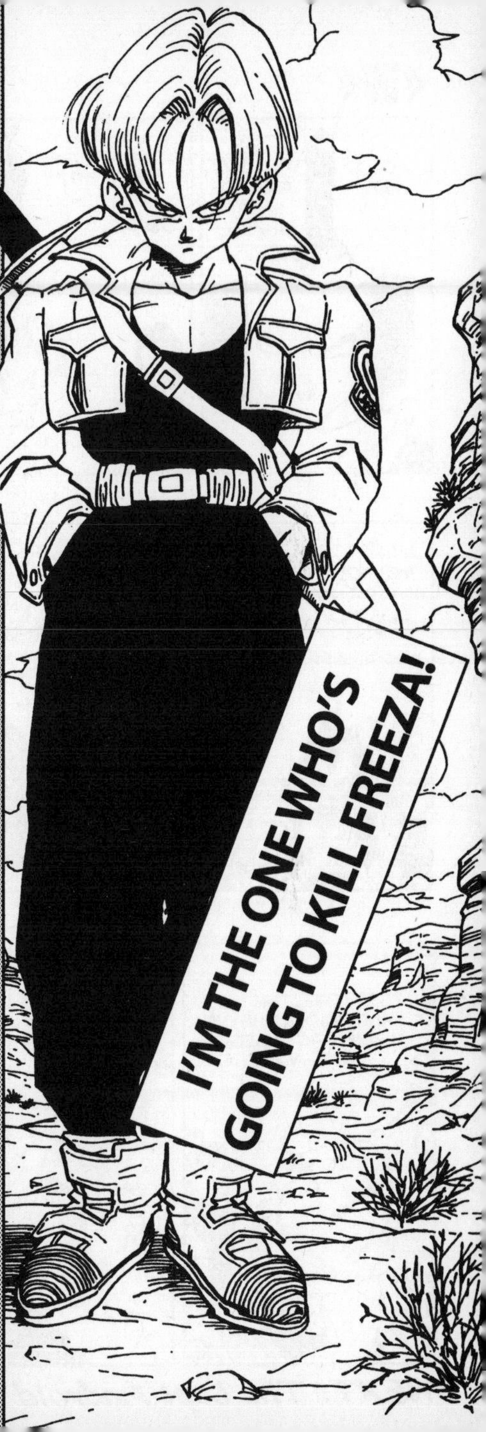
I'M THE ONE WHO'S GOING TO KILL FREEZA!

# DRAGON BALL

## DBZ:139 • Son Goku Comes Home

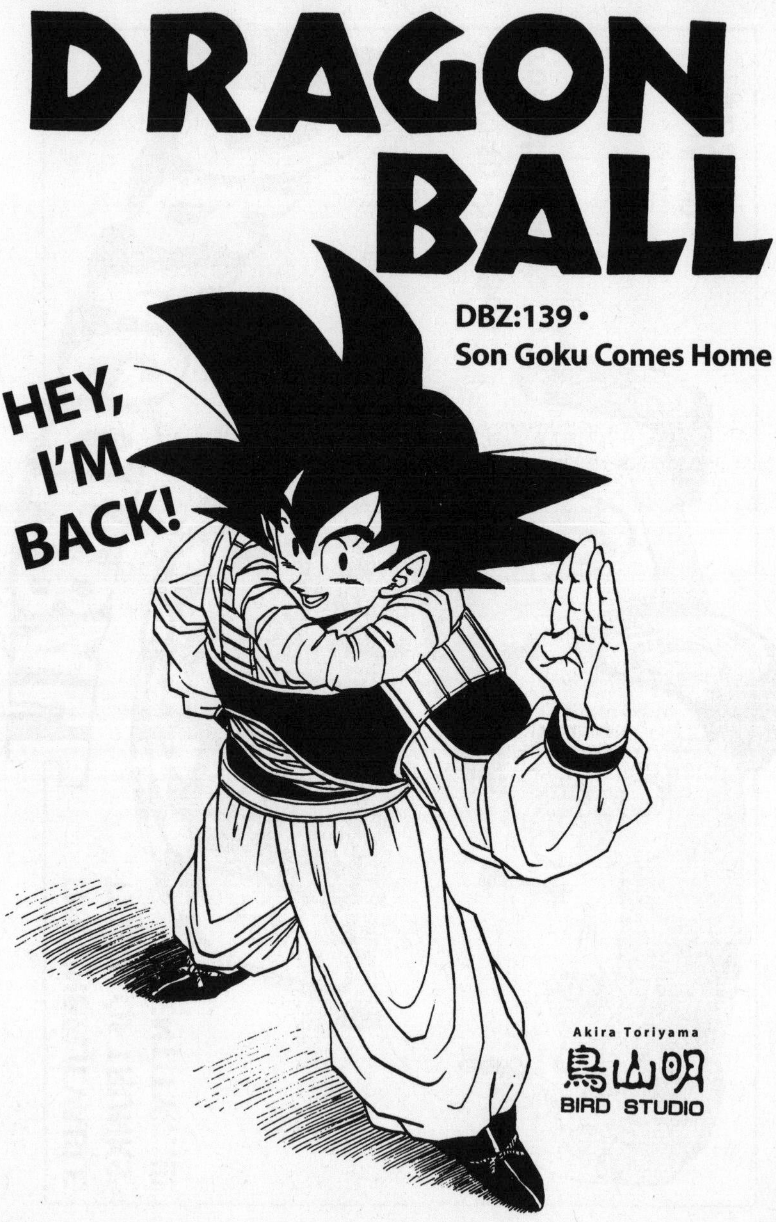

HEY, I'M BACK!


Akira Toriyama
鳥山明
BIRD STUDIO

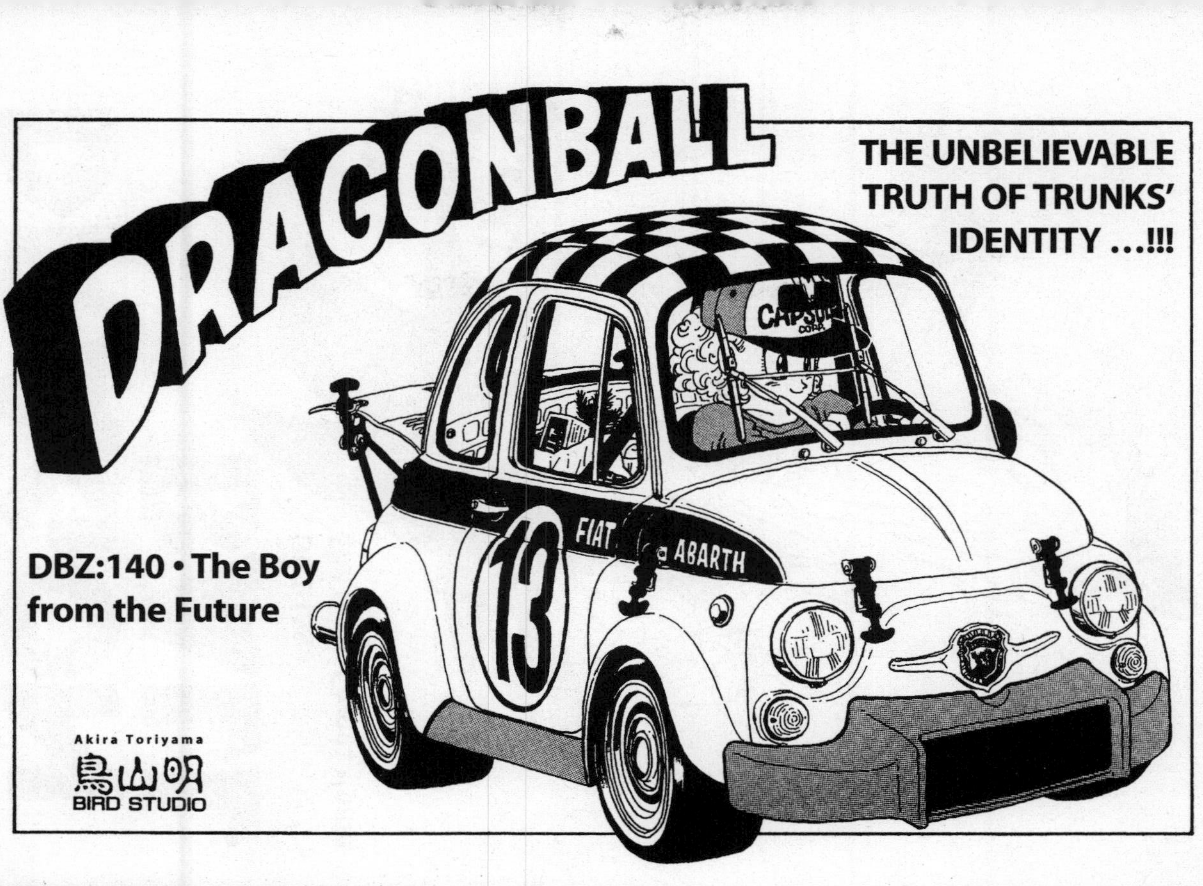
DRAGONBALL
THE UNBELIEVABLE TRUTH OF TRUNKS' IDENTITY ...!!!
CAPSULE CORP.
13
FIAT
ABARTH
DBZ:140 • The Boy from the Future
Akira Toriyama
鳥山明
BIRD STUDIO

# DRAGON BALL

## BALL

**DBZ:141 •**

### The Terrifying Message

Akira Toriyama

鳥山明
BIRD STUDIO

TRUNKS BRINGS A WARNING FROM THE FUTURE!!!

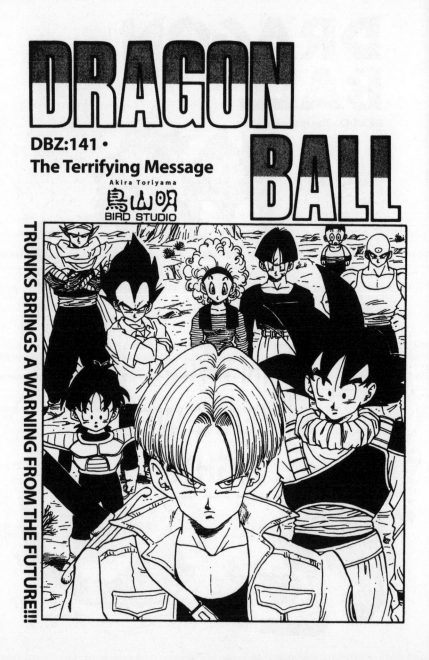

# DRAGON BALL

Akira Toriyama
鳥山明
BIRD STUDIO

## DBZ:142 • The Risky Decision

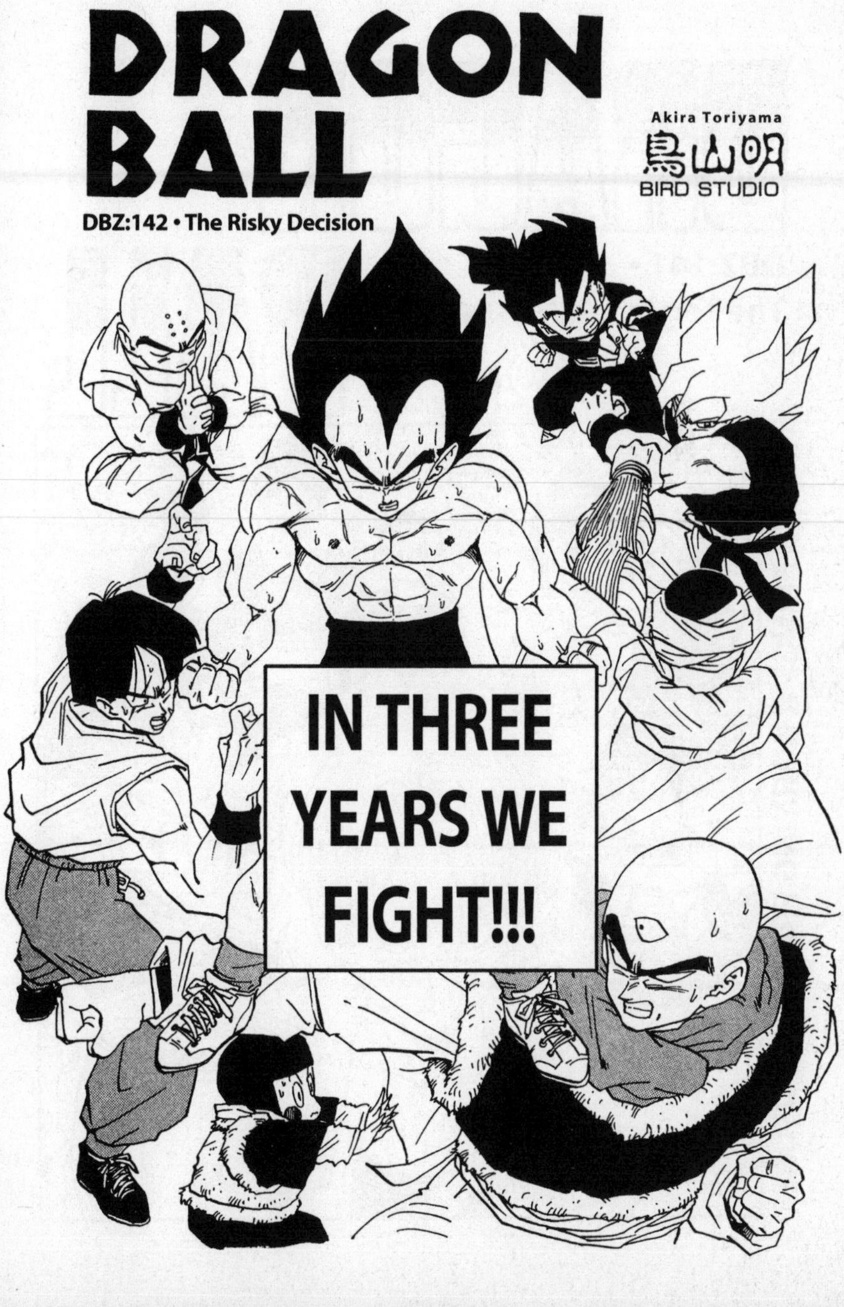
IN THREE YEARS WE FIGHT!!!

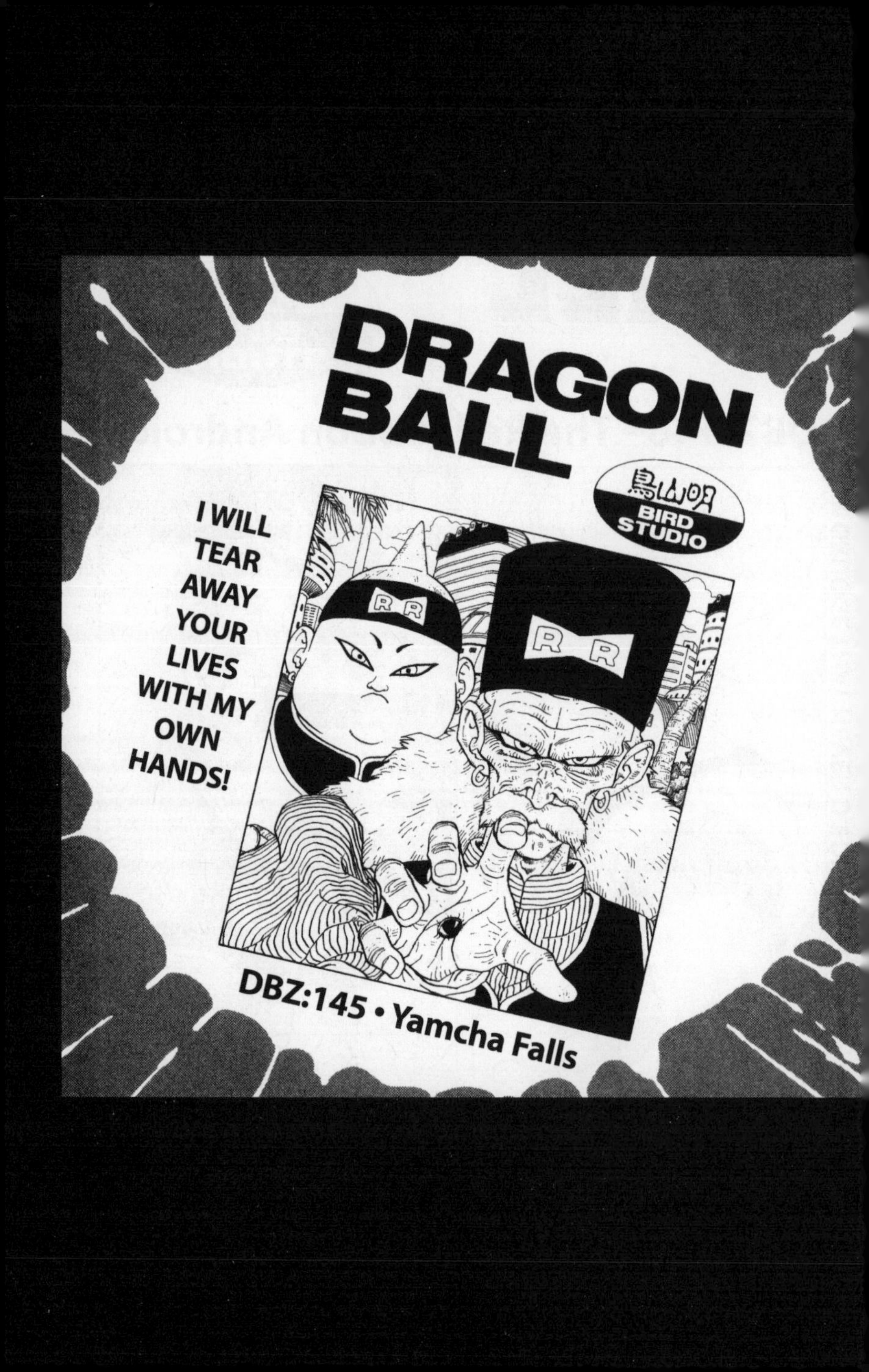
DRAGON BALL
鳥山明
BIRD STUDIO
I WILL TEAR AWAY YOUR LIVES WITH MY OWN HANDS!
DBZ:145 • Yamcha Falls

# DRAGON BALL

鳥山明 BIRD STUDIO

## DBZ:146 • The Red Ribbon Androids

THE GRUDGE THAT NEVER DIED!!! "I'LL BE YOUR OPPONENT!!!"

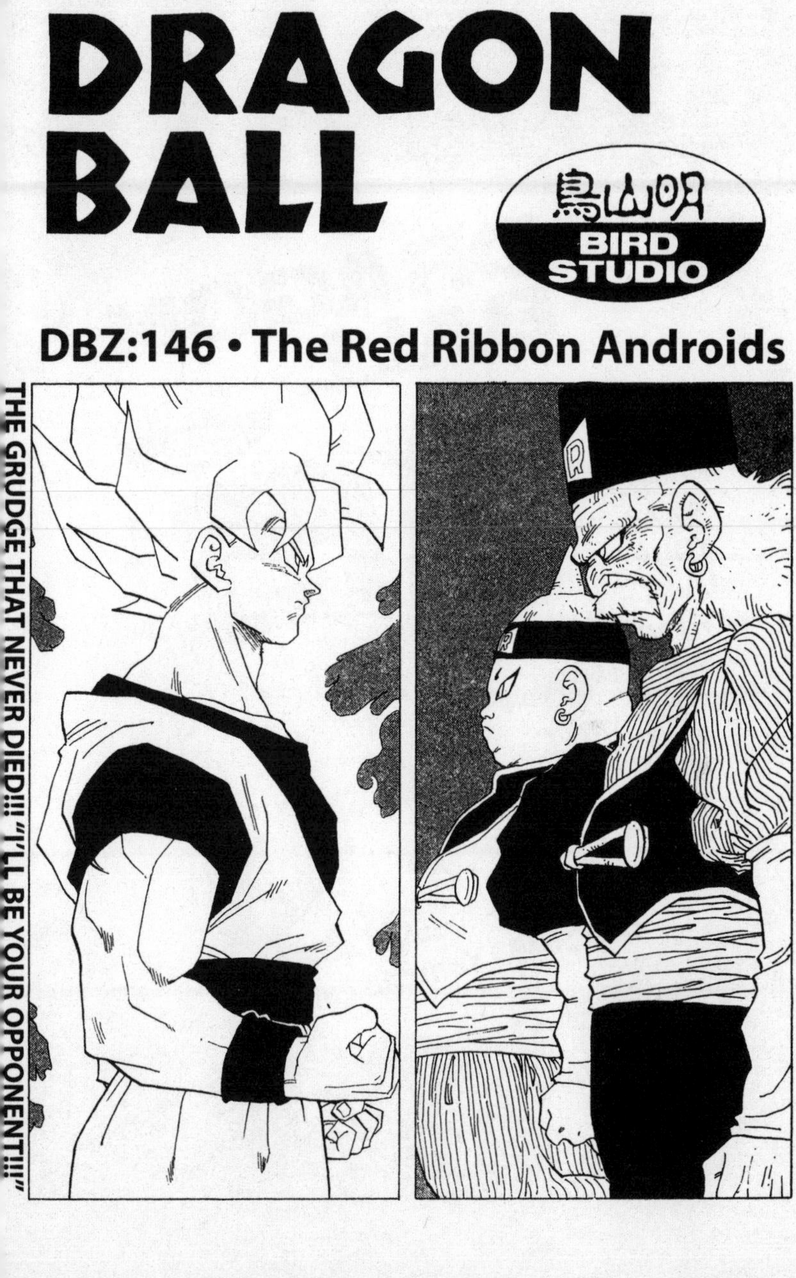

# DRAGON BALL

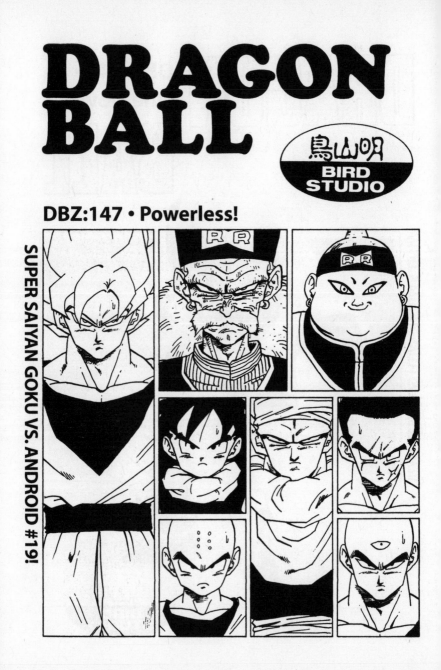

BIRD STUDIO

**DBZ:147 • Powerless!**

SUPER SAIYAN GOKU VS. ANDROID #19!

# DRAGON BALL

## DBZ:148 • One Down…

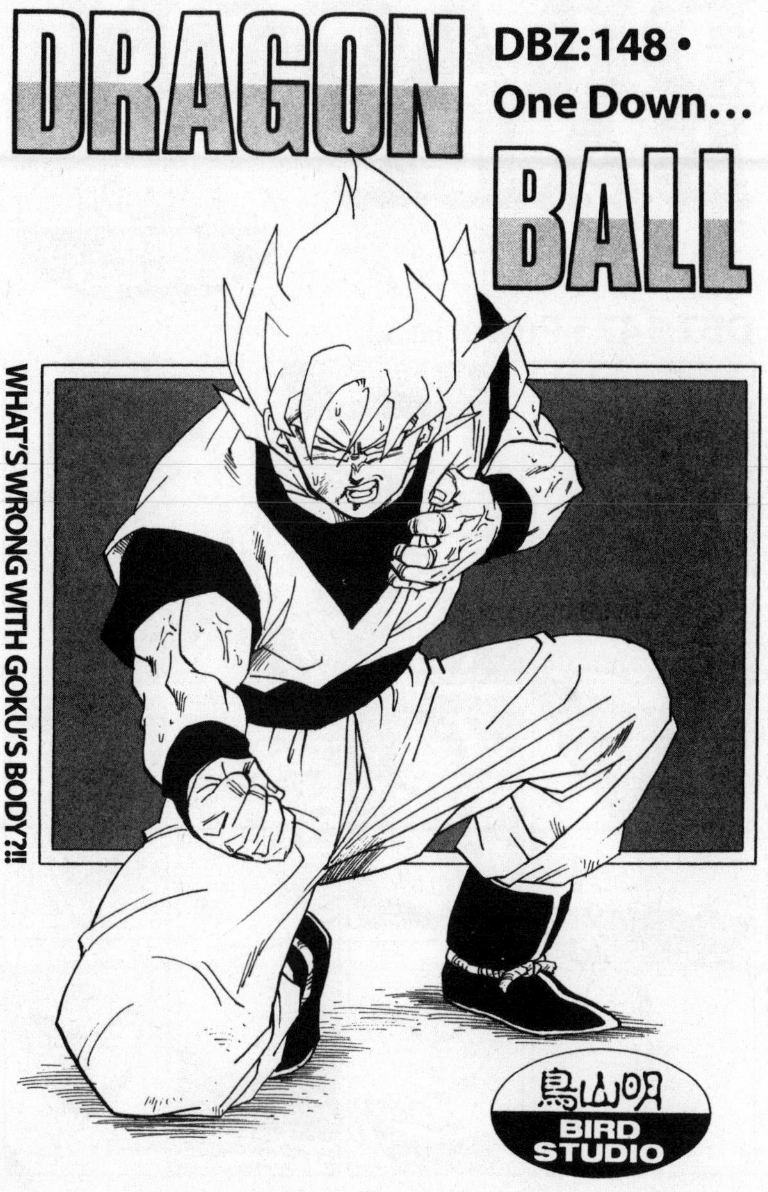

WHAT'S WRONG WITH GOKU'S BODY?!!

鳥山明

BIRD STUDIO

# DRAGON BALL

**DBZ:151 •**

**A Change of Plans**

EVEN #20 CAN'T HANDLE VEGETA!!!

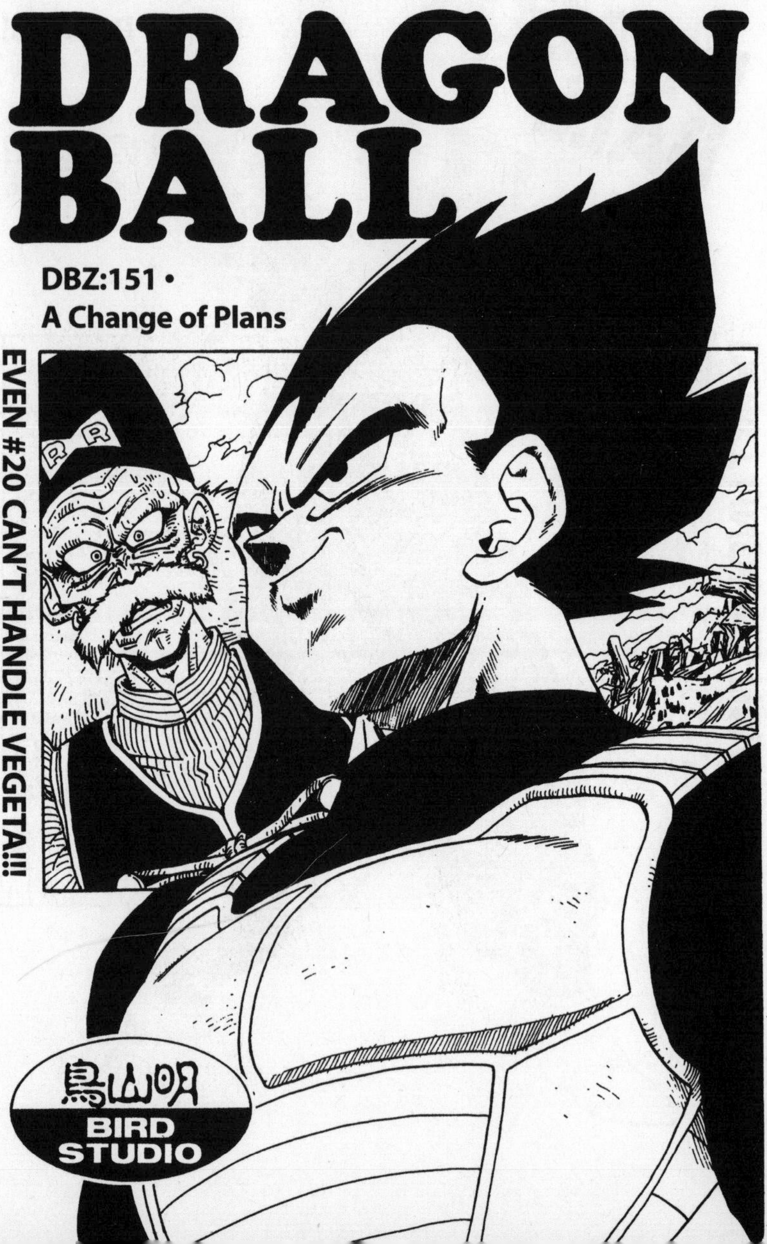

鳥山明
BIRD STUDIO

# DRAGON BALL

## DBZ:152 • Trunks Returns!

Akira Toriyama
鳥山明
BIRD STUDIO

DON'T UNDERESTIMATE ME!

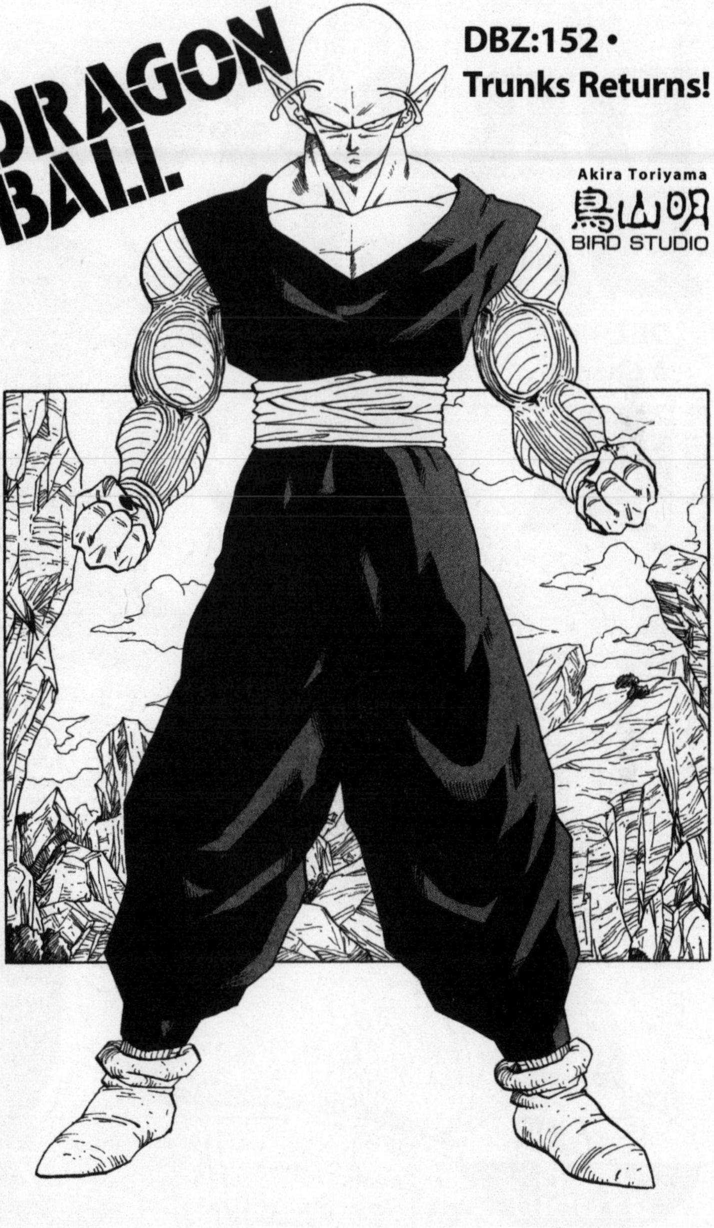

# DRAGON BALL

WHO ARE THESE ANDROIDS...?

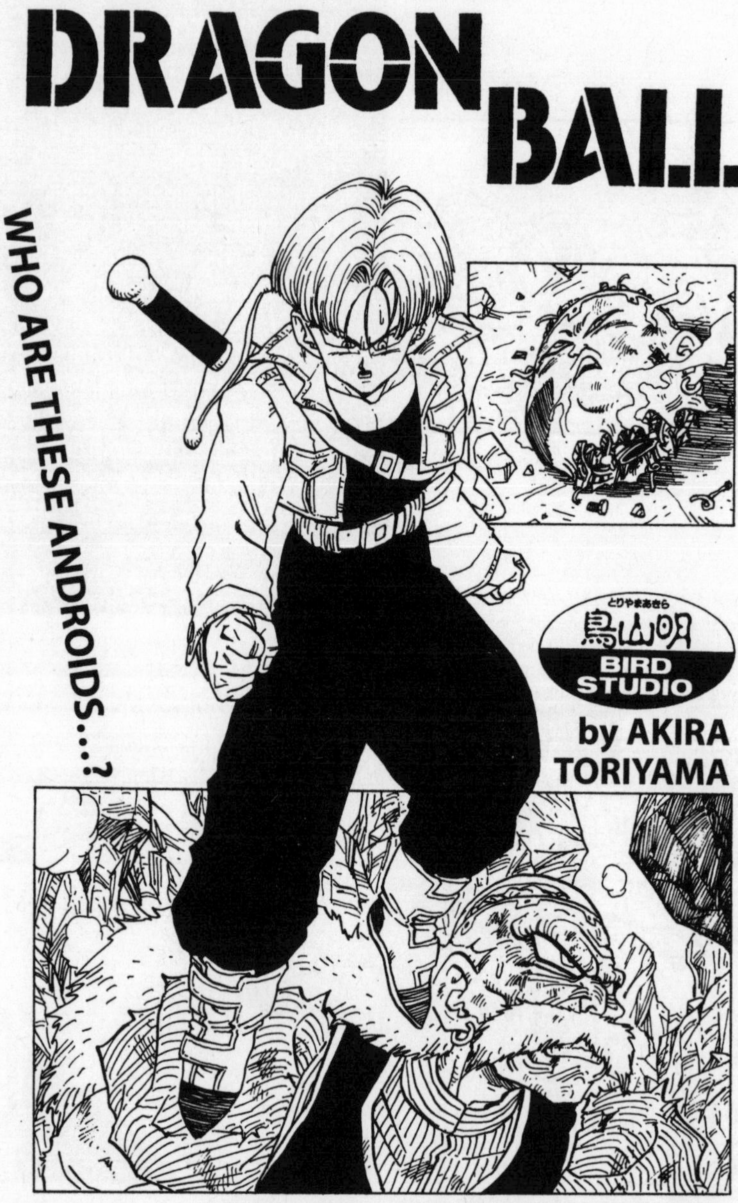

とりやまあきら
鳥山明
BIRD STUDIO

by AKIRA TORIYAMA

## DBZ:153 • A Sound of Thunder

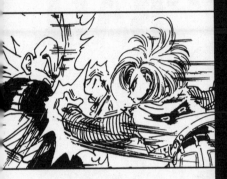

## IN THE NEXT VOLUME...

Androids #17 and #18 betray
their creator, and release the
untested experimental model
#16! Vegeta challenges the
androids all by himself—but is
even a Super Saiyan strong
enough to stop them before they
can kill Son Goku? To become
stronger, Piccolo asks Kami-sama
to fuse with him, to turn them
into the most powerful Namekian
who ever existed! But something
even worse than the androids is
about to be unleashed...

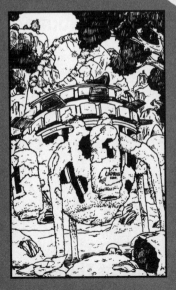

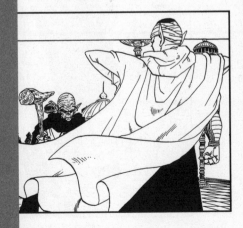

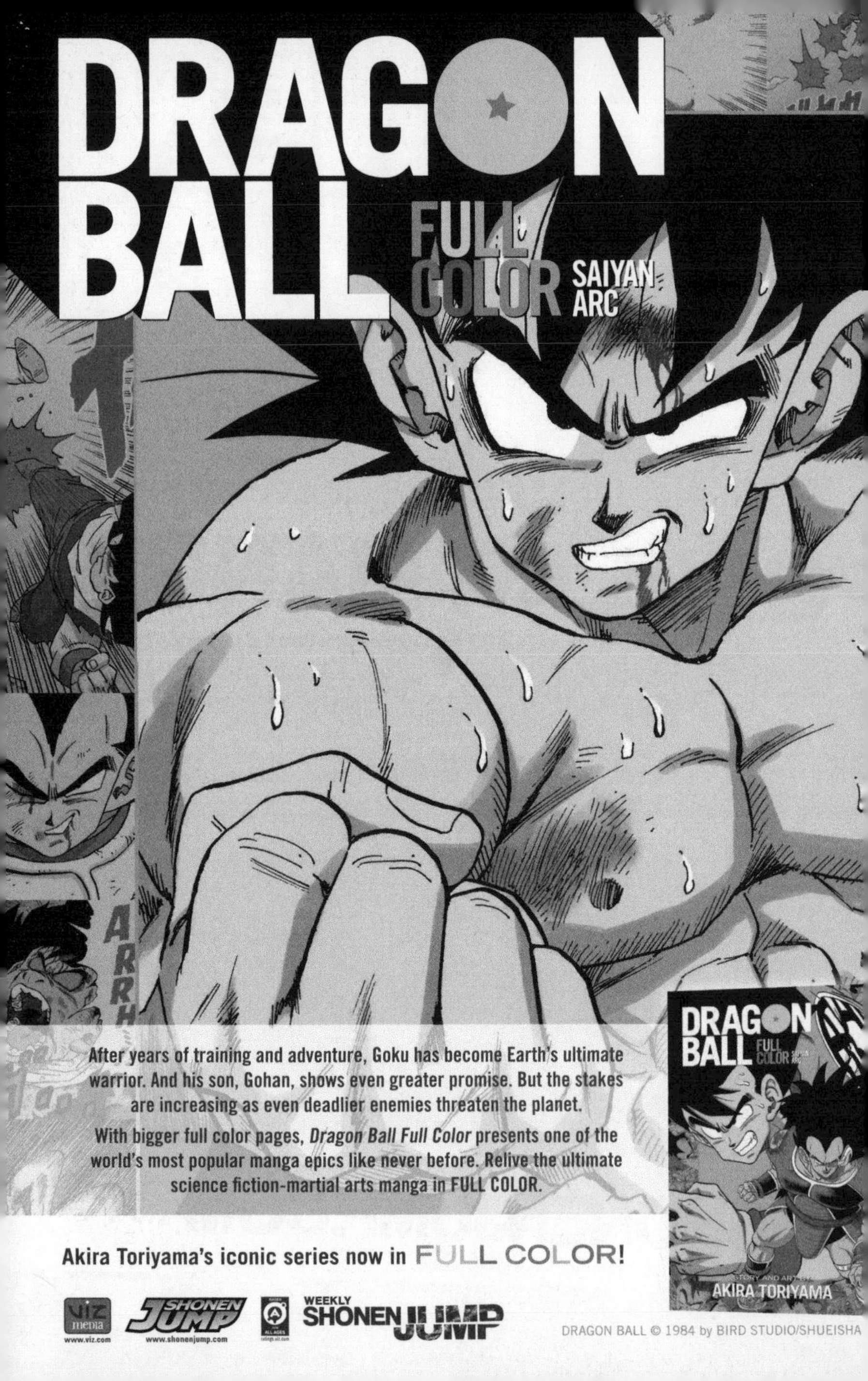
DRAGON BALL
FULL COLOR SAIYAN ARC
ARRH
After years of training and adventure, Goku has become Earth's ultimate warrior. And his son, Gohan, shows even greater promise. But the stakes are increasing as even deadlier enemies threaten the planet.
With bigger full color pages, Dragon Ball Full Color presents one of the world's most popular manga epics like never before. Relive the ultimate science fiction-martial arts manga in FULL COLOR.
DRAGON BALL FULL COLOR SAIYAN ARC
STORY AND ART BY AKIRA TORIYAMA
Akira Toriyama's iconic series now in FULL COLOR!
viz media
www.viz.com
SHONEN JUMP
www.shonenjump.com
ALL AGES
WEEKLY SHONEN JUMP
DRAGON BALL © 1984 by BIRD STUDIO/SHUEISHA

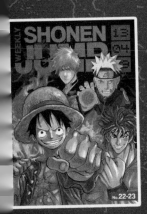
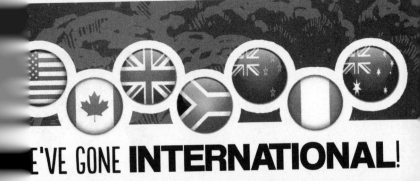

# You're Reading in the Wrong Direction!!

1
2
3
1
2
3
4
5
6

**W**hoops! Guess what? You're starting at the wrong end of the comic!

...It's true! In keeping with the original Japanese format, Akira Toriyama's world-famous **Dragon Ball Z** series is meant to be read from right to left, starting in the upper-right corner.

Unlike English, which is read from left to right, Japanese is read from right to left, meaning that action, sound effects and word-balloon order are completely reversed...something which can make readers unfamiliar with Japanese feel pretty backwards themselves. For this reason, manga or Japanese comics published in the U.S. in English have traditionally been published "flopped"–that is, printed in exact reverse order, as though seen from the other side of a mirror.

By flopping pages, U.S. publishers can avoid confusing readers, but the compromise is not without its downside. For one thing, a character in a flopped manga series who once wore in the original Japanese version a T-shirt emblazoned with "M A Y" (as in "the merry month of") now wears one which reads "Y A M"! Additionally, many manga creators in Japan are themselves unhappy with the process, as some feel the mirror-imaging of their art skews their original intentions.

In recognition of the importance and popularity of **Dragon Ball Z**, we are proud to bring it to you in the original unflopped format.

For now, though, turn to the other side of the book and let the adventure begin...!

–Editor

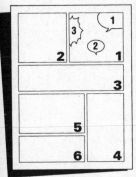

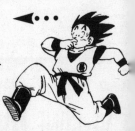